Essential Clinical Social Work Series

Series Editor

Carol Tosone

For further volumes:
http://www.springer.com/series/8115

Joanna Ellen Bettmann • Donna Demetri Friedman
Editors

Attachment-Based Clinical Work with Children and Adolescents

 Springer

Editors
Dr. Joanna Ellen Bettmann
College of Social Work
University of Utah
Salt Lake City, Utah, USA

Donna Demetri Friedman
Silver School of Social Work
New York University
New York, USA

ISBN 978-1-4614-4847-1   (hardcover)   ISBN 978-1-4614-4848-8 (eBook)
ISBN 978-1-4614-9381-5   (softcover)
DOI 10.1007/978-1-4614-4848-8
Springer New York Heidelberg Dordrecht London

Library of Congress Control Number: 2012952410

Springer is part of Springer Science+Business Media (www.springer.com)

Contents

Contributors

Beatrice Beebe College of Physicians & Surgeons at Columbia University, New York State Psychiatric Institute, New York, NY, USA

Ozlem Bekar Department of Psychology, The New School for Social Research, New York, NY, USA
Relationships for Growth and Learning Program, JBFCS, New York, NY, USA

Susanne Bennett The National Catholic School of Social Service, The Catholic University of America, Washington, DC, USA

Anni Bergman The Anni Bergman Parent Infant Program, New York University Postdoctoral Program in Psychotherapy and Psychoanalysis, New York Freudian Society, Institute for Psychoanalytic Training and Research, New York, NY, USA

Joanna Ellen Bettmann College of Social Work, University of Utah, Salt Lake City, UT, USA
Open Sky Wilderness Therapy, Durango, Colorado, USA

Inga Blom The New York Psychoanalytic Institute and Lenox Hill Hospital, New York, NY, USA

Wendy Whiting Blome National Catholic School of Social Service, The Catholic University of America, Washington, DC, USA

Elizabeth Buckner Riverdale Mental Health Association, Bronx, NY, USA

Stephanie Carlson Riverdale Mental Health Association, Bronx, NY, USA

Sara Deutsch Riverdale Mental Health Association, Bronx, NY, USA

Miriam Hernandez Dimmler Child Trauma Research Program, San Francisco General Hospital, San Francisco, CA, USA

Leyla Ertegun Riverdale Mental Health Association, Bronx, NY, USA

Mayra Estrada Riverdale Mental Health Association, Bronx, NY, USA

Emily Fried Early Childhood Center, Albert Einstein College of Medicine, Bronx, NY, USA

Donna Demetri Friedman Riverdale Mental Health Association, Bronx, NY, USA
Silver School of Social Work, New York University, NY, USA

Geoff Goodman Clinical Psychology Doctoral Program, Long Island University,
Brookville, NY, USA

Nadine Burke Harris Bayview Child Health Center, California Pacific Medical
Center, San Francisco, CA, USA

Isaac Karikari College of Social Work, University of Utah, Salt Lake City, UT,
USA

Alicia F. Lieberman Child Trauma Research Program, San Francisco General
Hospital, San Francisco, CA, USA

Tina Lupi Private Practice, New York, NY, USA

Hillary Mayers Riverdale Mental Health Association, Bronx, NY, USA

Anne Murphy Department of Pediatrics, Albert Einstein College of Medicine,
Bronx, NY, USA

Ruth P. Newton Newton Center for Affect Regulation, La Jolla, CA and St. Vincent
de Paul Village, San Diego, CA, USA

Todd S. Renschler Child Trauma Research Program, San Francisco General
Hospital, San Francisco, CA, USA

Allan N. Schore Department of Psychiatry and Biobehavioral Sciences, UCLA
David Geffen School of Medicine, Los Angeles, CA, USA

Rebecca Shahmoon-Shanok Institute for Infants, Children and Families, Jewish
Board of Family and Children's Services, New York, NY, USA

Howard Steele Department of Psychology, New School for Social Research, New
York, NY, USA

Miriam Steele Department of Department of Psychology, New School for Social
Research, New York, NY, USA

Mark Sturgeon Riverdale Mental Health Association, Bronx, NY, USA

Suzi Tortora Dancing Dialogue: Healing and Expressive Arts, New York, NY, USA

Attachment-Based Clinical Work with Children and Adolescents

Joanna Ellen Bettmann and Donna Demetri Friedman

Attachment theory was founded on the notion that childhood relational experiences create lasting impacts on our expectations for future relationships, emotion regulation, and even general mental health. Bowlby believed that humans' needs for relationships were instinctual and survival-driven (Bowlby 1958). Considering other research and other species, Bowlby concluded that we need our mothers, our primary caregiver, without whom we will die. He conceptualized that infant crying, suckling and clinging cemented the child's tie to the mother (Bowlby 1958).

Bowlby also made assertions about what happened to children who lacked empathic caregivers. In "Forty-Four Juvenile Thieves: Their Characters and Home-Life," Bowlby (1944/1946, p. 20) argued that maternal attitudes toward their children—both conscious and unconscious—impacted the child's development: "... in several cases sympathetic discussions with the mothers of the children revealed that their apparent love for their child was only one aspect of their feelings for him. Often an intense, though perhaps unadmitted, dislike and rejection of him also came to light". He drew links between those maternal feelings and children's delinquency. He also posited that children's emotional trauma "mean far more to children than most grown-ups conceive possible" (Bowlby 1944/1946, p. 20). Bowlby's declaration about the impact of caregivers and trauma on children was novel and added significantly to the prevailing dialogue on the mental health of children.

Where children were once thought to be simply resilient blank slates, Bowlby encouraged practitioners to see children as organizing themselves around their caregivers in such a way that negatively impacts to children's personalities was possible if stable, available, empathic caregivers were not there. Bowlby created a theory

J. E. Bettmann (✉)
College of Social Work, University of Utah, Salt Lake City, UT, USA

Open Sky Wilderness Therapy, Durango, Colorado, USA
e-mail: Joanna.Schaefer@socwk.utah.edu

D. D. Friedman
Riverdale Mental Health Association, Bronx, New York, NY, USA

Silver School of Social Work, New York University, New York, NY, USA

J. E. Bettmann, D. D. Friedman (eds.), *Attachment-Based Clinical Work with Children and Adolescents,* Essential Clinical Social Work Series, DOI 10.1007/978-1-4614-4848-8_1, © Springer Science+Business Media New York 2013

1

which allowed practitioners to see children's wounds more clearly. His work, along with the video contributions of James and Joyce Robertson, made the impacts of problematic caregiving visible on our child populations.

The implications of Bowlby's ideas continue to resound through the mental health community. The years since have yielded ground-breaking research defining attachment types (Ainsworth et al. 1978), exploring the longitudinal stability of such types (Hamilton 2000; Grossman et al. 2005; Waters et al. 2000; Weinfield et al. 2004) and the implications of such findings for clinical settings (Sable 2000; Slade 2008; Wallin 2007). While we know now that much of what Bowlby posited was true, we are still discovering the value of such findings for our clinical work with children and adolescents. Our book explores how attachment theory is being used in clinical settings throughout the country. It presents chapters relevant to work with infants and toddlers, children and adolescents. How can we translate what we know about attachment theory and research into practice? Our chapter authors have attempted to answer this question.

Inga Bloom and Anni Bergman offer the first chapter which compares and contrasts Margaret Mahler's theory of separation–individuation and John Bowlby's attachment theory. This chapter entitled, "Observing Development: A Comparative View of Attachment Theory and Separation–Individuation Theory," highlights how these theories contradict or compete with each other. While they were developed in different contexts, use different methodological approaches, and emphasize different aspects of psychological development, the two theories share a number of important aspects. This is an important chapter because there is renewed interest in understanding how these theories can together explain the process of child development. Both theories place emphasis on real events in the infant's life. In addition, both theories were pioneering in their reliance on observation. Their shared prospective rather than retrospective approaches are also unique. A deeper understanding of how these theories complement each other informs our use of them in clinical work with children and adolescents.

In the next chapter entitled "Securing Attachment: Mother–Infant Theory and Research Informs Attachment-based Clinical Work with Children," Donna Demetri Friedman, Leyla Ertegun, Tina Lupi, Beatrice Beebe, and Sara Deutsch show how early theorists paved the way for a deeper understanding of the importance of the parent–child relationship (Bowlby 1958, 1960; Winnicott 1953, 1956, 1965). This chapter traces how theory led to research and how that, in turn, impacted clinical work with children. The authors present a case example to illustrate how mother–infant research informs a parent–child treatment approach. The case is analyzed in relation to mother–infant theories and research, and clinical implications are discussed.

In the next chapter entitled "Using Modern Attachment Theory to Guide Clinical Assessments of Early Attachment Relationships" by Allan Schore and Ruth Newton, the authors present a review of recent research on mother–infant right brain-to-right brain interaction and development. The chapter offers a case example to illustrate these clinically important neurobiologic concepts. A critical component of this chapter is its description of modern attachment theory's combination of biology and psychoanalysis and how its concepts can be used in clinical work with children.

In the next chapter, "From Out of Sight, Out of Mind to In-Sight and In Mind: Enhancing Reflective Capacities in a Group Attachment-based Intervention," Anne Murphy, Miriam Steele, and Howard Steele describe the Group Attachment-based Intervention (GABI), an attachment-based clinical intervention for high-risk families with very young children. The goals of the intervention are to enhance the security of familial attachment relationships and to reduce stress in the family. Importantly, this chapter illustrates how this intervention is implemented and how clinicians are trained. Reflective functioning is the guiding principle in both the clinical work and supervision. The authors presented clinical vignettes to illustrate the work with children and their families.

The following chapter, "Becoming Baby Watchers: An Attachment-based Video Intervention In a Community Mental Health Center," by Donna Demetri Friedman, Sara Deutsch, Leyla Ertegun, Stephanie Carlson, Mayra Estrada, Mark Sturgeon, Hillary Mayers, and Elizabeth Buckner, begins with a description of an evidenced-based, attachment-focused video intervention for caregivers and babies called *Chances for Children* that was originally developed for adolescent mothers and their babies. This chapter highlights attachment-based clinical work with children using a video intervention with the caregiver–child dyad, rather than group intervention as in the previous chapter. This chapter addresses the theoretical underpinnings of this intervention and presents three case vignettes with high-risk dyads. The authors also explore clinical and training implications of the intervention.

The next chapter is entitled "Trauma Focused Child–Parent Psychotherapy in a Community Pediatric Clinic: A Cross-Disciplinary Collaboration," by Todd Renschler, Alicia Lieberman, Miriam Hernandez Dimmler, and Nadine Burke Harris. This chapter introduces a different dyadic intervention, this time involving a cross-disciplinary collaboration. The intervention uses a community pediatric clinic as the intervention port of entry for vulnerable families. The authors present an innovative model of community-based, multi-disciplinary collaboration among pediatricians, social workers, and clinical psychologists working together to address the impact of trauma on the physical and mental health of their patients.

The next chapter focuses on the specific population of children in foster care or adoptive homes. Given that children in foster care often have attachment difficulties, this is a critical chapter. "Restoring Safety" by Julie Ribaudo explores the integration of infancy studies, brain development, attachment theory, and models of infant and child therapy to address the needs of young children in foster or adoptive homes following experiences of abuse and neglect. This chapter describes in detail the case of a child and his foster/adoptive parents. The example encompasses the work of managing and containing a child's feelings, as well as the support given to the foster parents who later adopted him.

This next chapter entitled "The Essential Role of the Body in the Parent–Infant Relationship: Nonverbal Analysis of Attachment" by Suzi Tortora moves us into the important domain of somatic-based, attachment-oriented clinical work with children. It covers nonverbal aspects of clinical work and teaches the reader about how nonverbal dialogue and analysis can be used as therapeutic tools to repair attachment relationships. This chapter presents the *Ways of Seeing* dance movement psychotherapy program, based on nonverbal analysis, infant mental health theory, and research. The author also discusses a specific, dyadic, nonverbal analysis system called Dyadic, Attachment-based, Nonverbal, Communicative Expressions (D.A.N.C.E.) as a way to observe the attachment relationship. Finally, the author presents an illustration of her model using a clinical vignette.

The next chapter addresses the role of peers as important attachment figures. The chapter is entitled "Gems Hidden in Plain Sight: Peer Play Psychotherapy Nourishes Relationships and Growth Across Developmental Domains Among Young Children" by Rebecca Shahmoon-Shanok, Ozlem Bekar, Emily Fried and Miriam Steele. The chapter presents the intervention of Peer Play Psychotherapy (PPP) which is offered within some preschool settings. This chapter summarizes the model's unique intervention tool and its effectiveness. The authors present evidence of the intervention's success at engaging high-risk families in treatment. They also describe reflective supervision for the therapeutic staff as a central component of the intervention. The chapter concludes with a case vignette that provides descriptions of the interactions between two children within a typical PPP group to illustrate how it works.

The next chapter makes significant contribution by addressing the clinical needs of prepubertal children. "Impact of Intervention Points of Entry on Attachment-based Processes of Therapeutic Change with Prepubertal Children," by Geoff Goodman, describes that although attachment-based interventions with mothers and infants are becoming more widely available, attachment-based intervention with prepubertal children are lacking. This chapter remedies this lack by discussing the potential intervention points with this population. It conveys the importance of including the child as well as parents in treatment. The author highlights that therapists must reflect on their own attachment patterns as well as the children's. The author uses two clinical cases to illustrate challenges in this work. The chapter concludes with an emphasis on choosing a unique point of entry based on the needs of the child.

The next chapter focuses on attachment-based clinical work with adolescents. "Attachment Processes in Wilderness Therapy," written by Joanna Bettmann and Isaac Karikari, highlights out-of-home treatment for adolescents. This chapter is crucial given the clinical challenges presented by this population. It addresses how treatment can enhance the attachment bonds between family members even when the treatment is residential, by definition keeping the adolescent and his family apart. It addresses the unique challenge of residential treatment programs in which adolescents are far from their familiar environments and relationships, a distance which evokes adolescents' strong attachment needs and their need for new relationships within the treatment setting. The chapter explores how programs can support adolescents' attachment needs in the context of out-of-home care. This chapter presents a reconceptualization of adolescent dynamics in wilderness therapy settings, exploring how acting-out adolescent behaviors can be understood in the context of attachment dynamics.

The final chapter in our book on attachment-based clinical work with children and adolescents addresses unique issues regarding barriers in implementing these important interventions, focusing on the child welfare system. "Implementing Attachment Theory in the Child Welfare System: Clinical Implications and Organizational

Considerations," is written by Susanne Bennett and Wendy Whiting Blome. This chapter explains how research demonstrates the relationship between disorganized attachment and mental health issues for abused and neglected children. It also describes how child welfare administrators have placed increased emphasis on the implementation of practices that promote positive parent–child attachments. This chapter points out that the child welfare system has not systematically addressed the organizational challenges of implementing evidence-based practices or addressing the impact of disrupted parent–child attachments. The authors explore the internal and external pressures on child welfare agencies that promote or discourage the implementation of attachment-based clinical work with children. Importantly, the chapter closes by offering recommendations for agencies and clinicians.

The chapters in this book address attachment-based clinical work with infants, toddlers, children, adolescents, and their family members. This book represents both qualitative and quantitative approaches, including research as well as clinical case examples to illustrate its varied approaches. The book highlights how attachment theory and research informs emerging practice approaches. The book can be useful to clinicians working with difficult, traumatized or stressed children and their families. Attachment principles are as useful to understanding populations in pain now as they were when Bowlby proposed his notions in "Forty-Four Juvenile Thieves" so many years ago. The novel approaches represented in this book should serve as both an inspiration and a guide to clinicians in integrating attachment into practice.

References

Ainsworth, M. D. S., Blehar, M. C., Waters, E., & Wall, S. (1978). *Patterns of attachment: A psychological study of the strange situation*. Hillsdale: Erlbaum.

Bowlby, J. (1944/1946). Forty-four juvenile thieves: Their characters and home-life. *International Journal of Psycho-analysis, 25,* 19–53. (Reprinted as monograph. London: Bailiere, Tindall & Cox).

Bowlby, J. (1958). The nature of the child's tie to the mother. *International Journal of Psycho-analysis, 39,* 350–373.

Bowlby, J. (1960). Separation anxiety. *Psychoanalytic Study of the Child, 15,* 9–20.

Bowlby, J. (1980). Attachment and loss. *Loss: Sadness and depression* (Vol. 3). London: Hogarth Press and Institute of Psycho-Analysis.

Grossman, K. E., Grossman, K., & Waters, E. (Eds.). (2005). *Attachment from infancy to adulthood: The major longitudinal studies*. New York: Guilford.

Hamilton, C. E. (2000). Continuity and discontinuity of attachment from infancy through adolescence. *Child Development, 71*(3), 690–694.

Sable, P. (2000). *Attachment and adult psychotherapy*. Northvale: Jason Aronson.

Slade, A. (2008). The implications of attachment theory and research for adult psychotherapy: Research and clinical perspectives (pp. 762–782). In J. Cassidy & P. R. Shaver (Eds.), *Handbook of attachment: Theory, research and clinical applications*. New York: Guilford.

Wallin, D. J. (2007). *Attachment in psychotherapy*. New York: Guilford.

Waters, E., Hamilton, C. E., & Weinfield, N. S. (2000). The stability of attachment security from infancy to adolescence and early adulthood: General introduction. *Child Development, 71*(3), 678–683.

Weinfield, N. S., Whaley, G. J. L., & Egeland, B. (2004). Continuity, discontinuity, and coherence in attachment from infancy to late adolescence: Sequelae of organization and disorganization. *Attachment & Human Development, 6*(1), 73–97.

Winnicott, D. W. (1953). Transitional objects and transitional phenomena. *International Journal of Psychoanalysis*, 34, 89–97.

Winnicott, D. (1956). Primary maternal preoccupation. In *Collected papers* (pp. 53–58). New York: Basic Books.

Winnicott, D. (1965). *The maturational processes and the facilitating environment*. New York: International Universities Press.

Part I
Attachment Theory and Research with Children

Observing Development: A Comparative View of Attachment Theory and Separation–Individuation Theory

Inga Blom and Anni Bergman

The establishment of a sense of separateness from, and relation to, a world of reality, particularly with regard to the experiences of one's own body and to the principle representative of the world as the infant experiences it, the primary love object ... is never finished. (Mahler et al. 1975, p. 3).

Attachment theory and psychoanalysis are enjoying a reconciliation. After decades of mutual antagonism, clinicians and researchers alike have renewed interest in examining common underpinnings of attachment theory and psychoanalytic theories of development, evaluating overlapping concepts to determine how these theories can be mutually enhancing. This reconciliatory work appears to be primarily the impetus of attachment researchers, students of psychoanalysis themselves, who are curious about the internal worlds of the infants, and children they evaluate (e.g., Fonagy and Target 2007; Fonagy et al. 2002; Steele and Steele 1998).

Fonagy et al. (2002) attribute this interest partly to the surge of relational psychoanalytic work in the United States, which prioritizes the impact of real relationships in contrast to classical psychoanalysis, which focuses on fantasy. Also, while attachment researchers offer abundant demonstrations of the centrality of the attachment system for psychological functioning throughout life, the limitations of attachment theory are also known (Fonagy and Target 2007). For example, an infant who demonstrates an avoidant attachment organization in infancy will likely demonstrate a dismissing attachment organization in adulthood, which includes discomfort with intimacy and minimization of the importance of emotions and emotional life. However, why one dismissing infant develops strategies like idealization to manage these discomforts, and another uses devaluation and derogation, is not well elucidated in attachment theory. Additionally, there are a number of individuals who defy predic-

I. Blom (✉)
The New York Psychoanalytic Institute and Lenox Hill Hospital, New York, NY, USA
e-mail: dringablom@gmail.com

A. Bergman
The Anni Bergman Parent Infant Program, New York University Postdoctoral Program in Psychotherapy and Psychoanalysis, New York Freudian Society, Institute for Psychoanalytic Training and Research, New York, NY, USA
e-mail: annirink@gmail.com

J. E. Bettmann, D. D. Friedman (eds.), *Attachment-Based Clinical Work with Children and Adolescents,* Essential Clinical Social Work Series, DOI 10.1007/978-1-4614-4848-8_2, © Springer Science+Business Media New York 2013

tion and whose adult attachment organizations are different from their infant ones. Thus, while comprehensive, attachment theory is not developmental and therefore has some limits to its capacity to explain the intricacies of human functioning and experiencing. Psychoanalytic approaches assume the existence of universal development tasks and lines from infancy to adulthood, but approach understanding from the perspective of individual experience and individualized dynamics.

These and other issues contribute to the momentum to look beyond what is observable for a better understanding of the myriad factors that motivate what is observed. For example, the concepts of mentalization and reflective functioning describe capacities initially inferred from behavior and later from language, and which contribute much to variability in attachment capacities (Fonagy et al. 2002). The psychoanalytic concept of defenses, including lower and higher level defenses such as identification, internalization, introjection, reaction formation, and compromise formation, further explain why one individual develops idiosyncratic ways of being in the world within a specific family context.

While attachment theory currently enjoys a long era of empirical support for its relevance to a number of capabilities across the lifespan (e.g., Bartholomew 1993; Hazan and Shaver 1987; Kirkpatrick 2004), clinicians are showing increased interest in better understanding the transmission gaps. Transmission gaps refer to those babies whose attachment organization seems out of sync with their caregivers, those whose development proceeds in unexpected ways, and those families where siblings bear little resemblance to each other (van IJzendoorn et al. 2000). For example, attachment theory cannot explain why a boy has a secure attachment relationship with his mother while his sister is intensely anxious. These questions become particularly important for clinicians interested in understanding why an individual with a particularly troubling childhood demonstrates resilience, effective coping, and the capacity for intimacy and success, while another whose childhood does not include obvious stressors struggles to form and sustain relationships. A case study later in this chapter will help to illustrate how one sister's relative neglect ultimately resulted in greater mental health.

For their part, psychoanalysts are open to understanding early development in an integrated way that incorporates knowledge from the biological sciences, and are more accepting of the utility of empirical findings in clinical work (e.g., Fonagy and Target 2007). In recent decades, prolific psychoanalytic researchers like Beatrice Beebe and Daniel Stern delineated the fundamental importance of baby watching for clinical work with adults and children and integrated attachment theory and psychoanalytic theory in clinically relevant ways (Beebe 2005; Stern 1985). Beebe demonstrated that it is possible to measure qualities of infant attachment as early as 4 months of age (Koulomzin et al. 2002). She since used her findings to inform an analytically oriented approach to treating traumatized mothers (Beebe 2005). This closer collaboration between attachment theorists and psychoanalysts enhances both research and clinical work. This was demonstrated in a particularly poignant way in work with mothers who lost their partners following 9/11 and their children (e.g., Beebe and Jaffe 2011).

Attachment theory's explication of intergenerational transmission of attachment organization illuminates aspects of identification and defensive processes, including similarities between parents, children, and siblings that often seem hard to define or explain (e.g., Fonagy et al. 1991). In part, this is due to attachment theory's emphasis on the adaptive function of attachment organizations, such as the infant's pull to maximize contact and closeness with caregivers that contributes to patterns of behavior that are less adaptive in other circumstances. Attachment theory helps to explain, for example, why a new mother behaves with her child in ways she thought she never would—in the distant, awkward or overly involved way her mother treated her, for example. It might also help to clarify why a psychotherapy patient who is consciously motivated to ameliorate persistently unfulfilling relationships has trouble understanding the emotional needs of the people with whom he wants to be involved.

Separation–individuation theory provides concepts to understand a person's sense of themselves, as effectual or ineffectual, as confident or uneasy. It helps explain how siblings have dissimilar recollections of parental figures, and how people experience similar early circumstances in incompatible ways. This includes how a mother's involvement changes as her child becomes less dependent, how battles for autonomy or control between a child and his mother may develop over the course of early development, or how a child's gender affects a mother's attitude. These early experiences impact an individual's capacity for a stable sense of self and other in different ways over the course of a lifetime. This chapter examines aspects of attachment theory and separation–individuation theory relevant to these considerations and analyzes points of theoretical convergence and divergence.

For all of their differences, these two orientations are mutually enhancing. Each theory encompasses ideas about the development of self and affect regulation, but with different emphases. For example, affect regulation figures large in attachment research (Fonagy and Target 2007), while the development of the self is a focus of separation–individuation theory (Mahler et al. 1975). A clinician might conceptualize a psychotherapy patient's tendency to angrily fixate on daily phone conversations with her mother as representative of preoccupied attachment organization or as a failure of individuation which has made it hard for her to establish a sense of herself independent from her mother's close presence. Each perspective offers an entry into the psychological functioning and experiencing of the patient, and together provides ways to address both the patient's actual experiences and subjective reality. A close examination of these theories in a collaborative way reveals new possibilities for clinical understanding and directions for empirical work.

Origins and Methods

Events in the first months of life signal the beginning of normal and pathological identity formation (Mahler and McDevitt 1980). Attachment theory and separation–individuation theory each offer a compelling point of entry into the vast complexity of how the sense of self and other develops. Margaret Mahler and John Bowlby, the originators of separation–individuation theory and attachment theory respectively, began their ground-breaking work when each realized the enormous contributions of the real relationship between children and their caregivers to physical, psychological and interpersonal growth and development, in infancy and beyond. Independently, they sought knowledge of how development unfolds in the real world, and how life events—big or small, preventable or avoidable, familial or cultural—facilitate or impede development. From these basic points of origin, two revolutionary theories emerged that continue to impact the conceptualization, diagnosis, and treatment of a range of difficulties and disturbances.

In the 1950s, after years of working with developmental disturbances, Mahler and her team, which included analysts, pediatricians, researchers, and teachers, created a naturalistic setting, one that would allow for systematic study of development over time, as intact and undisturbed by scientific manipulation as possible (Mahler et al. 1975). They did not want to study psychological phenomena in isolation, but rather as they emerged in tandem with other developmental achievements. Mahler and her team fashioned the Master's Children's Center (MCC), created for the purposes of providing treatment to psychotic children and researching normal development, with the goal of facilitating "freely naturalistic observations which achieved a considerable degree of interrater reliability" (Mahler and McDevitt 1980, p. 396). In this setting, infants interacted with caregivers, strangers, and children in an environment that was relatively familiar to them. After observing nuances of behavior across various situations, Mahler and her team formulated a comprehensive theory of infant development.

A toddler room added later facilitated observation of children away from mothers, as mothers and babies left the baby room with different degrees of ease of separation (Mahler et al. 1975). Mahler and her team discussed observational data daily, weekly and monthly. Mahler's emphasis on beginning her formulations with "the earliest average mother–infant and mother–toddler interaction *in situ*" (Mahler (1986b) p. 222, italics in original) was quite revolutionary, and highly contentious in the analytic community. For example, predominant psychoanalytic ideas about development that came from the fantasy life of adult patients, at the time considered the only way into the mental life of young children. Professionals and the general public then held the opposite view, that much of what happens in the first years of life is inconsequential, inaccessible by language or memory. Nowadays these ideas seem impossibly archaic, which highlights how researchers like Mahler and Bowlby impacted mainstream culture.

Throughout Mahler's separation–individuation research, mothers and infants participated in psychological and developmental examinations by professionals who documented the children's development. Importantly, none of the children exhibited significant delays or impairments. This normalcy united these children for Mahler in contrast to the seriously disturbed children with whom she had previously worked. Senior researchers conducted interviews with parents and visited homes to learn about their perspectives and beliefs, and what happened in life beyond the center. All information contributed to the team's formulations about the separation–individuation subphases. Mahler and her team thus developed separation–individuation theory and modified it as their knowledge accumulated (Coates 2004; Mahler et al. 1975).

Mahler's research rationale is developed in a parallel fashion to John Bowlby's and Mary Ainsworth's seminal works. Bowlby's impetus for better understanding how children cope with separations emerged from two places: observations of hospitalized children's reactions to separations from caregivers and of the juvenile delinquency that seemed connected to familial separations as a result of World War II (Bowlby 1939; Bowlby and Robertson 1952). He was motivated to understand day-to-day events that could be traumatic. Departing from his original psychoanalytic frame, Bowlby became captivated by advances in ethology, biology, and cognitive science which seemed to offer avenues for understanding the complexity of his patient's lives (Coates 2004).

Attachment theory's Strange Situation procedure, now the gold-standard laboratory-based assessment of early attachment, grew out of Mary Ainsworth's knowledge accumulated from years of unstructured home observations in Uganda and Baltimore (Ainsworth 1978; Cassidy 1999; Main 2000). Prolonged direct observation in naturalistic settings is the best way to assess both attachment and separation–individuation phenomena (Waters et al. 2000), but this kind of observation is costly and time consuming. Ainsworth (1978) therefore developed the Strange Situation as a brief, yet comprehensive, tool for capturing internalized representations of attachment relationships before the development of language and symbolization. She focused on a child's behavior when reunited with the caregiver after brief separations, as these moments offered a glimpse into the child's internal world, including reflections of expectations about the caregiver's capacities, availability, and consistency. The Strange Situation is designed to elicit internal working models (IWMs) in children between 12 and 18 months of age (Ainsworth et al. 1978). It consists of eight episodes during which researchers observe a baby's reactions to sequences of separations and reunions with his primary caregiver. At times, a stranger is present with the baby, alone or with mother.

Observations of infants across a range of naturalistic settings, in places as diverse as Uganda and Baltimore, showed Ainsworth how secure and insecure attachment patterns manifest in behavior. Thus, she created a scenario to elicit these behaviors (Bretherton 1992). Mahler's observational work shares much with Ainsworth's, including a focus on stranger anxiety, reactions to separation and reunion, and the mutual focus on caregiver and child. However, the Strange Situation was the first standardized, laboratory-based method for evaluating these aspects of early development.

Separation–individuation theory describes an unfolding process, elaborating several points of entry for looking at a range of psychological and behavioral phenomena that develop and change across time and contexts (Solnit 1982). These phenomena include ways of coping with separations and reunions, interacting with familiar and unfamiliar adults and peers, psychomotor skills, and modes of communication. This theory does not employ a system of categorization or definitive scales of measurement. This theoretical framework contrasts with attachment theory, which relies on the Strange Situation and the Adult Attachment Interview (AAI) as measures of attachment organization. Notably, attachment theory is not a developmental theory while separation–individuation theory is.

Separation–individuation theory influenced the integration of infant-observation into clinical, theoretical and empirical work; Mahler's emergence at the forefront of developmental research in the 1960s energized the belief that "direct 'baby-watching' might supplement the observational opportunity of clinical psychoanalysis itself" (Pine 1994, p. 512). Mahler's formulations were dialectic, and her theory offered a glimpse into the origins of many clinical phenomena observed on the couch, as well as some hope for achieving resolution for long ago traumas.

Object constancy, the ultimate psychological achievement in Mahler's theory, is rarely if ever fully achieved (Mahler et al. 1975). This suggests, on the one hand, that normal development allows for many stumbling blocks that do not necessarily preclude successful functioning. It also suggests that structural psychological vulnerabilities are inevitable. Based on the contemporaneous achievement of a stable, positive sense of self and competence, the developmental accomplishment of object-constancy is the result of a balanced interaction between cooperative and competitive inter- and intra-personal dynamics.

Mahler's goal was to illuminate origins of psychological health and maladjustment, and to build a bridge between adult functioning and childhood experiences. However, she did not develop methods for evaluating separation, individuation, and the capacity for object-constancy throughout life. Many prominent analytic authors have applied separation–individuation theory to their clinical work, but this has been done predominantly through case study research and writing (e.g., Bergman and Fahey 2005; Kramer 1992; Olesker 1998; Olesker 2011; Pine 1994; Tyson 2005).

Views on Early Infancy

Separation–Individuation Theory

Separation–individuation theory describes four subphases of development, preceded by what Mahler called symbiotic and normal autistic phases that mark the months immediately following birth (Mahler et al. 1975). These earliest phases are perhaps the most controversial aspects of separation–individuation theory and various authors refute them (Blum 2004). The symbiotic phase follows the boundary-less autistic phase, beginning around the second month. This phase is marked by "dim awareness of the need-satisfying object" (Mahler et al. 1975, p. 44), in which the infant is aware that stimulation and the satisfaction of basic needs like hunger and warmth originate from sources beyond his or her physical self. At this stage, a mother's behavior and sensitivity determines the nature of the infant's experiences. Still absent, however, is a specific relationship between mother and infant, which includes the dyadically co-constructed interactions observed in later phases.

While Mahler eventually reconsidered how unified mother and baby initially are, she remained firm in her belief that the infant remains in a state of dual-unity or merger (Mahler et al. 1975) until the separation–individuation phase begins. Borrowing the term symbiosis from biology, Mahler (1967) emphasized that in the first weeks of life mother and baby exist as a functional unit of two organisms to their mutual advantage. She used symbiosis as a metaphor to capture a state of undifferentiation in which the child has not yet developed the capacity to discriminate "I" from "not-I." Mother and baby are one from the baby's perspective (Mahler 1986a).

Mahler emphasized the young infant's absolute dependence. She believed that children lacked the capacity to express demands and negotiate environmental cues. Differences in holding behavior, including aspects of breast-feeding, availability, and closeness, are fundamental precursors that determine how the co-constructed interaction between mother and child unfolds later (Mahler et al. 1994) and the child's emotional regulation (Tyson 1991). For Mahler, the mother's way of being shapes the infant's dawning awareness of physical and psychological boundaries. Gradually, the infant develops complex and idiosyncratic mechanisms for navigating separation and individuation (Mahler and Furer 1963). For example, the infant's preferential smiling signals the advent of a particular bond between mother and child (Mahler et al. 1975). At 4 to 5 months, the infant moves into the first subphase of separation–individuation, and begins the journey to selfhood and separateness.

Subsequent theorists working in the separation–individuation theory tradition argued that a core self is present at birth, citing neurological and observational evidence that indicates that the infant is born equipped with particular ways of negotiating the environment (Pine 1994; Tyson 1991). How temperament influences infant behavior and development continues to be debated, as babies act and react in ways that appear unrelated to caregiving or are different from siblings who share the same parents (van IJzendoorn et al. 2000). Mahler repeatedly emphasized how complicated the development of a sense of self and other is, influenced by myriad factors over years. She stated that the "biological birth of the human infant and the psychological birth of the individual are not coincident in time. The former is a dramatic, observable, and well-circumscribed event; the latter is a slowly unfolding intrapsychic process" (Mahler et al. 1975, p. 3). While Mahler might not take issue with the concept of an infant born in an active state of engagement with his environment, her focus was on how the infant transitioned from dependence to relative independence and to an autonomous sense of self.

Attachment Theory

Attachment theory promotes a different view of a baby's behavior in the first few months of life. Attachment theorists maintain that the infant arrives with active strategies for engaging with the external world (Ainsworth 1969; Bowlby 1969/1982). This thinking marked a dramatic departure from Bowlby's analytic training, as historically psychoanalysts thought of the baby's earliest experiences as driven by need-gratification, for example the need for food. They believed the baby was oriented in a boundary-less way to the breast (Ainsworth 1969). Early object relations theorists held the notion that some aspects of relationships, such differentiation and distinctness in the mind of the infant, existed from the very beginning of life. They framed the baby's experience as one of always being in-relationship rather than one of purely physical need-states (Winnicott 1964).

Attachment theory emphasizes the biologically based behavioral system with which the baby enters the world (Bowlby 1969/1982). From this perspective, the infant is born equipped with an arsenal of tools—crying, clinging, and sucking—employed to keep the caregiver in close proximity. Bowlby argued that the infant's new behaviors oriented the child to maintaining safety, sustenance, and proximity, as baby and mother worked out their own relational system.

Bowlby (1969/1982) was one of the first to challenge the view that interpersonal ties between baby and mother arise out of the gratification of primary drives. Bowlby proposed that the baby is motivated by a behavioral system designed to forge the mother–infant connection. "The concept of the behavioral system involves inherent motivation. There is no need to view attachment as the by-product of any more fundamental processes or 'drive'" (Cassidy 1999, p. 5). Psychoanalysts focused on Freud's belief that pleasure is the governing force in the newborn's world, an approach in which babies are perceived as motivated by maximizing pleasure and minimizing displeasure (Freud 1971). This belief includes the notion that the mother's ability to satisfy the baby's demands governs the first months of life; this includes decreasing displeasure while increasing positive feelings of comfort and satiety and maximizing the baby's perception that his demands for pleasurable stimuli are met. However, attachment theorists noticed that attachment occurs often enough in unfavorable circumstances, with or without pleasure. Babies of neglecting/rejecting caregivers are no less desiring of their mothers than those with attentively attuned mothers; they adapt to develop strategies to maximize proximity to a range of less-than-optimal circumstances (Bowlby 1969/1982).

Transitioning from Babyhood to Infancy

Even with different ideas of what happens in early infancy, both attachment theory and separation–individuation theory emphasize perception and psychomotor ability as integral to the unfolding dynamics emerging in the mother–child relationship.

Separation–Individuation Theory's View

Mahler took Freud's statement that the ego is first and foremost a body ego very seriously (Mahler and McDevitt 1982; Tyson 1992). The experience of a separate and consistent self and other begins tactilely and visually, as the infant begins to recognize variations in physiological stimulation signaling "me" and "not-me." What

Mahler referred to as hatching signals the first subphase of separation–individuation, differentiation, and the development of the body image (Mahler et al. 1975). We see hatching in the infant's increased alertness and responsiveness to changing stimuli. The infant is now capable of a more "permanently alert sensorium" and attention is increasingly directed outward, "combined with a growing store of memories of mother's comings and goings, of 'good' and 'bad' experiences" (Mahler et al. 1975, pp. 53–54). The baby's rapidly expanding activities initially belong to what Mahler called customs inspection, which refers to the baby's thorough visual and tactile investigation of immediate objects and surroundings. At first, the baby distinguishes what is familiar from what is unfamiliar and then between various sources of stimulation and excitement. In this process, adults can recognize the baby's developing cognition and emotion.

During this stage, the child and mother work out a system of predictable signals and responses and the mother selectively responds to her child's cues. Prior to this, the mother manages her baby's activities and experiences around her own conscious and unconscious needs (McDevitt 1980). Often during this subphase, mothers claim to have special knowledge of their infant's needs and intentions that is unavailable to anyone else. While a mother's experience of bonding with her infant is important, more important is the extent to which mothers can appropriately, adequately, and without too much self-preoccupation, respond to infants' individualized needs. An infant's progress can be hastened or delayed by his mother's particular ministrations, and separation and individuation can be differentially affected. For example, a mother's distractibility and unavailability can lead her baby to display signs of hatching too early, possibly compromising basic trust and self-confidence (Mahler et al. 1975).

As the child's physical capabilities develop, he exerts more influence on the unfolding separation–individuation process. A balance between the infant's need for mother's caregiving and exploration of the outside world becomes more important. Physiological, cognitive, and emotional development may derive from environmental deficiencies and/or stimulation. For example, "children who achieve premature locomotor development . . . may become prematurely aware of their own separateness much before their individuation . . . has given them the means with which to cope with this process" (Mahler 1972b, p. 490). Mothers can be more or less comfortable with aspects of their child's development, for example, hastening an infant's independent locomotion before he is equipped psychologically to handle the physical distance and independence that crawling and walking bring. A child's ability to navigate the next subphase, which is essential for social and emotional functioning, depends on the extent to which his mother's availability matches his needs.

During the practicing subphase, the normally developing child feels increasingly competent as a separately functioning individual, and is able to experience "a love affair with the world" (Greenacre 1957 as cited in Mahler 1972b, p. 491). Exuberance and excitement are characteristic of this phase, as the child, with his rapidly developing capacity for movement, is overjoyed by his own abilities. During this time, children seem impervious to stumbles and pains, and caregivers often find themselves chasing after toddlers who have no sense of potential mishaps or awareness of their watchful eyes.

Walking has enormous significance for development (Blum 2004; Mahler et al. 1994). The extent to which a child is able to confidently go out into the world depends on a foundation of basic safety provided by the mother, as well as the child's expectation of the mother's availability. Fear that the mother will be disapproving, will disappear, or will be disappointed can have a detrimental effect on the child's capacity to negotiate the environment and establish a sense of stability and security. The mother's ability to convey expectation and confidence in the child lays the foundation for the child's self-esteem, autonomy, and sense of separateness (Mahler et al. 1994). The mother's capacity to sustain availability and attunement to the child's needs during this time also influences the tremendous changes in the second year of life. Following the practicing phase, toddlers undergo the rapprochement subphase, in which toddlers must find ways to manage conflicting experiences, emotions, and desires. The outcome of the separation, individuation process is, ideally, "the establishment of a sense of separateness from, and relation to, a world of reality, particularly with regard to the experiences of one's own body and to the principal representative of the world as the infant experiences it, the primary love object" (Mahler et al. 1975, p. 420). The child who successfully navigates the separation–individuation process has internalized conflicting aspects of self and other as components of a worthwhile object and is able to engage in the world with flexibility, autonomy, and relatedness.

Attachment Theory's View

Attachment theorists have a different view of these first months. They focus on behavioral patterns that become predictable over time, noticing what is consistent in caregiver–child interactions. Bowlby believed that a child's behavioral patterns originate in an evolutionarily based species-characteristic behavior system (Ainsworth 1969; Bowlby 1969/1982). At birth, the infant employs behaviors designed to facilitate proximity and connectedness with caregivers. An infant employs increasingly sophisticated strategies to achieve these goals, strategies determined by accumulated interactions with caregivers and expectations in reciprocity. Attachment theorists refer to these behaviors and strategies as goal-corrected behaviors (Bowlby 1969/1982). Towards the end of the first year of life, simpler behavioral sequences are gradually subsumed into more complex sequences and cognitive structures begin to exert influence. Emotions play a role in appraising behavioral outcomes and inform internalization. The infant does not consciously think of strategies and outcomes. These are automatic, outside of awareness, but driven by cognition and affect. The secure-base function of the attachment system, which provides the infant with a sense of safety with which to enter into and explore the world, is reminiscent of the love-affair of the practicing subphase. However, attachment researchers emphasize the infant's constant awareness of the presence and availability of the caregiver. In their view, the infant is always alert to his safety and security, never oblivious to the availability of primary caregivers.

A key developmental window opens around the end of the first year. Behavioral patterns observed around 12–18 months in the presence of caregivers are manifestations of infants' IWMs of attachment. Main et al. (1985) defined IWMs as "a set of conscious and/or unconscious rules for the organization of information relevant to attachment and for obtaining or limiting access to that information, that is, to information regarding attachment-related experiences, feelings, and ideations" (p. 92). By 1 year of age, the infant internalizes a range of expectations—expectations of availability, attention, understanding, and protection.

IWMs are specific to attachment figures. Attachment researchers show that a mother's attachment history and contemporaneous attachment representations shape her infant's behavior. The infant's behavioral patterns in this context are stable, predictable, and consistent by 12 months (Main 1985; Fonagy et al. 1991). In all interactions, a child's behaviors are context-specific; they are initially designed to ensure the proximity of an attachment figure and become embedded in expectations of how available an attachment figure is. The infant adjusts his behaviors to his caregiver's responses, learning which behaviors are more effective in times of need (Bowlby 1969/1982; Cassidy 1999). Thus, he learns how to minimize his own distress and maximize experiences of feeling loved, competent, and protected, by favoring behaviors that facilitate positive and minimize negative encounters with his caregivers. A generalized representation of experiences in a specific caregiving context guides the infant, and eventually the adult (Main et al. 1985).

As development proceeds, the child makes use of a growing number of strategies for a growing range of goals. As Cassidy (1999) states, "an infant may maintain a stable internal organization of the attachment behavioral system in relation to the mother over time and across context, yet the specific behaviors used may vary greatly" (p. 5). Similarly, Bowlby (1969/1982) noted that although infants' behaviors may differ in their appearance, their intended effect may be the same. For example, crying, reaching, and crawling each facilitate proximity and communicate the need for protection or soothing.

The infant whose behavior shows greater flexibility is more likely to succeed in his proximity-seeking goal and to do so quickly. At the same time, caregiver attunement and availability determine some portion of the infant's capacity to be flexible. A child's confidence that caregivers will respond to his attempts to establish contact depends on what restrictions those caregivers place on his ability to attract attention and what kind of attention, positive or negative, he gets. Children increasingly rely on mental representations, formed from their own relational histories, when organizing their behavior in relation to their caregivers. The more that these representations reflect reality, one in which a loving, sensitive, and available mother is at hand, the better equipped that child is to cope with the demands of growing up (Bowlby 1969/1982; Cassidy 1999; Marvin and Britner 1999). Children are always in states of attachment, but the activation of attachment behaviors is situational, based on specific needs for specific individuals to provide comfort, protection or reassurance (Cassidy 1999).

Mary Ainsworth's groundbreaking observational work culminated in the identification of several distinct patterns of attachment behaviors observable in infants over the world: secure, resistant/ambivalent, avoidant, disorganized (Ainsworth et al. 1978; Ainsworth 1978). These patterns reflect a parent's responsiveness clearly in, but not limited to, moments of separation (Kobak 1999). Attachment organizations differ in how the child manages the distress of separation in an organized and systematic way. In other words, attachment organizations are defined by the extent to which a child openly exhibits distress, actively seeks refuge with his/her mother without ambivalence, and copes with the stress of separation while engaging with the world.

Attachment researchers use the Strange Situation to elicit IWMs between 12 and 18 months of age. This experimental, laboratory-based procedure captures separations and reunions between infants and their caregivers, during which a stranger is sometimes present, or when infant is left alone for brief periods (Ainsworth 1978; Kobak 1999; Waters et al. 2000; Sroufe 2003). Organized patterns of attachment are consistent in several significant ways. Secure infants make overtures to their mothers on reunion and are comforted by physical contact with her. Avoidant infants appear unmoved by separation and reunion experiences; these infants avoid or ignore mother on reunion, and their detachment increases with every separation. Resistant/ambivalent infants often seem clingy, are the most overtly distressed by the whole experience, and are difficult to comfort. They may appear angry and simultaneously needy and rejecting; they are more likely to elicit mother's proximity than to seek it.

Attachment behaviors convey information about the quality of the caregiving environment. Once formed, IWMs are increasingly resistant to change (e.g., Bowlby 1969/1982; Waters et al. 2000). An infant's attachment organization at 1 year of age correlates with a host of developmental sequelae along dimensions of affect regulation, sociability, likeability, adjustment and psychopathology (Kobak 1999; Fonagy et al. 2002). The nature and organization of IWMs may be inferred from observing a child's behavior in a variety of situations, such as when they are close to and away from caregivers.

Toddlerhood

Attachment theory's focus remains on IWMs throughout childhood. The theory focuses on how IWMs develop and how qualities of IWMs influence myriad aspects of development, including school performance and peer relationships. By contrast, separation–individuation theory examines how the development of autonomous thoughts, feelings, and actions continues to unfold throughout childhood. This process is the experience of becoming a separate person.

The third subphase of the separation–individuation process begins around the middle of the second year. Mahler emphasized the centrality of ambivalence during this subphase, which she called rapprochement (Mahler 1972b; Mahler et al. 1975). As the infant becomes more active in the world beyond mother, and has a wider variety of experiences with others and objects, he is gradually more aware of his own fallibility. The exuberance and omnipotence characteristic of the practicing subphase give way to a painful knowledge of limitations. The infant is faced with the dilemma of wanting to move further out into the world he has come to love while knowing that he is still very much dependent on mother's help and support. "Incompatibilities and misunderstandings between mother and child can be observed at this period even in the case of the normal mother and her normal toddler" (Mahler 1972a, p. 337). The mother is perplexed by her child's sudden neediness and the incomprehensible demands for attention and consolation typical for the 2-year old. The infant is also negotiating affective and cognitive aspects of his representation of mother, as he is able to sustain impressions and experiences increasingly over time. The child is confused and conflicted by positive and negative experiences of self and others; these experiences require attentive parenting to navigate effectively. During this phase, mother and child are no longer able to function as a dual unit (Mahler et al. 1975) and must recognize each other as separate, with at times complementary and at times distinct needs and desires (Mahler 1972b). Infants must also contend with the unmistakable reality that their mother's attentions are needed and demanded elsewhere. Mothers must adjust to infants' abilities to master tasks on their own.

Mahler (1972b) noted that the "mother's continual emotional availability is essential if the child's autonomous ego is to attain optimal functional capacity" (p. 495). The optimally emotionally available mother is not the same mother who immediately meets her toddler's demands. Mothers necessarily fail at times. Thus, learning how to tolerate frustration is an important developmental task for the toddler. The toddler struggles with the wish for his mother to regulate his frustration and the wish to employ his own capacity for self-regulation. At this point in development, fathers can be particularly important sources of relief and support for the mother, and a stimulating, less-conflicting, parental figure to the child (Mahler et al. 1975; McDevitt and Mahler 1980).

The rapprochement crisis refers to the height of this phase. This crisis carries a lot of weight during childhood and beyond as the origin of potential for adaptive functioning and psychopathology. The extent to which the toddler can learn to manage frustration and move toward integrating conflicting mental representations with adequate modeling and commiseration from his/her mother informs to what extent experienced anxiety inhibits psychological functioning and interpersonal competence.

Colarusso (1992) notes that when

> ... mother is available and actively participates with encouragement and enthusiasm, the toddler is emotionally refueled and ready to venture again, alone into the ever-expanding world. But even under the best of circumstances both mother and child experience intervals of ambivalence and frustration as they repeatedly work through the intense feelings of reunion and separation. (p. 49)

The toddler who is "not so fortunate in his development" suffers an intensified rapprochement crisis, is afflicted by increased ambivalence and splitting of the object world (McDevitt and Mahler 1980, p. 413). In less than optimal circumstances, the child's ambivalence toward competence versus dependence, good versus bad other, separation and merger, persists and inhibits the child's potential for integrated self-

and object-constancy, which would permit flexible and satisfying engagement with the world.

At this phase of development, both attachment theory and separation–individuation theory outline the mother's changing tasks, which expand beyond the role of safe-haven and secure-base. She becomes increasingly responsible for framing internal and external experiences through language: "The mother with the child creates a narrative about the child, about the mother, about their being together. This narrative is woven into the child's emerging representation of self and the outside world. The mother takes on the new role of organizer into language of her child's affective life" (Bergman and Harpaz-Rotem 2004, p. 564). Also, the toddler's image of the mother must be re-negotiated often, as her omnipotence wanes and misunderstandings between them necessitate repair. In optimal circumstances, these changes and their accompanied negotiations proceed smoothly, but conflict is inevitable. The nature and organization of the child's behavior during this time will reveal the extent to which he recognizes his mother as a dependable participant in his development who helps to navigate the rapprochement crisis while reflecting his own competence and capacities for autonomy.

Separation–individuation theory took for granted that some kind of attachment existed between the mothers and babies observed at the Master's Center. The original research team set out to describe the spectrum of normal experiences where some mutuality between mother and child exists. Mahler also turned her attention to separation, but not separation in the literal sense of babies being left or abandoned as had captured Bowlby's attention. Mahler started with the supposition that babies develop along predictable lines. In the course of development, they have to deal with the fact that separation from mother is a given, unavoidable, and frequent fact of life. From this perspective, separation is thought of in very small terms, such as going to sleep at night or when mother leaves the room. When separation is understood in these terms, separation–individuation meets attachment theory at the point where the accumulated experiences of these minor and momentary, although sometimes prolonged, but essentially unavoidable separations, define the quality of interaction between mother and child, and contribute to the infant's emerging understanding of both the self and mother as separate entities (Stern 1985).

Rather than focusing on the interpersonal domain, Mahler looked at the intra-person process of becoming a separate person. Attachment theory links this process of becoming a separate person to the quality of attachment, which defines much of how a person experiences himself and others. Mahler did not negate the importance of the primary relationship to that process of separating, but her main focus was always the child and his ability to establish "a sense of separateness from and relation to a world of reality, particularly with regard to the experiences of one's own body and to the principal representative of the world as the infant experiences it, the primary love object" (Mahler et al. 1975, p. 420). Mahler thought that a child's internalized primary love object, which determines so much about the sense of self, was based on a real relationship with her mother. But she also believed that the task of the child is to separate and to be an individual although the intrapsychic process of separateness reverberates throughout life and is constantly being reorganized.

Beyond Infancy

The fourth subphase of the separation–individuation phase of development is termed"on the way to object-constancy," which emphasizes that this process has repercussions throughout life (Mahler et al. 1975). The hallmark of object-constancy is the achievement of "a mostly 'good,' loving image" that functions to provide the child with a sense of security and comfort just as the actual mother had. The child internalizes the image of the mother as part of the self (Tyson 2005, p. 71). The child optimally experiences mother and self as primarily good and capable, even if negative, hostile, or deficient experiences of functioning occurred. Good self-esteem and generally positive expectations of the world then characterize the child's behavior. Object-constancy is thus conceptually similar to attachment theory's notion of IWMs of attachment experiences.

Embedded in the notion of object-constancy is the concept of self-constancy, which refers to the child's achievement of a sense of separateness and uniqueness, uncompromised by intimacy. Self-constancy signals organized and stable individuality. As Mahler et al. (1975) explained, at this stage "both inner structures—libidinal object-constancy as well as a unified self-image based on true ego identifications—should have their inception" (p. 118). In the face of environmental pressures and trauma, including those originating in the specific mother–child and father–child relationships, the infant is at risk for compromised psychological functioning. Mahler argued that unfavorable conditions threaten the persistence of omnipotence, paranoia, grandiosity, and magical thinking, elaborated and amplified from the toddler's worldview. The capacity for object- and self-constancy means the difference between an approach to life characterized by adequate self-assertion—reasonable compromise formation—and one defined by rigid, underdeveloped, infantile defenses (McDevitt and Mahler 1980).

At this point in development, attachment theory focuses on how the attachment system overlaps with other systems important in a child's world. Attachment-related behaviors in infancy are not the same as those of the older toddler and young child, whose capacity for representations and symbolic thought takes over what used to be accomplished by physical proximity. For example, a 4 year-old knows that mother exists even when she is not immediately at hand and can be reassured by a memory, phone-call or substitute object. Social relationships with peers and other adults become crucial to a child's world and sense of self. The child's attachment organization serves as model for most other relationships, but not exclusively so, as other people occupy different roles from the provider of a safe haven and secure base.

Object-Constancy

The concept of object-constancy has been central in psychoanalytic and developmental theory for many decades. Yet what is meant by object-constancy remains poorly defined (Burgner and Edgecumbe 1972; McDevitt 1975; Tyson 1996). That an individual's capacity for object-constancy says something about his psychological functioning is well-established (Tyson 1996), but when and how this can be evaluated is unclear. The literature upholds a double meaning that suggests, on the one hand, that object-constancy is a developmental achievement and, on the other, that it is a lifelong process. In light of this ongoing debate, Solnit (1982) and Tyson (1996) emphasize the function of object-constancy.

By most accounts, Hartmann (1952) introduced object-constancy into the psychoanalytic literature without providing a clear definition or explication (McDevitt 1975; Tyson 1996). Many psychoanalytic writers delineate the domain of object-constancy (Fraiberg 1969; Burgner and Edgecumbe 1972; McDevitt 1975; Solnit 1982; Tyson 1996) by separating what components of it belong to different developmental and academic domains, such as perception, cognition, affect regulation, interpersonal functioning, psychopathology, etc. As Burgner and Edgcumbe (1972) emphasize,

> The term *object constancy* is a confusing one because of its links with the narrowly defined concept of perceptual constancy derived from academic psychology, whereas psychoanalysts are essentially interested in the establishment of a specific level of object relationships to animate objects and in the first instance, to one specific and preferred object. (p. 327, italics in original)

Pioneering perspectives on object-constancy include the notion of object permanence (Piaget 1936), the concept of libidinal object-constancy (Fraiberg 1969; Gergely 2000), and the description of developmental tasks in the fourth subphase of separation–individuation, as well as object-constancy which shapes the subjective experience of self and other in relational contexts throughout the lifespan (Mahler et al. 1975). Piaget defined object-permanence as when an infant can recognize that an object still exists even when it is not in sight, around 8 months of age. It is not until about 18 months of age, however, that a child develops the capacity for evocative memory (Fraiberg 1969). Therefore, depending on the definition used, a child's capacity for object representations develops somewhere between 5 months and 3 years of age.

The 1-year old knows in some way that his mother exists even when they are separated. He employs strategies to bring her near when she strays from view. Thus, libidinal object-constancy has primacy over other object representations. The infant first develops a specific representation of mother before other people and objects (Fraiberg 1969). Libidinal object-constancy belongs to the interpersonal world of human relationships, and has broader implications for socioemotional development. Spitz (1957) uses the child's ability to recognize a stranger as not-mother—evident through the display of stranger anxiety—as the hallmark of object constancy "*in regard to the libidinal object*" (Fraiberg 1969, p. 17, italics in original). This ability also marks the beginning of a stable image in which positive and negative aspects of mother begin to be assimilated. However, Fraiberg (1969) makes the point that stranger anxiety does not mark the achievement of evocative memory, the child's ability to sustain the image of mother when faced with a stranger, and thus be comforted. It is not clear whether loving mother and stranger can both exist in the child's mind. Thus, a child who becomes anxious when faced with people other-than-mother has not yet achieved libidinal object-constancy.

Need states play an important role in defining object-constancy. The child's need for mother to fulfill various desires, such as protection or sustenance, and her capacity to comply enough are essential components of libidinal object-constancy as distinct from object-constancy for the inanimate object. A transitional/substitute object might take on some of these properties under certain circumstances. The emotional context of object-constancy, in the psychoanalytic sense, emphasizes that an attachment to the libidinal object is transformed from one based on need to a more purely psychological attachment and identification. Put differently, the libidinal object exists psychologically, an existence that is independent of its physical presence, and independent of an immediate (physical) need for it. Moreover, the internalized libidinal object provides the infant with information about himself, as lovable or valuable or essential, in a way that any inanimate object cannot.

Burgner and Edgecumbe (1972) offer the term "capacity for constant relationship" (p. 328) as a way to clarify object-constancy from a psychoanalytic perspective. They define this term by stating that "in the second half of the second year of life, psychic maturation is sufficiently advanced for the individual both to begin to recognize and to begin to tolerate such a conflictual feeling state toward the one object" (Burgner and Edgecumbe 1972, p. 328). An essential component of a constant relationship is the ability to stay in relationship even when the other (object) is lacking, unsatisfactory or even abusive (e.g., Fraiberg 1969). Similarly, early in her work, Mahler (1968) stated, "[b]y object constancy we mean that the maternal image has become intrapsychically available to the child in the same way as the actual mother had been libidinally available—for sustenance, comfort and love" (p. 222).

Mahler's conceptualization of object-constancy, and its particular emphasis on a consistent (integrated) representation of mother is controversial, even within the analytic community (Tyson 1996). Attachment theorists, who place the achievement of stable IWMs as a task of the first year, question her timeline which focuses on a rapprochement phase that needs to be successfully negotiated before object-constancy is possible (Gergely 2000; Lyons-Ruth 1991). These controversies highlight Mahler's comprehensive approach, with emphasis on the physical, psychological, motor, and perceptual processes through which a sense of self and other emerge. Solnit (1982) stressed that while object-constancy is not a psychic structure, as a capacity that resides in the ego, it has structural qualities and can act as a precondition for other cognitive and emotional capacities. Mahler began with object permanence as a prerequisite for object-constancy, putting the ability to retain a positively cathected internalized representation of mother in the face of conflict as the signal of the capacity for object-constancy.

According to separation–individuation theory, a child's capacity for object-constancy emerges around his second birthday (Mahler et al. 1975; McDevitt 1975). By this time, a child has more sophisticated strategies for existing as a separate individual in his own world, and for managing pleasure and anxiety on his own. From a different but parallel perspective, the child of this age achieves some capacity for autonomous affect regulation. "A great merit of the object-constancy concept lies in its ability to help us understand the development of a self-regulatory capacity" (Tyson 1996, p. 175). The capacity to maintain a complex yet stable representation of another person coincides with the capacity to maintain and regulate complex representations of one's self.

Nowadays, clinicians generally accept the notion that object-constancy is a process that spans development. Focusing on different points along the developmental continuum required the use of different evaluative criteria for object-constancy. While attachment researchers have developed ways to capture and evaluate security of attachment at different points in time, determining success or quality in the broader domain of object-constancy remains elusive. One way to consider how the concepts of IWMs and object-constancy overlap is to recall that the former emphasizes representations of interactions and how these representations influence relationships with particular objects, while the latter emphasizes internalized objects and how internalized objects inform interpersonal functioning. But both concepts organize behaviors and experience, knowledge of self and other.

Representations of interactions with one person can, for the infant, exist before the conscious attribution of those interactions to the same person. Attachment theory demonstrates that infants have predictable expectations of their caregiver's behaviors and preferences, long before language organizes thoughts and experiences. Thus, IWMs are precursors to object-constancy. The parallel experience of self that accompanies the achievement of object-constancy is not a necessary feature of IWMs. As indicated previously, one thing that separates separation–individuation theory from attachment theory is its original focus on the emerging sense of self, of separateness, and independence. In an optimal environment, children will achieve an understanding of their separateness and uniqueness. As Mahler et al. (1975) explained, during the phase of development where the capacity for object-constancy emerges "both inner structures—libidinal object constancy as well as a unified self-image based on true ego identifications—should have their inception" (p. 118). Ideally, the child has internalized a generally good and loving image that provides a sense of security and comfort similar to the actual mother.

Alongside this achievement, the infant should internalize loving aspects of mother as part of the self, so that a confident, good sense of the self endures (Tyson 2005). Integral to all conceptualizations of object-constancy is that it "is a milestone capacity in the development of object relations. Its achievement requires the intimacy and continuity of affectionate care that enables the child to move from need-satisfying limitations to the capabilities associated with object constancy, capabilities that can be characterized as ego functions" (Solnit 1982, p. 216). As a developmental milestone that emerges in the context of adequate caregiving, the capacity for object-constancy is reflected in an individual's moment-to-moment ability to cope with an ever growing range of experiences across the lifespan.

Evaluating Object Constancy: From Infancy to Adulthood

Researchers evaluate IWMs in infants using the Strange Situation procedure, but no instrument exists for evaluating the separation–individuation process. Solnit (1982) stated that object constancy "can be 'measured' in terms of the young child's tolerance for separation from the primary love object" (p. 211). While this sounds like the Strange Situation, he is not referring to an orchestrated scenario at a particular moment, but instead to the child's overall behavior patterns both when he is close to and separated from mother. These behavior patterns may include the extent to which a child tries to avoid separation and behaves in a way meant to keep his mother close, the extent to which a child will seek out others when his mother is present and/or absent, and the extent to which a child behaves differently when his mother is around. There are innumerable indicators of a child's emotional experience with and without mother, his ability to regulate the emotions that come with separations, and how well he engages with reality beyond his caregivers.

Toward the end of the second year, the normally developing child demonstrates tolerance for separation in familiar environments (Mahler et al. 1975). Settlage et al. (1991) suggest further that the child's ability to engage in play and exploration independently from mother and without signs of distress portrays a state of internal regulation. However, a child should not necessarily be calm or distressed when separated from mother—much depends on the circumstances of the separation (e.g., is the child sick, in familiar surroundings, with unfamiliar others, in conflict with peers, told of mother's departure, reacting to a prolonged separation, etc.).

Assessing independence and autonomy remains a controversial subject (e.g., Lyons-Ruth 1991), but the notion that children develop highly personalized strategies to manage separations is not. What signals an optimally developing capacity for object constancy is the extent to which children can manage emotions in ways that permit engagement in the world. This capacity affects myriad aspects of successful development and functioning throughout life. A child who is too dependent on mother and a child who avoids contact are functioning with mental representations of self and other that are conflicted and poorly defined. In short, determining to what extent a child is on the path to the capacity for object-constancy is necessarily complex, and requires a sophisticated understanding of the tasks of development and a thorough understanding of the child and his circumstances. Thus, evaluating the capacity for object-constancy typically occurs in clinical settings in the context of concern from caregivers about whether things are as they should be.

It is possible for clinicians to identify aspects of adaptive and maladaptive functioning, wherever in the lifespan an individual is. Much has been written in psychoanalytic literature about the application of separation–individuation subphases to phenomena of adolescence (e.g., Blos 1967) and adulthood (Colarusso 2000). However, object-constancy is only assessed clinically through a consideration of an individual's capacity to pilot their life, including work, recreation, and relationships, in ways that permit a consistent and stable sense of self and other.

Attachment researchers focused on developing methods to examine IWMs at different points across the lifespan for decades. In part, this is because the attachment system takes a backseat to other systems after infancy, when the proximity of caregivers is of less immediate concern, and thus attachment representations and their influence are obscured. A large body of work pertains to how attachment organizations relate to attachment styles in intimate relationships (e.g., Bartholomew 1993; Hazan and Shaver 1987), which indicates that relationships with romantic partners are influenced both in complementary and compensatory ways by how earliest experiences have been internalized.

In adulthood, attachment patterns can be evaluated using The AAI (Hesse 1999; Main et al. 2008). The AAI offers a compelling point of entry for examining how attachment experiences continue to resonate, in both conscious and unconscious ways (Main et al. 2002). In the same way that behavioral observations offer entry into the internal worlds of infants, the AAI provides access to internalized representations of self and other in adulthood. The AAI offers insight into what defenses are at work by highlighting the "individual differences in deeply internalized strategies for regulating emotion and attention in response to the discussion of attachment" (Main et al. 2008, p. 37). How the AAI, with its careful attention to both the content and form of language, can be used to examine reverberations of separation–individuation phenomena is one more task for this era of reconciliation.

Contrast Between the Two Theories

Separation–Individuation Theory's Critics

The proliferation of attachment research and theory over the past several decades is due in part to the advent of methods like the Strange Situation and the AAI, which evaluate attachment-related constructs. These tools make attachment theory laboratory-friendly and contribute to research on culture-bound elements of the attachment system on a global scale (van IJzendoorn and Kroonenberg 1988; van IJzendoorn and Sagi 1999). However, separation–individuation theory is more difficult to assess and observe systematically.

Attachment theory and separation–individuation theory examine similar phenomena through different lenses. Separation–individuation theory emphasizes that while early events lay a foundation for selfhood and patterns of perceiving and relating, our way of being in the world is highly individualized and always unfolding (Mahler et al. 1975). Attachment theory, in contrast, focuses on what is species-specific relational behavior and how much of what happens is resistant to change after the first or second year of life (Bowlby 1969/1982). While these perspectives are not mutually exclusive, the potential for collaboration has been challenged over the years.

Several attachment researchers, focusing on incompatibilities between separation–individuation theory and attachment theory, argue that separation–individuation theory normalizes behaviors that attachment theory understands differently (Lyons-Ruth 1991; Gergely 2000). For example, the concept of the rapprochement crisis marks an important point of disagreement between attachment theory and psychoanalytic theories. Mahler described the rapprochement crisis as an integral part of normative development. However, this crisis may be linked to insecure attachment, as her explication seems to refer to qualities of the anxious/ambivalent attachment organization in infancy (Lyons-Ruth 1991). Attachment theorists argue that a rapprochement crisis in the context of a secure attachment is untenable. They take issue with a necessarily stormy rapprochement subphase that seems to normalize pathological behaviors on behalf of both mother and infant (Gergely 2000; Lyons-Ruth 1991).

While some children exhibit more intense struggles around separateness and autonomy, separation–individuation theory agrees that this subphase can be navigated more quietly (Mahler et al. 1975). What has occurred before this point between mother and child will determine the nature and intensity of the rapprochement crisis. The mother's capacity for flexible attunement facilitates an optimal experience for the child. This relational stance approximates the basic features of secure attachment, which provides a solid foundation for the inevitable trials of early development.

Notably, insecure attachments fall in the domain of organized (versus disorganized) attachment (Main 2000). Dismissing/avoidant and anxious/ambivalent attachment patterns all represent organized, adaptive, and predictable strategies for negotiating a particular developmental context, in contrast with disorganized attachment. Moreover, attachment researchers highlight the inherent functionality of insecure attachment patterns as essential strategies developed to maximize caregiver attentiveness in particular caregiving environments (Fonagy and Target 2007). Therefore, closer examination reveals the two theories have much in common regarding what are considered optimal and pathological behaviors and interactional patterns, throughout infancy.

Mahler included a wide range of developmental phenomena in The Psychological Birth of the Human Infant (Mahler et al. 1975). She was not focused on describing optimal development but rather the vicissitudes of normal development. She sought to capture development as it occurred in a non-clinical context, emphasizing that a great deal of normal developmental phenomena are not synonymous with ideal developmental phenomena. "Mahler's interest was less on the optimal circumstances for development of the self and more on the internal forces driving the toddler toward the realization of the separate self, even in circumstances of *less than optimal availability* of the mother" (Bergman and Harpaz-Rotem 2004, p. 561, italics in original).

Attachment Theory's Critics

The psychoanalytic community accused Bowlby of promoting a reductionistic and mechanistic stance. Critics denounced him for ignoring the nuances of the interpersonal arena while trying too hard to find universal, biologically based truths (Fonagy and Target 2007). One of his adversaries was Anna Freud. For example, when discussing a paper Bowlby published in The Psychoanalytic Study of the Child Anna Freud (1960) said:

> Not that, as analysts, we do not share Dr. Bowlby's regard for biological and behavioral considerations. But taken by themselves, not in conjunction with the mental representations of the drives . . . . Equally we do not deal with the happenings in the external world as such but with their repercussions in the mind, i.e., with the form in which they are registered by the child . . . . (p. 54)

Even after years of additional research and theorizing, Gilmore (1990) criticized Bowlby's "adevelopmental perspective" while acknowledging his contributions to understanding child development (p. 497). She said, "he seems to minimize the extraordinarily complicated interaction of constitutional endowment, maturational sequencing and differentiation, experience (both internal and external), and gradually evolving and increasingly complex psychic structure" (p. 497). The fact that Bowlby was an analyst by training seemed to add insult to injury for the psychoanalytic community, as he rejected the possibility of aggressive and sexual drives in infancy, which analysts had fought hard to establish in mainstream science and culture.

More recently, Bergman and Harpaz-Rotem (2004) noted that some of these disagreements are now less critical, as it is more clear how attachment theory and separation–individuation theory both enhance our understanding of the first and crucial years of human development from a different point of reference. Anna Freud seemed to suggest that Bowlby's emphasis on scientific discovery had gone too far afield, as he unfairly accused the analytic community of ignoring biology while failing himself to appreciate the individual's subjective experience.

In contrast, Mahler explicitly upheld classical drive theory and ego psychology (Ainsworth 1969). While Bowlby worked hard to obscure his psychoanalytic roots, Mahler presented her ideas with the desire to be incorporated into psychoanalytic canon. The result was that neither Bowlby nor Mahler was initially well-received. Where Mahler sought to understand the developmental experiences of a group of normal children who epitomized normalcy at a particularly sociocultural moment as completely as she could, Bowlby sought to highlight vicissitudes of specific aspects of development across all children.

Common Ground Between the Two Theories

While attachment and separation–individuation theory developed using different methods and frameworks, the theories share some fundamental foundations (Coates 2004; Fonagy 1999; Steele and Steele 1998). Settlage et al. (1991) point out that "attachment theory research and psychoanalytic developmental research have thus come to share a focus on the process of psychic structure formation in the context of early parent–infant interaction" (p. 1006). Both theories provide greater understanding of the interplay between shared developmental needs and individual circumstances over the course of development. Bowlby challenged the psychoanalytic establishment while Mahler worked hard to gain acceptance for her new ideas in the same community (Coates 2004). Yet attachment theory and separation–individuation theory overlap in their rejection of classical psychoanalytic theory. When Bowlby and Mahler began their research, clinicians believed that psychoanalytic research was impossible; the clinical psychoanalytic situation was considered the only entry into an understanding of people's inner worlds (Bergman and Harpaz-Rotem 2004). Mahler's formulations, derived from observations of mothers and babies together, were thus a radical departure from classical psychoanalysis. At the same time, Bowlby emphasized what happens between mother and child in explanations of psychic structure, experience, and relational dynamics in the developing child (Blum 2004; Bowlby 1979; Coates 2004). Mahler's and Bowlby's pioneering efforts to consider the real life circumstances of the children they encountered, along a spectrum from typical or normal to atypical or deprived, was unusual for their time and initially met with skepticism (Coates 2004).

Basic principles shared by separation–individuation and attachment theory include the following:

1. An emphasis on real events and interactions, captured in descriptive, observational data.
2. An emphasis on the developmental achievement of a representational system of self and other, originating in mother–child interactions, that is dynamic and resistant to change, and continues to organize experience throughout life.
3. A focus on how the development of language and motor skills influences relationships and the quality of the interaction between mother and child.
4. An appreciation for the many environmental, inter- and intra-psychic events that influence the psychological foundation established in early childhood.
5. An apprec.ation for what both caregiver and child bring to the interaction, and how each influences development. This includes the belief that mother is not solely responsible for all positive and/or negative elements of early experiences and achievements.
6. The proposition that the infant in his own right is highly influential in the development of the relationship with the primary caregiver.
7. An understanding that the quality of the interaction between caregiver and child influences myriad aspects of social and relational development, including affect regulation, self-esteem, peer relationships, and psychopathology throughout life.
8. A belief that the capacity for self-awareness, self-reflection, and mentalization emerges out of a sufficiently attuned, flexible, and mutually enhancing mother–infant relationship.
9. A belief that psychological health comes from an early environment that is good enough, but not perfect. For example, moments of misattunement and frustration are necessarily part of early life and serve to promote healthy development if managed properly by a consistent caregiver.
10. A primary infant–caregiver relationship is fundamental to representation and experience of self and other. This fundamental relationship becomes generalized, although other relationships and subsequent experiences also continue to shape and inform identity and experience.

Separation–individuation theory and attachment theory both emphasize that children's behaviors are organized around relationships with caregivers and that identifying patterns and tendencies illuminates how a child understands and perceives himself and his environment. Both theories also emphasize the primacy of reciprocal aspects of the mother–child relationship and look to what both mother and baby bring to the interaction. The hallmarks of a secure attachment and a successful separation–individuation process is a balance of autonomy and relatedness, the capacity to be with and rely on another while maintaining a clear sense of self and regulating emotions appropriately. "The goal of separation-individuation theory is to understand the intra-psychic process of each child on the way to reaching object constancy . . . Attachment theory has enriched our understanding of developmental processes, but it has not contradicted the basic steps of development as articulated by separation–individuation theory" (Bergman and Harpaz-Rotem 2004, p. 557). Self-regulation and affect-regulation are fundamental to the mother–child interaction (Fonagy et al. 2002).

Attachment theory and separation–individuation theory both promote the idea that a mother's overall parenting attitude is consistent over time. However, much variability in parental behaviors is possible, especially in an insecurely attached mother. For example, a mother's ability to delight in her child and to understand her child might change with time (Mahler et al. 1975). Both Bowlby and Mahler agreed that consistency is critical for optimal development, and this is especially true in regards to the mother's flexible, predictable, and understanding attitude towards her infant. In the context of this good-enough mother–child relationship, intrapsychic development proceeds smoothly along predictable lines. However, in the face of relational uncertainty, the journey to adolescence can be complicated and painful.

Attachment theory traditionally focuses on stability over time, and more recently considered what might change within a caregiving situation or family over time, what can contribute to changes in internal representations and thus patterns of attachment (van IJzendoorn et al. 2000). Separation–individuation theory starts from the assumption that some variability is inevitable and looks to how infant and mother work together to establish the kind of consistency and stability that is essential for self and object-constancy, and for providing a foundation for future growth, development, and adaptive functioning (Blum 2004).

A Case Study: Anna and Wendy W.

The case described here comes from a larger research project that incorporated observational data from the MCC and used psychoanalytic perspectives on development and attachment theory in a collaborative way (Blom 2009). The first author reexamined observational data of infants who attended the MCC, using a coding system based in the child development literature, including the literature reviewed earlier in this chapter. This reexamination provided a detailed story of the participants' early experiences from about 18 to 24 months of age, and an overview of each child's developing capacity for representations of self, other, and relationships. The first author then interviewed several of these original participants using the AAI and administered several self-report questionnaires that assessed self-esteem, psychological symptoms, and life-events. AAIs were examined for overall attachment classification, and also for sub-classifications, individual experiencing scales, and content, all of which was incorporated into a story of the participants' adult functioning.

The following case study draws on data from two subjects who were sisters. Using an approach to data analysis that integrates separation–individuation theory, attachment theory, and related work, it is possible to examine these sisters' infancies and adult lives in a systematic and empirically based way. This follow-up work illustrates the benefits of integrating theoretical orientations and highlights the nuances of normal development.

Often in clinical work, there is a tendency to believe we can know what came before with adult patients and what will come with child patients. These are potentially dangerous tendencies. The story of these two sisters shows that very early experiences and ways of being get carried forward into adulthood and also that sometimes things change over time in sometimes unexpected ways. Similarly, what might appear as positive or negative aspects of early relationships can end up having the reverse effect over time. The study epitomizes attachment theory's emphasis on continuity/inflexibility of mental representations while offering an opportunity to examine transmission gaps, in the context of important dissimilarities in the sisters' interactions with and internalizations of their mother.

Anna and Wendy W. in Infancy

The W. family was active at the MCC for many years. Anna's attendance began when she was less than a year old. In intake materials, Mrs. W. described her as "cunning, endearing, lovable, shy, sensitive, robust, even-tempered." Wendy was born when Anna was 28 months old. Observers often noted a change in enthusiasm in Mrs. W. after Wendy's birth. She described her second daughter as "her child."

Observations of Anna described her as very other-directed, which seemed to emerge from her mother's inconsistent attention and frequent requests for her to perform for observers. Anna regularly sought others in her mother's absence and was attentive to what was happening around her, independently of her mother's presence. However, Mrs. W. showed little spontaneous interest in Anna, who seemed almost desperate to engage her mother when she was close by. Anna was observed to struggle with conflicting emotions when faced with reunions, and worked to avoid separations. She persisted in seeking contact with Mrs. W. even when faced with her mother's irritation. Overall, Anna's behavior was characterized by a desire to be with her mother and those at the center, and to solicit positive attention.

This example illustrates a typical observation of Anna:

> Anna selected one of the books and brought it over to her mother. She climbed onto Mrs. W.'s lap and Mrs. W. asked her, 'wee wee? Do you want to wee wee? Are you sure?' Anna shook her head. Whenever Anna would start to fuss, Mrs. W. would read a few lines of the book, but then go right back to her talk with the others. At one time, when Mrs. W. stood up, Anna tried to climb into her mother's chair. Mrs. W. lifted her out, saying 'I have to read my paper.' Anna looked at a book by herself on the floor.

Mrs. W.'s preparations for separations sometimes elicited Anna's obvious distress, which kept Mrs. W. close for a little longer. Additionally, small frustrations inhibited

Anna's ability to explore. Anna's object constancy at this time was characterized by a precarious sense of others as available. Awareness of changes to her environment and her mother's proximity, rather than allowing Anna to shift her attention and regulate corresponding emotions, had the effect of destabilizing her sense of security.

Wendy, Anna's younger sister, was described as an attractive and active little girl who, like Anna, had to work hard to solicit her mother's attention and maintain engagement. However, unlike Anna who could involve herself in a range of activities with various people, Wendy was more exclusively focused on her mother and on those adults whom her mother preferred. Thus, Wendy often engaged in behaviors that elicited Mrs. W.'s attention in indirect ways, like needing help or exuberance. Wendy's high level of activity developed as a way to get her mother's attention, positive or negative.

Mrs. W. was often described as playing it up for observers, and as showing annoyance when Wendy's attempts to engage her interrupted other activities. For example, at age two, an observer noted that when Wendy "ran to her and clung to her leg, Mrs. W. at first did not react to this … but when she saw she was being observed, she leaned down to be more affectionate with Wendy."

In Wendy's internal world, she was an extension of her mother's social persona, and love depended on being sufficiently entertaining. In contrast to Anna, Wendy typically became sad and withdrawn in her mother's absence. Mrs. W.'s attention and was not based in an intrinsic valuing of Wendy's own experience, and thus Wendy's experience was dependent on her mother's state of mind. Wendy's activity appeared in the context of a distracted and self-centered maternal figure. Her early behavior suggested inconsistent and unpredictable object relationships. Wendy had difficulty occupying herself and regulating emotions and interactions, without her mother's direct feedback or participation.

Wendy was often intense, aggressive and oppositional, or inconsolable. She could also be "adorable" and "flirtatious." For example, at 19 months old, an observer described witnessing how "very frequently strangers would come up to her, talk to her, and say what a beautiful child she was." When her mother was close by Wendy sought out substitute adults almost twice as often as when her mother was absent. She seemed to recognize that it was often easier to seek contact with a familiar adult than with her mother. Likewise, interactions with observers seemed to catch her mother's attention in ways that Wendy's direct appeals did not. When Wendy succeeded in getting recognition and praise from others, her mother was particularly animated and attentive. She learned how to coax her mother into an observing state. While she had developed a clear representation of her mother's wants and needs, Wendy's sense of self and of her own needs and preferences seemed diminished. Wendy was occasionally playful but she was more typically described to have "no real relationships" with the other children, and had trouble comprehending that others might want to seek her out.

Internal conflict and confusion related to self-efficacy emerged as, for example, distressed outbursts served to engage mother at one moment and annoy her the next. The observations indicate the absence of reliable strategies for negotiating contact, separations, and reunions. Wendy did not often look for her mother, suggesting she had learned that such efforts were futile. Similarly, Wendy at times displayed no awareness of her mother's departure. All of this indicates an internalized sense of self as undervalued, and an internalized representation of the other as selectively responsive to direct and indirect appeals.

When attending to her daughter, Mrs. W. tended to adopt a sarcastic voice and to mock direct expressions of need—at times in frustration and at other times as entertainment. However, she could also be more attentive and less sarcastic when she thought others were not around. Thus Wendy internalized attachment needs as undesirable things to avoid conveying to others. Her behavior overall indicated that she had internalized a maternal object, who valued Wendy to the extent that she could function as an extension of her mother's social world and minimally intrude on her mother's own needs and interests.

Overall, the observational data presented two very different little girls, and their unfolding interactions with an ambivalent mother who clearly favored her younger daughter. A close examination of phenomena elucidated by both separation–individuation theory and attachment theory, including separations, reunions, appeals for attention, interactions with peers and adults, and behavioral strategies used to manage closeness and distance from caregivers, facilitated a complex understanding of the W. girls. With this knowledge, their adult functioning is expectable and surprising in a number of ways.

Anna and Wendy W. in Adulthood

Anna's follow-up material was strikingly consistent with the observational data in terms of her ongoing struggle for a sense of efficacy and acceptance, in particular when faced with challenging family circumstances. At age 46 she stated, "I am an overachiever who always feels a little incompetent, but rationally I know that I do more than most people." Similarly, she reported difficulty balancing her own emotional needs in the face of others'. Endorsing a moderate degree of psychological distress characterized by self-doubt and hopelessness, her capacity for object constancy was compromised. These were maybe expectable outcomes based on what was observed when she was a child.

However, in the context of these internal conflicts, Anna conveyed a strong sense of self, including an awareness of her difficulties and appreciation for her abilities. She offset daily challenges with a sense of pleasure and satisfaction in many areas of her life. Overall, Anna had a fairly reasonable and balanced understanding of herself and important others in spite, or perhaps because of, her sensitivity to interpersonal dynamics.

Notably, Anna's AAI received a secure classification, even though the content of her recollections was less than ideal and reminiscent of the observational data. Anna described her early relationship with her mother as "distant," "adversarial," "creative," and "strained." She explained by saying: "my memories are more memories of things that didn't happen." For example, she had no memories of being held as a child. However, she was an active and collaborative participant in the interview process and conveyed a realistic and balanced perspective of her experiences in infancy, and a clear valuing of attachment relationships.

Furthermore, Anna was also able to separate childhood experiences from her adult perspective, and keep them in mind when caring for her own children. She described not being able to leave her baby alone when distressed because it did not seem right "from a baby perspective." Therefore, in spite of a difficult and neglectful early relationship with her mother, Anna developed curiosity about herself and relationships that promoted an autonomous approach to her own parenting. Her focus on maintaining closeness and negotiating intimacy facilitated significant emotional development and capacity for affect regulation. Her insecurities and tendency to minimize or restrict unpleasant early experiences did not overwhelm her in a way that inhibited closeness and engagement. Given her mother's difficulty in understanding Anna's behavior, and her inconsistent and highly context-dependent attention, Anna's insecurities were perhaps expectable, while her competencies and resilience were not.

As expected, Wendy's adult perspective and psychological functioning was quite different from Anna's, but in unexpected ways. The preferred daughter who focused so much energy and attention on her mother, Wendy had an AAI which was classified as derogating/dismissing. She revered independence and scorned closeness with others. She claimed she was unable to recall specific details of longstanding relationships. While Wendy demonstrated some perceptiveness when she evaluated her mother's behavior and described her experiences, she utilized psychological defenses of minimization, devaluation, and isolation of affect when she was stimulated by current and past experiences with family members. For example, Wendy described seeing film of herself as a young child, visibly very upset when separated from her mother; however, she did not remember ever feeling that distressed, and denied having the same "problem" as childhood peers who had trouble separating from their parents for extended periods. When upset as a child, Wendy described rocking herself alone for hours, highlighting her experience that others were not sources of comfort or consolation.

Closer analysis of Wendy's recollections revealed continuity between the early observations and her adult perspective. While dependence and intimacy were explicitly discouraged in the W. family, Wendy remembers feeling as if her mother needed her close by. This resonates with when Wendy was observed to function as an extension of her mother. Wendy used "needy" to characterize their early relationship. To illustrate, she described:

> ... being up in my mother's room and she's busily doing stuff and I'm sitting there and coloring and she's just ignoring me, she doesn't say anything about the work I'm doing . . . . But she wants me to do it in her room with her so I want her to pay attention to me, but she's not – but I can't go somewhere else, because she needs me to be there to keep her company.

This illustrates persistent contradictory and conflicting internalized object representations: On the one hand, Wendy was needed by her mother and discouraged from exercising autonomy; at the same time, she was actively rejected. Likewise, she wanted to be attended to by her mother, but could not ask directly for attention and felt ignored.

As an adult, Wendy related that her thinking has been "very black and white" and that like her parents "I'm somewhat guarded." She described an ongoing effort to establish appropriate boundaries with her parents and with others. She continued to feel as if her mother's happiness was dependent on her own success. Although working hard to gain her mother's affections was a source of regret and frustration, it remained an active part of her emotional life.

On self-report measures, Wendy skipped questions about intimate relationships; she endorsed problems expressing feelings, and a tendency to distance herself from others. She was very concerned with losing her independence. She endorsed a high degree of self-esteem, and it is likely that defensiveness related to accomplishments and abilities led Wendy to exaggerate feelings of self-worth. This is consistent with a dismissing AAI in which the importance of positive appraisals from others is minimized as a defensive strategy to avoid feeling rejected or neglected. Mrs. W.'s conditional attention appears to have contributed to Wendy's difficulty trusting those around her to be consistent, available, and valuing of her experiences.

Overall, Wendy seemed to identify with her mother's habit of extracting herself from interpersonal scenarios when called upon to attend to the emotional needs of another, as well as Mrs. W.'s tendency to focus on how others function for her. She actively devalued positive aspects of closeness and dependency, emphasized her ability to take care of herself, and talked about relationships in terms of personal gain. She said: "I'm secretive, I mean I always sort of think you can manipulate people to do what you want .... I've been in a lot of relationships with people I shouldn't have been for very long 'cause they weren't gonna give me what I want." The little girl who tried hard to entertain her mother, and whose engagement with her surroundings was so dependent on her mother's presence, learned how to repress the need for intimacy.

Discussion

Anna and Wendy showed a range of ways of interacting with their mother, coping with separations, and being with other children and adults. This variability appears to be founded on differences in the achievement of an internalized stable and loving image (of self and other) and the ability to rely on that image when mother was physically or psychologically unavailable (Mahler et al. 1975). Analysis of the observational data revealed aspects of internal representations and provided insight into the development of strategies for negotiating closeness and distance. Development, in the context of a good enough mother should ensure that a child engages in the world with flexible, successful strategies. Neither Anna nor Wendy demonstrated this as children. The optimal relationship in infancy (and throughout life) is a balance of closeness and independence. Over-reliance on one behavioral strategy—like seeking a mother-substitute when mother is physically or psychologically unavailable—is insufficient.

The child who has internalized an available and loving caregiver should be able to engage in his environment with flexibility and find ways of meeting developmental needs across contexts.

The ability to review several months of observational data facilitated a comprehensive understanding of Anna and Wendy's early development, which highlights the importance and utility of a psychoanalytic approach to early development, especially in the context of understanding a child's functioning and development. One observation, no matter how detailed, can only reveal so much about a child's internal world. A sick child might stay close to mother one week and be more independent the next; an argument at home can linger in interactions somewhere else. Thus, being able to enter into the day-to-day patterns of relating and interacting between mothers and children allows for a more valid and reliable perspective. The importance of understanding context is of value for clinical work, especially the understanding that children behave differently in different situations. This perspective counteracts trends in attachment theory, which relies on the Strange Situation for data about a child's internal representations, and also traditional psychoanalysis, as influential analysts like Melanie Klein were largely unconcerned with a child's actual mother or real circumstances.

After considering early observational data, it seems that both Anna and Wendy demonstrated highly conflicted internalized representations of early relationships that contributed to a range of interpersonal problems. How these sisters dealt with their mothers' psychological unavailability and the kinds of efforts they did or did not make to establish connection with her and others was less than optimal in both of them. While both girls worked hard to elicit their mother's attention, Anna's seemed to employ a more flexible resignation that appeared to maintain some kind of contact while minimizing explicit rejection. Anna persisted in appealing to mother, but was often satisfied with momentary or peripheral contact. In contrast, Wendy showed more ambivalence, often demanding attention and proximity from mother only to turn away when she received it. Mrs. W. responded to these appeals differently, depending in part on who was close by. These dynamic aspects of early life contributed to each daughter's development in unique ways. We might have predicted that they both would provide insecure AAIs and further that Anna would be distant and removed in relationships and Wendy demanding and clingy.

Similarities and differences between Anna's interactions with her mother and Wendy's interactions with her mother are plentiful. On the one hand, Mrs. W. did not seem to change much from Anna's infancy to Wendy's—she could be observed reading the paper, trading recipes, flirting with observers throughout her time there—and yet she clearly favored Wendy and interactions with her daughters were described very differently. The notion that a mother is different with her children is not a surprising one from a clinical perspective. However, from a developmental standpoint and from the perspective of attachment theory and research, differences in recollections, identifications, and internalized aspects of early life were quite unexpected. Particularly unexpected was how the favored daughter seemed to end up the worse for it. This point is worth emphasizing: In this familial context, less attention was a good thing.

Psychoanalytic theory helps to explain these dynamics. The potential for change in mothers over time is an important factor was a central concern for Mahler and her team, and highlights a major contribution of separation–individuation theory. In addition to a mother's general consistency and flexibility, what a mother learns from parenting one child that influences her relationship with the next, and why a mother focuses more on one child's development than another's, are dynamic issues. Winnicott (1964) believed that the capable, or practiced, mother is not necessarily the best one. But with time, some mothers may learn how to better put aside their needs and anxieties. Whether this happened for Mrs. W. is debatable, but her special kind of delight in her youngest daughter was at least clear.

Other analytic writers have explored the reciprocal nature of development for mothers and siblings and focus on the increased demands that come with a sibling. These demands also arise from an older child who tends to regress, to become more needy, and/or to withdraw (Kris and Ritvo 1983). A mother is faced with a new "internal psychological dilemma" in regards to how she will love her different children (Kris and Ritvo 1983, p. 13). Mrs. W. was open about her preference for Wendy, even in Anna's presence. How this translated into meaningful differences in her interactions with her children, and consequently their developing internal representations of self and other, is less clear. She seemed to take a more active interest in Wendy, yet without being necessarily more attuned to her. Mrs. W.'s affinity for Wendy may have been beneficial for Anna in the end. In the end, Mrs. W.'s decreased focus on Anna likely facilitated her development in ways that allowed for a secure attachment organization in adulthood.

Attachment theory is becoming more focused on these issues and ideas. In their meta-analysis, van IJzendoorn et al. (2000) examined the attachment organizations of three groups of mothers and siblings from different countries, and evaluated a number of other dimensions, including maternal sensitivity, gender, and the age difference between children. Their data indicated that a child's attachment organization can change with the birth of a sibling, with only modest rates of attachment concordance between siblings, including twins. Maternal sensitivity was a factor, but only in that maternal insensitivity explained a large portion of the concordance of siblings with insecure attachment organizations. While counterintuitive for attachment theory, these results are hardly surprising from a psychoanalytic perspective, which has always emphasized the unique, highly individualized nature of relationships.

For Mrs. W. and her daughters, an integrative approach to understanding their lives revealed surprising and unsurprising aspects of their experiences and recollections years after the initial observations were recorded. A comprehensive exploration of these continuities and discontinuities benefits from an integrative approach based in psychoanalytic ideas and attachment research and that enhances a truly developmental perspective. Psychoanalytic principles, and specifically those elaborated by separation–individuation theory, provide a dynamic framework to understand the range of experiences that can inform typical development. Important to keep in mind is that normal is synonymous with optimal. Attachment theory illuminates how patterns of thought and behavior are transmitted between parents and children and provides a framework for anticipating what is typical or expectable in a range of circumstances. Together, these approaches provide complementary and mutually enhancing facts and principles, filling in gaps for each other, and offering new direction for future work.

Acknowledgments The authors gratefully acknowledge the contributions of Adriana Lis and Claudia Mazzeschi to the original research project that informed the development of this chapter, in addition to the contributions of Miriam Steele, whose ongoing guidance is invaluable.

References

Ainsworth, M. D. S. (1969). Object relations, dependency, and attachment: A theoretical review of the mother child relationship. *Child Development, 40,* 969–1025.
Ainsworth, M. D. S. (1978). *Patterns of attachment: A psychological study of the strange situation.* Hillsdale: Lawrence Erlbaum Associates.
Ainsworth, M. D. S., Blehar, M., Waters, E., & Wall, S. (1978). *Patterns of attachment.* Hillsdale: Lawrence Erlbaum Associates.
Bartholomew, K. (1993). From childhood to adult relationships: Attachment theory and research. Learning about relationships. In S. Duck (Ed.), *Learning about relationships, understanding relationship processes* (Vol. 2) (pp. 30–62). Thousand Oaks: Sage.
Beebe, B. (2005). Mother-infant research informs mother-infant treatment. *Psychoanalytic Study of the Child, 60,* 7–46.
Beebe, B., & Jaffee, J. (2011). Description of the project: A longitudinal prevention project for mothers pregnant and widowed in the World Trade Center tragedy of September 11, 2001, and their young children. *Journal of Infant, Child and Adolescent Psychotherapy, 10,* 156–169.
Bergman, A., & Fahey, M. (2005). Observations and representations of the earliest relationship: A view from separation-individuation and attachment. In S. Akhtar & H. Blum (Eds.), *The language of emotions: Development,* psychopathology, and technique (pp. 139–150). New York: Jason Aronson.
Bergman, A., & Harpaz-Rotem, I. (2004). Revisiting rapprochement in light of contemporary developmental theories. *Journal of the American Psychoanalytic Association, 52,* 555–569.
Blom, I. (2009). A longitudinal study evaluating early observations and representations of relationships: Separation individuation theory and attachment theory in a qualitative approach (Doctoral dissertation). *The New School for Social Research,* New York, NY.
Blos, P. (1967). The second individuation process of adolescence. *The Psychoanalytic Study of the Child, 22,* 162–186.
Blum, H. (2004). Separation-individuation theory and attachment theory. *Journal of the American Psychoanalytic Association, 52,* 535–553.
Bowlby, J. (1939). Evacuation of small children [Letter to the editor]. *The British Medical Journal, December,* 1202.
Bowlby, J. (1969/1982). *Attachment and loss volume 1: Attachment.* New York: Basic Books.
Bowlby, J. (1979). *The making and breaking of affectional bonds.* London: Routledge.
Bowlby, J., & Robertson, J. (1952). A two-year-old goes to the hospital. *Psychoanalytic Study of the Child, 7,* 82–94.
Bretherton, I. (1992). The origins of attachment theory: John Bowlby and Mary Ainsworth. *Developmental Psychology, 28,* 759–775.
Burgner, M., & Edgecumbe, R. (1972). Some problems in the conceptualization of early object relationships—Part II: the concept of object constancy. *Psychoanalytic Study of the Child, 27,* 315–333.
Cassidy, J. (1999). The nature of the child's ties. In J. Cassidy & P. R. Shaver (Eds.), Handbook of attachment (pp. 3–20). New York: Guildford.

Coates, S. W. (2004). John Bowlby and Margaret S. Mahler: Their lives and theories. *Journal of the American Psychoanalytic Association, 52*, 571–601.

Colarusso, C. (2000). Separation-Individuation phenomena in adulthood: General concepts and the fifth individuation. *Journal of the American Psychoanalytic Association, 48*, 1467–1489.

Colaruso, C. (1992). *Child and adult development: A psychoanalytic introduction for clinicians.* New York: Springer.

Fonagy, P. (1999). Points of contact and divergence between psychoanalytic and attachment theories: Is psychoanalytic theory truly different? *Psychoanalytic Inquiry, 19*, 448–480.

Fonagy, P., & Target, M. (2007). The rooting of the mind in the body: New links between attachment theory and psychoanalytic thought. *Journal of the American Psychoanalytic Association, 55*, 411–456.

Fonagy, P., Steele, M., & Steele, H. (1991). Maternal representations of attachment during pregnancy predict the organization of infant-mother interaction at one year of age. *Child Development, 62*, 891–905.

Fonagy, P., Gergely, G., Jurist, E., & Target, M. (2002). *Affect regulation, mentalization and the development of the self.* New York: Other Press.

Fraiberg, S. (1969). Libidinal object constancy and mental representation. *The Psychoanalytic Study of the Child, 24*, 9–47.

Freud, A. (1960). Discussion of Dr. John Bowlby's paper. *Psychoanalytic Study of the Child, 15*, 53–62.

Freud, A. (1971). The infantile neurosis—Genetic and dynamic considerations. *Psychoanalytic Study of the Child, 26*, 79–90.

Gergely, G. (2000). Reapproaching Mahler: New perspectives on normal autism, symbiosis, splitting and libidinal object constancy from cognitive developmental theory. *Journal of the American Psychoanalytic Association, 48*, 1197–1228.

Gilmore, K. (1990). A secure base. Parent-child attachment and healthy human development: By John Bowlby. *Psychoanalytic Quarterly, 59*, 494–498.

Hartmann, H. (1952). *Essays on ego psychology.* New York: International University Press.

Hazan, C., & Shaver, P. R. (1987). Romantic love conceptualized as an attachment process. *Journal of Personality and Social Psychology, 25*, 511–524.

Hesse, E. (1999). The adult attachment interview: Historical and current perspectives. In J. Cassidy and P. Shaver (Eds.), *Handbook of attachment* (pp. 395–433). New York: Guilford.

Kirkpatrick, L. A. (2004). *Attachment, evolution and the psychology of religion.* New York: Guilford.

Kobak, R. (1999). Separation and the emotional dynamics of attachment. In J. Cassidy & P. Shaver (Eds.), *Handbook of attachment* (pp. 88–105). New York: Guilford.

Koulomzin, M., Beebe, B., Anderson, S., Jaffe, J., Feldstein, S., & Crown, C. (2002). Infant gaze, head, face and self-touch at 4 months differentiate secure vs. avoidant attachment at 1 year: A microanalytic approach. *Attachment and Human Development, 4*, 3–24.

Kramer, S. (1992). Nonverbal manifestations of unresolved separation-individuation in adult psychopathology. In S. Kramer & S. Akhtar (Eds.), *When the body speaks: Psychological meanings in kinetic cues* (pp. 1–19). Northvale: Jason Aronson.

Kris, M., & Ritvo, S. (1983). Parents and siblings—Their mutual influences. *Psychoanalytic Study of the Child, 38*, 311–324.

Lyons-Ruth, K. (1991). Rapprochement or approchement: Mahler's theory reconsidered from the vantage point of recent research on early attachment relationships. *Psychoanalytic Psychology, 8*, 1–23.

Mahler, M. S. (1967). On human symbiosis and the vicissitudes of individuation. *Journal of the American Psychoanalytic Association, 15*, 740–763.

Mahler, M. S. (1968). *On human symbiosis and the vicissitudes, Vol. 1: Infantile psychosis.* Madison: International Universities Press.

Mahler, M. S. (1972a). On the first three subphases of the separation-individuation process. *International Journal of Psycho-Analysis, 53*, 333–338.

Mahler, M. S. (1972b). The rapprochement subphase of the separation-individuation process. *Psychoanalytic Quarterly, 41,* 487–506.

Mahler, M. S. (1986a). On human symbiosis and the vicissitudes of individuation. In P. Buckley (Ed.), *Essential papers on object relations* (pp. 200–221). New York: New York University Press.

Mahler, M. S. (1986b). On the first three subphases of the separation-individuation process. In P. Buckley (Ed.), *Essential papers on object relations* (pp. 222–232). New York: New York University Press.

Mahler, M. S., & Furer, M. (1963). Certain aspects of the separation-individuation phase. *The Psychoanalytic Quarterly, 32,* 1–14.

Mahler, M. S., & Furer, M. (1968). *On human symbiosis and the vicissitudes of individuation.* New York: International University Press.

Mahler, M. S., & McDevitt, J. (1980). The separation-individuation process and identity formation. In S.I. Greenspan & G. H. Pollock (Eds.), *The course of life: Psychoanalytic contributions toward understanding personality development* (pp. 395–406). Bethesda: NIMH.

Mahler, M. S., & McDevitt, J. (1982). Thoughts on the emergence of a sense of self, with a particular emphasis on the body self. *Journal of the American Psychoanalytic Association, 30,* 827–848.

Mahler, M. S., Pine, F., & Bergman, A. (1975). *The psychological birth of the human infant.* New York: Basic Books.

Mahler, M. S., Pine, F., & Bergman, A. (1994). Stages in the infant's separation from the mother. In G. Handel & G. G. Whitchurch (Eds.), *The psychosocial interior of the family.* (4th ed., pp. 419–448). Hawthorne: Aldine de Gruyter.

Main, M. (2000). The organized categories of infant, child, and adult attachment: Flexible vs. inflexible attention under attachment-related stress. *Journal of the American Psychoanalytic Association, 48,* 1055–1096.

Main, M., Kaplan, N., & Cassidy, J. (1985). Security in infancy, childhood and adulthood: A move to the level of representation. In I. Bretherton & E. Waters (Eds.), *Growing points of attachment theory and research. Monographs of the Society for Research in Child Development* (Vol. 50) (1–2, serial no. 2009), (pp. 66–104), Hoboken: Wiley.

Main, M., Goldwyn, R., & Hesse, E. (2002). *Adult attachment scoring and classification system.* Unpublished manuscript.

Main, M., Hesse, E., & Goldwyn, R. (2008). Studying differences in language usage in recounting attachment history: An introduction to the AAI. In H. Steele & M. Steele (Eds.), *Clinical applications of the adult attachment interview* (pp. 31–68). New York: Guilford.

Marvin, R. S., & Britner, P. A. (1999). Normative development: The ontogeny of attachment. In J. Cassidy & P. R. Shaver (Eds.), *Handbook of attachment: Theory, research, and clinical applications* (pp. 44–67). New York: Guilford.

McDevitt, J. (1975). Separation-individuation and object constancy. *Journal of the American Psychoanalytic Association, 23,* 713–742.

McDevitt, J. (1980). The role of internalization in the development of object relations during the separation-individuation phase. In R. Lax, S. Bach & J. A. Burland (Eds.), *Rapprochement: The critical subphase of separation-individuation.* New York: Jason Aronson.

McDevitt, J., & Mahler, M. S. (1980). Object constancy, individuality and internalization. In S. I. Greenspan & G. H. Pollock (Eds.), *The course of Life: Psychoanalytic contributions toward understanding personality development* (pp. 407–424). Bethesda: NIMH.

Olesker, W. (1998). Conflict and compromise in gender identity formation: A longitudinal study. *Psychoanalytic Study of the Child, 53,* 212–230.

Olesker, W. (2011). The story of Sam: Continuities and discontinuities in development. Transforming into and out of a perversion. *The Psychoanalytic Study of the Child, 65,* 48–78.

Piaget, J. (1963). *The origins of intelligence in children.* New York: Norton.

Pine, F. (1994). Mahler's Concepts of "Symbiosis" and Separation-Individuation: Revisited, Revaluated, Refined. *Journal of the American Psychoanalytic Association, 52*(2), 511–553.

Settlage, C. F., Bemesderfer, S., Rosenthal, J., Afterman, J., & Spielman, P. M. (1991). The appeal cycle in early mother-child interaction: Nature and implications of a finding from developmental research. *Journal of the American Psychoanalytic Association, 39*, 987–1014.

Solnit, A. J. (1982). Developmental perspectives on self and object constancy. *Psychoanalytic Study of the Child, 37*, 201–218.

Spitz, R. A. (1957). *No and yes: On the genesis of human communication.* New York: International Universities Press.

Sroufe, J. W. (2003). Appendix: The infant and adult attachment categories. In M. Cortina & M. Marrone (Eds.), *Attachment theory and psychoanalytic process* (pp. 470–476). London: Whurr.

Steele, H., & Steele, M. (1998). Attachment and psychoanalysis: Time for a reunion. *Social Development, 7*, 92–119.

Stern, D. (1985). *The interpersonal world of the infant.* New York: Basic Books.

Tyson, P. (1991). Psychic structure formation: The complementary roles of affects, drives, object relations, and conflict. In T. Shapiro (Ed.), *The concept of structure in psychoanalysis* (pp. 73–98). New York: International Universities Press.

Tyson, P. (1992). The challenges of psychoanalytic developmental theory. *Journal of the American Psychoanalytic Association, 50*, 19–52.

Tyson, P. (1996). Object relations, affect management and psychic structure formation: The concept of object constancy. *Psychoanalytic Study of the Child, 51*, 172–189.

Tyson, P. (2005). Separation-individuation, object constancy and affect regulation. In S. Akhtar and H. Blum (Eds.), *The language of emotions: development, psychopathology and technique* (pp. 69–82). New York: Jason Aronson.

van IJzendoorn, M. H., & Kroonenberg, P. (1988). Cross-cultural patterns of attachment: A meta-analysis of the strange situation. *Child Development, 59*(1), 147–156.

van IJzendoorn, M. H., & Sagi, A. (1999). Cross-cultural patterns of attachment: Universal and contextual dimensions. In J. Cassidy & P. Shaver (Eds.), *Handbook of attachment: Theory, research, and clinical applications* (pp. 713–734). New York: Guilford

van IJzendoorn, M. H., Moran, G., Belsky, J., Pederson, D., Bakermans-Kranenburg, M. J., & Kneppers, K. (2000). The similarities of siblings' attachment to their mother. *Child Development, 71*, 1086–1098.

Waters, E., Merrick, S., Treboux, D., Crowell, J., & Albersheim, L. (2000). Attachment security in infancy and early adulthood: A twenty-year longitudinal study. *Child Development, 71*, 684–689.

Winnicott, D. W. (1964). *The child, the family and the outside environment.* Harmondsworth: Penguin.

Securing Attachment: Mother–Infant Research Informs Attachment-Based Clinical Practice

Donna Demetri Friedman, Leyla Ertegun, Tina Lupi, Beatrice Beebe and Sara Deutsch

Introduction

Early theorists paved the way for an understanding of the importance of the parent–child relationship (Bowlby 1958, 1960; Fairbairn 1963; Spitz & Cobliner 1965; Winnicott 1956, 1965). Bowlby, an avid student of nature and of Darwin's nineteenth century theory of evolution, shifted research in infant development away from Sigmund Freud's concentration on the primacy of individual human instinctual endowment. He instead emphasized consideration of the significant role played by the caregiver. Similarly, Ainsworth et al. (1978) upheld that maternal sensitivity is central to infant attachment security. Bowlby (1958, 1969) believed that infant attachment behaviors are used to maintain proximity to and contact with the primary caretaker, contributing to a bond that ties infant and caregiver. Alertness to infant signals, appropriateness and promptness of response, flexibility, and capacity to negotiate conflicting goals are aspects of maternal sensitivity (Jaffe et al. 2001).

Winnicott (1965), also an influence on researchers in the United States, used "holding" (p. 44) to describe a state similar to what Bowlby (1958) referred to as "a secure base" (p. 11). "Holding" designates a nurturing and regulating provision, first from the primary caretaker, and gradually from the greater environment. The "holding" state sustains and protects the proper conditions for the infant's gradual incorporation of elements essential to development, producing the least possible interference with a "good enough" (Winnicott 1965, p. 145) natural progression. Equanimity hinged to sensitive caregiving in a climate of well-timed mutual exchanges between infant and

D. D. Friedman (✉) · L. Ertegun · S. Deutsch
Riverdale Mental Health Association, Bronx, New York, NY, USA

Silver School of Social Work, New York University, New York, NY, USA
e-mail: donnademetrif@msn.com

T. Lupi
Private Practice, New York, NY, USA

B. Beebe
College of Physicians & Surgeons at Columbia University, New York State
Psychiatric Institute, New York, NY, USA

J. E. Bettmann, D. D. Friedman (eds.), *Attachment-Based Clinical Work with Children and Adolescents,* Essential Clinical Social Work Series,
DOI 10.1007/978-1-4614-4848-8_3, © Springer Science+Business Media New York 2013

caregiver contributes to the infant's progressive development (Beebe 2003, 2005; Brazelton et al. 1974; Stern 1971, 1977; Trevarthen 1977, 1998).

"Good enough" mothering suggests a maternal manner that is positioned to balance patient attentiveness, lack of intrusiveness, attuned and contingent interaction, and the capacity to facilitate development through a system of well-timed corrections of interaction errors (Cohn and Tronick 1988; Lyons-Ruth 1999). A hallmark of "good enough" mothering is that it also includes the capacity to tolerate the infant's need for gradual experiences of separateness and self-regulation, as exemplified by an infant's need to look away when overstimulated. For example, when an infant averts its gaze from her, a "good enough" mother understands that this action likely evidences the infant's overstimulation and allows a temporary break in the interaction—rather than viewing the looking-away as a form of rejection or a failure on her part to keep the infant interested.

Parent–Infant Research

In the 1960s, Ainsworth conducted a seminal longitudinal study of 26 pairs of mothers and babies in their natural settings. Trained observers visited the subjects in their homes in Baltimore, Maryland for four hours at a time, every three weeks during the first year, making notes on the infants' behavior and mothers' sensitivity in responding to the infants (Ainsworth and Wittig 1969). Ainsworth and Wittig developed a laboratory experiment, the Strange Situation, to observe babies' responses to several discrete situations: being in a new place, meeting an adult stranger, being separated from their mothers for a brief period, and being left alone in an unfamiliar place for a brief period. Experienced coders then used scales to rate the intensity of interactive behavior in four areas: proximity and contact seeking; contact maintaining; resistance; and avoidance (Ainsworth and Wittig 1969).

Using the coded observations, Ainsworth categorized patterns of attachment into three major groups: secure, anxious/avoidant, and anxious/ambivalent. Securely attached infants are able to use the attachment figure as an effective secure base from which to explore the world. When separated from the mother, secure babies approach the mother upon reunion and seek a degree of proximity to soothe themselves.Anxious-avoidant babies are covertly anxious about the attachment figure's responsiveness and have developed defensive strategies for managing their anxiety. Upon the attachment figure's return, these babies act in a detached way, failing to greet the mother, ignoring her overtures and acting as if she is of little importance. Anxious-ambivalent babies upon reunion with their mothers both resist and cling, often displaying anger toward the mother (Ainsworth and Wittig 1969).

Ainsworth's work became the pivotal force for an enormous surge in infancy research in the United States. Following in Ainsworth's footsteps, psychologists conducted the first wave of important infancy research, which then provoked interest among others working with children and their mothers (Beebe 2003, 2005; Sroufe 1985; Waters et al. 2000). Notably, later research suggested that infant attachment security predicted several developmental outcomes including school performance, affect regulation, and psychopathology (Arend et al. 1979; Erickson et al. 1983; Kobak and Sceery 1988; Lewis et al. 1984; Lyons-Ruth et al. 1993; Sroufe 1985). Further, infants of depressed mothers are at risk for insecure attachments (Murray and Cooper 1997).

As the theoretical thinking shifted from the individual psychoanalytic perspective to the attachment based parent–child perspective, Stern (1971, 1974, 1995) and others (Beebe 2003, 2005; Giannino and Tronick 1988) pioneered the microanalytic investigation of bi-directionality in the parent–infant relationship. Stern described bidirectional attributes such as contingency in which each dyadic partner's behavior predicts the other's behavior. Optimal cueing within a dyad occurs when sensitive, well-timed responsiveness results in correspondence of affect states in both members of an interactive pair. Beebe (2003) commented on the value of attaining this coordination: "It indicates that each partner senses an ongoing willingness (or unwillingness) to be influenced, as well as an ongoing impact (or failure of impact) on the other" (p. 52). This mutual exchange fosters what Fonagy and Target (1998) termed mentalization. In other words, the mother's mind is open to her infant, creating the kind of equilibrium that Tronick and Weinberg (1997) asserted is required for infants to begin to find their own sense of agency.

Jaffe et al. (2001) conceptualized interactive regulation on a continuum, with an optimum midrange and two poles. The two poles were defined by excessive or inhibited monitoring of the partner. At age four months, midrange coordinated interpersonal timing (CIT) predicted secure attachment, while low and high extreme CIT predicted insecure attachment. Jaffe et al. (2001) consider that both infant and caregiver create this coordination of communication, espousing a dyadic systems view.

Beebe and many of her colleagues concluded that the mutual regulation system between mother and baby functions optimally when each member of the dyad shifts and adjusts to the other's cues without the rigidity or choreography implied by tight coordination. Instead, such regulation occurs through the flexibility of attunement, with mothers adjusting according to the perceived tempo and affective state of the infant (Beebe and Gerstman 1980; Beebe and Lachmann 1994, 1998; Tronick and Giannino 1986; Tronick and Weinberg 1997). These studies supply evidence that corroborates the perception that an infant's security is positively linked to its mother's sensitive handling of cues, but in a manner that is neither too tightly matched, nor escalates arousal or neglects to provide an appropriate response.

Tronick's (2007) Mutual Regulation Model sees infants as part of a dyadic communicative system. Within this system, the infant and adult mutually regulate and scaffold their engagement with each other by communicating their own intentions and responding to one another. Tronick created the face-to-face/still-face (FFSF) paradigm, which is based on the idea that if infants are regulating themselves and the state of interaction by responding to the adult's regulatory input, then when the adult communication is perturbed, the infant should respond by attempting to correct it. The research indeed showed that in this situation the infants attempted to solicit the mother's attention and when she did not respond they eventually looked away, withdrew or showed anger or sad affect (Tronick 1989; Tronick and Cohn 1989).

The internal processing of experience also plays an important role in psychic organization. In an ideal parenting situation, a responsive mother accurately registers the meaning of visual cues communicated by her infant and responds by increasing or decreasing the level of stimulation she is providing. Infants then respond accordingly. This interactive contingency—involving each partner's use of self- and mutual-regulation maneuvers—characterizes mother–infant interactions (Tronick and Weinberg 1997). Infants need to develop their own sense of reality and agency. This sense is born of dyadic attempts to repair the minor disruptions that inevitably occur in the ordinary interplay between mother and child (Tronick and Weinberg 1997). Infants' psychic organization rests on the co-creation of mental representation within the dyadic system. Mothers' and infants' states of mind are built together by their attempts and failures to understand each other.

Current researchers and theorists state that "good enough" mothering (Winnicott 1965, p. 145) is most correctly understood as a co-construction by mother and infant, not the work of mother alone. Cohn and Tronick (1988) assert that coordination of infant and mother is bi-directional. Jaffe and Beebe's research presents the additional conclusion that "good enough" mothering (Winnicott 1965, p. 145) is not simply a matter of bi-directionality, but also a function of the degree and intensity of the coordination (Jaffe et al. 2001). Too much or too little coordination is not "good enough" mothering. Mutual regulation patterns are most effective for building stable and beneficial internal representations when these patterns are flexible. "Good enough" mothering permits the infant to sustain its own self-regulation while staying in optimal contact with its reliable attachment figure, with allowances made for the infant's rudimentary autonomy.

Mother–Infant Research Predicts Attachment

Beebe et al. (2010) predicted 12-month insecure attachment outcomes, specifically resistant and disorganized attachment patterns, from a microanalysis of 4-month old infant–mother face-to-face communication. The results show that more contingency is not necessarily better in relation to attachment security. Beebe et al. (2010) found that infants with anxious-ambivalent/resistant attachment styles have dysregulated tactile and/or spatial exchanges with their caregivers. The "chase and dodge" pattern that characterizes this attachment style originates in maternal impingement ("chase") which babies orient themselves away from ("dodge"), generating approach–withdrawal patterns. The strategy used by these infants for managing maternal touch is to tune it out; however, doing so compromises their ability to communicate about maternal touch. Beebe et al. (2010) propose that these infants have difficulty feeling sensed and known when maternal spatial/tactile impingements occur.

Conflict in the context of distressed infants is the central feature of disorganized attachment. Failures of maternal affective correspondence and lowered maternal contingent coordination are present in infants exhibiting a disorganized attachment style. These maternal deficiencies compromise infant interactive agency and emotional coherence. In contrast to resistantly attached babies who have difficulty in feeling sensed and known by the mother, disorganized infants in states of distress experience not sensing and knowing their own internal state (Beebe et al. 2010). In disorganized attached infants, maternal response to distress may lead such infants to develop an internal working model of confusion about their own basic emotional organization, and to a disturbance of the fundamental integration of their selfhood.

Beebe and others use a dyadic systems approach, examining contributions of both infant and mother, and of self and interactive contingency across multiple communication modalities to the process of attachment formation (Beebe et al. 1992, 2000; Jaffe et al. 2001; Sander 1977; Tronick 1989). While these researchers emphasize locating the source of difficulty in a dyad either by finding a problem in one partner or the other, Beebe et al. (2010) focus on both partners.

Bowlby (1958, 1969, 1973) also held a systems view. He considered patterns of relational behavior, what activated and terminated them, and their function within the social context. His attachment theory is consistent with a model of mutual regulation in mother–infant research in that mother and infant both contribute in essential ways to the attachment relationship.

Beebe's research focus on mutual regulation has significant implications for attachment-based clinical work. Mutual regulation is based on the premise that a mother understands her child's needs in part because of what is activated in her own attachment system. Treatment informed by Beebe's findings on mutual regulation provides tools for parents to better mobilize their inner resources in the service of strengthening the attachment relationship.

The Use of Video in Mother–Infant Research

Interventions using videotape have played a crucial role in mother–infant research (Beebe et al. 1985, 2008; Beebe and Stern 1977; Tronick et al. 1978; Tronick and Weinberg 1997). The use of video cameras, playback equipment, and computers for managing data and computing statistical results has contributed dramatically to the volume of infant research produced in the past four decades (Beebe 2000, 2003; Field 1981, 1994; Stern 1974, 1985; Tronick 1989, 2001; Weinberg et al. 1998). Infancy research, now international in scope, benefits from tremendous advances in technology.

The Use of Video in Clinical Interventions

The use of video by the "Great Baby Watchers" (Guedeney and Guedeney 2010, p. 3), Brazelton, Stern, Beebe, and Tronick, gave insight into the way parent–infant interaction develops and paved the way for numerous attachment-based interventions using video as a primary tool. Beebe and Stern (1977) began using video in parent–infant psychotherapy in order to help improve the mother–infant face-to-face interaction and maternal attunement. Fraiberg (1980) used film to assess and intervene with high-risk infants and their mothers. McDonough (1993) was one of the first clinicians to use video to engage hard-to-reach families.

More recently, interventions using video include the "Circle of Security" project (Marvin et al. 2002, p. 107). This intervention model uses videotape to establish an assessment of secure base behavior that can be used in group or individual sessions, educating parents using their reactions to the strange situation with their child with the goal of strengthening the attachment relationship. Lyons-Ruth et al. (2005) and Slade (2008) use video in interactional guidance with high-risk dyads to increase self-reflective functioning in the mother.

The use of video, an outgrowth of mother–infant research, is now a major tool for psychotherapeutic intervention and prevention. It allows clinicians to spot brief and meaningful events that can be reviewed with the parents. It thus provides an opportunity to focus on the young child's reactions and interactions within the context of developing relationships. In the midst of a difficult relationship, parents are often unable to perceive the positive aspects of their interactions. In such cases, video enables parents to take note of both their behaviors that enhance and impede the attachment relationships with their children.

Using Mother–Infant Research in Clinical Practice

Beebe's (2003) mother–infant research has had a far-reaching influence on clinical intervention strategies. Her 2003 study of 4-month old infants and mothers confirms the importance of early intervention for parent–child dyads. While attachment theory has informed clinical practice in a variety of settings since its inception, only recently has knowledge about the intricacies of the interaction between caregivers and babies in the first few months of life been applied in clinical settings. The following case example illustrates just such an application. The treating therapist for this case example was the first author. This case was videotaped as part of the treatment, and video feedback sessions took place with both parents. The therapist paid special attention to the developing attachment relationships between these adopted children and their parents.

Background

Ariel was adopted at the age of 13 months by an American couple from New York City. The couple had tried to get pregnant for a long time and finally decided to adopt a Caucasian baby from Russia. They are Jewish, he from South America and she from the United States. When Ariel was first adopted, both of her parents were at home with her. Her adoptive mother had taken family leave from her job for three months. Her adoptive father works at home, so he was with Ariel until she started nursery school. When Ariel's mother returned to work, the transition was difficult for all of them. According to her parents, Ariel began to show more significant signs of separation anxiety about a year after the adoption.

Ariel first came to the first author when she was having difficulty at age 3, while in nursery school. Every day at dismissal, she refused to put on her jacket. Her parents reported that she seemed to have lots of sensory issues. She did not like the way her clothes felt. Everything she wore bothered her. Getting Ariel dressed in the morning also became difficult. She did not like the drive to school because she did not want to get into her car seat. She would throw a tantrum if her parents tried to force her to do these things. She had bad dreams at night. When they brought her to family gatherings where there were many adults, Ariel became hyperactive and oppositional.

Her parents described the process of adopting Ariel from the orphanage. Their first trip to Russia was to meet her and to discuss the adoption with the administration there. It was difficult for them because they got to spend time with her, but then had to leave her there until they returned several months later to take her home. Ariel lived in one of the baby houses with many other children, all of them slept in the same room. According to her parents, the children's physical needs were met en masse. They were all put on the toilet together. No child left the bathroom until they all went. Her parents also speculated that the orphanage staff did not attend to the children's individual needs and preferences in terms of comfort, feeding, playing, and face-to-face interaction.

Ariel's parents described her as a cheerful girl who was curious and interested in the toys that they brought her when they met her in Russia. Upon adoption, Ariel's parents changed her name: As in the Jewish tradition, she was named after her father's deceased grandmother. This is a great source of pride for her adoptive father. When they left the orphanage they traveled with her in a car that did not have a car seat, and then flew home to the United States. Ariel had never been in a car or a plane before. Initially, her parents brought her to visit a neighbor who spoke Russian, so that she would still be exposed to her native language. They soon stopped doing this however, because they did not think Ariel was responding favorably to it. Ariel's connection to her homeland was thus ended fairly early into her life in the United States. My reaction was that I (the first author) felt that Ariel's parents minimized how much this exposure meant to her and it was not clear what it meant to the parents. I also felt angry at them for changing her name. By one year, children know their names.

Ariel's parents were very interested in managing her oppositional behavior when they first came to me. As they described their understanding of her presenting problems, I felt it was important for them to consider the possibility that her early experiences in the orphanage might have impacted how she was responding to her current environment. Initially, they were resistant to considering this and we worked together to imagine what her first year of life might have been like. They were so happy to have become parents that it was difficult for them to see the transition for Ariel as anything but positive. In addition, they felt that she could not remember her time at the orphanage.

We spent many sessions discussing the care that Ariel probably received in her early months and her parents slowly began to make connections to her symptoms. I learned from them about the uniformity with which all of the children were bathed, clothed, fed, and put to bed. We discussed the possible connections between her reactions to grown-ups coming together. We wondered if for Ariel "big things happen" when the big people get together. Her father began to wonder if her aversion to the car seat, which is not so unusual, might have been connected to her early experience of them whisking her away in a car. The focus of the treatment was encouraging and supporting the reflective functioning of both parents. I found it frustrating that often they were not attuned to Ariel's feelings and focused instead on her misbehavior. I sometimes felt reluctant to point this out to them, but I felt that Ariel needed me to do so. Her parents trusted me and felt I had been helpful, so they listened and seemed genuinely to want to understand Ariel's experience despite their own frustration.

As one might have expected, Ariel always needed to be in control, which was particularly challenging for her parents. Over time, they began to understand that her need for control was perhaps a result of her early attachment issues, that Ariel acted in an overly confident manner which served to mask her attachment anxiety. As her parents began to understand her symptoms and their potential meaning, they felt less upset and angry by her behavior. They were able to be more empathic and to give her choices and opportunities to be in control, while still setting limits and boundaries. Her symptoms began to lessen and her parents began to feel more confident in their parenting.

Ariel's controlling behavior was particularly evident in the videotaped sessions with her parents. As we viewed together the videotape of her playing with them, we discussed reasons why she might need to be in control. Her parents developed the capacity to reflect during these sessions on what her early life was like. They speculated that very often there were things being done to her rather than her being given the opportunity to have her own sense of agency.

When Ariel was about 5 years old, her parents decided to adopt another child. This time it was a boy, from the same orphanage in Russia. While we spent a good deal of time discussing how to prepare her for her brother's arrival, Ariel had understandable reactions to sharing her home with a new 13-month old. While she was very protective of him, she also began to display aggressive, oppositional, and fearful behavior. She struggled with the idea that there would be enough love for both of them, and she was able to express this directly. As her behavior escalated, her parents had difficulty controlling their own frustration and anger. Again, it was a challenge for them to see her behavior as something they should expect. They felt she was being willful and manipulative. We returned to some of our earlier discussions about Ariel's early experience and how this new sibling might threaten her sense of attachment security.

Meeting Ariel

My initial reaction to meeting Ariel was that she was charming and adorable. I noted that I felt this more strongly than I typically did with other children I worked with, and sensed that this countertransference was important to examine. As I reflected on this, I realized others responded similarly to her in the waiting room: People seemed drawn to Ariel. Ariel also appeared older than her stated age in terms of her relatedness to relative strangers. I wondered if this ease was a façade underneath which she might actually feel anxious. As I examined my own feelings, I realized that I was disturbed by her pseudo-maturity. Given her lack of wariness towards strangers, her seemingly outward lack of anxiety and her pseudo-maturity, I wondered if she had an avoidant-anxious attachment style.

Becoming Attached: Keeping Mommy and Me Together

In one session, Ariel drew a picture of two figures that she described as herself with Mommy. She then took glue and proceeded to put clear tape across the figures. As I looked to her mother and father, they both smiled. I said to Ariel, "Mommy and Ariel are together. You taped them together." She smiled and said, "Yes, Mommy and Ariel are together." In a collateral session with her parents, we explored the meaning of this action. Ariel's mother said she felt it was significant, but did not quite know what it meant. We discussed the idea that perhaps Ariel was telling us that she never wanted her mother to go away. We discussed how difficult it was sometimes for both Ariel and her mother when her mother left for work, but this was also a positive sign that Ariel feels attached to her.

The session in which Ariel made this drawing was one of the most poignant moments in the early treatment. As she carefully drew, I felt tenderness and warmth toward her. I felt that I was sharing a very special moment between Ariel and her parents. I smiled as I witnessed this and felt like I was being let in. I felt hope for Ariel as I realized that she was becoming attached to her new mother. I saw that her mother had tears in her eyes as she smiled as well.

Separation During a Vulnerable Time: A Break in Treatment

I worked with Ariel from the time she was 3 years old until she was about 4.5 years old, when her symptoms had abated. While I encouraged her parents to continue in treatment as they were considering adopting another child, they felt that our work was done. I felt some anger toward them for this because I was concerned about the impact of the adoption on Ariel and had hoped to assist them in helping her. We did discuss this prior to their leaving and I expressed that they were always welcome to call and/or return. I suspected they would return and felt that we had developed a good enough alliance that when they felt they could use my help they would ask for it. I respected their need to be separate from me at this vulnerable time, while worrying about Ariel. Countertransferentially, this termination was also difficult as I felt that the timing of Ariel's separation from me would complicate the arrival of her brother.

The Betrayal: Ariel Gets a Baby Brother

Ariel was 5 years old when her parents adopted their second child. She returned to treatment when she was 5.5 years old, as she began to once again have symptoms of not feeling comfortable in her clothes and shoes. Ariel's new brother Jacob was 13 months old when adopted from the same orphanage. While Ariel stated that she was happy to get a sibling, she seemed worried, jealous, and angry.

When her parents talked about adopting another child, I felt protective of Ariel. They seemed to dismiss her concerns and focused on the practical aspects of the adoption process. I anticipated that Ariel would regress and worry about what the arrival of another child would mean for her relationship to her parents. I worried that she would feel like her parents did not have enough love and attention to give to both her and her brother or worse that they would give her away. While this is a normal concern for all children who first become a sibling, Ariel's reality that her own biological parents had given her up for adoption made this threat more significant.

Night Terrors

When they returned to treatment, Ariel's parents expressed a need for help with both children and with their own adjustment to the difficulty of caring for more than one child. I felt a sense of relief that the family had returned because I had felt worried for Ariel. Although her parents were coming to discuss Ariel's response to her new brother, they also wanted help with their new son. My initial response to little Jacob was very similar to my initial reactions to Ariel. He was adorable and very competent. Everyone in the waiting area was drawn to him. Again I wondered what was happening internally for Jacob. Was he anxious beneath his façade of confidence?

His parents described Jacob's night terrors, how he would wake up in the middle of the night and how difficult it was to soothe him. I tried to imagine what his experience was like in his new home and wondered what his sleeping arrangements had been like in the orphanage. I realized that his parents had not been thinking about his transition in this way. I asked them what they knew about his early experience. I had the feeling that they wanted to put this behind them and in doing so, were not attuned to Jacob's feelings. I was initially frustrated with them as I had hoped that our previous work would have translated into greater insight during the transition for their new child. At times, I felt that the mom was defensive. I felt that the parents wanted to understand their children, but found it difficult to do so.

The parents explained that Ariel and Jacob slept in the same room. I asked them if Jacob could see Ariel from his crib in the middle of the night when he woke up. They looked at me puzzled and asked "why?" I explained that I suspected that the children in the orphanage may have slept in a large room together and that the children might have felt comforted by having each other. The parents explained that Jacob slept with a large teddy bear, and that the way he slept with it told them that he had perhaps shared a crib with another baby. I smiled at Jacob's father who seemed pleased to have figured this out.

That night they moved Jacob's crib and put a nightlight in the room so that he could see Ariel in her bed when he woke up at night. They also had Ariel lay down on the bed before Jacob fell asleep so that he could see that she was there. What they figured out was that he did not know his sister slept in the room because she went to bed later than he did. Jacob did not have night terrors after this.

Falling Apart

One session, I came out to get Jacob and his parents in the waiting room and found Jacob lying in the hallway crying. His parents looked paralyzed. They were ten feet away from him as he kicked and screamed on the floor. I slowly moved toward them, and they explained that, when this happens, Jacob does not want them near. I lowered my body as I slowly moved toward him. I said, "Jacob is very upset right now and he is having a hard time letting mommy and daddy comfort him but they are right here with him." While I spoke, I matched his facial affect and I encouraged his parents to approach him slowly. As they moved toward him, he began to calm down and eventually he let his mother pick him up. This felt like an important moment for all of us as Jacob was calmed, and his parents felt more competent in their ability to soothe him.

You Are Scaring Me

There were several sessions in which Ariel showed me her anger and underlying fear. In one session, she wanted to throw a ball to me and began doing so very hard, to the point of frightening me. I asked if she could throw it less hard because it frightened me. Initially, this was hard for her to do. We talked about what it feels like to be frightened. At this point, Ariel hid her own fear, but had induced it in me. Not long after that session, she had a nightmare that a vicious animal was going to devour her. It was terrifying to her. Upon further exploration, I discovered that both of her parents had been pretty scary lately in their attempts to discipline her. I discussed this with them alone and then we talked with Ariel about how they would try very hard not to yell because they understood that it frightened her. When I met with her parents, we wondered about Ariel's early life at the orphanage and hypothesized that it was traumatizing. Perhaps her father's yelling was triggering this early trauma and frightening her.

The next session, Ariel announced that she figured out how to stop the bad dreams. She said she was sleeping with her stuffed animal and, as long as she did, she felt better. I asked her how she figured this out, and she responded that after last week she was thinking about it. I hoped this meant Ariel felt effective in communicating her fear. I worried, however, that she might believe that she had to figure out how to soothe herself and, like many avoidant children, had had to take care of her own needs. I expressed how positive it was that she comforted herself with the stuffed animal and that she also let me know how scared she was. I told her it was helpful because we could let her parents know what scares her and then they could respond. Ariel did not behave aggressively toward me in that session or in any subsequent sessions.

Later in the treatment, Ariel announced that parents do not always do what they are supposed to, even if you tell them. She explained that her father had been yelling again. Ariel began to exhibit a new symptom at this point: a tick in which she would incessantly wipe her eye with her index finger. When I observed this, it looked as though she were wiping away tears. I asked Ariel how she felt about her father yelling even after we talked about it. She looked at me and stated it made her mad. I validated this feeling and then looked at her very sad face; I found myself matching the sadness in my own expression. We looked at one another for a while that way until Ariel said, "and maybe it makes me sad too." We were later able to share her feelings with her parents and they were able to validate them as well. The tick subsided.

As I worked with Ariel and Jacob, I often wondered what their early caregiving was really like. Were they responded to when in distress? Were they helped to regulate their internal states of arousal or were they left to self-regulate? What was the early face-to-face interaction like? The use of videotape in this case helped the parents to see how they were interacting with the children, both verbally and nonverbally. We imagined together what each child felt during their first year of their life. As a result, Ariel and Jacob's parents were able to create a different, more attuned relationship with them as the attachment between them developed.

Analysis of the Case

The case of these adoptees illustrates how the use of an attachment-based intervention informed by parent–Infant theory and research can make a significant difference in the lives of very young children. The clinical approach in this case is based on Bowlby's theory of attachment. Ariel, in her first year of life, did not have a consistently and sensitively attuned primary caregiver. Being treated like all of the other children in the orphanage in terms of toileting, bathing, holding, and feeding, created an attachment style in which she needed to be pseudo-independent. Her avoidant attachment style served her well, as she was not too demanding (Ainsworth and Wittig 1969). This coping strategy, along with her charming personality, likely helped her create proximity to the orphanage caregivers. Over time, Ariel began to develop a more positive attachment relationship with her parents. She demonstrated her attachment through her drawing of her mother and herself taped together.

Her parents' consistent, sensitive caregiving paved the way for Ariel to expect something different in terms of an attachment relationship. She was able to express her needs more directly, first through her actions and behavior and later with words.

Understandably, in times of transition or change, she felt less secure, more anxious, and became symptomatic. These times of regression were opportunities for her adoptive parents to demonstrate a concern for her experience of the situation and attend to Ariel with a relatedness that contrasted with how she had been responded to in her first year of life.

Winnicott's (1965) theory on holding and creating a facilitating environment is relevant in this case. Ariel's issues with her clothing not feeling right and her refusal to wear her coat are examples of difficulty in early holding environments. The uniformity with which each child was clothed in the orphanage is an example of a lack of sensitivity to children's needs. Ariel is a child who gets overheated more quickly than other children but her early caregivers did not take this into consideration. In addition, multiple caregivers do the actual holding of the children in the orphanage and apparently less frequently than needed. Helping her parents understand this allowed them to individualize her care and provide a new holding environment for her. Her parents were mindful of her unique needs and tailored their responses to her as a result. For example, they allowed her to wear shorts until late in the fall because she tended to be hot much of the time. In addition, her parents held her literally when she sought comfort but also respected her need at times for space. They allowed her to make her own choices about clothing, food, toys, etc. They provided a safe, consistent, and stable home with extended family, friends, and a strong community.

Tronick and Giannino's (1986) concept of rupture and repair applies to this treatment case. Empathic attunement to moments when Ariel frightened the therapist repaired her early ruptures of being frightened by allowing the therapist to feel the way she had. This use of projective identification allowed the therapist to interpret Ariel's fear and repair the rupture regarding her adoptive father frightening her.

Facilitating the parents' ability to mentalize the states of their children was especially helpful in this treatment (Fonagy and Target 1998). Watching the videotapes together was an important tool in facilitating the parents' ability to imagine what Ariel was thinking and feeling and what she had experienced early in her life. Once they were able to envision the lives of their children in the orphanage and its impact on their emotional states, the parents focused less on behavior and more on understanding the meaning of the behavior and the feelings behind it.

These are examples of how attachment-based clinical work can be highly effective with at-risk children using multiple theoretical perspectives and research. There is tremendous opportunity to help families using this approach. Specialized training in this work is necessary in order for clinicians to be able to maximize positive outcomes.

Conclusion

This chapter demonstrates how mother–infant theorists and researchers have influenced clinical practice. It traces how the research on attachment and mother–infant face-to-face interaction is being used to intervene and prevent difficulties in the parent–infant relationship. It highlights how videotape, once primarily used in observation and research, is now used in clinical settings. It demonstrates that videotape can serve as a useful clinical intervention; as with research, the ability to see what the naked eye cannot, or to see their interaction with their child after the actual moment, provides rich insight for parents and clinicians alike.

The case example demonstrates that with this knowledge base and the ability to videotape, less than optimal early parent–infant relationships can be repaired. Engaging parents in the process of understanding the meaning of their children's behavior and helping them to better attune, hold, and nurture their young children is both possible and potentially quite effective. The early attachment relationships that are forged in the first year of life can be modified through different patterns of caregiving. Supporting families in providing "good enough" parenting is possible when the clinician is working from a perspective of attachment. A "secure base" (Bowlby 1958, p. 11) can be created with the caregivers within the context of the therapeutic work, providing the groundwork for the child to attain more positive outcomes in the future. The earlier the clinician intervenes, the more opportunity there is to minimize negative effects and optimize the child's potential. This is a hopeful prospect.

References

Ainsworth, M. D. S., & Wittig, B. A. (1969). Attachment and exploratory behaviour of one-year-olds in a strange situation. In B. M. Foss (Ed.), *Determinants of infant behavior* (pp. 113–136). London: Methuen.

Ainsworth, M. D. S., Blehar, M. C., Waters, E., & Wall, S. (1978). *Patterns of attachment: A psychological study of the strange situation.* Hillsdale: Lawrence Erlbaum.

Arend, R., Gove, F., & Sroufe, A. (1979). Continuity of individual adaptation from infancy to kindergarten: A predictive study of ego resilience and curiosity in preschoolers. *Child Development, 50,* 950–959.

Beebe, B. (2000). Co-constructing mother–infant distress. *Psychoanalytic Inquiry, 20,* 421–440.

Beebe, B. (2003). Brief mother–infant treatment: Psychoanalytically informed video feedback. *Infant Mental Health Journal, 24,* 24–52.

Beebe, B. (2005). Mother–infant research informs mother–infant treatment. *Psychoanalytic Study of the Child, 60,* 7–46.

Beebe, B., & Gerstman, L. (1980). The packaging of maternal stimulation in relation to infant facial-visual engagement: A case study at four months. *Merrill-Palmer Quarterly, 26,* 321–339.

Beebe, B., & Lachmann, F. M. (1994). Representation and internalization in infancy: Three principles of salience. *Psychoanalytic Psychology, 11,* 127–165.

Beebe, B., & Lachmann, F. M. (1998). Co-constructing inner and relational processes: Self and mutual regulation in infant research and adult treatment. *Psychoanalytic Psychology, 15,* 480–516.

Beebe, B., & Stern, D. (1977). Engagement-disengagement and early object experience. In M. Freedman & S. Grenel (Eds.), *Communicative structures and psychic experiences* (pp. 33–55). New York: Plenum.

Beebe, B., Jaffe, J., Buck, K., Chen, H., Cohen, P., Feldstein, S., et al. (2008). Maternal depressive symptoms at 6 weeks predict mother-infant self- and interactive contingency. *Infant Mental Health Journal, 29,* 442–471.

Beebe, B., Jaffe, J., Feldstein, S., Mays, K. & Alson, D. (1985). Interpersonal timing: The application of an adult dialogue model to mother-infant vocal and kinesic interactions. In T. M. Field & N. A. Fox (Eds.), *Social perception in infants* (pp. 61–82). Hillsdale: Analytic Press.

Beebe, B., Jaffe, J., & Lachmann, F. M. (1992). A dyadic systems view of communication. In N. Skolnick & S. Warshaw (Eds.), *Relational perspectives in psychoanalysis* (pp. 61–81). Hillsdale: Analytic Press.

Beebe, B., Jaffe, J., Lachmann, F. M., Feldstein, S., Crown, C., & Jasnow, J. (2000). Systems models in development and psychoanalysis: The case of vocal rhythm coordination and attachment. *Infant Mental Health Journal, 21*, 99–122.

Beebe, B., Jaffe, J., Markese, S., Buck, K., Chen, H., Cohen, P., Bahrick, L., Andrews, H., & Feldstein, S. (2010). The origins of 12-month attachment: A microanalysis of 4-month interaction. *Attachment and Human Development, 12*, 3–141.

Bowlby, J. (1958). The nature of the child's tie to his mother. *International Journal of Psychoanalysis, 39*, 350–373.

Bowlby, J. (1960). Separation anxiety. *Psychoanalytic Study of the Child, 15*, 9–20.

Bowlby, J. (1969). Attachment. In *Attachment* and loss, *Vol. 1*. London: Hogarth Press and the Institute of Psycho-Analysis.

Bowlby, J. (1973). Attachment and loss. In *Separation: Anxiety and anger, Vol. 2*. London: Hogarth Press and Institute of Psycho-Analysis.

Brazelton, T. B., Kowslowski, B., & Main, M. (1974). The origins of reciprocity: The early mother-infant interaction. In M. Lewis & L. Rosenblum (Eds.), *The effect of the infant on its caregivers* (pp. 49–76). New York: Wiley.

Cohn, J. F., & Tronick, E. Z. (1988). Mother-infant interaction: Influence is bidirectional and unrelated to periodic cycles in either partner's behavior. *Developmental Psychology, 24*, 386–392.

Erickson, M., Sroufe, A., & Egeland, B. (1983). The relationship between quality of attachment and behavior problems in preschool in a high-risk sample. In I. Bretherton & E. Waters (Eds.), *Growing points in attachment theory and research. Monographs for the Society for Research in Child Development* (Vol. 50, 1–2, Serial No. 209).

Fairbairn, W. R. D. (1963). Synopsis of an object-relations theory of the personality. *International Journal of Psychoanalysis, 44*, 224–225.

Field, T. (1981). Infant gaze aversion and heart rate during face-to-face interactions. *Infant Behavior and Development, 19*, 307–315.

Field, T. (1994). The effects of mother's physical and emotional unavailability on emotion regulation. *Monograph of the Society for Research in Child Development, 59*, 208–227.

Fonagy, P., & Target, M. (1998). Mentalization and the changing aims of child psychoanalysis. *Psychoanalytic Dialogues, 8*, 87–114.

Fraiberg, S. (1980). *Clinical studies in infant mental health: The first year of life*. New York: Basic Books.

Giannino, A., & Tronick E. Z. (1988). The mutual regulation model: The infant's self and interactive regulation and coping and defensive capacities. In T. Field, P. McCabe & N. Schneiderman (Eds.), *Stress and coping* (pp. 47–60). Hillsdale: Lawrence Erlbaum Associates.

Guedeney, A., & Guedeney, N. (2010). The era of using video for observation and intervention in infant mental health. *The Signal, 18*, 1–14.

Jaffe, J., Beebe, B., Feldstein, S., Crown, C. L., & Jasnow, M. D. (2001). Rhythms of dialogue in infancy. *Monograph of the Society for Research in Child Development, 66*, 1–131.

Lewis, M., Feiring, C., McGuffog, C., & Jaskir, J. (1984). Predicting psychopathology in six year olds from early social relations. *Child Development, 55*, 123–136.

Lyons-Ruth, K. (1999). The two-person unconscious: Intersubjective dialogue, enactive relational representation, and the emergence of new forms of relational organization. *Psychoanalytic Inquiry, 19*, 576–617.

Lyons-Ruth, K., Alpern, L., & Repacholi, B. (1993). Disorganized infant attachment: Classification and maternal psychosocial problems as predictors of hostile-aggressive behavior in the preschool classroom. *Child Development, 64*, 572–585.

Lyons-Ruth, K., Yellin, C., Melnick, S., & Atwood, G. (2005). Expanding the concept of unresolved mental states: Hostile/helpless states of mind on the adult attachment interview are associated and infant disorganization. *Development and Psychopathology, 17*, 1–23.

Marvin, R., Cooper, G., Hoffman, K., & Powell, B. (2002). The circle of security project: Attachement-based intervention with caregiver-pre-school dyads. *Attachment & Human Development, 4*, 107–124.

McDonough, S. (1993). Interaction guidance. In C. Zeanah (Ed.), *Handbook of infant mental health* (pp. 414–426). New York: Guilford.

Murray, L., & Cooper, P. (1997). *Postpartum depression and child development.* New York: Guilford.

Sander, L. (1977). The regulation of exchange in the infant-caretaker system and some aspects of the context-content relationship. In M. Lewis & L. Rosenblum (Eds.), *Interaction, conversation, and the development of language* (pp. 133–156). New York: Wiley.

Slade, A. (2008). The implication of attachment theory and research for adult psychotherapy. In J. Cassidy & P. R. Shaver (Eds.), *Handbook of attachment* (pp. 762–782). New York: Guilford.

Spitz, R. A., & Cobliner, W. G. (1965). *The first year of life.* New York: International Universities Press.

Sroufe, A. (1985). Attachment classification from the perspective of infant-caregiver relationships and infant temperament. *Child Development, 56*, 1–14.

Stern, D. (1971). A microanalysis of the mother-infant interaction. *Journal of the American Academy of Child Psychiatry, 10*, 501–507.

Stern, D. (1974). Goal and structure of mother-infant play. *Journal of the American Academy of Child Psychiatry, 13*, 402–421.

Stern, D. (1977). *The first relationship.* Cambridge: Harvard University Press.

Stern, D. (1985). *The interpersonal world of the infant.* New York: Basic Books.

Stern, D. (1995). *The motherhood constellation.* New York: Basic Books.

Trevarthen, C. (1977). Descriptive analyses of infant communicative behavior. In H. R. Schaffer (Ed.), *Studies in mother-infant interaction* (pp. 227–270). London: Academic.

Trevarthen, C. (1998). The concept and foundations of infant intersubjectivity. In H. Schaffer (Ed.), *Intersujective communication and emotion in early ontogeny* (pp. 15–46). Cambridge: Cambridge University Press.

Tronick, E. Z. (1989). Emotions and emotional communication in infants. *American Psychologist, 44*, 112–119.

Tronick, E. Z. (2001). Emotional connections and dyadic consciousness in infant-mother and patient-therapist interactions. *Psychoanalytic Dialogues, 11*, 187–194.

Tronick, E. Z. (2007). *The neurobehavioral and social-emotional development an infants and children.* New York: Norton.

Tronick, E. A., & Cohn, J. F. (1989). Infant-mother face-to-face interaction: Age and gender differences in coordination and the occurrence of miscooridination. *Child Development, 60*, 85–92.

Tronick, E. Z., & Giannino, A. (1986). Interactive mismatch and repair: Challenges to the coping infant. *Zero to Three: Bulletin of the National Center for Clinical Infant Programs, 5*, 1–6.

Tronick, E. Z., & Weinberg, M. K. (1997). Depressed mothers and infants: Failures to form dyadic states of consciousness. In L. Murray & P. Cooper (Eds.), *Postpartum depression and child development.* New York: Guilford.

Tronick, E. Z., Als, H., Adamson, L., Wise, S., & Brazelton, T. (1978). The infant's response to entrapment between contradictory messages in face-to-face interaction. *Journal of American Academy of Child and Adolescent Psychiatry, 17*, 1–13.

Waters, E., Merrick, S., Treboux, D., Crowell, J., & Albersheim, L. (2000). Attachment security in infancy and early adulthood: A twenty-year longitudinal study. *Child Development, 7*, 684–689.

Weinberg, M. K., Tronick, E. Z., Cohn, J. F., & Olson, K. L. (1998). Gender differences in emotional expressivity and self regulation during early infancy. *Developmental Psychology, 35*, 175–188.

Winnicott, D. (1956). *Collected papers.* New York: Basic Books.

Winnicott, D. (1965). *The maturational processes and the facilitating environment.* New York: International Universities Press.

Using Modern Attachment Theory to Guide Clinical Assessments of Early Attachment Relationships

Allan N. Schore and Ruth P. Newton

Introduction

In an editorial of a recent issue of the *Journal of Child Psychology and Psychiatry* entitled "Developmental neuroscience comes of age," Leckman and March (2011) describe "the phenomenal progress of the past three decades in the developmental neurosciences" (p. 333). Summarizing the critical meaning of this rapidly expanding body of research for a deeper understanding of human development, they assert,

> Over the past decade it has also become abundantly clear that . . . the in utero and immediate postnatal environments and the dyadic relations between child and caregivers within the first years of life can have direct and enduring effects on the child's brain development and behavior . . . Indeed, the enduring impact of early maternal care and the role of epigenetic modifications of the genome during critical periods in early brain development in health and disease is likely to be *one of the most important discoveries in all of science* that have major implications for our field. (p. 334, emphasis added)

Leckman and March conclude that "A scientific consensus is emerging that the origins of adult disease are often found among developmental and biological disruptions occurring during the early years of life" (p. 333). Similarly, in the psychiatric literature Insel and Fenton (2005) assert, "Most mental illnesses . . . begin far earlier in life than was previously believed" (p. 590).

In fact, recent approaches integrating neuroscience and pediatrics focus on reducing significant stress and adversity in the early periods of childhood (Shonkoff et al. 2009). Attempting to forge tighter links between advances in developmental theory and research with innovative clinical applications, Shonkoff (2011) calls for "early childhood policy and practice" to have a better understanding "of the extent to which

A. N. Schore (✉)
Department of Psychiatry and Biobehavioral Sciences, UCLA David Geffen School
of Medicine, Los Angeles, CA, USA
e-mail: aschore@ucla.edu

R. P. Newton
Newton Center for Affect Regulation, La Jolla, and St. Vincent de Paul Village,
San Diego, CA, USA

J. E. Bettmann, D. D. Friedman (eds.), *Attachment-Based Clinical Work with
Children and Adolescents,* Essential Clinical Social Work Series,
DOI 10.1007/978-1-4614-4848-8_4, © Springer Science+Business Media New York 2013

early experiences are incorporated into the developing brain, for better or for worse" (p. 982). He suggests that "interventions that enhance the mental health, executive function skills, and self-regulation capacities of vulnerable mothers, beginning as early as pregnancy, suggest promising strategies to protect the developing brains of their children" (p. 983). Congruent with this proposal, researchers studying the developmental neurobiological basis of human attachment assert, "Understanding the motivational basis of healthy and at-risk parenting may open new theoretical vistas and clinical opportunities and may lead to the construction of more specific interventions that can target disruptions to maternal–infant bonding at an earlier stage and in a more accurate manner" (Atzil et al. 2011, p. 11).

Thus, the next step forward would create more efficient programs of early intervention and prevention which require that clinicians working with children under five incorporate recent data from neuroscience on brain development into their clinical assessments of primary attachment relationships. Because development in infancy occurs within the relational context of nonverbal, implicit nonconscious infant/caregiver attachment dynamics, clinicians assessing these early relationships must also be able to integrate recent advances in developmental psychoanalysis and neuropsychoanalysis on the early relational development of the unconscious mind into their early interventions. In line with current relational psychoanalytic approaches, clinicians must do more than objectively observe a particular maternal–infant relationship. Rather they need to act as participant–observers who intersubjectively join, feel, attune to, and resonate with the nonverbal, implicit world of affective communications that lie at the core of the mutually constructed attachment system.

Stern (2005) states, "Without the nonverbal it would be hard to achieve the empathic, participatory, and resonating aspects of intersubjectivity. One would only be left with a kind of pared down, neutral 'understanding' of the other's subjective experience" (p. 80). This dictum applies directly to clinical mother–infant attachment assessments. Alluding to the limitations of relying too heavily on adult verbal mechanisms in understanding infancy, he beautifully describes the impact of learning verbal language on the nonverbal child "whose comfortable, rich, implicit, pre-verbal world is fractured into unrecognizable pieces by attaching language to his implicit experiences . . . The loss is of wholeness, felt truth, richness and honesty" (Stern 2004, p. 144). It is this implicit world—prior to language—that clinicians assess, especially in cases where a preverbal infant does not have a comfortable relationship with his primary attachment caregiver.

Modern attachment theory (Schore and Schore 2008) advances Bowlby's (1969) basic tenet that attachment is biological in nature and in the service of infant protection to the primacy of the attachment relationship in emotional regulation, the structural connectivity of the right hemisphere, and the development of the implicit self. This expansion of Bowlby's seminal ideas allows for "new understandings in clinical assessments, shaping therapeutic interventions from relevant theory, and providing a unique awareness of the adaptive nonconscious functions of the implicit self" (Schore and Schore 2008, p. 17). As opposed to classical attachment theory which focuses on behavioral and cognitive development in infancy, modern attachment theory describes the earliest stages of social and emotional development, emphasizing the central roles of affect communication and affect regulation (Schore and Schore 2008).

In contrast to cognitive developmental psychological theories, regulation theory integrates developmental affective psychology and affective neuroscience in order to generate more complex psychobiological models of not just the infant's developing mind, but mind/brain/body. In this interpersonal neurobiological perspective, the nonconscious interactive regulation of not behavior but affective arousal, especially states of autonomic arousal, lies at the core of the bodily based attachment dynamic. We suggest that the significant advances in developmental neuroscience can directly inform and even significantly alter our assessments and therapeutic interventions with high risk infants and their primary caregivers. Thus, therapists treating young children and their families can now use clinical models grounded in robust scientific evidence showing the inseparable nature of brain development and lived experience within the primary attachment relationship (Schore 1994, 2001a, b, in press).

Modern attachment theory posits that the hard wiring of the infant's developing right brain, which is dominant for the emotional sense of self, is influenced by implicit intersubjective affective transactions embedded in the attachment relationship with the mother (Schore 1994, 2005). Developmental intersubjective studies conclude that implicit, nonconscious processing of nonverbal affective cues in infancy 'is repetitive, automatic, provides quick categorization and decision-making, and operates outside the realm of focal attention and verbalized experience' (Lyons-Ruth 1999, p. 576). Neuroscience now reveals that the medial orbitofrontal cortex of adults rapidly and thereby implicitly responds to the image of an infant's face in 130 ms, beneath levels of conscious awareness (Kringelbach et al. 2008). These authors conclude, the orbitofrontal cortex expresses a specific and rapid signature for parental instinct. We suggest that in order to assess any infant–mother system of attachment communications, the clinician must be able to not only be aware of but enter into this rapid-acting nonverbal realm of implicit relational knowledge. The clinician's own right brain instinctive psychobiological attunement to the moment-to- moment implicit bodily based affective communication of both mother and infant is thus essential in the evaluation of the development of a young child under 5.

Regulation theory also integrates developmental psychoanalytic data back into attachment models, thereby focusing on both the development of the mind and unconscious processes. Schore (1991–2012) offers clinical data and experimental research documenting that the experience-dependent maturation of the right brain equates with the early development of the biological substrate of the human unconscious. This developmental neuropsychoanalytic conception is echoed in recent neuroscientific writings by Tucker and Moller (2007): "The right hemisphere's specialization for emotional communication through nonverbal channels seems to suggest a domain of the mind that is close to the motivationally charged psychoanalytic unconscious" (p. 91). The psychoanalytic perspective of modern attachment theory thus dictates that the early structural and functional development of the human unconscious occurs in a critical period of infancy, and that this emerging mind/body system is impacted, for better or worse, by its emotional interactions embedded in the attachment relationship with the mother's unconscious mind/body system.

Schore (1994, 2003a, 2011, 2012) also cites ongoing interdisciplinary data indicating that nonverbal right brain functions underlie what psychoanalysis has long described as primary process operations. Indeed, Schore and Schore (2008, p. 14) propose that "during heightened affective moments ... right brain dialogues between the relational unconscious of both the patient and therapist (*like the attachment communications of the infant and mother*) are examples of 'primary process communication' (Dorpat 2001)." Dorpat further proposes,

> The primary process system analyzes, regulates, and communicates an individual's relations with the environment ... [A]ffective and object-relational information is transmitted predominantly by primary process communication. Nonverbal communication includes body movements (kinesics), posture, gesture, facial expression, voice inflection, and the sequence, rhythm, and pitch of the spoken words. (Dorpat 2001, p. 451)

Note that these same communications are transacted in the attachment relationship the clinician is attempting to assess. This means that, in an assessment of an attachment dyad, the clinician attends not to the mother's left brain secondary process expressions, but to her and her infant's right brain primary process expressions.

The major goal of this chapter is to offer the reader recent knowledge about the structural development and unique functional activities of the early developing right brain (Schore 1994, 2001a, b). Indeed the now well-established principle that the right hemisphere is in a critical growth period from the last trimester of pregnancy to 2.5–3 years of age (Chiron et al. 1997; Mento et al. 2010), suggests that the experience-dependent maturation of the right hemisphere is the primary developmental task of the first 3 years of life (Newton 2008a). The dynamic forces of brain development, the unfolding of critical periods, the impacting of attachment by epigenetics, and lived experience occur within this foundational socio-emotional developmental period. The attachment relationship occurs in the nonverbal body-world between the infant and the primary caregiver, usually the mother. According to Bowlby (1969), attachment is an evolutionary driven biological system designed to protect the infant from predation, and therefore it represents the primary force for development. Infants without attachments fail to thrive and often die (Robertson 1952; Spitz 1947). The rhythmic developmental movement between survival-security and exploration etches a template in the brain for the rest of the life span. The quality of maternal response thus directly impacts her child's future self development and the ability to intersubjectively be with another.

Both experimental research and clinical data emphasize the critical importance of the "good-enough" (Winnicott 1965, p. 145), psychobiologically attuned caregiver who can sensitively respond to her infant's needs, that is, receive and meaningfully process her infant's affective attachment communications and regulate them. Our interpersonal neurobiological perspective describes how the mother's ability to down-regulate stressful high arousal states through soothing and up-regulate stressful low arousal states in play states acts as an epigenetic mechanism by which the connectivity between the central nervous system (CNS) and autonomic nervous system (ANS) in the infant's developing emotional right brain is enhanced. Optimal interactive arousal regulation allows for more complex right brain functions, expressed in more efficient strategies of affect regulation, attachment security, and a burgeoning positive sense of self. This security in turn allows the child to explore by playfully looking, listening, feeling, smelling, studying, reaching, holding, transferring objects from hand to hand, and experiencing what can be created from objects in the physical and social environment. When caregivers scaffold age-appropriate levels of exploration, the typical and rhythmic developmental movement of moving outward for exploration and returning inward for safety is seen in children and is the hallmark of emotional security. When caregivers support this natural life rhythm, the mind/brain/body of the securely attached child passes through the ensuing developmental stages toward more complex human growth and development.

But as clinicians know, attachment histories can be regulated or dysregulated, secure, or insecure. Current research supports what clinicians have long known—"all mothers are not created equal" (Barrett and Fleming 2011, p. 368).

> The interaction between a mother and her infant can be like a dance. There are routines, standards and missteps, there is give and take, there is unparalleled intimacy, there are often vast differences in skill level and motivation, there is learning . . . . This dance can be beautiful, it can be tender, it can be awkward, it can be difficult. And sometimes it just does not occur. (Barrett and Fleming 2011, p. 368)

Frequently, this latter dynamic presents itself as high risk dyads that require clinical assessments. Regulation theory can assist therapists in intervening in a misattuned infant/caregiver relationship by providing a lens for observing, experiencing, and evaluating the communication of affects and the regulation of affective arousal between the mother's and infant's right brains. Through the therapist's own right brain connection to the infant's and the mother's right brains, she can assess (1) the dyadic strength and attunement of caregiver/infant nonverbal communications of eyes, facial expressions, voice prosody, gesture, and touch, (2) the caregiver's ability to regulate infant hypo-and hyper arousal, (3) the caregiver's support of exploration, (4) the impressions of the attachment relationship based upon both caregiver and infant behavior, and (5) the knowledge of developmental stages as they relate to brain development. A fundamental tenet of modern attachment theory dictates that the early developing right brain which is involved in survival functions is shaped by attachment dynamics. Thus the evolutionary mechanism of attachment is critical to more than just the development of overt behaviors and cognitive mental functions; it is critical to developing organismic psychobiological capacities that are essential for adaptive functioning (Schore 1994, 2001b, 2003a).

In this chapter, we will offer a review of recent research on mother–infant right brain-to-right brain visual, auditory, and tactile attachment communications, and on the interpersonal neurobiological mechanisms that facilitate or inhibit experience-dependent maturation of the infant's developing right brain. We then utilize regulation theory to model the brain/mind/body neurodynamics of a relational sequence between a 7-month-old infant and his mother, and finally, offer some thoughts about the unique contributions of regulation theory's integration of biological and psychological domains in constructing more effective models of early assessment, intervention, and prevention. We shall suggest that in applying the subjective trans-theoretical lens of regulation theory to the clinical evaluation of the mother–infant relationship, the assessment technique is not as important as the assessment process.

Recent Studies of Right Brain-to-Right Brain Attachment Communications

In 1996, Schore proposed the interpersonal neurobiological principle that "[T]he self-organization of the developing brain occurs in the context of a relationship with another self, another brain" (p. 60). Thus from the perspective of modern attachment theory, a central question is: How are intersubjective emotional attachment communications transmitted between the mother's and the infant's right brains?

At about the same time that Bowlby was describing affective attachment communications of facial expression, posture, and tone of voice, Brown and Jaffe's (1975) developmental neuropsychological research indicated, "The right hemisphere can be considered dominant in infancy, for the type of visual and acoustic communication which is relevant for the prelinguistic child" (Brown and Jaffe 1975, p. 108). Following Bowlby's lead, Schore (1994) suggested that, during attachment episodes of visual–facial, auditory–prosodic, and tactile–gestural affective communications, the psychobiologically attuned caregiver regulates the infant's internal states of arousal.

> The infant's early maturing right hemisphere, which is dominant for the child's processing of visual emotional information, the infant's recognition of the mother's face, and the perception of arousal-inducing maternal facial expressions, is psychobiologically attuned to the output of the mother's right hemisphere, which is involved in the expression and processing of emotional information and in nonverbal communication. (Schore 1994, p. 63)

A large body of developmental neurobiological studies supports the hypothesis that the attachment mechanism is embedded in infant–caregiver right brain-to-right brain affective transactions (Schore 1994, 2003a, 2011).

Visual–Facial Attachment Communications

Research now clearly demonstrates that face-to-face mutual gaze is critical to early social development (Trevarthen and Aitken 2001). The development of the capacity to efficiently process information from faces requires visual input to the right (and not left) hemisphere during infancy (Le Grand et al. 2003). At 2 months of age, the onset of a critical period during which synaptic connections in the developing occipital cortex are modified by visual experience (Yamada et al. 2000), infants show right hemispheric activation when exposed to a woman's face (Tzourio-Mazoyer et al. 2002). Using electroencephalography (EEG) methodology, Grossmann et al. (2007) report that 4-month-old infants presented with images of a female face gazing directly ahead show enhanced gamma electrical activity over right prefrontal areas. Recent near-infrared spectroscopy (NIRS) research (perhaps the most suitable of all neuroscience methodologies applicable to human infants) reveals that specifically the 5-month-olds' right hemisphere responds to images of adult female faces (Nakato et al. 2009; Otsuka et al. 2007). By 6-months, infants show a right lateralized left gaze bias when viewing faces (Guo et al. 2009), right temporal activation when looking at angry faces (Nakato et al. 2011), and a significantly greater right frontotemporal activation when viewing their own mother's (as opposed to a stranger's) face (Carlsson et al. 2008).

In total, these research data mean that the future capacity to process the essential social information expressed in face-to-face communications, a central aspect of all later intimate relationships is dependent upon caregiver/infant eye contact and visual gazing during this critical period. Thus, how often and in what contexts the mother and infant look (and not look) directly at each other is of key importance to a clinician when evaluating an infant's development and the health of the dyadic relationship. When there is mutual infant/caregiver visual gazing that looks and feels natural to the clinician, the clinician knows that likely the infant's brain is developing well in this area.

Auditory–Prosodic Attachment Communications

Ongoing studies of prenatal, perinatal, and postnatal auditory–prosodic attachment communications also highlight the role of the right brain. In an EEG study of auditory pitch processing in preterm infants born at 30 gestational weeks, Mento et al. (2010) conclude, ". . . the earlier right structural maturation in foetal epochs seems to be paralleled by a right functional development" (p. 1). A functional magnetic resonance imaging (MRI) study of 1- to 3-day-old newborns reports that music evokes right hemispheric activation in the auditory cortex (Perani et al. 2010). Using NIRS with 2–6-day-old neonates, Telkemeyer et al. (2009) observe "responses to slow acoustic modulations are lateralized to the right hemisphere" (p. 14726). This same optical brain imaging technology reveals that prosodic processing of emotional voices in 3-month-old (Homae et al. 2006) and 4-month-old infants (Minagawa-Kawai et al. 2011) activates the right temporoparietal region. Grossmann et al. (2010) report that 7-month-old infants respond to emotional voices in a voice-sensitive region of the right superior temporal sulcus, and happy prosody specifically activates the right inferior frontal cortex. These authors conclude, "The pattern of finding suggests that temporal regions specialize in processing voices very early in development and that, already in infancy, emotions differentially modulate voice processing in the right hemisphere" (p. 852). This research shows that the emotional quality of what infants hear in the early stages of infancy affects the development of the auditory processing areas of the right hemisphere.

The caregiver's use of infant-directed speech ("motherese") is critical for the development of the child's prosodic–emotional functions. Compared to adult-directed speech, motherese is higher in pitch, has a wider pitch range, and exhibits exaggerated pitch contours. In addition it is shorter, slower, and separated by longer pauses than adult speech (Fernald 1989; Stern et al. 1983). Developmental neuroscience research demonstrates that 7- to 9-month-old infants show greater activation to maternal infant-directed speech in the right temporal area than 4- to 6-month old infants (Naoi et al. 2011). In 11-month-old infants, the voice of a woman's infant-directed speech (i.e., with somewhat exaggerated prosody), elicits a right-lateralized event-related potential (Thierry et al. 2003). Clinically, these studies indicate the importance of assessing not the verbal content but the melody of the mother's voice, and whether or not she's using infant-directed versus adult directed speech in her interactions with her child, especially in playful contexts. This use of infant-directed speech is essential to the development of the infant's right temporal areas and her burgeoning ability to read the emotional tone of others' voices, an essential element of adaptive social relationships.

Tactile–Gestural Attachment Communications

Tactile–gestural attachment communications found in touch affect the developing right hemisphere (Sieratzki and Woll 1996). The authors assert that the emotional impact of touch is more direct and immediate if an infant is held on the left side of the body. Because the left side of the body projects directly into the right hemisphere, infants cradled on the left receive direct input into their developing right brain (Bourne and Todd 2004; Huggenberger et al. 2009; Reissland et al. 2009). In contrast, mothers classified as depressed and those with a history of domestic violence show right sided cradling (Weatherill et al. 2004).

Other studies demonstrate the essential role of maternal touch on human infant development in the first year of life (Ferber et al. 2008; Jean et al. 2009). Touch allows the infant and mother to create a system of "touch synchrony" to alter vagal tone and cortisol reactivity (Feldman et al. 2010, p. 271). The dyad thus uses interpersonal touch as a communication system (Gallace and Spence 2010), especially for the communication and regulation of emotional information (Hertenstein 2002; Hertenstein and Campos 2001). High levels of tactile stimulation and mutual touch occur in breastfeeding (Lavelli and Poli 1998). Lehtonen et al.'s (2002) research observed an increase in EEG amplitude in right posterior cortical areas in 6-month-old infants during the intense somatosensory tactile contact of breastfeeding. This research supports the infant's need for affectionate touch for healthy right hemisphere development, which can be observed in an infant/caregiver assessment.

With respect to gestures, Nagy (2006) demonstrates a "lateralized system for neonatal imitation" and concludes, "The early advantage of the right hemisphere (Chiron et al. 1997; Schore 2000; Trevarthen 2001) in the first few months of life may affect the lateralized appearance of the first imitative gestures" (p. 227). Moreover, Montirosso et al. (2010, p. 108) document left-sided regulatory gestures (right hemisphere controlled) when infants are stressed. Summarizing their work on gestures, they state,

> Infants cope with the emotional distress caused by unresponsive mothers through self-regulation behaviors associated with a greater activation of the right hemisphere. In sum, this finding supports the view that during a stressful condition there is a state-dependent activation of the right hemisphere . . . . More generally these findings suggest that the right hemisphere is more involved in the social and biological functions regarding infant caregiver emotional bonding (Schore 2005; Siegel 1999). (Montirosso et al. 2010, p. 108)

Role of Maternal Psychobiological Attunement in Infant Right Brain Development

Confirming this relational neurobiological model, Noriuchi et al. (2008) report interesting results in recent functional magnetic resonance imaging (fMRI) studies of mother–infant emotional communication. They found activation of the mother's right orbitofrontal cortex during moments of maternal love triggered by viewing a video of her own infant. Another NIRS study of infant–mother attachment at 12 months shows right orbitofrontal activation in the mother when viewing a video of her smiling infant. The authors conclude, "our results are in agreement with that of Schore (1999, 2000) who addressed the importance of the right hemisphere in the attachment system" (Minagawa-Kawai et al. 2009, p. 289).

In the course of these right brain-to-right brain transactions, the infant forms an internal working model of his or her attachment relationship with the primary caregiver that is stored in right lateralized nonverbal implicit-procedural memory. These interactive representations encode strategies of affect regulation and contain coping mechanisms for maintaining basic regulation and positive affect in the face of environmental challenge. At the most fundamental level, attachment represents the biological connection between the infant and mother. What is learned in emotionally laden attachment transactions and imprinted into the emotional right brain is stored not in conscious verbal declarative memory, but in nonconscious implicit-procedural memory where biologically wired instincts are interacting with the lived experience embedded in the primary caregiver/infant bodily-based nonverbal relationship. It is this implicit, nonverbal world that the clinician is accessing and assessing.

Therefore, mother's psychobiological attunement to the infant's arousal and psychobiological state occurs in nonverbal communications of eyes, faces, voice prosody (infant-directed speech), and touch, and in body-based transactions in which she intuits what the infant feels and needs in the moment. Attuned sensitivity of caregivers is amply supported by research as being the one factor consistently associated with secure attachment (Ainsworth et al. 1978; De Wolff and van IJzendoorn 1997; van IJzendoorn and De Wolff 1997). Psychobiologically attuned mothering represents a right brain process. If all that parents do to respond to an infant's nonverbal communications were done by the left brain (adult-directed speech), there would be a narrow focus on the details of parenting without the emotional elements; this would be stressful to both caregiver and infant. In a functional magnetic resonance study of maternal communication within the attachment relationship, Lenzi et al. (2009) offer data "supporting the theory that the right hemisphere is more involved than the left hemisphere in emotional processing and thus, mothering" (p. 1131). Yet clinicians often see mothers who are trying to parent exclusively with their left brains, that is, mothers who focus more on the non-relational tasks of infant care rather than the nonverbal communications of the infant.

McGilchrist (2009) describes the differences between the two hemispheric processors: "The world of the left hemisphere, dependent on denotative language and abstraction, yields clarity and power to manipulate things that are known, fixed, static, isolated, decontextualized, explicit, disembodied, general in nature, but ultimately lifeless" (p. 174). In contrast, "the right hemisphere ... yields a world of individual, changing, evolving, interconnected, implicit, incarnate, living beings within the context of the lived world, but in the nature of things never fully graspable, always imperfectly known—and to this world it exists in a relationship of care" (p. 174). This essential human capacity of the right brain optimally evolves in an interpersonal context of a secure attachment bond, a relationship of care.

Current Studies of Attachment and the Experience-Dependent Maturation of the Right Brain

In the aforementioned editorial by Leckman and March (2011), the authors describe "A complex, dynamic story is unfolding of evolutionarily conserved genetic programs that guide mammalian brain development and how our in utero and our early postnatal interpersonal worlds shape and mold the individuals (infants, children, adolescents, adults and caregivers) we are to become" (p. 333). The shaping of brain development by our early interpersonal worlds is an essential focus of the field of interpersonal neurobiology (Schore 2003a). Indeed, over the last two decades our understanding of how brain development is impacted by early experience has been radically transformed.

The brain has a bottom up (caudal to rostral) developmental trajectory with the lower and phylogenetically older brain systems maturing first (Gogtay et al. 2004). During prenatal and postnatal critical periods, the rate of synaptogenesis (the formation of synapses) is estimated at 40,000 new synapses every second (Lagercrantz and Ringstedt 2001). In a structural MRI study of the human brain from birth to two, Knickmeyer et al. (2008) report, "Total brain volume increased 101 % in the first year, with a 15 % increase in the second ... The volume of the subcortical area (including brainstem) increased by 130 % in the first year and by 14 % in the second year" (p. 12178). Thus, the developmental stage of infancy is a critical stage for both cortical and subcortical brain development. We also know that this growth is not just genetically encoded. Rather it is epigenetically influenced and requires human interaction. Both variations in maternal caregiving and caregiver maltreatment are now seen as epigenetic modifications that regulate gene activity in the developing brain (Roth and Sweatt 2011). This means that the quality of the primary attachment experience affects synaptogenesis and brain volume. Clinicians therefore need to be especially able to assess the quality of infant/caregiver relationships and provide interventions when needed.

Schore (1994) proposed that attachment experiences specifically influence the maturation of the early developing right brain Subsequently, Sieratzki and Woll (1996) asserted, "The role of the right hemisphere is crucial in relation to the most precious needs of mothers and infants" (p. 1747). Chiron et al. (1997) also published a study asserting, "The right brain hemisphere is dominant in human infants" (p. 1057). Studies of the unique functions of the right brain subsequently increased (Schore 2001a, 2003a). Braun et al. (2002) assert, "The right and left human brain hemispheres differ in macrostructure, ultra-structure, physiology, chemistry, and control of behavior" (p. 97). Indeed, a number of anatomical and imaging studies now show earlier maturation of the right hemisphere in prenatal and postnatal stages of human development (Gupta et al. 2005; Howard and Reggia 2007; Sun et al. 2005). This research supports the earlier work of Previc (1991), who suggested that the origins of cerebral asymmetry emanate in the intrauterine environment and that the prenatal positioning of the fetus in the womb allows the inward facing left ear to receive a greater amount of vestibular stimulation and thus an earlier organization of the right hemispheric vestibular cortex, a brain system involved in emotion processing (Carmona et al. 2009). For clinicians, this means that early emotional processing appears to begin in utero. Therefore, assessing emotional well-being of the mother-to-be in pregnancy is critical.

There is now an emerging consensus that "the emotional experience(s) of the infant ... are disproportionately stored or processed in the right hemisphere during the formative stages of brain ontogeny." (Semrud-Clikeman and Hynd 1990, p. 198). The experiences the infant has in his or her interactions with the primary caregiver affect the development of the right hemisphere which is the foundation for self-development (Devinsky 2000; Devue et al. 2007; Kaplan et al. 2008). Over the course of the first year, increasingly complex right brain-to-right brain attachment communications first imprint the right posterior cerebral areas involved in sensory processing (e.g., right occipital, right fusiform gyrus, right superior temporal sulcus, right temporoparietal regions) and later right anterior cerebral areas. Classical studies reveal regional differences in the time course of cortical synaptogenesis (Huttenlocher 1990) and that the metabolic activity that underlies regional cerebral function is ontogenetically highest in the posterior sensorimotor cortex and only later rises in anterior cortex (Chugani and Phelps 1986). Indeed, although a period of synaptic excess occurs at 4-months in visual cortex, a similar process does not onset in the prefrontal anterior cortex until the end of the first year of human life (Huttenlocher 1979). Because of these critical periods of brain development that are wiring the somatosensory and visual cortices, particularly in the right hemisphere, clinicians need to assess not only the quality and amount of caregiver/infant eye gazing and nonverbal auditory communication, but also the quality and amount of sensitive interpersonal touch the infant is receiving.

Maternal–infant emotional transactions, however, allow for more than the maturation of cortical connections within the right cerebral hemisphere that are dependent upon caregiver/infant experience. In line with the principle of the sequential caudal to rostral structural development of the brain, bodily based attachment transactions also imprint cortical–subcortical connections of the right brain, which is deeply connected into emotion processing limbic system. Recall Bowlby's (1969) original description of mother–infant attachment communications that are "accompanied by the strongest of feelings and emotions, happy or the reverse" (p. 242). Basic research in developmental neuroscience now demonstrates, "The functional maturation of limbic circuits is significantly influenced by early socio-emotional experience" (Helmeke et al. 2001, p. 717). Using fMRI research, Dapretto et al. (2006) contend, "Typically developing children can rely upon a right hemisphere-mirroring neural mechanism—interfacing with the limbic system via the insula—whereby the meaning of imitated (or observed) emotion is directly felt and hence understood" (p. 30). Attachment studies strongly support Panksepp's (2008) bold assertion of the primacy of affective neuroscience: "Now cognitive science must re-learn that ancient emotional systems have a power that is quite independent of neocortical cognitive processes" (p. 51). In other words, what is learned cognitively and stored in the left hemisphere has little to do with the affective relational, two person experiences stored in the right hemisphere. Clinicians can only assess these patterns through their own implicit right brain connections with their clients, that is, by accessing their own bodily based instinctive responses.

A prime example of an ancient emotional system is the ANS, "the physiological bottom of the mind" (Jackson 1931), and a central component of the human stress response. Studies indicate that maternal care within the attachment relationship shapes the infant's hypothalamic–pituitary–adrenocortical (HPA) stress regulating axis (Gunnar 2000) and that epigenetic programming of maternal behavior alters the development of HPA responses to stress through tissue-specific effects on gene transcription (Weaver et al. 2004). The cortical and subcortical systems of the right brain are known to play a dominant role in regulating the HPA axis and in mediating the human stress response. Indeed, the right hemisphere, more so than the left, is central to the control of vital functions supporting survival and enabling the organism to cope with stresses and challenges (Wittling 1997).

Bodily based attachment communications between the infant and primary caregiver act as an epigenetic mechanism that imprints the circuits of the stress regulating system. Studies now indicate that during early critical periods, prenatal and postnatal interpersonal events wire the connectivity of structures in the developing CNS with the sympathetic and parasympathetic branches of the evolving ANS. According to McGilchrist (2009, p. 437), "The right hemisphere is . . . more closely in touch with emotion and the body (therefore with the neurologically 'inferior' and more ancient regions of the central nervous system)." There is now consensus that the right brain plays a greater role than the left in autonomic arousal and therefore the somatic aspects of emotional states. Porges (2007) concludes, "Consistent with the views that the right hemisphere appears to play a greater role in affect, especially the adaptive expression of negative affect, the right hemisphere also appears to have a greater role in regulation of cardiac function presumably via shifts in (parasympathetic) vagal regulation" (p. 126).

Regulation theory asserts that the attuned caregiver's dampening of negative affect arousal, as well as enhancing positive affective arousal, entrains a balance between the energy-expending sympathetic and energy-conserving parasympathetic branches of the infant's ANS, thus creating optimal arousal ranges associated with focused attention, homeostatic visceral–somatic processing and secure attachment. Slade (2005) articulates the importance of the infant's developing the capacity of "experiencing the links between, affect, behavior, the body, and self-experience" (p. 271). We suggest that "the body" specifically refers to the functions of the ANS, the system of peripheral neurons that controls in an involuntary fashion, visceral organs, the cardiovascular system, and effectors in the skin. In classical writings, Basch (1976) speculated that "the language of mother and infant consists of signals produced by the autonomic, involuntary nervous system in both parties" (p. 766). These infant and mother bodily based affective autonomic signals need to be incorporated into clinical treatment models so that therapists can evaluate the strength and the quality of the synchrony between the caregiver/infant affective signals.

The ANS harnesses and regulates the energy in the body needed for life processes (Recordati 2003). The sympathetic nervous system (SNS) is triggered when more energy is needed in the body, and the parasympathetic nervous system (PNS) is triggered for balancing energy or energy renewal. The Polyvagal theory proposed by Porges (1995, 2001, 2009) suggests that the vagus nerve, a cranial nerve that connects the face, heart, and viscera and controls facial expression, vocalization, and listening is the newest phylogenetic circuit that evolved for social communication. The social engagement system (called the ventral vagal system) is myelinated, enabling it to respond quickly, but it can only be used when a person is feeling safe within their optimal arousal range. If a person senses a threat, even unconsciously, the SNS mobilization system then prepares the body for flight or fight by increasing energy. Should the danger be a life threat with no possibility of escape, a phylogenetically older unmyelinated vagus system (called the dorsal vagal system) controlled by the PNS can take control and put the body into a freeze or feigning death state by shutting down the brain. In animals, this feigning death state appears to function as a possible survival mechanism as some predators become disinterested in an animal that appears dead (Levine 1997). Schore (2009) equates this immobilized dorsal vagal state with dissociation, described as detachment from an unbearable situation (Mollon 1996), the escape when there is no escape (Putnam 1997) and a last resort defensive strategy (Dixon 1998).

As the SNS response is associated with increased arousal or hyperarousal with increased respiration and heart rate whereas the PNS is associated with decreased arousal or hypoarousal with a decrease in respiration and heart rate, the quality of the co-regulation experience lived in the early attachment relationship entrains set-points within the developing ANS. Optimal arousal ranges are created when good-enough sensitive parenting occurs so that an infant and young child does not spend large amounts of time in hyperaroused or hypoaroused states. Specifically, caregivers try to soothe crying infants so that they are not in long hyperaroused states and play with their infants so they are not in long hypoaroused states. These caregiver responses are associated with creating optimal arousal ranges in the ANS.

On the other hand, chronic hyperarousal can be imprinted into infants who use their inborn attachment signaling for their primary caregiver by crying, but whose caregivers respond sometimes, but the infant never knows when. This dynamic could contribute to the infant's brain being organized more toward the SNS side of arousal because the infant has developed a nonconscious survival strategy that hyperactivates the biological attachment system. Conversely, some infants learn not to use their inborn attachment signals to cry when needing their primary caregiver because crying has been chronically responded to harshly or not at all or the caregiver is too frightening. Such infants may develop a nonconscious survival strategy that deactivates the attachment system with an ANS organized more toward the PNS side of arousal. Infants and young children coping with frightening behavior in their caregivers possess subcortical circuits that fire repeatedly to protect the child from danger. Since infants can't remove themselves from danger, dissociation and the auto-regulation of the PNS is often the outcome. Sadly, an unseen and unheard baby may have a better chance of surviving in family systems where trauma and violence are the norm. The biological attachment instinct that emits stressful regulatory signals of active protest by crying can thus be facilitated or inhibited by the primary caregiver. This essential instinct can be reshaped and altered by the demands of the lived environment.

Furthermore, during early critical periods these transactions shape the cortical–subcortical stress regulating circuits of the developing right brain. Indeed, basic research now establishes that optimal stress regulation is dependent on "right hemispheric specialization in regulating stress—and emotion-related processes" (Sullivan and Dufresne 2006, p. 55). Schore (2001a) proposes that critical periods for the development and connectivity of the regulatory centers in the right hemisphere occur within the attachment relationship during infancy. Specifically, the amygdala and insula, subcortical structures capable of harnessing the ANS in the service of survival, function at birth. At 3 to 9 months of age, the anterior cingulate (medial frontal cortex), a cortical-limbic structure that is associated with responsivity to social cues, comes online, giving the infant greater regulatory capacity when there is good-enough caregiver co-regulation. From 10 to 12 months of age, the regulatory center in the orbitofrontal cortex begins its developmental growth period. This ventromedial prefrontal cortex, especially in the right hemisphere, is the executive control center for emotion. With optimal attachment experiences, the vertical axis that connects the orbitofrontal cortex with its interconnected subcortical areas gets well developed, allowing the right orbitofrontal cortex to regulate the amygdala (see Barbas 2007, and Schore 2001a, 2012 for a more in-depth discussion). Indeed, for the rest of the life span the right, and not left, lateralized prefrontal regions are responsible for the regulation of affect and stress (Cerqueira et al. 2008; Schore 1994; Sullivan and Gratton 2002; Wang et al. 2005). These data clearly indicate that the right orbitofrontal cortex is considered the highest regulatory center in the brain and its connectivity is associated with the emotional regulation that is commonly found in secure children.

We suggest that the in utero and postnatal dyadic relations between the child and caregiver have enduring effects on brain development. We further propose that these effects are elucidated by a deeper understanding of the interpersonal neurobiological mechanisms by which the early attachment relationship acts as the germinal matrix of right brain development. The best current description of the path of neurodevelopment is that it is "malleable" (Leckman and March 2011, p. 333). The attachment relationship shapes, for better or worse, the child's capacity for resilience or a predisposition for psychopathology.

Application of Regulation Theory to Clinical Assessment

The maternal attuned nonverbal communications needed to optimally facilitate the early development of the infant's right hemisphere require that the caregiver is able to implicitly and intuitively use her own right hemisphere and her own instincts in the service of co-creating the attachment bond. This principle of right brain dominance is true for clinicians as well. Therapists using regulation theory in work with young children and their families use their own carefully honed clinical instincts. Specifically, they use their own right brains to intuitively read and assess the nonverbal communications of the body-world of an infant/caregiver dyad (Newton 2008b; see Schore and Schore 2008 and Schore 2011 for discussions of the neurobiology of clinical intuition). This often private right hemisphere world is inextricably tied to the true nature of the primary attachment relationship. But it can be missed if therapists observe only the infant's overt behaviors and only interact verbally with the caregiver (see Newton 2008a). Shai and Belsky (2011) assert:

> Whereas verbal manifestations of the parent's representation of the child may be meaningful, and thereby developmentally significant for the older child, it is unlikely that the preverbal infant could directly experience such mentalizing in a semantically meaningful way. Moreover, verbal parental mentalizing cannot illuminate the process by which parents' mental capacities actually affect the infant ... (p. 2)

Since clinicians' own use of their right brains is so critical in assessing and treating young children and their families, the second author will often playfully insist that interns "Train your left hemisphere to sit on command," meaning focus on your initial spontaneous instinctive bodily based responses.

As a part of her initial evaluation of a dyadic infant/caregiver relationship, the second author begins all assessments with a 5 min structured and 5 min unstructured play experience between caregiver and child. For infants under 12-months of age, only the play experience is used. With consent, these sessions are videotaped to be used in intervention if needed. Clinicians watching the play session are accessing their own right hemispheres and using their instincts to see, feel, and evaluate the quality and intensity of the caregiver's attunement, misattunement, and repair of the infant's regulated and dysregulated affective communications as there are no verbal interactions between the caregiver and clinician at this point in the observation.

In this approach, the assessment technique is not as important as the assessment process. The interdisciplinary lens of regulation theory illuminates how one's subjectivity and implicit corporeal self is used in assessment and treatment at all stages of the lifespan, including infancy. The following vignette is offered to demonstrate the approach of regulation theory.

Clinical Assessment of an Infant–Mother Dyad

Jonathan was a cute 7-month-old infant who was accompanied by his mother to an initial evaluation through a specialized birth to 5 training program at St. Vincent de Paul Village, a large homeless rehabilitation center in downtown San Diego. Jonathan's mother had been homeless since he was 4 months old, having left Jonathan's father due to domestic violence. Jonathan and his mother were referred by the onsite childcare program staff who were concerned about his lack of facial expression and vocalizations. He also appeared withdrawn. The observer in the program noted "at times, he seems to be staring off into space, and he doesn't seem to respond much when his mother picks him up." The evaluation began with a 5 min play session with the clinician, while training interns observed from behind a one-way mirror. As per protocol for the Parent–Child Early Relational Assessment (Clark 1985), his mother was asked to play with Jonathan like she usually does. Jonathan sat on a blanket covering mats on the floor with his mother. On the blanket were a number of infant banging toys including rattles, blocks, and an infant mirror.

His mother first picked up the infant rain stick rattle and began upending it to make sound. She shook the rattle close to his face, and Jonathan turned his head away. She then picked up another rattle asking, "What's this? What's this?" Jonathan reached for the rattle at the top when mother said, "No, hold it like this" and clasped his hand around the handle. Mother then picked up two rattles together and shook them close to Jonathan's face. Jonathan responded by turning his head and body toward the door. She quickly dropped one rattle for another, shaking the rattles intensely and close to his face. From behind the one-way mirror, the second author was beginning to feel tense as mother showed no signs of being aware that her son was overstimulated even when he was clearly doing his best to signal to his mother that he was overaroused by turning his head and then his body away from his mother.

Jonathan then reached for the rain stick and began to explore it when his mother grabbed the other end and began pulling it away from him. Jonathan looked away, then down. His mother began pulling it out of his hand saying in a rising shrill tone, "Gimme, gimme, gimme. Mine, mine, mine." His mother then moved toward him, dangling her hair in his face laughing louder saying, "I'm going to get you." She then added a growl to her voice and began to laugh in a rhythmic decrescendo. Jonathan's body stilled and he began to collapse his body away from his mother. In response, his mother used all the rattles, shaking them around Jonathan's face saying, "Hey, right over here." It appeared she was trying to recapture his attention. He made no sounds. He did not smile and his eyes were fixed. His body alternated between still and jerky.

Jonathan tried to look at his mother when she showed him the infant mirror. He appeared to have a beginning smile for her and began patting the mirror, however, his mother then took it from him and asked if he wanted to crawl. At this point, his mother changed Jonathan to a crawl position.

After this initial observation, the testing team engaged with the infant while mother was interviewed at a distance but within sight of the infant. During the testing which used the Bayley Scales of Infant Development II (BSID-II: Bayley 1993), Jonathan sat on the blanket and interacted with the toys given by the intern examiner who also sat on the floor at a distance of about 3 ft. Jonathan studied the ring and easily transferred it between hands and shook the bell multiple times while cooing and babbling. He smiled a number of times at the examiner. He did not look at his mother during the half hour testing even though she was sitting approximately 4 ft away to his right; he appeared to stiffen when she picked him up at the end of testing. Jonathan's BSID-II cognitive and motor scores were in typical ranges for his age. The Behavioral Rating Scale showed delays, which supported our clinical observations that the socio-emotional developmental domain was delayed. Given that Jonathan showed more typical relational interaction with the intern than his mother, we now had both observational and testing data that supported an optimistic beginning of an intervention with the attachment relationship.

Assessment of Parental Nonverbal Communication and Infant Dissociation

In the assessment of the dyad, our treatment team perceived that Jonathan's mother was attempting to play with him, yet she could not read his face, his lack of vocalization and eye contact, and his striking head and whole body gestural turns away from his mother to reduce the increasing stimulation. Nor did she understand his body collapse was a last ditch effort to reduce stimulation. Jonathan had little facial expression during this 5 min play interaction that indicated he was enjoying the play. His exploration with his mother was lifeless, halting, slow moving, jerky, and peppered with many gaze and body aversions. At 7 months, a baby's right brain should be reading his caregiver's face, eyes, voice prosody, gesture, and touch.

Earlier we cited research showing infants at this age express right temporal activation when looking at an angry face (Nakato et al. 2011). Jonathan's mother's face was contorted much of the time and her voice showed a deficit in infant-directed speech. In fact her prosody (rising shrill tone) was clearly scary especially when she began growling and laughing loudly in a repetitive pattern that sounded frighteningly eerie. Her tactile–gestural expressions lacked "touch synchrony" and instead was combative and competitive as she tried to pull items away from him and change his posture when no signal was given to do this. His mother's behavior was intense and Jonathan showed signs of being over-stimulated and hyper-aroused, yet he did not cry or complain. Instead he tried to modulate the over stimulation by looking down, turning his body away and withdrawing, fixating his eyes in a dissociative stare, and eventually collapsing his body away from his mother.

Because there was no caregiver interactive regulation of Jonathan's nervous system that moved into critically high and aversive SNS hyperarousal, Jonathan's own body began auto-regulating the hyperarousal through dissociation and eventual shut-down. This shut-down is a function of the parasympathetic nervous system when there is life threatening fear with no escape. Not only was his mother intrusively amplifying his state of accelerating hyperarousal, she appeared not to sense that there was any need for repair. Research shows that when mothers are stressed, such stress interferes with their parenting of infants (Suter et al. 2007). Mothers in states of ultra-high or ultra-low states of dysregulated arousal become less sensitive as caregivers, more autocratic, and less able to pick up subtle infant emotional communications. If caregivers become so overwhelmed that they cannot regulate their own stress state, they cannot act as a regulator of their babies' states. Thus, the first treatment goal was for Jonathan's mother to become aware of his thresholds for arousal dysregu-lation and behavioral disorganization. A further therapeutic goal was to reduce her own arousal in order to expand her ability to read her son's nonverbal communi-cations. The therapeutic focus on the infant included attention to his dysregulated hyperarousal that resulted in dissociative hypoarousal as the only available strategy of affect regulation.

According to Schore (2002), pathological dissociation is manifested in a mal-adaptive highly defensive rigid, closed self system, one that responds to even low levels of intersubjective stress with parasympathetic dorsal vagal parasympathetic hypoarousal, heart rate deceleration, and passive disengagement. This fragile un-conscious system is susceptible to relational stress-induced mind/body metabolic collapse and thereby a loss of energy-dependent synaptic connectivity within the right brain, expressed in a sudden implosion of the implicit self and a rupture of self-continuity. As the right hemisphere mediates the communication and regulation of emotional states, a chronic rupture of intersubjectivity in the mother/infant rela-tionship is accompanied by an instant dissipation of safety and trust in the dyad and a sense of fear and danger in the infant.

Jonathan's dissociative stares, lack of eye contact and vocalization, relational withdrawal, slow gestural movements, and body collapse all point to Jonathan's body moving into the dorsal vagal function of the PNS. Clinicians trained to understand the role of this autonomic survival strategy and to recognize how infants appear in this state of frozen fear recognize this immobilization as his ANS responding to a life threatening situation that must be addressed. Indeed, very recent research from neuroscience and child psychiatry now shows that under severe interpersonal stress or relational trauma, an infant does not cry, but will disengage and shut down. If it becomes chronic, this relational withdrawal is the most pathological of all infant responses to stress. In this involuntary disengagement from the social environment, the infant is still and silent.

These observations of a mother and her 7-month infant are very similar to the characterization of intrusive mothers and their 4–6-month-old infants by Atzil et al.

(2011). Using fMRI they document that these mothers show significant right amygdala activation associated with fear and anxiety while watching videos of their own infants interacting with them. The authors interpret this neural activation pattern as underlying "insufficient behavioral inhibition, which may lead to excessive, non-modulated maternal behavior typical of the intrusive style" and "behaviors . . . marked by overstimulation, excessive parenting, and miscoordination" (p. 10).

Note the similarities also to Shai and Belsky's (2011) videotape of a 6-month-old and a psychobiologically misattuned mother who cannot read her infant's kinesthetic responses to her dysregulating interventions. They document that when the mother moves into the infant's personal space, the infant shrinks his body so that his shoulders, arms, and legs come close to the body center in an enclosing movement, thereby withdrawing from the mother's stimulation. During withdrawal, the infant's muscles tense. When the mother moves away from him he twists his torso away from her. As this continues she presses his arms to the floor, restricting his efforts to move away. Subsequently the infant brings his arms towards his belly, attempting to block the stimulus. The authors note these defensive movements signal the infant's desperation and distress. Ultimately, the infant's body stiffens and is turned away from the mother, yet despite these signals the mother continues her stimulation.

A deeper understanding of Jonathan's responses to his emotionally dysregulating caregiver (dissociative stilling and body collapse while interacting with her and body stiffening upon reunion) is also informed by Beebe and colleagues' (2010) studies of mothers of 4-month-old infants who later show disorganized attachment. They observe that the mothers of these infants are overwhelmed with their own unresolved abuse or trauma and therefore cannot bear to intersubjectively engage with their infants' distress. Because these mothers are unable to regulate their own distress, they cannot regulate their infant's distress. These mothers are unable to allow themselves to be emotionally affected by their infant's dysregulated state, thus they shut down emotionally closing their faces, looking away from the infant's face and failing to coordinate with the infant's emotional state. Beebe interprets this fearful maternal behavior as a defensive dissociation, a strategy that protects the mother from the facial and visual intimacy that would come from joining the infant's distressed moments. This type of mother thus shows disrupted and contradictory forms of affective communication (intrusiveness and disengagement), especially around the infant's need for comfort when distressed (Beebe et al. 2010).

Schore (2001b) describes the intergenerational transmission of not just the intense emotional distress of relational trauma, but of the defensive response of pathological dissociation. Over the ongoing period of relational trauma in this case the mother's disengagement and detachment from an unbearable situation has been matched by the infant's disengagement, detachment, and withdrawal. Milne et al. (2009) describe the long-term negative developmental impact of social withdrawal and depression in 6-month-old infants. They conclude, "A withdrawal response in infancy is problematic behavior . . . not because it leads to later withdrawal per se, but because of the compounding effects on development of not being present in the interpersonal space—the space upon which much of infant development depends" (p. 165).

Guedeney et al. (2008) report a study of relational withdrawal in infants aged 14–18 months. This withdrawal reaction reflects inadequate parent–infant interactions and is a feature of disorganized attachment. Guedeney et al. (2008) note, "Sustained withdrawal behavior may be viewed as a chronic diminution of the attachment system, which is gradually generalized into a diminished engagement and lowered reactivity to the environment as a whole" (p. 151). They conclude, "Withdrawn social behavior from as early as 2 months of age, indicated by a lack of either positive (e.g., smiling, eye contact) or negative (e.g., vocal protestations) behavior, is more akin to a state of learned helplessness and should alert the clinician to the possibility that the infant is not displaying age-appropriate emotional/social behavior" (p. 151).

Notably, the childcare program referred Jonathan for evaluation because he had minimal facial expression, minimal vocalizations, and appeared withdrawn. Since his evaluation in a more optimal relational context showed normative cognitive and motor development, his lack of reactivity on the childcare site provided some support for a likely history of diminished caregiver attention to his attachment needs. Thus, the second treatment goal was for the mother to recognize her infant's dissociative withdrawal as a cue to not increase but decrease her stimulation and provide more physical and psychological space between them when they played.

Caregiver Support for Exploration

The attuned caregiver not only down regulates stressful negatively charged arousal, she also up regulates positive arousal necessary for exploration. The developmental concern for Jonathan was not only his mother's overstimulating-to-frightening behavior but also her clasping his hand around the rattle and misinterpreting Jonathan's collapsing behavior as an infant-generated desire to crawl. Responding to an infant's exploratory behavior with chronic misidentification of infant intent and feelings can lead to the infant's creation of a false self based more on the expectations and definitions from parents than the infant's own true bodily based self expressions (Newton 2006).

Winnicott (1960/1965) speculated the deadness of the false self was a defensive structure developed within the early infant relationship with the caregiver. He stated, "The mother who is not good enough ... substitutes her own gesture which is to be given sense by the compliance of the infant. This compliance on the part of the infant is the earliest stage of the False Self, and belongs to the mother's inability to sense her infant's needs" (p. 145). Most clinicians treating adults will often recognize the profound differences between a client's conceptual or false self versus their true self. Sadly, a false self can develop when a child has experienced little to no accurate labeling of their intrinsic psychobiological nature, visceral feeling, and relational intent.

A typically developing 7-month-old is generally quite content to explore by reaching, holding, transferring objects from hand to hand, looking, studying, and experiencing what can be created from the object when feeling secure-enough in the environment. For Jonathan, his mother was doing the experiencing for him, by showing him the toys without letting him take the initiative to explore them himself. However, when he was tested with the intern examiner who did not encroach on his space, Jonathan's exploration was more typical for his age. He was delighted with the discovery that he could make the bell ring, and he cooed and wiggled a number of times as he did so. The intern examiner was equally delighted in Jonathan's exploration and vocalizations giving Jonathan a matched, attuned, and affectively resonant dyadic interaction.

Jonathan's play with his mother was in stark contrast with his more robust exploration that included vocalizations with an attuned intern. When his mother saw Jonathan play with the intern, she appeared hurt by what she saw and this clinician felt a great sadness and empathy for her when she said, "He doesn't play like that with me." Our observations, that Jonathan could form a relational bond with a non-intrusive adult and that his mother could subjectively experience the differences between his play with her and feel saddened by this, were positive prognostic signs for a therapeutic intervention. It was easy for the team to see that the intervention that would likely make the most change in the dyad was helping mother give her son more space when he plays and helping her to learn to understand and respond to his right brain nonverbal signals.

In all developmental assessments after the family leaves, the second author asks the team, "How do you feel now?" and "How does it feel to be with this dyad?" This is because training using regulation theory focuses on the clinician's own intersubjective body-based somatic markers and affective responses (Newton 2008b; Schore 2009, 2011). The subsequent discussion integrated subjective observations and feelings with other objective assessments. Out of this dialogue, the team created an intervention plan. Some of the words the interns used to describe their feelings were "shell-shocked," "dazed," and "angry." The words they used to describe the infant's subjective states were "exhausted," "scared," "confused," and "sad." For training interns, it is often easier to focus on the infant's distress without seeing the mother's responses as likely reflecting her own attachment experiences. When expanding the focus into mother's past and current trauma however, there was a noticeable and appropriate shift toward a more empathetic appreciation of the mother's stressful state. The third treatment goal was to help mother engage in nonintrusive play by following Jonathan's lead and amplifying his states of regulated positive arousal.

Impressions of the Attachment Relationship

The attachment impressions observed in Jonathan's play interaction with his mother was that of childhood disorganization. When his mother could not read his gaze aversions, lack of eye contact, vocalization, and whole body turns away from her, Jonathan used a dissociative defense to cope with intense arousal followed by a body collapse when he could no longer continue the engagement. Because his mother was looming over Jonathan while shaking rattles close to his face and using voices that included growling, there was ample observational evidence to support this impression.

According to Main and Solomon (1990), disorganized attachment behavior in infants is often seen as odd, anomalous, contradictory, and/or disoriented behavior, often lasting for only a few seconds, that appears to "lack a readily observable goal, intention, or explanation" (p. 122). Hesse and Main (2000, p. 1097) describe disorganized behavior as a "collapse in behavioral and attentional strategies." Disorganized attachment behaviors are thought to represent the untenable position of a stressed infant seeking his caregiver for protection and soothing with his attachment system fully activated while at the same time being fearful of the same caregiver, a condition that Hesse and Main (2006) term "fright without solution" (p. 311). Importantly, Hesse and Main (1999) note that disorganization and disorientation is phenotypically similar to dissociative states.

Our observations of Jonathan and his mother call to mind another aspect of Beebe's important research in this area. In a comprehensive study of 84 four-month-old infant–mother dyads whose communications and interactions were videotaped and rated, Beebe et al. (2010) found that mother–infant communications at 4 months predicted both insecure-resistant (C) and disorganized (D) attachment at 12 months of age. Specifically what predicted disorganized attachment was *"not being sensed and known* by the mother (p. 7) . . . and *confusion in sensing and knowing himself"* (p. 119, italics in the original). Furthermore, all communication modalities were affected, such as "attention, touch . . . spatial orientation as well as facial and vocal affect, and facial–visual engagement" (p. 119). These authors conclude that "Aspects of the phenomena of 12-month C and D attachment are thus *already in place at 4 months"* (p. 119, italics in the original).

Disorganized attachment is a serious childhood indicator for immediate parent–child intervention. This attachment pattern is highly associated with unresolved loss and trauma in adults and frightening, threatening, and dissociative behavior in parents (Hesse and Main 2000, 2006; Main and Hesse 1990). Jonathan's mother had come from a violent relationship with Jonathan's father and also indicated that she experienced attachment trauma in her own childhood. It is well known that the intergenerational transmission of attachment trauma is high, thus increasing the risk if no intervention is offered (Benoit and Parker 1994; Lieberman et al. 2011).

The previously cited fMRI study by Atzil et al. (2011) also documented that mothers who are in synchrony with their 4–6 month old infants have brain responses that show a "clearer organization" across time periods whereas intrusive mothers had brain responses that show "greater cross-time disorganization" (p. 1). A clinician trained in regulation theory knows quite well the development trajectory for Jonathan if no immediate assistance is given to him and his mother. Jonathan is in high-risk: his mother has a history of unresolved childhood trauma, was in a violent relationship and then became homeless when he was 4 months old, and at 7 months, he showed many signs of childhood disorganization. This may have been overlooked by a therapist focused mainly on mother's verbal narrative of her attachment experiences and history. Jonathan himself tells the true story that "this is the way it is with mother" through his nonverbal communications. Fortunately, we heard his message. The fourth treatment goal then was to have mother in individual psychotherapy for trauma resolution as well in Healthy Relationships, a psychoeducational group focused on developing healthy relationships.

Knowledge of Developmental Stages and Brain Development

Knowing the developmental stages and their correspondence with brain development, helps the clinician evaluate the impact of relational trauma behavior on the maturing brain (Schore 2010a, b). For example, in the case of Jonathan, the second author wondered how often and how intensely his amygdala, the major fear center in the brain, was firing to protect him from his mother's intense interactions and from the violence he possibly experienced between his parents. Since these traumatic experiences occurred in a critical period of brain development, these dysregulating events could, and if chronic would, be training the amygdala toward chronic survival reactions, such as characterological dissociation. The arousal dysregulation could also reduce the set point of the HPA and interfere with the ability of the right brain to process stress and nonverbal affect communications.

These events could also negatively impact development of the right insula (thereby causing a deficit in empathy), the right anterior cingulate (causing a deficit in affiliative behaviors), and, if the attachment pattern is unchanged, the later maturing right orbitofrontal cortex (resulting in deficits in affect and stress regulation). There is evidence that children raised in severely depriving situations have brains with smaller overall gray and white matter volumes, yet larger amygdala volumes especially in the right hemisphere (Mehta et al. 2009; Schore 2001b). There are also now a number of imaging studies that show amygdala—orbitofrontal disconnections (New et al. 2007), hyper amygdala reactivity (Donegan et al. 2003), and abnormal brain asymmetries in teens and adults diagnosed with borderline personality disorder (Chanen et al. 2008; Irle et al. 2005). Perhaps most strikingly, a very recent study reports that a phenotype of early infancy identified at 4 months predicts individual differences in reactivity of the right amygdala to faces almost two decades later in adults (Schwartz et al. 2011). This rapidly growing body of research emphasizes the important need for clinical assessment and early intervention for chronically misattuned caregiver–infant communications that are found in contexts of relational attachment trauma.

A 7-month-old baby is typically curious about his environment, interested in the sounds he can make through banging, studying toys, reaching and exploring with hands and sometimes mouth, looking down at the floor when something falls off a table, and babbling. Most 6–7 month olds are good-natured. Their range of emotions tends to be positive, displaying frequent smiling and laughter. But they can also feel angry and frustrated if things do not go as expected (Newton 2008a). Within this same 7-month period, the regulatory centers in the anterior cingulate are maturing. When optimally functioning, this medial frontal limbic structure, which has direct bidirectional connections with the amygdala, regulates autonomic and endocrine functions. It is also involved in conditioned emotional learning, vocalizations associated with expressing internal states, assessments of motivational content, and assigning emotional valence to internal and external stimuli, and human maternal behavior (Devinsky et al. 1995; Lorberbaum et al. 2002; Schore 2001a). If the relationship itself triggers fear responses more than positive interactions, the anterior cingulate may not acquire the robustness needed to down-regulate the amygdala. A weakened connection in the anterior cingulate could also mean a weak connection to the orbitofrontal cortex, the highest emotional regulation center in the brain. This weakness would mean that without a functional change in his mother's regulatory capacity, Jonathan's future development toward emotional regulation would be comprised.

Although Jonathan's communication and exploration improved when interacting with an affectively attuned intern, Jonathan's mother appeared to have no understanding that her son needed her interactive regulation and resonant attunement to support his brain growth and social–emotional development. The fifth treatment goal then was to give his mother some basic information about the critical role of attunement, affect-arousal regulation, security, exploration, and play in brain development.

Interventions Informed by Regulation Theory

Observations based upon the clinical integration of attachment, regulation, and developmental neuroscientific theories set up interventions that target all aspects of the dyadic system at different levels of mind/brain/body in both mother and infant. Jonathan's disorganized attachment is a known risk factor for later forming psychopathologies (Sroufe et al. 2005), as well as future deficits in right brain social–emotional processing (Schore 2001b, 2003b). His use of relational withdrawal and dissociative defenses indicated that his emotional and social development was seriously at risk. Thus, immediate intervention targeted at helping his mother change as indicated in the five treatment goals, was needed.

The use of regulation theory to guide both the observations and theoretical orientation of the assessment specifically informs the clinician regarding risk level. Jonathan's development was at risk for a vulnerability to later psychopathologies. Thus, an approach to helping his mother and the dyad, change their dysregulating affective dynamics was needed immediately. This intervention was timely, not only because of the ongoing relational traumatic context of the insecure attachment bond, but because it was occurring in a period of maximal plasticity, the human brain growth spurt.

Although this paper is focused on assessment, we offer a general broad overview of the mother–infant therapeutic interventions that followed. In any intervention with mothers and infants, a primary mechanism is co-constructing an empathic intersubjective connection with the mother. In light of this mother's trauma history, this involved some clinical skill. The developing therapeutic alliance allows the clinician to act as a psychobiological regulator of the mother's dysregulating affective arousal underlying the stressful affects she is experiencing and defending against in the insecure attachment relationship (e.g., fear, aggression, and shame). This right amygdala-driven state of hyperarousal interferes with her receiving and resonating with the nonverbal right brain signals Jonathan is communicating. Once this arousal can be interactively regulated within the clinician–caregiver relationship, the mother's right orbitofrontal and medial frontal areas become more able to resonate with the infant's distress, form a two-way psychobiological feedback loop with him, and create a more efficient system of rupture and repair. By increasing the mother's regulatory capacities, the therapist can help the mother become a more effective interactive regulator of her infant's negative affects.

According to the protocol of the second author, the interventions in this case included review of videos taken during the initial evaluation and other dyadic therapy sessions (Newton 2008b). Neuroimaging research demonstrates that videos of both positively and negatively valenced social interactions directly activate right hemispheric circuits (Semrud-Klikeman et al. 2011). Thus video review is a particularly helpful support for dyadic therapy as caregivers are less stressed and generally in their more optimal range of arousal themselves when not interacting with their child (Clark 1985; Newton 2008b). Using video feedback as a part of treatment also has been found to be an effective treatment for mothers with insecure attachment (Bakermans-Kranenburg et al. 1998). For parents with unresolved relational trauma, it is often easier to wonder about what can be seen in a tape when the sound is off. This is because ANS arousal associated with trauma can be easily triggered by sound.

Over the course of the relational intervention, Jonathan's mother learned how to implicitly match his vocalizations with expressive and warmer voice prosody, facial expression, and interpersonal touch. As she began to work through her complex feelings about Jonathan's father in individual therapy, she improved in her ability to play with her son using appropriate voicing and following his lead. This therapy would have continued but Jonathan and his mother left the village, transitioning from homelessness to living with her sister, a very positive change for both.

Prevention: Enhancing the Future Developmental Trajectory of the Right Brain

A number of disciplines stress the importance of early intervention: infant mental health, child psychology and psychiatry, developmental psychoanalysis, pediatrics, clinical social work, and developmental neuroscience. Authors in this latter field assert,

> The large increase in total brain volume in the first year of life suggests that this is a critical period in which disruption of developmental processes, as the result of innate genetic abnormalities or as a consequence of environmental insults, may have long-lasting or permanent effects on brain structure and function ... Although the first year of life may be a period of developmental vulnerability, it may also be a period in which therapeutic interventions would have the greatest positive affect. (Knickmeyer et al. 2008, p. 12179–80)

Regulation theory indicates that early interventions which attempt to optimize infant brain development need to utilize assessments of caregiver–infant right brain-to-right brain communication and regulation systems. Thus, clinical training needs to include a neuropsychoanalytic knowledge base of brain development as it unfolds within the developmental stages as well as a relational psychoanalytic focus on the clinician's use of their own instincts, that is, their own right brain. What aspects of the attachment communications and how the clinician uses her own subjectivity to evaluate the intersubjective strengths and deficits are critical to an informative assessment. Schore (in press) proposes that, in the first year of life, evolving right lateralized visual–facial, auditory–prosodic, and tactile-gestural functions of the human social brain can be assessed over the pre- and postnatal stages of infancy to appraise the ongoing status of emotional and social development. Indeed, current developmental neuroscience concludes that the strong and consistent predominance for the right hemisphere emerges postnatally (Allman et al. 2005) and so this increasing right lateralization trend should be evaluated in infants.

More specifically, in reference to evolving visual–facial functions, Mento et al. (2010) assert, "the right hemisphere would sustain the functions necessary for the survival of the species, such as visuospatial or emotional processes. Consequently the earlier and faster development of the neural substrates underlying these functions is needed to prevent possible impairment during infancy and childhood" (p. 7). In regard to auditory–prosodic processing, Grossmann et al. (2010) argue that in postnatal periods, "responses to voices and emotional prosody ... might thus serve as one of potentially multiple markers that can help with an early identification of infants at risk for neurodevelopmental disorders" (p. 856). And in terms of tactile–gestural functions, Montirosso et al. (2010) propose that studies that simultaneously measure gesture and brain functions "would also be useful with samples of high risk-infants whose behavior and brain organization may be compromised" (p. 109). On the matter of high-risk infants, Schore (2010a) concludes,

> Recent models of early life trauma are altering their focus from deficits in later matur-ing conscious, verbal, explicit and voluntary behavior, to impairments of early maturing nonconscious, nonverbal, implicit and automatic adaptive social emotional functions ... Developmental neuroscience is now moving from studies of later maturing left brain con-scious verbal cognitive processes into the early preverbal development of adaptive emotion processing right brain systems in pre- and postnatal periods. (p. 144)

Regulation theory asserts that therapeutic interventions that take place within criti-cal periods can positively impact the experience-dependent maturation of developing brain systems (Schore 1994, 2001b, 2011). Indeed, an early therapeutic interven-tion aimed towards increasing maternal sensitivity with a different high risk group (preterm infants) documents enhanced maturation and connectivity of white mat-ter and improved cerebral micro-structural development (Milgrom et al. 2010). The therapeutic goals of that study is also focused on increasing maternal sensitivity and regulation and were very similar to our model: training the parent to recognize signs of infant stress, shut-down mechanisms, alert-available behavior quality of motor behaviors, facial expressions, posture/muscle/tone; how to optimize interactions and avoid overwhelming infants; touch, vocal, visual and multisensory stimulation, and normalizing parental feelings.

At the beginning of this chapter, we suggested that the transformation of classical attachment theory into modern attachment theory alters our clinical approaches to the assessment and treatment of developmental disturbances in early childhood. Shai and Belsky (2011) argue that "Parental reflective functioning (Slade 2005) concerns the parent's capacity to think reflectively about, and articulate verbally, the child and his mental states as motivators of behavior" (p. 2). They suggest that exclusive reliance on verbal processes does not capture the embodied relational perspective for investigating parent–infant interaction. Modern attachment theory focuses on the nonverbal communication of affective states and the relational regulation of the infant's developing brain/mind/body. Clinical assessments and interventions grounded in regulation theory are centered in the clinician's own bodily based affective responses and instincts, that is, in their own right brain nonverbal functions.

A fundamental theme of this chapter is that nonverbal psychobiological attachment communications are located in the right brain. Regulation theory attempts a deeper understanding of critical intersubjective forces that operate at implicit levels of all emotional relationships, beneath the exchanges of language and explicit cognitions. This theoretical perspective attempts to elucidate the interpersonal neurobiological mechanisms that underlie changes in "implicit relational knowing" (Boston Change Process Study Group 2007, p. 845) which is encoded in the right brain (Schore 2003a). Infant researchers now assert, "Preverbal communication ... is the realm of non-consciously regulated intuitive behavior and implicit relational knowledge. Whether information is transferred or shared, which information gets across, and on which level it is 'understood,' *does not necessarily depend on the sender's intention or conscious awareness*" (Papousek 2007, p. 258, emphasis added). Recall, the adult orbitofrontal cortex rapidly and thereby implicitly responds to the image of an infant's face in 130 ms, beneath levels of conscious awareness (Kringelbach et al. 2008).

We suggest that attachment interventions that attempt to expand the mother's mentalization functions and conscious awareness of intentions are too focused on the caregiver's left brain. Indeed, neuroimaging research indicates that reflective mentalization is associated with activation of the left inferior frontal gyrus, left posterior superior temporal sulcus, and left temporoparietal function (Nolte et al. 2010). Recall the fMRI study of maternal attachment communication by Lenzi et al. (2009) that documents the mother's right hemisphere is more involved than the left in emotional processing and mothering. That study also reports that maternal reflective function involved in empathically ascribing her baby's emotion correlates with activation of her right anterior insula, a right lateralized cortical area involved in viscera motor integration and the interoceptive state of the body. In line with regulation theory, these authors conclude that increased activity in the right insula in more empathic mothers represents a greater ability to bodily feel the infant's emotions.

Supporting this idea, a recent study of mothers of young infants looking at photographs of infant facial expressions found no correlation between recognition of infant cues of emotion and either maternal mentalization or executive functioning ability (Turner et al. 2008). These researchers also report "no significant relationship were found between bonding scores and performance on the executive functioning and mentalization measures" (p. 499), which, they say, suggests that these factors are unrelated. We propose this is because executive functions and mentalization are functions of the left brain, while facial emotion recognition and bonding are right brain functions. These and the above research data clearly imply that interventions should focus not so much on the primary caregiver's left brain explicit, rational verbal metacognitions, theory of mind, and executive functions, but on her right brain abilities to intuitively read her infant's nonverbal signals and her interoceptive bodily based responses to these communications, and then to implicitly regulate his states of affective arousal. The clinician's trust and use of her own interoceptive bodily based responses, intuition, and instinct that helps foster a right-brain to right-brain connection is thus essential to the assessment process.

From the perspective of interpersonal neurobiology, models of effective early intervention in the period of the brain growth spurt (the last trimester of pregnancy through the second year) are equated with prevention. For clinicians, an optimal connectivity of the right brain is a prime generator of emotional wellbeing and is the socio-emotional foundation upon which all other development rests (Newton 2008a). Although the right brain initially evolves in prenatal and postnatal critical periods in infancy, it continues to enter later growth spurts (Thatcher 1997). The attachment relationship sets the developmental trajectory of the right brain at later stages of life and in this manner, attachment experiences influence all later development.

In all stages of human development, the bodily based functions of the emotional, social right brain hemisphere are centrally involved in attachment, attentional processes, autonomic functions, and stress regulation. A healthy right brain is also involved in imagery, play, humor, affiliation, novelty, context, empathy, creativity, metaphor, intuition, and the feeling laced communications found in eyes, faces, voices, body movements, gestures, and touch (Schore 2003a, b, in press). The right lateralized system is dynamic, nonlinear, integrative, and is the source of what Fogel and Garvey (2007, p. 256) describe as "aliveness." The developing right brain, the biological substrate of the human unconscious, is malleable and indelibly shaped by dyadic attachment transactions. Given the fact that both research and clinical data demonstrate the essential role of this hemispheric system in survival functions, a central tenet of modern attachment theory dictates that the right brain must be a fundamental focus of early clinical assessment, intervention, and prevention programs. Advances in theory, research, and clinical models are converging to emphasize that relational affective communications and interactive regulation lie at the core of the attachment relationship. This clearly means that early assessment and treatment should also be relational.

References

Ainsworth, M. D. S., Blehar, M. C., Waters, E., & Wall, S. (1978). *Patterns of attachment: A psychological study of the Strange Situation.* Hillsdale: Erlbaum.

Allman, J. M., Watson, K. K., Tetreault, N. A., & Hakeem, A. Y. (2005). Intuition and autism: A possible role for Von Economo neurons. *Trends in Cognitive Sciences, 9,* 367–373.

Atzil, S., Hendler, T., & Feldman, R. (2011). Specifying the neurobiological basis of human attachment: Brain, hormones, and behavior in synchronous and intrusive mothers. *Neuropsychopharmacology.* doi:10.1038/npp.2011.172.

Barbas, H. (2007). Flow of information for emotions through temporal and orbitofrontal pathways. *Journal of Anatomy, 211,* 237–249.

Barrett, J., & Fleming, A. S. (2011). Annual research review: All mothers are not created equal: Neural and psychobiological perspectives on mothering and the importance of individual differences. *Journal of Child Psychology and Psychiatry, 52,* 368–397.

Basch, M. F. (1976). The concept of affect: A re-examination. *Journal of the American Psychoanalytic Association, 24,* 759–777.

Bayley, N. (1993). *The Bayley scales of infant development*—2nd ed. San Antonio: Pearson.

Beebe, B., Jaffe, J., Markese, S., Buck, K., Chen, H., Cohen, P., Bahrick, L., Andrews, H., & Feldstein, S. (2010). The origins of 12-month attachment: A microanalysis of 4-month mother-infant interaction. *Attachment & Human Development, 12,* 3–142.

Benoit, D., & Parker, K. C. H. (1994). Stability and transmission of attachment across three generations. *Child Development, 65,* 1444–1456.

Boston Change Process Study Group. (2007). The foundational level of psychodynamic meaning: Implicit process in relation to conflict, defense and the dynamic unconscious. *International Journal of Psychoanalysis, 88,* 843–860.

Bourne, V. J., & Todd, B. K. (2004). When left means right: An explanation of the left cradling bias in terms of right hemisphere specializations. *Developmental Science, 7,* 19–24.

Bowlby, J. (1969). *Attachment and loss,* (Vol. 1). *Attachment.* New York: Basic Books.

Braun, C. M. J., Boulanger, Y., Labelle, M., Khiat, A., Dumont, M., & Maillous, C. (2002). Brain metabolic differences as a function of hemisphere, writing hand preference, and gender. *Laterality, 7,* 97–113.

Brown, J. W., & Jaffe, J. (1975). Hypothesis on cerebral dominance. *Neuropsychologia, 13,* 107–110.

Carlsson, J., Langercrantz, H., Olson, L., Printz, G., & Bartocci, M. (2008). Activation of the right fronto-temporal cortex during maternal facial recognition in young infants. *Acta Paediatrica, 97,* 1221–1225.

Carmona, J. E., Holland, A. K., & Harrison, D. W. (2009). Extending the functional cerebral systems theory of emotion to the vestibular modality: A systematic and integrative approach. *Psychological Bulletin, 135,* 286–302.

Cerqueira, J., Almeida, O. F. X., & Sousa, N. (2008). The stressed prefrontal cortex. Left? Right! *Brain, Behavior, and Immunity, 22,* 630–638.

Chanen, A. M., Velakoulis, D., Carison, K., Gaunson, K., Wood, S. J., Yuen, H. P., Yucel, M., Jackson, H. J., McGorry, P. D., & Pantelis, C. (2008). Orbitofrontal, amygdala and hippocampal volumes in teenagers with first-presentation borderline personality disorder. *Psychiatry Research: Neuroimaging, 163,* 116–125.

Chiron, C., Jambaque, I, Nabbout, R, Lounes, R, Syrota, A, & Dulac, O. (1997). The right brain hemisphere is dominant in human infants. *Brain, 120,* 1057–1065.

Chugani, H. T., & Phelps, M. E. (1986). Maturational changes in cerebral function in infants determined by 18 FDG positron emission tomography. *Science, 231,* 840–843.

Clark, R. (1985). *The parent-child early relational assessment.* Unpublished instrument. Madison: Department of Psychiatry, University of Wisconsin Medical School.

Dapretto, M., Davies, M. S., Pfeifer, J. H., Scott, A. A., Sigman, M., Bookheimer, S. Y., & Iacoboni, M. (2006). Understanding emotions in others: Mirror neuron dysfunction in children with autism spectrum disorders. *Nature Neuroscience, 9,* 28–31.

Devinsky, O. (2000). Right cerebral hemisphere dominance for a sense of corporeal and emotional self. *Epilepsy & Behavior, 1,* 60–73.

Devinsky, O., Morrell, M. J., & Vogt, B. A. (1995). Contributions of anterior cingulate cortex to behaviour. *Brain, 118,* 279–306.

Devue, C., Collette, F., Balteau, E., Degueldre, C., Luxen, A., Maquet, P., & Bredart, S. (2007). Here I am: The cortical correlates of visual self-recognition. *Brain Research, 1143,* 169–182.

De Wolff, M. S., & van IJzendoorn, M. H. (1997). Sensitivity and attachment: A meta-analysis on parental antecedents of infant attachment. *Child Development, 68,* 571–591.

Dixon, A. K. (1998). Ethological strategies for defense in animals and humans: Their role in some psychiatric disorders. *British Journal of Medical Psychology, 71,* 417–445.

Donegan, N. H., Sanislow, C. A., Blumberg, H. P., Fulbright, R. K., Lacadie, C., Skudlarski, P., Gore, J. C., Olson, I. R., McGlashan, T. H., & Wexler, B. E. (2003). Amygdala hyperreactivity in borderline personality disorder: Implications for emotional dysregulation. *Biological Psychiatry, 54,* 1284–1293.

Dorpat, T. L. (2001). Primary process communication. *Psychoanalytic Inquiry, 3,* 448–463.

Feldman, R., Singer, M, & Zagoory, O. (2010). Touch attenuates infants' physiological reactivity to stress. *Brain and Behavior, 13,* 271–278.

Ferber, S. G., Feldman, R., & Makhoul, I. R. (2008). The development of maternal touch across the first year of life. *Early Human Development, 84,* 363–370.

Fernald, A. (1989). Intonation and communication intent in mothers' speech to infants. Is the melody the message? *Child Development, 60,* 1497–1510.

Fogel, A., & Garvey, A. (2007). Alive communication. *Infant Behavior & Development, 30,* 251–257.

Gallace, A., & Spence, C. (2010). The science of interpersonal touch: An overview. *Neuroscience and Biobehavioral Reviews, 34,* 246–259.

Gogtay, N., Giedd, J. N., Lusk, L., Hayashi, K. M., Greenstein, D., Vaituzis, A. C., Nugent III, T. F., Herman, D. H., Clasen, L. S., Toga, A. W., Rapoport, J. L., & Thompson, P. M. (2004). Dynamic mapping of human cortical development during childhood through early adulthood. *Proceedings of the National Academy of Sciences, 101,* 8174–8179.

Grossmann, T., Johnson, M. H., Farroni, T., & Csibra, G. (2007). Social perception in the infant brain: Gamma oscillatory activity in response to eye gaze. *Social Cognitive and Affective Neuroscience, 2,* 284–291.

Grossmann, T., Oberecker, R., Koch, S. P., & Friederici, A. D. (2010). The developmental origins of voice processing in the human brain. *Neuron, 65,* 852–858.

Guedeney, A., Foucault, C., Bougen, E., Larroque, B., & Mentre, F. (2008). Screening for risk factors of relational withdrawal behavior in infants aged 14–18 months. *European Psychiatry, 23,* 150–155.

Gunnar, M. R. (2000). Early adversity and the development of stress reactivity and regulation. In C. A. Nelson (Ed.), *The Minnesota symposium on child psychology,* Vol. 31, *The effects of early adversity on neurobehavioral development* (pp. 163–200). Mahweh, NJ: Erlbaum.

Guo, K., Meints, K., Hall, C., Hall, S., & Mills, D. (2009). Left gaze bias in humans, rhesus monkeys and domestic dogs. *Animal Cognition, 12,* 409–418.

Gupta, R. K., Hasan, K. M., Trivedi, R., Pradhan, M., Das, V., Parikh, N. A., & Narayana, P. A. (2005). Diffusion tensor imaging of the developing human cerebrum. *Journal of Neuroscience Research, 81,* 172–178.

Helmeke, C., Ovtscharoff, W., Poeggel, G., & Braun, K. (2001). Juvenile emotional experience alters synaptic inputs on pyramidal neurons in the anterior cingulate cortex. *Cerebral Cortex, 11,* 717–727.

Hertenstein, M. J. (2002). Touch: Its communicative functions in infancy. *Human Development, 45,* 70–94.

Hertenstein, M. J., & Campos J. J. (2001). Emotion regulation via maternal touch. *Infancy, 2,* 549–566.

Hesse, E., & Main, M. (1999). Second-generation effects of unresolved trauma as observed in non-maltreating parents: Dissociated, frightened and threatening parental behavior. *Psychoanalytic Inquiry, 19,* 481–540.

Hesse, E., & Main, M. (2000). Disorganized infant, child, and adult attachment: Collapse in behavioral and attentional strategies. *Journal of the American Psychoanalytic Association, 48,* 1097–1127.

Hesse, E., & Main, M. (2006). Frightened, threatening, and dissociative parental behavior: Theory and associations with parental Adult Attachment Interview status and infant disorganization. *Development and Psychopathology, 18,* 309–343.

Homae, F., Watanabe, H., Nakano, T., Asakawa, K., & Taga, G. (2006). The right hemisphere of sleeping infants perceives sentential prosody. *Neuroscience Research, 54,* 276–280.

Howard, M. F., & Reggia, J. A. (2007). A theory of the visual system biology underlying development of spatial frequency lateralization. *Brain and Cognition, 64,* 111–123.

Huggenberger, H. J., Suter, S. E., Reijnen, E., & Schachinger, H. (2009). Cradling side preference is associated with lateralized processing of baby facial expressions in females. *Brain and Cognition, 70,* 67–72.

Huttenlocher, P. R. (1979). Synaptic density in human frontal cortex—Developmental changes and effects of aging. *Brain Research, 163,* 195–205.

Huttenlocher, P. R. (1990). Morphometric study of human cerebral cortex development. *Neuropsychologia, 28,* 517–527.

Insel, T. R., & Fenton, W. S. (2005). Psychiatric epidemiology. It's not just about counting anymore. *Archives of General Psychiatry, 62,* 590–592.

Irle, E., Lange, C., & Sachsse, U. (2005). Reduced size and abnormal asymmetry of parietal cortex in women with Borderline Personality Disorder. *Biological Psychiatry, 57,* 173–182.

Jackson, J. H. (1931). *Selected writings of J.H. Jackson* (Vol. I). London: Hodder and Soughton.

Jean, A. D. L., Stack, D. M., & Fogel, A. (2009). A longitudinal investigation of maternal touching across the first 6 months of life: Age and context effects. *Infant Behavior and Development, 32,* 344–349.

Kaplan, J. T., Aziz-Zadeh, L., Uddin, L. Q., & Iacoboni, M. (2008). The self across the senses: An fMRI study of self-face and self-voice recognition. *Social Cognitive and Affective Neuroscience, 3,* 218–223.

Knickmeyer, R. C., Gouttard, S., Kang, C., Evans, D., Wilber, K., Smith, J. K., Hamer, R. M., Lin, W., Gerig, G., & Gilmore, J. H. (2008). A structural MRI study of human brain development from birth to 2 years. *The Journal of Neuroscience, 28,* 12176–12182.

Kringelbach, M., Lehtonen, A., Squire, S., Harvey, A. G., Craske, M. G., Holliday, I. E., et al. (2008). A specific and rapid neural signature for parental instinct. *PLoS One, 3,* 1–6.

Lagercrantz, H., & Ringstedt, T. (2001). Organization of the neuronal circuits in the central nervous system during development. *Acta Paediatrica, 90,* 707–715.

Lavelli, M., & Poli, M. (1998). Early mother-infant interaction during breast- and bottlefeeding. *Infant Behavior & Development, 21,* 667–684.

Leckman, J. F., & March, J. S. (2011). Editorial: Developmental neuroscience comes of age. *Journal of Child Psychology and Psychiatry, 52,* 333–338.

Le Grand, R., Mondloch, C. J., Maurer, D., & Brent, H. P. (2003). Expert face processing requires visual input to the right hemisphere during infancy. *Nature Neuroscience, 6,* 1108–1112.

Lehtonen, J., Kononen, M., Purhonen, M., Partanen, J., & Saarikoski, S. (2002). The effects of feeding on the electroencephalogram in 3- and 6-month-old infants. *Psychophysiology, 39,* 73–79.

Lenzi, D., Trentini, C., Pantano, P., Macaluso, E., Iacaboni, M., Lenzi, G. I., & Ammaniti, M. (2009). Neural basis of maternal communication and emotional expression processing during infant preverbal stage. *Cerebral Cortex, 19,* 1124–1133.

Levine, P. A. (1997). *Waking the tiger. Healing trauma.* Berkeley: North Atlantic Books.

Lieberman, A. F., Chu, A., Van Horn, P., & Harris, W. W. (2011). Trauma in early childhood: Empirical evidence and clinical implications. *Development and Psychopathology, 23,* 397–410.

Lorberbaum, J. P., Newman, J. D., Horwitz, A. R., Dubno, J. R., Lydiard, R. B., Hamner, M. B., et al. (2002). A potential role for thalamocingulate circuitry in human maternal behavior. *Biological Psychiatry, 51,* 431–445.

Lyons-Ruth, K. (1999). The two-person unconscious: Intersubjective dialogue, enactive relational representation, and the emergence of new forms of relational organization. *Psychoanalytic Inquiry, 19*(4), 576–617.

Main, M., & Hesse, E. (1990). Parents' unresolved traumatic experiences are related to infant disorganized attachment status: Is frightened or frightening parental behavior the linking mechanism? In M. Greenberg, D. Cicchetti, & E. M. Cummings (Eds.), *Attachment in the preschool years.* Chicago: University of Chicago Press.

Main, M., & Solomon, J. (1990). Procedures for identifying infants as disorganized/disoriented during the Ainsworth Strange Situation. In M. Greenberg, D. Cicchetti, & E. M. Cummings (Eds.), *Attachment in the preschool years.* Chicago: University of Chicago Press.

McGilchrist, I. (2009). *The master and his emissary.* New Haven: Yale University Press.

Mehta, M. A., Golembo, N. I., Nosarti, C., Colvert, E., Mota, A., Williams, S. C. R., Rutter, M., & Songua-Barke, E. J. S. (2009). Amygdala, hippocampal and corpus collosum size following severe early institutional deprivation: The English and Romanian Adoptees Study Pilot. *Child Psychology and Psychiatry, 50,* 943–951.

Mento, G., Suppiej, A., Altoe, G., & Bisiacchi, P. S. (2010). Functional hemispheric asymmetries in humans: Electrophysiological evidence from preterm infants. *European Journal of Neuroscience, 31,* 565–574.

Milgrom, J., Newnham, C., Anderson, P. J., Doyle, L. W., Gemmill, A. W., Lee, K., Hunt, R. D., Bear, M., & Inder, T. (2010). Early sensitivity training for parents of preterm infants: Impact on the developing brain. *Pediatric Research, 67,* 330–335.

Milne, L., Greenway, P., Guedeney, A., & Larroque, B. (2009). Long term developmental impact of social withdrawal in infants. *Infant Behavior and Development, 32,* 159–166.

Minagawa-Kawai, U., Matsuoka, S., Dan, I., Naoi, N., Nakamura, K., & Kojima, S. (2009). Prefrontal activation associated with social attachment: Facial-emotion recognition in mothers and infants. *Cerebral Cortex, 19,* 284–292.

Minagawa-Kawai, Y., Van Der Lely, H., Ramus, F., Sato, Y., Mazuka, R., & Dupoux, E. (2011). Optical brain imaging reveals general auditory and language-specific processing in early infant development. *Cerebral Cortex, 21,* 254–261.

Mollon, P. (1996). *Multiple selves, multiple voices: Working with trauma, violation and dissociation.* Chichester: Wiley.

Montirosso, R., Borgatti, R., & Tronick, E. (2010). Lateral asymmetries in infants' regulatory and communicative gestures. In R. A. Lanius, E. Vermetten, & C. Pain (Eds.), *The impact of early life trauma on health and disease: The hidden epidemic* (pp. 103–111). Cambridge: Cambridge University Press.

Nagy, E. (2006). From imitation to conversation: The first dialogues with human neonates. *Infant and Child Development, 15,* 223–232.

Nakato, E., Otsuka, Y., Kanazawa, S., Yamaguchi, M. K., Watanabe, S., & Kakigi, R. (2009). When do infants differentiate profile face from frontal face? A near-infrared spectroscopic study. *Human Brain Mapping, 30,* 462–472.

Nakato, E., Otsuka, Y., Kanazawa, S., Yamaguchi, M. K., & Kakigi, R. (2011). Infants' neural responses to facial expressions using Near-Infrared Spectroscopy. *Journal of Vision, 10,* 575. doi:10.1167/10.7.575.

Naoi, N., Minagawa-Kawai, Y., Kobayashi, A., Takeuchi, K., Nakamura, K., Yamamoto, J., et al. (2011). Cerebral responses to infant-directed speech and the effect of talker familiarity. *NeuroImage, 59*(2), 1735–1744.

New, A. S., Hazlett, E. A., Buschsbaum, M. S., Goodman, M., Mitelman, S. A., Newmark, R., Trisdorfer, R., Haznedar, M. M., Koenigsberg, H. W., Flory, J., & Siever, L. J. (2007). Amygdala-prefrontal disconnection in Borderline personality disorder. *Neuropsychopharmacology, 32,* 1629–1640.

Newton, R. P. (2006). Speaking out of both sides of the mouth: The unnoticed road to childhood disorganization. *Psychologist-Psychoanalyst, 26,* 17–21.

Newton, R. P. (2008a). *The attachment connection.* Oakland: New Harbinger.

Newton, R. P. (2008b). Dyadic therapy for homeless parents and children. In C. Schaefer, J. McCormick, P. Kelly-Zion, & A.Ohnogi (Eds.), *Play therapy for very young children.* Lanham: Rowman & Littlefield.

Nolte, T., Hudac, C., Mayes, L. C., Fonagy, P., Blatt, S. J., & Pelphrey, K. (2010). The effect of attachment-related stress on the capacity to mentalize: An fMRI investigation of the biobehavioral switch model. *Journal of the American Psychoanalytic Association, 58,* 566–573.

Noriuchi, M., Kikuchi, Y., & Senoo, A. (2008). The functional neuroanatomy of maternal love: Mother's response to infant's attachment behaviors. *Biological Psychiatry, 63,* 415–423.

Otsuka, Y., Nakato, E., Kanazawa, S., Yamaguchi, H. K., Watanabe, S., & Kakigi, R. (2007). Neural activation to upright and inverted faces in infants measured by near infrared spectroscopy. *Neuroimage, 34,* 399–406.

Panksepp, J. (2008). The power of the word may reside in the power of affect. *Integrative Psychological and Behavioral Science, 42,* 47–55.

Papousek, M. P. (2007). Communication in early infancy: An arena of intersubjective learning. *Infant Behavior & Development, 30,* 258–266.

Perani, D., Saccuman, M. C., Scifo, P., Spada, D., Andreolli, G., Rovelli, R., Baldoli, C., & Koelsch, S. (2010). Functional specializations for music processing in the human newborn brain. *Proceedings of the National Academy of Sciences, 107,* 4758–4763.

Porges, S. W. (1995). Orienting in a defensive world: Mammalian modifications of our evolutionary heritage. A Polyvagal Theory. *Psychophysiology, 32,* 301–318.

Porges, S. W. (2001). The polyvagal theory: Phylogenetic substrates of a social nervous system. *International Journal of Psychophysiology, 42,* 123–146.

Porges, S. W. (2007). The polyvagal perspective. *Biological Psychology, 74,* 116–143.

Porges, S. W. (2009). The polyvagal theory: New insights into adaptive reactions of the autonomic nervous system. *Cleveland Clinic Journal of Medicine, 76*(Suppl 2), S86–90.

Previc, F. H. (1991). A general theory concerning the prenatal origins of cerebral lateralization in humans. *Psychological Review, 98,* 299–334.

Putnam, F. W. (1997). *Dissociation in children and adolescents: A developmental perspective.* New York: Guilford.

Recordati, G. (2003). A thermodynamic model of the sympathetic and parasympathetic nervous systems. *Autonomic Neuroscience: Basic and Clinical, 103,* 1–12.

Reissland, N., Hopkins, B., Helms, B., & Williams, B. (2009). Maternal stress and depression and the lateralization of infant cradling. *Journal of Child Psychology and Psychiatry, 50,* 263–269.

Robertson, J. (1952). *A two-year-old goes to hospital.* [Film]. New York: New York University Film Library.

Roth, T. L., & Sweatt, J. D. (2011). Annual research review: Epigenetic mechanisms and environmental shaping of the brain during sensitive periods of development. *Journal of Child Psychology and Psychiatry, 52,* 398–408.

Schore, A. N. (1994). Affect regulation and the origin of the self: The neurobiology of emotional development. Mahweh: Erlbaum.

Schore, A. N. (1996). The experience-dependent maturation of a regulatory system in the orbital prefrontal cortex and the origin of developmental psychopathology. *Development and Psychopathology, 8,* 59–87.

Schore, A. N. (1999). Commentary on emotions: neuro-psychoanalytic views. *Neuropsychoanalysis, 1,* 49–55.

Schore, A. N. (2000). Attachment and the regulation of the right brain. *Attachment & Human Development, 2,* 23–47.

Schore, A. N. (2001a). Effects of a secure attachment relationship on right brain development, affect regulation, and infant mental health. *Infant Mental Health Journal, 22,* 7–66.

Schore, A. N. (2001b). The effects of early relational trauma on right brain development, affect regulation, and infant mental health. *Infant Mental Health Journal, 22,* 201–269.

Schore, A. N. (2002). Dysregulation of the right brain: A fundamental mechanism of traumatic attachment and the psychopathogenesis of posttraumatic stress disorder. *Australian & New Zealand Journal of Psychiatry, 36,* 9–30.

Schore, A. N. (2003a). *Affect regulation and the repair of the self.* New York: Norton.

Schore, A. N. (2003b). *Affect dysregulation and disorders of the self.* New York: Norton.

Schore, A. N. (2005). Attachment, affect regulation, and the developing right brain: Linking developmental neuroscience to pediatrics. *Pediatrics in Review, 26,* 204–211.

Schore, A. N. (2009). Attachment trauma and the developing right brain: Origins of pathological dissociation. In P. F. Dell & J. A. O'Neil (Eds.), *Dissociation and the dissociative disorders: DMS-V and beyond* (pp. 107–141). New York: Routledge.

Schore, A. N. (2010a). Synopsis. In R. A. Lanius, E. Vermetten, & C. Pain (Eds.), *The impact of early life trauma on health and disease: The hidden epidemic* (pp. 1142–1147). Cambridge: Cambridge University Press, 142–147.

Schore, A. N. (2010b). Relational trauma and the developing right brain. The neurobiology of broken attachment bonds. In T. Baradon (Ed.), *Relational trauma in infancy* (pp. 19–47). London: Routledge.

Schore, A. N. (2011). The right brain implicit self lies at the core of psychoanalysis. *Psychoanalytic Dialogues, 21,* 75–100.

Schore, A. N. (in press). Bowlby's environment of evolutionary adaptedness: Recent studies on the interpersonal neurobiology of attachment and emotional development. In D. Narvaez, J. Panksepp, A. Schore, & T. Gleason (Eds.), *Evolution, early experience and human development: From research to practice and policy.* New York: Oxford University Press.

Schore, A. N. (2012). *The science of the art of psychotherapy.* New York: Norton.

Schore, J. R., & Schore, A. N. (2008). Modern attachment theory: The central role of affect regulation in development and treatment. *Clinical Social Work Journal, 36,* 9–20.

Schwartz, C. E., Kunwar, P. S., Greve, D. N., Kagan, J., Snidman, N. C., & Bloch, R. B. (2011). A phenotype of early infancy predicts reactivity of the amygdala in male adults. *Molecular Psychiatry.* doi:10.1038/mp.2011.96.

Semrud-Clikeman, M., & Hynd, G. W. (1990). Right hemisphere dysfunction in nonverbal learning disabilities: Social, academic, and adaptive functioning in adults and children. *Psychological Bulletin, 107,* 196–209.

Semrud-Klikeman, M., Fine, J. G., & Zhu, D. C. (2011). The role of the right hemisphere for processing of social interactions in normal adults using functional magnetic resonance imaging. *Neuropsychobiology, 64,* 47–51.

Shai, D., & Belsky, J. (2011). When words just won't do: Introducing parental embodied mentalizing. *Child Development Perspectives, 0,* 1–8. doi:10.1111/j.17508606.2011.00181.x.

Shonkoff, J. P. (2011). Protecting brains, not simply stimulating minds. *Science, 333,* 982–983.

Shonkoff, J. P., Boyce, W. T., & McEwen, B. S. (2009). Neuroscience, molecular biology, and the childhood roots of health disparities building a new framework for health promotion and disease prevention. *Journal of the American Medical Association, 301,* 2252–2259.

Siegel, D. J. (1999). *The developing mind: Toward a neurobiology of interpersonal experience.* New York: Guilford.

Sieratzki, J. S., & Woll, B. (1996). Why do mothers cradle their babies on the left? *Lancet, 347,* 1746–1748.

Slade, A. (2005). Parental reflective functioning: An introduction. *Attachment and Human Development, 7,* 269–281.

Spitz, R. A. (1947). *Grief: A peril in infancy.* [Film]. New York: New York University Film Library.

Sroufe, L. A., Egeland, B., Carlson, E. A., & Collins, W. A. (2005). *The development of the person: The Minnesota study of risk and adaptation from birth to adulthood.* New York: Guilford.

Stern, D. (2004). *The present moment in psychotherapy and everyday life.* New York: Norton.

Stern, D. (2005). Intersubjectivity. In E. S. Person, A. M. Cooper, & G. O. Gabbard (Eds.). *Textbook of psychoanalysis* (pp. 77–92). Washington, DC: American Psychiatric Publishing.

Stern, D., Spieker, S., Barnett, R. K., & MacKain, K. (1983). Intonation contours as signals of maternal speech to prelinguistic infants. *Developmental Psychology, 18,* 727–735.

Sullivan, R. M., & Gratton, A. (2002). Prefrontal cortical regulation of hypothalamic-pituitary-adrenal function in the rat and implications for psychopathology: Side matters. *Psychoneuroendocrinology, 27,* 99–114.

Sullivan, R. M., & Dufresne, M. M. (2006). Mesocortical dopamine and HPA axis regulation: Role of laterality and early environment. *Brain Research, 1076,* 49–59.

Sun, T., Patoine, C., Abu-Khalil, A., Visvader, J., Sum, E., Cherry, T. J., Orkin, S. H., Geschwind, D. H., & Walsh, C. A. (2005). Early asymmetry of gene transcription in embryonic human left and right cerebral cortex. *Science, 17,* 1794–1798.

Suter, S. E., Huggenberger, H. J., & Schachinger, H. (2007). Cold pressor stress reduces left cradling preference in nulliparous human females. *Stress, 10,* 45–51.

Telkemeyer, S., Rossi, S., Koch, S. P., Nierhaus, T., Steinbrink, J., Poeppel, D., Obrig, H., & Wartenburger, I. (2009). Sensitivity of newborn auditory cortex to the temporal structure of sounds. *Journal of Neuroscience, 29,* 14726–14733.

Thatcher, R. W. (1997). Neuroimaging of cyclical cortical reorganization during human development. In R. W. Thatcher, G. Reid Lyon, J. Rumsey, & N. Krasnegor (Eds.), *Developmental neuroimaging. Mapping the development of brain and behavior* (pp. 91–106). San Diego: Academic Press.

Thierry, G., Vihman, M., & Roberts, M. (2003). Familiar words capture the attention of 11-month-olds in less than 250 ms. *NeuroReport, 14,* 2307–2310.

Trevarthen, C. (2001). Intrinsic motives for companionship in understanding: Their origin, development, and significance for infant mental health. *Infant Mental Health Journal, 22,* 95–131.

Trevarthen, C., & Aitken, K. J. (2001). Infant intersubjectivity: Research, theory, and clinical application. *Journal of Child Psychology and Psychiatry, 42,* 3–48.

Tucker, D. M., & Moller, L. (2007). The metamorphosis. Individuation of the adolescent brain. In D. Romer & E. F. Walker (Eds.), *Adolescent psychopathology and the developing brain. Integrating brain and prevention science* (pp. 85–102). Oxford: Oxford University Press.

Turner, J. M., Wittkowski, A., Hare, D. J. (2008). The relationship of maternal mentaliztion and executive functioning to maternal recognition of infant cues and bonding. *British Journal of Psychology, 99,* 499–512.

Tzourio-Mazoyer, N., De Schonen, S., Crivello, F., Reutter, B., Aujard, Y., & Mazoyer, B. (2002). Neural correlates of woman face processing by 2-month-old infants. *NeuroImage , 15,* 454–461.

van IJzendoorn, M. H., & De Wolff, M. S. (1997). In search of the absent father—meta-analysis of infant-father attachment: A rejoinder to our discussants. *Child Development, 68,* 604–609.

Wang, J., Rao, H., Wetmore, G. S., Furlan, P. M., Korczykowski, M., Dinges, D. F., & Detre, J. A. (2005). Perfusion functional MRI reveals cerebral blood flow pattern under psychological stress. *Proceedings of the National Academy of Sciences of the United States of America, 102,* 17804–17809.

Weatherill, R. P., Almerigi, J. B., Levendosky, A. A., Bogat, G. A., von Eye, A., & Harris, L. J. (2004). Is maternal depression related to side of infant holding? *International Journal of Behavioral Development, 28,* 421–427.

Weaver, I. C. G., Cervoni, N., Champagne, F. A., D'Alessio, A. C., Sharma, S., Seckl, J. R., Dymov, S., Szyf, M., & Meaney, M. J. (2004). Epigenetic programming by maternal behavior. *Nature Neuroscience, 7,* 847–854.

Winnicott, D. W. (1960/1965). Ego distortion in terms of true and false self. In D. W. Winnicott (Ed.), *The maturational processes and the facilitating environment. Studies in the theory of emotional development* (pp. 140–152). Madison: International Universities Press.

Winnicott, D. W. (1965). *The maturational processes and the facilitating environment. Studies in the theory of emotional development.* Madison: International Universities Press.

Wittling, W. (1997). The right hemisphere and the human stress response. *Acta Physiologica Scandinavica, Supplement, 640,* 55–59.

Yamada, H., Sadato, N., Konishi, Y., Muramoto, S., Kimura, K., Tanaka, M., Yonekura, Y., Ishii, Y., & Itoh, H. (2000). A milestone for normal development of the infantile brain detected by functional MRI. *Neurology, 55,* 218–223.

Part II
Attachment-Based Clinical Work with Children and Adolescents

Becoming Baby Watchers: An Attachment-Based Video Intervention in a Community Mental Health Center

Donna Demetri Friedman, Sara Deutsch, Leyla Ertegun, Stephanie Carlson, Mayra Estrada, Mark Sturgeon, Hillary Mayers and Elizabeth Buckner

Adolescent mothers are particularly at risk of attachment difficulties. Coley and Chase-Landale (1998) found that teenage mothers were more likely to experience attachment problems and that their infants are more likely to be recipients of reported child abuse and neglect, as well as to be placed in foster care, than are children of older mothers. In a study of 67 infants and their adolescent mothers, Hann et al. (1991) found that 62 % of these infants displayed disorganized attachment patterns, which also predicted future aggression. The mothers of disorganized infants showed less affection than mothers whose attachment relationships with their children were secure. The disorganized infants demonstrated the lowest frequency of initiating social interactions, while also tending to refuse more of their mothers' initiatives. Children of teenage mothers are also more likely to have behavior problems in pre-school (Leadbeater and Bishop 1994). In Leadbeater and Bishop's study, maternal reports on the Child Behavior Checklist/2–3 (*CBCL*/2–3) evaluated predictors of behavior problems in 83 pre-school children of adolescent mothers. The results indicated significant correlations between ratings on *CBCL*/2–3 and maternal depressive symptoms, social supports and life stress.

Adolescent motherhood is also linked to depression (Osofsky et al. 1993). Maternal depression produces negative consequences on infants and their development of a secure attachment style (Beebe et al. 2010). Interactions between depressed mothers and their infants are significantly more negative than those in a non-depressed population, and these infants appear to be more passive and helpless (Dodge 1990). Furthermore, infants of depressed mothers exhibit emotional dysregulation and diminished cognitive functioning (Whiffen and Gottlieb 1989; Cohn et al. 1990).

Teenage mothers often do not receive sufficient emotional support from the baby's father (Osofsky et al. 1993), and the father's support is a key factor impacting the

D. D. Friedman (✉) · S. Deutsch · L. Ertegun · S. Carlson · M. Estrada · M. Sturgeon · H. Mayers · E. Buckner
Riverdale Mental Health Association, Riverdale, Bronx, NY, USA
e-mail: donnademetrif@msn.com

D. D. Friedman
Silver School of Social Work, New York University, New York, NY, USA

J. E. Bettmann, D. D. Friedman (eds.), *Attachment-Based Clinical Work with Children and Adolescents,* Essential Clinical Social Work Series,
DOI 10.1007/978-1-4614-4848-8_5, © Springer Science+Business Media New York 2013

mother's capacity to foster a secure attachment to her child (Bowlby 1952). Adolescents' own families may respond negatively to their pregnancies, resulting in a lack of support from the teenage mother's own primary attachment figures. Such conflicts between the mother and her family, or mother and the baby's father, may lead to difficulties in her parenting in a sensitive, positive manner (Mayers et al. 2008).

The psychological stress of adolescent motherhood has a negative impact on the social and emotional development of both the mother and infant (Brooks-Gunn and Furstenberg 1986). To become a mother during adolescence interrupts the mother's developmental trajectory that includes separation from old attachments and the creation of new ones (Siegler 1997). Instead of transitioning toward being less dependent on her family, an adolescent mother may become more dependent on her family (Mayers and Siegler 2004). The adolescent developmental tasks of identity consolidation and increased independent functioning are thus often at risk of being compromised. In addition, their experiences of motherhood may not correspond with their fantasies of having a baby, often resulting in a disappointed, withdrawn, or rageful reaction that leads to a cycle of expectation and despair in the mother–child dyad.

Mayers and colleagues designed the *Chances for Children* Teen Parent–Infant Project (*CFC*: Mayers et al. 2008) to improve the attachment relationship between teenage mothers and their babies. They worked in collaboration with the Institute for Child, Adolescent, and Family Studies (ICAFS), a non-profit psychodynamic training institute for mental health professionals, and the New York City Department of Education's Living for the Young Family Through Education (LYFE) program. The LYFE program provides on-site daycare centers in selected inner-city high schools in order to enable teen mothers to attend classes. Mayers and colleagues thus had the opportunity to implement the *CFC* intervention with new mothers and their babies in the first years of their babies' lives. The founders of the project (seventh and eighth authors), both social workers, trained the LYFE program's social work staff in the model, and provided services in the schools for 7 years.

Chances for Children evolved to address the specific needs of each mother–child dyad, with particular attention to the effects of depression and parenting stress on vulnerable dyads. Its overall aim was to amplify mothers' understanding of their children's needs in order to bolster parenting skills. More specifically, the goal of the intervention was to increase positive interactions between mother and child, and to decrease negative ones. By helping mothers improve their ability to be sensitive to their babies' needs, the intervention sought to strengthen the attachment in the dyad. Concurrently, *CFC* provided the opportunity to diagnose and treat emotional illnesses of the mother, and to assess and intervene when babies show early signs of disturbed development (Mayers and Siegler 2004).

Theoretical Underpinnings of the Project

This strengths-based, early intervention model integrates a series of strategies designed to improve the attachment relationship between caregivers and their infants. It aims to provide coping skills for caregivers and to prevent disruptions in the parent–infant bond that could compromise the healthy development of both care-giver and child. Three components make up this model: individual, dyadic, and play therapy treatment for caregiver and child, parenting support groups, and support for the staff.

The mother–baby treatment component of the program is based upon several clinical approaches. The first of these approaches is psychodynamic psychotherapy, centered on the work of Fraiberg (1987) and Lieberman and Pawl (1993), which focuses on linking the past to the present. This model proposes to drive out the mother's "ghosts in the nursery," by helping the mother to identify experiences from her own infancy that may be impacting her current psychological state in relation to her baby (Fraiberg 1987, p. 387). The second of these approaches is a strength-based interaction guidance model derived from McDonough (2008) that incorporates videotape analysis feedback techniques used by Beebe (2003) to identify dyadic patterns of behavior. Third, the project utilizes the mentalization treatment technique originally conceptualized by Fonagy et al. (2002), which focuses on increasing caregivers' reflective functioning.

One of the key theoretical underpinnings of the *CFC* model is Tronick's concept of rupture and repair as the mechanism that allows for development to progress (Tronick 2007). He states,

> It is our hypothesis that reparation of interactive errors is the critical process of normal interactions that is related to developmental outcome rather than synchrony or positive affect per se. That is, reparation, its experience and extent, is the 'social-interactive mechanism' that affects the infant's development. (Tronick 2007, p. 283)

Therapists commonly observe how interactive and intersubjective ruptures can derail patients and therapists themselves. Yet these ruptures are clinical opportunities as well, for successful reparations teach infants and adults alike that relationships can be mended and survive.

As infant researchers and neurobiologists continue to explore the moment-to-moment exchanges between caregivers and their babies (Beebe 2003; Schore 2000; Tronick 2007), there is increasing scientific evidence for the co-creation of rela-tionships and attachments (Beebe 2000). For example, the same area of the brain (the orbitofrontal cortex) appears involved in both the comforting function of care-givers and in the attachment system in infants (Schore 2001). Researchers believe that something equivalent to a right hemisphere dialogue occurs between mother and infant that mediates attachment (Trevarthen 2001). Some further note that one out-come of a flexible dialogue between the right brains of a caregiver and her infant is a secure attachment (Schore 2006). Besides biological and physiological regulation, the mother–infant dyad also shares the regulation of moment-to-moment stimulus–response interactions that Stern terms affect attunements (Stern 1985). This finding is consistent with Schore's hypothesis that the formation of attachment bonds derives from a recurrent experience of affective rhythms that are appropriately and sensi-tively regulated, bringing about homeostasis. For this reason, Schore characterizes the attachment theory as essentially a regulatory theory and views the regulation of affect as the central organizing principle of development, motivation, and resilience.

CFC's Video Intervention

Several pioneers in the field of infant mental health paved the way for the use of video in clinical work with children. Spitz and Cobliner (1965); Bowlby (1973), and Robertson (1971) used film to deepen our understanding of early childhood development. Subsequently, Stern (1985); Brazelton et al. (1975); Tronick (2007), and Beebe (2000) used video in their research on mothers and infants and set the stage for the use of video in clinical interventions.

Building on these historical influences, the *CFC* intervention involves videotaping caregiver–infant dyads for 10 min of free-play, with the therapist instructing the caregiver to play with her child as she would at home. In a subsequent session, caregiver and therapist watch the videotape together and discuss it non-judgmentally, looking for strengths in the interaction. This perspective focuses on the positive aspects of the dyadic relationship, rather than on educative instruction or criticism. The mutual viewing experience allows for a therapist–caregiver alliance to develop, as the therapist begins to understand the caregiver's experience of her infant and to model reflection over reaction.

Mothers who participated in the original *CFC* Teen Parent–Infant Project intervention improved their interactions with their infants in the areas of responsiveness, affective availability, and directiveness (Mayers et al. 2008). Additionally, infants in the treatment group were found to increase their interest in mother, respond more positively to physical contact, and improve their general emotional tone. These findings remained even for mothers who were depressed, confirming that it is possible for a depressed mother to improve her interaction with her infant without specifically targeting her depression (Mayers et al. 2008).

CFC Project Training and Implementation in a Community Mental Health Center

The *CFC* intervention was originally designed to address the needs of adolescent mothers and their babies in a school-based setting, and was highly effective with that population. At-risk caregiver–infant dyads in an outpatient mental health setting are another population that would benefit from this intervention. Like teen-aged mothers, depressed mothers and their infants are at risk for insecure attachments (Murray and Cooper 1997). Other researchers studying at-risk mothers, those with histories of trauma, mental illness, and the negative effects of poverty, have focused upon attachment problems in this population (Sadler et al. 2006). As a result, the *CFC* project was introduced to a community mental health setting in New York City as a treatment and research model. This outpatient mental health agency houses a wide range of programs for adults, children, and adolescents, including a program for young children in its Early Childhood Center. The Early Childhood Team received extensive training in both parent–infant psychotherapy and video-intervention models, including studying the theoretical groundwork and technical issues involved in videotaping. *CFC*'s leaders integrated the approach into the agency's services with a team of social workers and psychologists. Parents with children ages 0 to 4 years old participated in video recording sessions to address their developmental, behavioral, or emotional concerns by assisting them in enhancing their connection.

The purpose of the *CFC* intervention in this setting was to improve caregiver–infant attachment by focusing on the strengths evidenced in the dyadic relationship. Clinicians videotaped the caregivers and their children in 10-min free-play interactions. For each videotaped session, clinicians subsequently viewed the video with caregivers, identifying positive elements manifested in the relationship with the infant. Some areas considered by the clinician in this strengths-based model included both the caregiver's and the infant's self-regulation techniques, and the dyad's interactions vis-a-vis gaze, facial expression, orientation, touch, and vocalizations. In building a positive therapeutic alliance with caregivers, clinicians invited caregivers to ponder the baby's emotional and mental state at various moments in the video. This aspect of the intervention helps develop reflective functioning, the capacity of mothers to reflect on their infants' experiences. Concurrently, clinicians focused on the mother's thoughts and feelings while watching the video together. The therapist's affective attunement to the caregiver provides a model for caregivers to learn how to attune more affectively to their infants. In the course of treatment, clinicians provide caregivers the space to reflect on their own early childhood experiences, supporting them while making links between the present and lurking demons from the past.

The *CFC* intervention implemented at the outpatient center in New York City included training seven staff members—five social workers and two psychologists. Over 30 families received this intervention. During this 2-year pilot project, the *CFC* model was successfully replicated. Families with 21 boys and 17 girls received services utilizing *CFC* dyadic treatment. Children's ages ranged from 1 month to 6 years; diagnoses in the families included: maternal post-partum depression, attachment disorder, separation anxiety, post-traumatic stress disorder, pervasive developmental disorders/autism, selective mutism, sleep problems, adjustment disorder, attention deficit hyperactivity disorder, opposition defiant disorder, and regulatory disorders.

Some of the specialized staff training of the *CFC* program included: experts in early childhood treatment attending team meetings, team visits to relevant professional conferences, and team members' receiving weekly individual supervision on their clinical work and specifically on their videotaping. In addition, the team met weekly as a group to discuss progress, obstacles, opportunities, outcomes, and countertransference.

Case Vignettes

The following three case vignettes illustrate the implementation of the *CFC* intervention in a community mental health setting. The team observed several positive outcomes across all three cases. In each case, the *CFC* video intervention appeared to strengthen the attachment between caregiver and baby. Clinicians helped caregivers heighten their understanding of their babies' affects, which resulted in their increasing positive interactions with their babies and decreasing negative ones. The first case provides an example of how *CFC* was used to treat a mother whose own childhood was marred with abuse and neglect, and who had difficulty in reading and attending to her daughter's emotional needs. The second case involves a father–son dyad that developed a more attuned bond through the father's recognition of the rigidity and directiveness with which he interacted with his son. The third vignette depicts how a single interaction captured on videotape and closely looked at, helped one mother–who was recovering from drug and alcohol addiction–begin to feel competent in her ability to comfort and soothe her son.

The Case of Laura and Mary

The fourth author began to work with Laura, aged 33, when Laura's daughter Mary was under a year old. Laura had a longstanding history of depression, emotional abuse, and neglect, starting in early childhood and continuing into her current marriage, for which she had been in traditional psychotherapy. As a mother, Laura felt frustrated and powerless, and described how Mary was often uncooperative and unresponsive to her. Instead, Mary seemed to tune her out and withdraw into her own world. Laura had little support in taking care of Mary, and although Laura's own mother provided some assistance, she often made Laura feel incompetent as a mother. The dyad seemed locked in a pattern of feeling alienated from one another.

Laura's childhood was characterized by poverty, alcoholism, and domestic violence between her parents. Laura's father drank regularly and beat her mother throughout Laura's early years. At the age of 13, during a particularly grueling fight, in which Laura thought that her mother's life was in danger, Laura stabbed her father in the leg. The notoriety that ensued left her feeling alienated from her community for the rest of her teenage years. Laura never completed high school.

Laura stated that she was ineffective at getting the people in her life to take her seriously. She used the refrain, "They take me for a joke" to describe how she felt about anyone she was intimately involved with, especially her husband, whom she believed was engaged in a long-term affair. Pre-dyadic work with Laura focused on helping her feel less depressed and powerless, and on having her begin to see her role in perpetuating some of the misery she currently experienced. The goal was for Laura to feel more optimistic and motivated to make both internal as well as behavioral changes toward her daughter. For example, Laura worried about how to manage Mary's apparent separation anxiety, which she described as Mary "having a panic attack when I leave out the door."

In the initial phase of dyadic treatment, Laura's capacity to bond with Mary was assessed by videotaping the dyad in free play. Laura appeared to relate to Mary as if she were a doll that had the power to become animated and attacking. Mary never referenced her mother. Though she would sit near her mother, there was no eye contact between them. During one early session, Laura was so unaware of her baby's cries that she laughed while her daughter was in tears. It also seemed at times that Laura felt her baby was persecuting her. For example, when Mary was struggling to get a toy she was interested in and that her mother was attempting to hide from her, Laura commented to Mary, "You're trying to beat me up." Unable to read Mary's communications, Laura did not respond empathically to Mary. On the other hand, Mary was on her way to becoming another victimizer in her mother's life.

Laura had no idea how to help Mary explore, how to help expand her play, or how to teach her. She did not understand that exploration was an important behavior for a baby to engage in. When Mary made moves toward creativity or exploration of her environment, Laura would attempt to engage Mary in a monotonous, repetitive task that was, predictably, rejected by Mary. When Mary expressed her discontent verbally, or made attempts through gestures to signal her desire to move to another activity, Laura perceived Mary as "having a temper tantrum."

Through the videotaping component of *CFC*, Laura, for the first time in her life, began to see and hear herself in a way that was different from her prior experience in her own individual treatment. Closeness had been painful and fraught with terror throughout Laura's early years, and dissociation continued to function to keep her emotions at bay. Emphasizing Laura's strengths helped her feel a sense of competence. Laura began to recognize that she could affect and was actively impacting her daughter. Viewing herself playing with Mary in a safe environment on videotape, Laura began to feel more hopeful. She began to reflect on her inaction, saw how her sense of powerlessness permeated her relationship with her baby, and resulted in her feeling ineffective as a mother.

For instance, as she viewed the videos Laura saw herself saying, "No, no" in a singsong manner, and making no eye contact with Mary. Mary, in turn, did not seek her mother's face. Over time, this changed. In fact, Laura began to laugh at herself as her capacity to tolerate positive affect grew. As Laura became more animated in an appealing way, Mary began to respond to her, to seek her face, to laugh with her. Laura was able to recognize that her "No" in the past did not communicate her intended message. In the therapy, Laura practiced saying "No" in a way that really meant "No," and played with various vocal intonations to listen for their different emotional effects. Laura identified the meaning and emotional resonance of her being able to say "No" and mean "No." With Mary present, Laura began to practice saying, "No" while leaning her body in closer toward her daughter to scaffold her as she explored her environment. Laura also learned to add eye contact, and saw how this elicited from Mary not only the previously missing mutual recognition of meaning, but also actual smiles of joy, as mother–daughter bonding occurred.

Mary's affect changed too. From relative flatness and preoccupation with searching for random objects to busy herself with, Mary became more active in seeking her mother's face and attention. Once Mary discovered how her mother was tuning in to her, she showed delight in finding her. The videotaping not only benefited Laura and Mary's relationship, it also helped to support Laura in believing that she might be capable of making changes in her other interpersonal relationships.

There are still some moments in which Laura plays in a way that is intrusive and confusing for Mary. However, as Laura becomes better able to read Mary's cues and act upon them, their relationship continues to improve. Through the *CFC* intervention, the dyad has built a much better base for their relationship. Viewing the videotapes and highlighting positive moments helped this mother to recognize and appreciate her own capacities as a parent. As this therapist held Laura in mind, she could keep her baby in mind. As a result, Mary demonstrated more relatedness, cooperative behavior, and collaborative and expanded play. Ultimately, both mother and baby achieved a sense of security and increased effectiveness as each began to re-find the other emotionally, as was demonstrated in the final videotape of the intervention. Mary's face was full of joy as Laura more naturally followed her baby's cues, enjoyed her time with her daughter, and openly registered emotions on her face. Laura had become capable of moments in which she could more fully relate to her daughter, and Mary now knew when she had found her mother. As psychoanalyst and pediatrician Donald Winnicott (1989) wrote, "It is a joy to be hidden, but a disaster not to be found" (pp. 185–186). Not only was Mary now able to find her mother, but she had the experience of being found.

The Case of Carlos and Carlitos

This case demonstrates an improvement in reflective functioning on the part of the care-giving father. In addition, the intervention helped this father become less directive in his style of play and learn to follow his son's lead in their interactions. The use of video here mobilized this father's awareness of his role in the healthy development of his son's self-esteem.

Carlos and Carlitos were self-referred to the fifth author, by Carlitos' mother, Andrea, a 28-year-old Dominican woman. Andrea felt that her child, Carlitos, age three, was perfectly normal, but that he grew very serious around his father, Carlos, a 43-year-old Dominican man. Andrea thought that Carlos' attitude about parenting and his beliefs about his role as a father were interfering with her son's normal social and emotional development. Carlos was raised in the old-fashioned strict Dominican way, in contrast to her own more open upbringing in an environment where children could express their feelings. Andrea's own father had been more fun and affectionate than her mother.

Andrea described how when Carlos arrived home, he usually went through his routine of settling in and then secluded himself in the bedroom. During this routine, Carlitos diligently followed his father around, stopping whatever game he was playing. Andrea felt that Carlitos should prefer to come back and play, but that perhaps he was afraid to do so. She knew from what she had read about child development that toddlers are generally silly, exuberant and even somewhat unruly. She worried that her son was becoming overly compliant out of fear and anxiety, especially when his father was around.

Since Carlos was primarily Spanish speaking, Andrea requested and secured a bilingual therapist because she knew that language and culture were going to play a role in the treatment. When Carlos and Andrea came in, the tension between them was quite palpable. Carlos was very polite and well spoken. He talked about his job as a construction site inspector with relish. In session, Andrea explained to him what her concerns about Carlitos were, how it seemed their son had quietly abdicated all agency and renounced having fun to follow his father around in the hope of gaining affection, or praise. Carlos seemed stumped and quietly rageful. He did not deny that he was a quiet man, that he wanted to arrive home to the calm he thought he deserved after a long day at work. He explained that Carlitos following him around was proof that his system of keeping order and control was working.

Emerging as well in this initial session was the marital disconnect of a couple with a significant age difference, as well as marked cultural and parenting differences. This therapist speculated that Carlitos' behavior around his father might also be an attempt at keeping the peace. Andrea and Carlos agreed to bring Carlitos for an initial session, following which Carlos and Carlitos would be videotaped in free play.

Carlitos appeared to be a normal, slightly shy 3 year-old. He separated from his mother nicely in the waiting room and entered the office exhibiting a mixture of excitement and anxiety, which rapidly gave way to Carlitos becoming constricted, almost frozen. He sat on his hands in a chair in front of the dollhouse. With some prompting he was able to explore it, asking questions about the different objects. It was clear Carlitos needed several sessions to help him not only learn to explore, but to construct a story. In subsequent sessions, still with prompting, he focused on the bathroom, putting father in the tub or placing every single object from the dollhouse on a truck, impossibly balancing items. In one session, he set up a scene of a family watching TV, a different and more hopeful theme, seeming to be a response to Carlos joining the family the previous weekend when they were all watching a movie. It appeared Carlitos was expressing that certain things were difficult to manage and balance, but good family moments made it better. Carlitos needed more of these moments, especially with his father, in order to lessen his anxiety and increase his sense of security.

Carlos' and Carlitos' play revealed significant problems, which coincided with Andrea's concerns. Carlos was extremely directive, causing Carlitos to give up minutes after the play began. Carlos was focused on fixing and putting things in order in the dollhouse. Carlitos quietly watched, moving his head yes or no, and barely touching the toys. When Carlitos decided to play parallel to his father, Carlos almost touchingly said, "Papi, you are not going to play with me?" then directed him to do so. Carlitos complied.

Carlos returned the following week for a feedback session during which he watched a selection of several positive videotaped moments of their interaction. After watching the first minute of the video, Carlos stated he did not feel that Carlitos was having fun. As the video rolled Carlos continued to insist that Carlitos did not look like he was enjoying their play. He also remarked on his own attitude, saying that he was being too bossy. Carlos asked what he could do, and seemed to understand the idea of following Carlitos, letting him lead the play. Carlos and Carlitos came for several subsequent videotaped sessions. Both father and son began to enjoy their interaction more as Carlos let his son lead the play. In their second session, for example, they played with a train set. Carlos began to play second engineer to his son's master engineer. Viewing the video, Carlos saw that he was still an active player, making train and truck sounds, but the difference now was that he helped Carlitos build ramps and praised Carlitos' designs and ideas. During another video feedback session, Carlos was able to see how he could also slip into the role of teacher, and identified how this disengaged Carlitos from their play.

Carlitos began to relax as his father became more approachable; he could be silly, for example, by freely putting a piece of track on his head without showing any fear of Carlos' reaction. As Carlos identified a negative aspect of his interaction with his son almost immediately after seeing the first video, the intervention was immediate in that Carlos quickly created a plan to change the tenor of their relationship. Through *CFC*, Carlos learned to follow his son's lead, rather than dictating the play or insisting on the proper use of toys. In response, Carlitos began to feel safe and comfortable enough to take agency in their co-constructed play. Carlos understood that allowing Carlitos to be a toddler and experience more positive feelings during their interactions would help his son develop a healthy sense of self-esteem, be more compliant with rules, and create a more satisfactory relationship with his parents. Through the *CFC* intervention and its lessening of Carlos' directiveness in play, Carlitos began to behave more authentically, as demonstrated by a marked change in his affect in session—Carlitos in the final videotapes was engaged and giggling wholeheartedly as he played with his father.

The Case of Rita and Michael

The last case example by the sixth author demonstrates how the *CFC* intervention strengthened the attachment between a mother and a son and improved this mother's ability to recognize a key positive interaction between them. Her own past experience interfered with her ability to see herself as a good mother, but through the intervention she was able to claim her role as a mother.

Rita is a 40-year-old Hispanic woman who lives with her husband, Miguel, and toddler son Michael. Rita came for treatment following inpatient psychiatric hospitalization, precipitated by a suicide attempt. Diagnosed as bipolar and bearing a long history of chemical dependency, Rita described her internal experience that led her to attempt to take her own life: "I am a work in progress and I have come a long way but I have been and I am so filled with rage and bad feelings about myself that when I tried to kill myself I genuinely thought that my husband and baby would be better off if I were not in the picture." From the outset it was clear that Rita could benefit greatly from engaging in dyadic therapy with her son Michael.

In the initial interview, Rita described her early life as secure and happy, and how she had enjoyed an intact family system. By the time Rita was 10, however, both of her parents had succumbed to alcoholism, becoming extremely abusive to one another and to Rita. The subsequent neglect and abuse resulted in Rita being removed from the home and sent to live in a group home at the age of 12.

As an adult, Rita contained all of the pain and loneliness, fear and rage that marked her internal life, in part through not only the exertion of her will, but also through her use of cocaine and other substances. Underneath the anesthetizing power of the substances and her own striving for achievement was a lonely little girl devastated by the loss of her family of origin to alcoholism. Rita managed to put down the drugs and alcohol on her own, but without a holding environment, the rage and despair that she kept so tightly held within led her to believe that her husband and child would be better off without her. By ingesting a lethal dose of prescription medication, Rita attempted to take her life.

Following inpatient hospitalization, Rita came to the clinic, was admitted for chemical dependency treatment and through her work in group and individual psychotherapy, began to gain safer access to her internal life. In the early stages of the dyadic therapy, Rita described how she felt she was unimportant to her toddler son. She disclosed her excruciatingly deep feelings of inferiority as a parent, especially in comparing her parenting abilities to those of her husband. "Miguel is very hands on and I am not," she would say, and go on to describe with an insight how her son had begun to become a symbol to her of her failings as a mother.

The initial sessions of dyadic play therapy between Michael and Rita evidenced a significant difference between Rita's perception of her relationship with Michael and what we, the mother and therapist together, were witness to in watching video footage of their interaction. The videotape of the third session showed Michael and Rita on the floor together, playing with various toys. The two are sitting facing each other, creating a warm and secure play space. In reviewing the video with Rita, it was easy to focus on her strengths as a mother, how she warmly followed and facilitated Michael's play. After watching the video with sound in real time, we watched the video again with no sound, and in slow motion. This allowed Rita to take in a powerful moment between herself and her son.

Picking up a toy airplane, Michael is making flying gestures as Rita follows his play and describes it back to her son. Michael, wanting to see the airplane actually fly, throws the toy across the room, where it lands underneath a table behind the camera and out of sight. Rita watches as Michael, in the process of retrieving the airplane, hits his head on the table. Viewing this in slow motion, Rita and I could see how her entire body tensed when Michael bumped his head. We continued to watch as she then waved her hand to motion Michael to return to her. Michael comes again into camera view as he seeks proximity to his mother, and sitting with his back slightly turned toward her, presents his head for his mother to soothe. Rita starts gently caressing and rubbing his head as a look of pure delight comes across Michael's face. Enjoying his return to this clearly secure base, and while continuing to enjoy the caress of his mother's touch on his head, Michael begins to shift his attention back to the toys. Following his cue that he no longer wishes the touch to continue, Rita withdraws her hand. Michael begins to rub his own head, but changes his mind and decides to search for his mother's hand, which he then places directly back on his head.

Viewing the video in slow motion with Rita, we were able to see that although Michael was perfectly able to rub his own head, he wanted his mother's soothing touch, and sought her out. While watching this moment with her, this therapist began speaking for Michael, "You see Mommy, I can easily rub my own head, but I want you to do it Mommy." When Rita resumed her caresses that unmistakable expression of joy returned to Michael's face. Rita's face conveyed a very similar expression as she observed and took in her son's enjoyment of her. Rita was beginning to recognize her strengths as a mother.

Analysis of the Cases

These three cases illustrate how the *Chances for Children* intervention can result in profound changes in attachment relationships. Each case depicts the ways in which the *CFC* intervention improved reflective functioning in the caregiver. The case of Laura and Mary illustrates how psychodynamic psychotherapy helped the mother begin to process her early trauma. The video feedback helped Laura recognize that the abuse and neglect in her childhood was hindering her ability to tolerate positive affect and be attuned to her child. Laura, previously traumatized by her past, also learned how to set limits with Mary in a clear, nonthreatening manner. After the intervention both members of the dyad showed more positive affect and mutual enjoyment. Carlos, through viewing his play with Carlitos on video, was able to identify his son's desire to please him at the expense of enjoying his play. The father's ability to examine his relationship with his son and to make such rapid change in his style of play highlights the efficacy of the mentalization component of this model (Fonagy et al. 2002). Carlos' ability to mentalize allowed Carlitos to gain agency and confidence. Playing the video of Rita and Michael in slow motion was instrumental in helping this mother to feel more competent; this case demonstrates the positive impact of videotape analysis feedback conducted from a strengths perspective (Beebe 2000; McDonough 2010). This case also exemplifies an instance of rupture and repair (Tronick 2007). Rita first stopped rubbing Michael's head when it seemed she had soothed him enough, and viewing the tape of how she subsequently successfully read his cue for her to continue was clearly highly empowering.

The three cases presented in this chapter demonstrate the versatility of the *CFC* intervention. The caregivers are from different cultural backgrounds. They struggle with a range of challenges including: early childhood trauma, substance abuse, depression, poverty, domestic violence, and foster care placement in childhood. They are all able to make use of the intervention and improve in a variety of important areas of parenting. They become better able to reflect, mentalize, wait, soothe, and play. All of these are important elements in improving the attachment relationship.

Clinical Implications

Learning and implementing the *CFC* video intervention can change the way clinicians deliver clinical services to caregivers and their young children. The use of video allows clinicians to help caregivers observe and be curious about their children, in a way that in the absence of video, could not be attained. Mothers often present to the clinic as fearful and anxious, as they are the ones generally criticized for the child's behavior. *CFC* focuses on the positive interactions reflected on tape, thus engaging the caregivers so that they can begin to pause and reflect upon their children's emotional states and respond in more attuned manners. While the *CFC* model is strength based, highlighting the importance of mentalization, prior caretaker trauma, and rupture and repair, the clinicians described in this chapter also utilized other elements of parent–infant psychotherapy. This includes psycho-educational information to parents about the importance of a nondirective approach to daily play, clinicians modeling nondirective play, caregiver skill building (e.g., limit-setting through practicing with using voice as in the case of Laura and Mary), and providing other developmental help (e.g., coordinating with early intervention workers and pediatricians, answering questions about developmental issues).

The *CFC* video intervention has been used with mothers, fathers, grandmothers, and foster parents. Engaging these caregivers in the filming and observing it with them helps initially to strengthen the therapeutic relationship and ultimately the attachment relationship. Joining the parent in the act of observing him/herself with the child creates a shared focus in the treatment. The therapeutic alliance is positively impacted by this joint attention on the caregiver–child interaction. The caregiver and the clinician become baby watchers together. Seeing oneself interact with his/her child is very powerful and therefore moves the treatment along more quickly than mere discussion. Focusing on the positive aspects of the interaction helps build caregiver's self-esteem, improves the quality of play, and paves the way for caregivers to identify areas that need improvement.

Training Implications

Several issues are important in transferring this early intervention model to other settings. Supervisors and other team members must maintain the cohesiveness of a special, *CFC* training group within the larger agency context. Most staff in mental health settings manage heavy caseloads and do not have time to stop and reflect on the complexities of most cases. Having to attend additional meetings initially seems almost impossible. Team members receive weekly individual and group supervision on their clinical work. Evaluating the videotapes in individual supervision and as a team contributes to the motivation of the team members to follow the protocol closely and to effectively evaluate their own work.

Thus, establishing a cohesive training group within a busy work setting is of paramount importance to the success of this model. The team must be able to bond through openness to acknowledging and discussing differences; they must recognize that despite their individualities, they had all once been infants themselves. The team must also connect through their ability to apply the key components of the *CFC* model, mentalization and containment, to the team itself. Team members should be encouraged to express their countertransference feelings in a nonjudgmental and safe atmosphere. Supervisors should take care to address and repair disruptions in the group, with team members' relationships with each other, and with their supervisors. Parent–infant work can result in significant transference issues (Trout 2007), as therapists shift between identifying with both child and parent roles. The ability of the team to contain members' negative affect, to allow team members to switch from a non-mentalizing to a reflective, mentalizing stance, promotes positive group interactions. This parallels and reinforces the therapists' work in attempting to hold in mind their caregiver–infant dyads.

Another key contributing factor in the development of each staff member's identity as an early childhood specialist is the group's participation in early childhood conferences. Interacting with other professionals with common interests and other skills and competencies solidifies each team member's identity as an early childhood expert. In addition, early childhood specialists in such areas as reflective functioning, trauma, attachment, maternal depression, movement therapy, and video feedback, greatly assist in the development of a common theoretical framework, and in turn, a common identity for clinicians.

The issue of recruitment of families and caregiver–child dyads is also important in utilizing this *CFC* model because many families are wary of mental health services for their young children. Team members can initially obtain referrals from other staff members within the agency itself by presenting at agency meetings and through word of mouth. Marketing materials describing the program should be developed and distributed to parents, staff, and community organizations. Team members can conduct individual meetings with local pediatricians, and preschool administrators and teachers. Some team members can serve as consultants to preschools and Headstart programs, conducting workshops on various early childhood topics while also promoting the video program. The specifics of how team members should discuss the benefits of the program to both parents and referral sources should be reviewed in team meetings. Team members become more enthusiastic about the program due to the successes that they observe, making it easier to recruit new families as the project continues. Families are also promised a CD of their play sessions at the end of the project; transportation by paid car service, should be made available for needier families.

Being trained in the use of videotaping and setting up the research protocol is crucial. Training in the use of video equipment is essential, and the fact that it is easier for some team members than others must be taken into consideration. This may require a few training sessions on the basic mechanics of handling the camera as well as using a TV to display the video to caretakers. Other issues that need to be addressed are designing consent forms, devising a standardized toy list by child's age that each team member is required to follow, labeling the videos, and transferring the pre and post videos from cameras to a central computer server.

Conclusion

The *CFC* model proves successful in both a school-based setting with teenage mothers and with an at-risk population of varying ages in a mental health clinic. It was implemented with families from diverse backgrounds and improved the attachment relationships between the caregivers and their children. Since the staff training that took place at our community mental health clinic, the intervention continues to be used clinically as an effective modality of treatment for infants, toddlers and their caregivers. Ongoing supervision is important to sustain the intervention. The three most critical elements necessary to implement the *Chances for Children* Training Program in order to offer the intervention are: enthusiastic support from the agency being trained, well-trained clinicians who are consistent and reliable, and sufficiently thorough outreach to have dyads to treat. Individuals and organizations wishing to learn more about the *Chances for Children* Training Program can contact the authors of this chapter.

References

Beebe, B. (2000). Co-constructing mother–infant distress: The microsynchrony of maternal impingement and infant avoidance in the face-to-face encounter. *Psychoanalytic Inquiry, 20*, 421–440.

Beebe, B. (2003). Brief mother–infant treatment: Psychoanalytically informed video feedback. *Infant Mental Health Journal, 24*, 24–52.

Beebe, B., Jaffe, J., Markese, S., Buck, K., Chen, H., Cohen, P., Bahrick, L., Andrews, H., & Feldstein, S. (2010). The origins of 12-month attachment: A microanalysis of 4-month interaction. *Attachment and Human Development, 12*, 3–141.

Bowlby, J. (1952). *Maternal care and mental health*. Northdale: Jason Aaronson.

Bowlby, J. (1973). *Attachment and loss: Vol. 2. Separation*. New York: Basic Books.

Brazelton, T. B., Tronick, E. Z., Adamson, C., Als, H., & Wise, S. (1975). Early mother-infant-reciprocity. In: *Parent-infant interaction. Ciba Foundation Symposium No. 33*. Amsterdam: Elsevier.

Brooks-Gunn, J., & Furstenberg, F. (1986). The children of adolescent mothers: Physical, academic and psychological outcomes. *Developmental Review, 6*, 224–251.

Cohn, J. F., Campbell, S. B., Matias, R., & Hopkins, J. (1990). Face-to-face interactions of postpartum depressed and non-depressed mothersinfant pairs at 2 months. *Developmental Psychology, 26*, 15–23.

Coley, R. L., & Chase-Lansdale, P. L. (1998). Adolescent pregnancy and parenthood: Recent evidence and future directions. *American Psychologist, 53*, 152–166.

Dodge, K. A. (1990). Developmental psychopathology in children of depressed mothers. *Developmental Psychology, 26*, 3–6.

Fonagy, P., Gergely, G., Jurist, E. L., & Target, M. (2002). *Affect regulation, mentalization, and the development of the self*. New York: Other Press.

Fraiberg, S. (1987). Ghosts in the nursery. In L. Fraiberg (Ed.), *Selected writings of Selma Freiberg* (pp. 100–136). Columbus: Ohio State University Press.

Leadbeater, B. J., & Bishop, S. J. (1994). Predictors of behavior problems in preschool children of inner-city Afro-American and Puerto Rican adolescent mothers. *Child Development, 65*, 638–648.

Lieberman, A. F., & Pawl, J. H. (1993). Infant–parent psychotherapy. In C. L. Zeanah (Ed.), *Handbook of infant mental health* (pp. 427–442). New York: Guilford.

Hann, D. M, Castino, R. J., Jarosinski, J., & Britton, H. (1991). Relating mothertoddler negotiation patterns to infant attachment and maternal depression with an adolescent mother sample. In J. Osofsky & L. Hubbs-Tait (Chairs), *Consequences of adolescent parenting: Predicting behavior problems in toddlers and preschoolers*. Symposium conducted at the biennial meeting of the Society for Research in Child Development, Seattle, WA.

Mayers, H., & Siegler, A. L. (2004). Finding each other: Using a psychoanalytic-developmental perspective to build understanding and strengthen attachment between teenaged mothers and their babies. *Journal of Infant, Child, and Adolescent Psychotherapy, 3,* 444–465.

Mayers, H., Hager-Budny, & Buckner, E. (2008). The *chances for children* teen parent-infant project: Results of a pilot intervention for teen mothers and their infants in inner city high schools. *Infant Mental Health Journal, 29,* 320–342.

McDonough, S. (2003). Interaction guidance: An approach for difficult to reach families. In C. H. Zeanah (Ed.), *Handbook of infant mental health,* 2nd ed., (pp. 485–493). New York: Guilford.

Murray, L., & Cooper, P. (1997). *Postpartum depression and child development.* New York: Guilford.

Osofsky, J., Hann, D., & Peebles, C. (1993). Adolescent parenthood: Risks and opportunities for mothers and infants. In C. L. Zeanah (Ed.), *Handbook of infant mental health* (pp. 106–119). New York: Guilford.

Robertson, J., & Robertson, J. (1971). Young children in brief separation: A fresh look. *Psychoanalytic Study of the Child, 26,* 264–315.

Sadler, L. S., Slade, A., & Mayes, L. C. (2006). Minding the baby: A mentalization-based parenting program. In J. G. Allen & P. Fonagy (Eds.), *Handbook of Mentalization based treatment* (pp. 271–288). West Sussex: Wiley.

Schore, A. N. (2000). Attachment and the regulation of the right brain. *Attachment & Human Development, 2,* 23–47.

Schore, A. N. (2001). The effects of a secure attachment relationship on right brain development, affect regulation, and infant mental health. *Infant Mental Health Journal, 22,* 7–66.

Siegler, A. (1997). *The essential guide to the new adolescence.* New York: Dutton.

Simpson, J. (1999). Attachment theory in modern evolutionary perspective. In J. Cassidy & P. R. Shaver (Eds.), *Handbook of attachment* (pp. 115–140). New York: Guilford.

Spitz, R. A., & Cobliner, W. G. (1965). *The first year of life.* New York: International Universities Press.

Stern, D. N. (1985). *The interpersonal world of the infant: A view from psychoanalysis and developmental psychology.* New York: Basic Books.

Trevarthen, C. (2001). The neurobiology of early communication: Intersubjective regulations in human brain development. In A. F. Kalverboer & A. Gramsbergen (Eds.), *Handbook on brain and behavior in human development.* Dordrecht: Kluwer Academic.

Tronick, E. (2007). *The neurobehavioral and social-emotional development of infants and children.* New York: W. W. Norton.

Trout, M. (1987). *Working papers on process in infant mental health assessment and intervention.* Champaign: The Infant-Parent Institute.

Whiffen, V. E., & Gottlieb, I. H. (1989). Infants of post-partum depressed mothers: Temperament and cognitive status. *Journal of Abnormal Psychology, 98,* 274–279.

Winnicott, D. W. (1965). *The maturational processes and the facilitating environment and the theory of emotional development.* The International Psycho-Analytic Library. London: The Hogarth Press and the Institute and Psycho-Analysis.

Trauma–Focused Child–Parent Psychotherapy in a Community Pediatric Clinic: A Cross-Disciplinary Collaboration

Todd S. Renschler, Alicia F. Lieberman, Miriam Hernandez Dimmler and Nadine Burke Harris

The integration of mental health services in primary health care clinics has the potential to create a coordinated approach to treatment that addresses the mental health origins of many leading medical problems. This integrated approach can serve an important preventive role in early childhood because long-term mental health and medical problems often originate in the first years of life. Early childhood mental health specialists, particularly social workers and child psychologists, can collaborate productively with primary health providers in the early identification and treatment of behavioral and mental health problems in families with young children (Groves and Augustyn 2004; Cohen et al. 2008).

Parents often develop a deep trust in the capacity of pediatricians to keep their child healthy and to address the child's illnesses, and this positive attitude often leads them to turn to the child's doctor for advice as the first recourse when facing troubling child behaviors at home or at school. In detailing a philosophy of holistic pediatric care, Brazelton (1992) highlights the importance of developing meaningful relationships with each family member in order to strengthen the pediatrician's understanding of the interpersonal and contextual dynamics that influence a child's growth and development. Because of this unique window into the child's first relationships, the community pediatric clinic holds special importance as a place for early identification of disturbances in the parent–child relationship and the effects of trauma (Groves and Augustyn 2011). Pediatricians, social workers, and psychologists embedded in the communities that they serve have an opportunity to better understand the ecological influences—such as socio-economic status, community violence, and trauma—that may have a negative impact on the parents' capacity to

The authors would like to thank Tipping Point Community for the generous support that made the work described in this chapter possible.

T. S. Renschler (✉) · A. F. Lieberman · M. H. Dimmler
Child Trauma Research Program, San Francisco General Hospital, San Francisco, CA, USA
e-mail: Todd.Renschler@ucsf.edu

N. B. Harris
Bayview Child Health Center, California Pacific Medical Center, San Francisco, CA, USA

J. E. Bettmann, D. D. Friedman (eds.), *Attachment-Based Clinical Work with Children and Adolescents,* Essential Clinical Social Work Series,
DOI 10.1007/978-1-4614-4848-8_6, © Springer Science+Business Media New York 2013

provide adequate care and which significantly shape the young child's early development. Cross-disciplinary collaboration builds long-lasting relationships that foster greater communication and the sharing of resources. The pediatrician's capacity to respond effectively is greatly enhanced when immediate referrals can be made to on-site social work and psychological services.

In this chapter, we describe a unique model of collaboration between pediatricians and mental health specialists at a pediatric clinic in San Francisco. Pediatricians at this clinic routinely screen for the kinds of traumatic experiences that have been shown to predispose children and parents to a variety of long-term physical and mental health problems and work with an integrated team of mental health professionals to proactively address these problems. We proceed by describing child–parent psychotherapy (CPP) as the treatment of choice for traumatized young children and parents, and assert the importance of thoughtful, well-timed engagement, and collaboration when working with marginalized populations. This model of collaborative treatment is proposed as having the potential of replication in communities facing similar challenges.

The Pediatric Clinic as Mental Health Setting

The Bayview Child Health Center (BCHC) is a pediatric clinic located in the Bayview Hunters Point neighborhood of San Francisco. Although historically a predominantly African American neighborhood, the Bayview is increasingly diversified with a growing percentage of Pacific Islander, Asian, Latino, and Caucasian residents. Although the neighborhood is ethnically and culturally diverse, many residents are affected by poverty, lack of access to health care, lack of education, and ongoing exposure to gang and drug related violence. One fifth of the neighborhood's residents live in poverty (Northern California Council for the Community 2004).

Community violence and other violent crimes affect many families who live in the neighborhood. In this context, ongoing stress and chronic intergenerational and complex trauma take a heavy toll on the physical and emotional wellbeing of the families seen by clinic staff. BCHC was established in 2007 to address health disparities and to reduce rates of asthma hospitalization and raise rates of immunization in a neighborhood that, at the time, had only one other pediatrician, but the largest number of children of any neighborhood citywide. The BCHC medical director quickly recognized the important influence of ongoing exposure to trauma on the physical and emotional well being of her patients (Burke et al. in press; Tough 2011).

BCHC staff strive to understand and address the impact of traumatic experiences on the physical and mental health of their patients, and the clinic was founded with the belief that physical and psychological services must be integrated in order to effect long lasting change. The clinic serves patients with a staff of two full-time pediatricians, three medical assistants, and one practice coordinator. The mental health team comprises one social worker, one master's level clinician working as a case manager and parent advocate, and two clinical psychologists. With private funding from Tipping Point Community, the clinic has established a partnership with the University of California, San Francisco, Child Trauma Research Program as part of an special initiative to provide on-site early childhood mental health services for children aged zero to five identified as having trauma exposure and/or behavioral and mental health problems. This initiative is part of a larger effort to more broadly implement trauma–focused CPP in collaboration with community agencies (Hernandez Dimmler et al. in press).

BCHC is first and foremost a primary care clinic with in-house mental health services as opposed to being a destination for patients seeking mental health care. The trauma screen devised by clinic pediatricians is based on the adverse childhood experiences (ACE) study (Felitti et al. 1998), a longitudinal study of more than 15,000 middle class, Kaiser Permanente patients that showed a correlation between adverse childhood experiences, such as sexual abuse, neglect and trauma, and risk for disease later in life.

The ACE screen is part of a comprehensive program intended to address the impact of adverse childhood experiences as a major risk factor for chronic disease (Burke et al. in press). Clinic pediatricians initially screen every patient for trauma including physical and sexual abuse, substance use, neglect, domestic violence, parental incarceration, history of mental illness, and past or current involvement of child protective services. Once pediatricians have administered the screen, they begin a consultation process with social workers and psychologists at the clinic to determine the appropriateness of a referral to mental health services.

This consultation process begins when pediatric staff present families at the multi-disciplinary rounds—a weekly consultation group that consists of a child and adolescent psychologist, a social worker and psychologist trained in child–parent psychotherapy, a case manager, and two pediatricians, in order to discuss patients and to strategize about how to effectively offer services. After an intervention plan is formulated, services are coordinated to address the physical and mental health needs of the child and family. These services may include referral for brief consultation with a staff therapist, case management, outside psychological, educational or neurodevelopmental assessment, and family, individual or child–parent psychotherapy.

In addition to providing a forum for discussion of families, the multi-disciplinary rounds process gives medical staff the opportunity to reflect on their experience of the traumatic material generated in their interviews with patients. Clinicians and care providers exposed to patients with traumatic histories are at risk of experiencing burnout as a result of secondary traumatization (Figley 1996; McCann and Pearlmann 1990). The collaboration between the mental health and pediatric teams seeks to encourage an organizational culture that values reflective capacity, self-care, and the mitigation of secondary traumatization. The multi-disciplinary rounds process intends to mitigate secondary traumatization by providing staff with a forum to reflect on the overwhelming or upsetting images and affect generated by the ACE screen.

The mental health team has weekly meetings intended to reflect on organizational process, presentation of challenging clinical material, and to discuss how to more effectively engage hard to reach families. The mental health team also provides in-service trainings to clinic staff related to mental health.

Viewing Trauma Through an Attachment Lens

Our interdisciplinary model of collaboration has roots in an ecological/transactional model of conceptualization and treatment (Cicchetti and Lynch 1993; Lieberman and Van Horn 2009). This approach assumes that healthy development and psychopathology are the result of the mutual influences between both risk and protective factors within the child such as genetic biology, and environmental influences such as the parent–child relationship, the family, community, and cultural context (Bronfenbrenner 1977). When considering the impact of trauma, our approach involves developing a better understanding of the quality of the child's primary attachment relationships as a significant part of the context in which the trauma occurred.

Trauma in the first 5 years of life is profoundly disruptive of a child's expected developmental trajectory and often has a negative impact on the parent–child relationship. Infants and young children may remember traumatic events long after they occur, and these memories can have profound effects on their play, development, and expectations of the caregiver (Gaensbauer 1995). Following a traumatic event, the parent's past and present circumstances—including early attachments and trauma history—influence their ability to function as a developmentally critical protective shield for their child (Freud 1926/1959). When past traumas or unresolved developmental conflicts are evoked by the present trauma, the parent may find it impossible to provide the sense of safety needed to regulate the child's fluctuating emotional and physiological states (Lieberman and Amaya-Jackson 2005; Scheeringa and Zeanah 2001). As a result, an attachment system that has evolved to provide protection, physiological and affective regulation, and a sense of safety for young children may become a source of fear, insecurity, and dysregulation.

When both caregiver and child experience a traumatic event—such as when a child witnesses domestic violence involving the parents—they may come to remind each other of the trauma. The parent's own symptoms of traumatic stress may be triggered when the child's dysregulated affect and behavior remind her of the event, and her own distress may interfere with her ability to respond supportively to the child (Lieberman and Van Horn 2005, 2008).

Trauma symptoms reflect the child's developmental stage, and in the first year of life may include prolonged and inconsolable crying, motor agitation, disorders of feeding and sleep, and blunted affect. In toddler and preschool age children symptoms may include reckless behavior, engaging in disinhibited or dangerous behaviors and precocity of self-care (Lieberman and Van Horn 2005; Scheeringa and Zeanah 1995a, b). According to the *Diagnostic Classification of Mental Health and Developmental Disorders of Infancy and Early Childhood-Revised* (DC: 0–3R), symptoms of Post Traumatic Stress Disorder (PTSD) in early childhood include re-experiencing the event through repetitive posttraumatic play, recurrent recollections of the event, nightmares, physiological distress, flashbacks or dissociation, as well as numbing of responsiveness, disruption of the child's development and increased arousal (National Center for Infants, Toddlers and Families 2005).

There is a striking similarity between the behavior of children classified as having a disorganized attachment relationship to their mothers and those who have experienced traumatic events. For example, children with a classification of disorganized attachment may appear disoriented in relation to their surroundings, show contradictory behaviors in rapid succession, may be inhibited in their exploration, and show dysregulation of affect. Similar behaviors are observed in children who experienced violence and chronic traumatic experiences, raising the possibility that exposure to trauma may be a factor in the etiology of disorganized attachment (Lyons-Ruth and Jacobvitz 1999; Lieberman and Amaya-Jackson 2005). The mutually influencing nature of attachment and trauma make it critical for mental health providers to be attentive to trauma history in the presence of a disorder of attachment. Some caregivers, especially those with histories of trauma themselves, may find it difficult to understand the connection between the traumatic event and the child's behavior and may mistake symptoms of traumatic stress as unexplained defiance, oppositional behavior, attention problems, rebelliousness or tantrums. The parent may then begin to make negative attributions about the child, coming to believe that the child is "bad," "angry," "a liar," or "manipulative" (Silverman and Lieberman 1999).

Since avoidance and minimization are two common mechanisms of psychological protection following a traumatic event, caregivers may also seek to downplay the significance of the trauma. Parents may have trouble speaking about the trauma directly with their children or believe that their children do not remember the trauma, even when the children's play indicates that they are remembering and reenacting traumatic events that occurred before the acquisition of language (Gaensbauer 1995). Alternatively, a caregiver may be affected by the trauma in such a way that their own anxiety, hyper vigilance, and misapprehension of danger leads them to become overly protective, anticipating danger when there is no realistic reason for it and over-interpreting developmentally expectable behaviors as manifestations of the traumatic exposure.

When a family seeks treatment or advice for a child's behavioral problems, they often do so without necessarily making an explicit connection between the behavior and the trauma. In part because of the disorganizing effects of trauma, parents may wait to seek treatment or advice until their child's behavior becomes severe enough at home or school that it begins to fundamentally disrupt the child or parent's ability to function.

In the setting of a community pediatric clinic, pediatricians are often the first provider to hear about these concerns, making them a particularly important part of the system of care and an influential figure in the referral process.

Although pediatricians have the opportunity to identify behavioral, emotional, and developmental problems in their earliest stages, they may be unaware of mental health resources in the communities they work or unsure of how to utilize available resources. As a result, they may feel pressure from parents to prescribe psychotropic medications to address the symptoms of depression, anxiety, or hyperactivity that may be linked to trauma, rather than referring to mental health providers. For this reason, there is a vital need for social workers, psychologists, and pediatricians to work together on an early intervention/prevention model of treatment as a way of addressing the needs of traumatized children.

Trauma–Focused Child–Parent Psychotherapy in the Pediatric Clinic

Child–parent psychotherapy is an evidence-based form of clinical intervention that focuses on improving relationships between parents and children aged zero to five and takes place in joint sessions with the parent and the child (Lieberman and Van Horn 2005, 2008; Lieberman et al. 2006). It is the treatment of choice for infants and young children who have experienced trauma. Contemporary CPP evolved from the groundbreaking work of Fraiberg (1980) who as a social worker and psychoanalyst was uniquely positioned to develop a model of treatment of infants and parents that was attuned to the intrapsychic "ghosts" of the parents past as well as to the concrete social and psychological needs of vulnerable young children (St. John and Lieberman in press). Psychotherapists trained in this approach take into account the type and severity of the traumatic event, the quality of the child and parent's individual functioning before the trauma, the quality of the attachment of both parent and child, and changes in the parent–child relationship since the traumatic event. One of the hallmarks of CPP is the routine integration of variety of clinical modalities such as developmental guidance, concrete assistance and advocacy, as well as perspectives informed by psychoanalytic theory, social learning theory, mindfulness, attachment theory, and cognitive-behavioral therapy.

Child–parent psychotherapy's goals include evaluating and strengthening the parent–child attachment and improving the overall emotional quality and sense of safety in the dyad (Lieberman and Van Horn 2009). In order to foster greater affective attunement and communication, therapists routinely offer translations of the child's behavior and affect during free play and parent–child interactions. This facilitates greater parental self-awareness and a deeper understanding of the child's subjectivity, both of which contribute to healthy parent–child relationships (Lieberman and Van Horn 2009). However, treatment is not limited to helping parents better understand and respond to their child's behavior. Thoughtfully timed provision of developmental guidance facilitates understanding and reduces anxiety, and concrete assistance with problems of daily living strengthens the therapeutic alliance and encourages self-care. Helping parents and children understand and make meaning of the trauma is a central focus of the work. This is achieved through the co-creation of a narrative that puts the traumatic events in context and allows parents and children to better understand the ongoing internal and external factors that trigger their symptoms (Lieberman and Van Horn 2009).

Engaging Hard to Reach Families

The mental health team originated with the understanding that the mental health needs of the community could only be met when those needs are identified and responded to flexibly and individually. Using a dual lens of attachment and trauma, psychotherapists at the clinic use a variety of means to understand and engage families.

Families who reside in marginalized communities affected by chronic violence, trauma, and poverty are often reluctant to engage in psychological treatment (Seligman and Pawl 1984; Kiefer 2000). Engagement with systems of care requires a level of trust and a stability of primary attachment relationships that is often absent in the families from such communities. Rates of missed appointments and unreturned phone calls are high. Because of unexpected moves, homelessness, financial stress, and other reasons, patients may change phone numbers frequently and working numbers are suddenly disconnected. Without a way of contacting or following up with a family, staff can become frustrated and disheartened.

BCHC was founded to facilitate an early intervention/prevention model of treatment in the service of a larger public health perspective. However, because of ongoing emotional and socioeconomic stress and lack of trust of systems of care, many families wait until symptoms are significant before coming to the clinic to see the doctor. Some African American families may be reluctant to seek mental health services once established at the clinic because of the longstanding stigma related to mental health services in the African American community (Sanders Thompson et al. 2004; Diller 1999).

Patients who have developed a strong bond with the pediatric staff including front desk staff and medical assistants tend to engage more readily. The front desk staff is crucial in building rapport with families and in helping them feel at ease and are often more aware of the life stories of the families served than members of either the pediatric or mental health teams. They observe families in the waiting room and often witness unfiltered interactions between family members. They often know how to contact a family when that family has been out of touch, for instance, because two family members had a falling out and the parent and child moved. In fact, many families come to think of clinic staff as being "like family." For this reason, clinic staff is a vital part of the dialogue between the pediatric staff and the mental health team. This strong rapport and sense of connection with the front desk staff is one important reason why families accept the clinic as a place for their child's mental health care.

Impediments to Engagement

Families who have been mandated by social services to attend therapy can be particularly reluctant to form a therapeutic alliance because of feelings of powerlessness and their association of the therapist with the social service agency. Although from the standpoint of the therapist, CPP is not a mandated service, psychotherapy is often a requirement for families where child abuse or neglect is suspected or has been confirmed and CPS is involved. There are significant challenges in developing a therapeutic relationship with a family when the family feels that the treatment has been forced upon them.

Similarly, not every family who has experienced trauma is ready for treatment. In fact, because avoidant behavior is common in families who have experienced trauma, the task of engagement becomes that much more difficult. These families may underreport adverse experiences, downplay symptoms, or minimize the pediatrician's concerns.

When speaking to a parent about mental health issues, the pediatrician takes care to address the patient's primary concern regarding the wellbeing of the family. Parents may present concerns about their child's behavior more readily than personal feelings of depression or anxiety. Pediatric staff has become attuned to the way that parents present their concerns and attempt to be respectful of the parent's level of functioning and readiness for treatment. This parallels the CPP assessment process, in which the therapist begins with the parent's primary concern about their child and proceeds from there.

Engaging multiply stressed families in child–parent psychotherapy often involves beginning with a family's greatest need rather than addressing the traumatic incident right away. This is especially true of families who have been referred, but are not seeking treatment. Families who live in poverty are often in ill health, lack adequate transportation and family support and are often uninterested in beginning a course of talk therapy. As a result, engaging families in the concrete aspects of their needs (i.e., physical health, services such as respite and daycare, and establishment of appropriate benefits) is often the most effective way to engage families in psychotherapy.

For example, following up on a referral by the child's pediatrician, a clinician was met with silence after presenting clinical services focused on trauma. After hearing that the overwhelmed mother's greatest concern was keeping her five children's clothes clean at home and that her rented washing machine had just broken and would be too costly to repair, the clinician offered to help the mother find a new one. The subsequent relationship that formed as a result of the clinician's genuine efforts on the family's behalf led to critical involvement when the family experienced a crisis. As in clinical social work, such concrete interventions are helpful when engaging patients from marginalized communities.

Concrete interventions may also occur in the context of advocacy. This includes interfacing with the legal system on behalf of patients, helping to review and complete important documents with patients, and clarifying important information with other caregivers and systems. When thoughtfully employed, such well-timed interventions may also be considered to be nonverbal interpretations (Renschler 2009).

Home visiting is another aspect of initial or ongoing engagement of families who are difficult to reach. For example, following a client's surgery for a debilitating leg injury, the clinician offered to travel to the family's home for therapy rather than allow the treatment to falter because of the patient's difficult life circumstances. The mother was touched by this accommodation, which allowed a deepening of the therapeutic relationship. Because the family lived in a dangerous neighborhood, the visits evoked the mother's protective feelings for the therapist, which allowed her to feel, and more deeply express, her feelings of vulnerability about herself and her child due to living in an area where community violence was common.

Culture and Class

Issues related to cultural differences between clinician and patient may present initial impediments to engagement. Despite this, there can be significant advantages to treatments that involve therapists and patients of different ethnicities. Clinicians, working in communities where the predominant ethnicity is different than their own, have a responsibility to develop the capacity to reflect on their own cultural background, biases, and assumptions and to seek out culturally appropriate consultation. It is the clinician's readiness to address issues of culture and class in treatment and supervision that determines in part whether treatment will falter due to cultural differences (Diller 1999). For this reason, reflective practice is vital to implementing a diversity-informed approach to mental health treatment (Gosh Ippen and Lewis 2011).

Some African American patients may feel that a white clinician cannot understand their experience or they may associate the white therapist with a system of care that has historically been anything but helpful (Williams 2008). However, it can be significant when a strong relationship is formed between a therapist and patient of different ethnicities in a spirit of mutual respect and collaboration. This is especially true of patients who have never had a close relationship with a person of another ethnicity. In one instance, an African American woman revealed to her white therapist that she had been taught to "never trust the white man and never tell the white man your problems." When she followed her African American pediatrician's advice and pursued treatment with a white therapist, the resulting relationship caused her to reflect that, "some things are more important than the color of your skin."

The clinician's willingness to engage in a thoughtful, self-reflective process around his or her own cultural biases, ethnic background, and socioeconomic status and how these elements differ from those of their patients is an important part of addressing issues of culture and class in child–parent psychotherapy. When therapists take this into account, they are better able to understand not just the larger cultural context of their patients and of the community, but the culture specific to the individual and the family as well. Ultimately, this approach facilitates flexible adaptation to the specific needs of each child, parent, and family (Lieberman 1990; Diller 1999; Devore and Schlesinger 1981).

Case Example

The following case example serves to illustrate the advantages to providing child–parent psychotherapy in the context of the community pediatric clinic. In this case, the referral from the pediatrician, typically a useful introduction to mental health services, was tainted by the pediatrician's earlier referral of the mother to child protective services on suspicion of neglect. This left the mother feeling betrayed, resentful, and reluctant to engage with services. As the clinician would learn, the mother's attachment history left her untrusting of close relationships and without close friends or significant family support. From an attachment perspective, the mother's capacity to be emotionally available and attunement to her own daughter improved as her she developed a strong relationship with the clinician. This relationship served to facilitate the gradual repair of longstanding hurts that had existed in her relationship with her own mother which impaired her own ability to be attentive to her daughter and left her without a healthy model of parenting. The co-location of medical and psychological services at the clinic allowed for the later repair of the damaged relationship with the pediatrician as well. As the mother's self-awareness increased by talking about herself in therapy, a new experience for her, she developed a greater capacity to nurture and respond to her daughter's changing needs. As the therapeutic relationship strengthened, a traumatic event involving mother and child threatened to damage the mother's fragile attachment to the therapist as well as to derail her growing bond with her child.

Presenting Problem

Charlene[1] was a 25-year-old, African American, first-time mother when she was referred with her 5-month-old daughter Nia, for CPP by Nia's pediatrician. Born 8 weeks premature at three pounds, Nia had been diagnosed with nonorganic failure to thrive after she continued to struggle to gain weight several months after being released from the hospital. For the first few months of Nia's life, the medical team at the clinic worked closely with the family to understand the causes of Nia's weight problems. According to the pediatrician, there was no known physiological reason that Nia should not be gaining weight, but she was increasingly concerned about Charlene. The staff observed that Charlene often seemed annoyed and overwhelmed by her daughter's cries. On several occasions, they witnessed Charlene telling her newborn to "shut up." At other times, her affect was flat and she seemed distracted and inattentive. Despite giving her careful instructions about how to feed and care for Nia, the pediatrician was concerned that Charlene's apparent postpartum depression was affecting her capacity to care for daughter.

After several weeks of unsuccessful psychosocial intervention, including concrete assistance, modeling, and detailed parenting instruction by the clinic case manager and medical staff, Nia's pediatrician recommended that she be hospitalized to further assess the cause of her failure to thrive. Nia gained a significant amount of weight during this four-day hospitalization but quickly lost these gains following her return

---

[1] In this case example, names and identifying information have been changed to protect the confidentiality of the patient and family.

home. In order to ensure greater supervision and care for this family, and from the pediatrician's perspective, to save Nia's life, the clinic case manager, at the request of the pediatrician, informed Charlene that they would be filing a report with child protective services (CPS) due to suspicion of neglect. At the time, Nia was under the third percentile for weight and was thought to be in considerable danger due to her low weight.

Following a team decision meeting arranged by the Child Protective Services social worker, and discussion of the case at multi-disciplinary rounds, child–parent psychotherapy was recommended to attempt to address both Charlene's possible postpartum depression as well as any other potential psychosocial causes for the Nia's failure to thrive. At the team meeting, Charlene's mother, whom Charlene and Nia lived with at the time, accused her daughter of neglectful behavior and publicly scolded her. She seemed angry with Charlene and insinuated that it might be better if Nia were removed from her care altogether. Despite this, CPS determined that as long as Charlene would agree to participate in a variety of supportive services—including child–parent psychotherapy—and if Nia began to gain weight, Nia would stay at home with Charlene. Charlene and Nia were then referred to a psychotherapist at the clinic who is trained in CPP.

Initial Assessment: Sharing the Mother's Perspective

When the clinician first met Charlene, Charlene was withdrawn and her affect was flat. In the initial sessions, she wore headphones over her ears with the volume turned loud enough that the clinician could hear the music. The clinician initially understood this to be a reflection of her depressed mood as well as her anger about being referred to therapy against her wishes. In fact, the clinician was aware that from Charlene's perspective, CPS was ordering her to attend psychotherapy or risk losing her baby. The clinician imagined how this might leave Charlene feeling powerless, undermined, angry, and potentially humiliated both as a mother and a new parent. Charlene insisted on referring to the clinician by his professional title and full last name.

As the therapy was considered mandatory, the task of building rapport and safety in the therapeutic relationship presented a special challenge. Initial attempts to engage Charlene and to establish rapport focused on acknowledging her lack of choice in coming to treatment and empathizing with her about the stress of CPS involvement. With this in mind, the clinician also attempted to find ways to offer her more choice within the framework of the treatment. The clinician focused a great deal in the first session on clarifying his role as separate from that of the pediatrician and the CPS social worker. He also focused on clarifying confidentiality and on helping Charlene—who had never seen a therapist before—know what information was considered private and when information would need to be shared. The clinician stressed that in the event that something needed to be shared, such as if he learned that a child was being hurt, he would always tell her what he was going to say first, and if possible, the two of them would tell someone about it together.

In the first session, rather than focusing on the presenting problem, which he imagined might have put Charlene on the defensive, the clinician focused on concerns she had about Nia and how things were going at home. The clinician said that even though he understood that it was not her idea to receive services, he thought that therapy could provide a space for her experience as a new parent and to talk about the things that had been stressful for her and Nia. The clinician also told Charlene that the three of them could work together to better understand some of the reasons for her child's difficulty with weight gain. Although guarded at first, Charlene seemed relieved. It would take many more weeks before she began to open up about feelings of betrayal by the pediatrician and her mother due to the CPS report.

As the clinician and Charlene completed the administrative paperwork necessary to begin work together, Charlene said that she felt that she and her daughter had spent more time in doctor's offices filling out paperwork and being examined than getting to know each other at home. The clinician took this as another opportunity to offer Charlene a choice with respect to the early treatment. A typical CPP assessment at CTRP lasts 5 to 6 weeks and involves a number of psychological measures that assess the functioning and the history of both parent and child. This process can evoke strong feelings in many parents and can be especially difficult when a parent feels disempowered and distrustful of the system of care. With this in mind, the clinician outlined the traditional assessment process but offered Charlene the option of choosing how she would like to proceed and inquired what if any questions she would like to learn more about her and her daughter. Charlene seemed surprised and asked if it would be okay to just start by talking and the clinician agreed to this. This approach reduced the sense of scrutiny and eased the feeling that she was at "another doctor's office." Charlene began by talking about her most immediate concern: Her frustration and exhaustion from Nia's frequent night waking.

Charlene reported being sleep deprived and considerably frustrated with Nia's waking. Early therapeutic work involved understanding and normalizing this behavior and helping Charlene to develop a consistent sleep routine for Nia. Discussions of sleep issues—a common complaint among new parents—allowed the clinician to express empathy and to collaborate with Charlene in a way that further strengthened the therapeutic relationship.

When, after a few sessions, the new sleep routine began to pay off with Nia sleeping longer stretches at night, the therapeutic relationship benefitted as a result. Discussion of Charlene's experience of exhaustion allowed her to vent about an issue that was neutral and less charged than the CPS report. It also led the clinician to inquire more about Charlene's supports at home and to wonder aloud why, although she lived with her mother and sister, she seemed to feel so alone and unsupported during a time when any new parent would need support.

Early Treatment: Ghosts in the Nursery Emerge

Charlene tentatively opened up about her relationship with her mother and the clinician began to learn more about her history. Ever since telling her mother that she was pregnant, Charlene felt that her mother had turned her back on her, offering more criticism and judgment than support. Similarly, Charlene said that her older sister often sided with her mother, leaving her feeling isolated and alone. She said that she did not know why Nia was born prematurely and did not gain weight. The clinician wondered initially about maternal substance use, but toxicology reports were negative. Charlene expressed concern that because of Nia's prematurity and lack of weight gain she would grow up being frail, vulnerable, and unable to protect herself as an adult. She presented herself as streetwise and tough, a former high school track star who said she would never let another person get the best of her. Still, the clinician wondered about Charlene's own feelings of vulnerability and how this might be influencing her fears about her daughter.

As they continued to form a therapeutic alliance, Charlene and the clinician worked together to develop a better understanding of the scope of their work. For Charlene, two of the most important initial goals were helping Nia get more sleep and better understanding the reasons for her difficulty in gaining weight. She also expressed frustration with the CPS case and mentioned wanting it to be closed. Several implicit goals began to emerge over the initial weeks of treatment: Helping Charlene navigate her role as a new parent, better understanding her relationship with her mother, and encouraging greater responsiveness and understanding in her relationship with her daughter. As the initial treatment progressed, Charlene became very explicit about wishing to have a different kind of relationship with her daughter than she had with her mother. This desire opened a pathway of discussion that encouraged a deepening of self-awareness and reflection.

After 2 months of treatment, Charlene seemed to feel better and made more eye contact during sessions. Nia, because of her prematurity and her struggles to gain weight, was still underweight and often slept during sessions. This sense of quiet initially created space for Charlene to reflect on her experience of herself and Nia without any pressure for her to be responsive to Nia's needs. As Nia, now 7 months old, began to be awake for more of the sessions, the clinician began to address her directly in order to acknowledge Nia's subjectivity and his awareness of her as a person with her own needs and desires separate from her mother's. Similarly, Nia's vocalizations and smiles became another opportunity for reflection about the meaning of her behavior and about Charlene's experience in relation to her.

Charlene's wearing earphones during sessions left the impression of someone who sought to tune out the world around her. As sessions progressed, Charlene began to take out one earpiece to listen but would leave the other in with music still playing. As Nia's curiosity and capacity to reach out and interact with her mother grew, she would often grab at the ear phones and pull them from her mother's ears as if to say to her mother that she wanted her to be more present and pay more attention to her.

After 3 months of weekly treatment, Charlene began to take her earphones off during sessions. During a collateral consultation with the pediatrician, the clinician learned that Nia's weight was beginning to stabilize. Because of her lingering negative feelings towards the pediatrician, Charlene was especially reluctant to reach out to her for advice or support. The clinician worked to facilitate a repair in the relationship by asking for information from the pediatrician at Charlene's request, and encouraging her to ask such questions herself when she was ready to do so.

Feeding became an important part of the sessions. At first it appeared that Charlene needed to show the clinician how well she was feeding Nia by methodically preparing and giving her the bottle during session. Little by little however, Charlene began to ask the clinician to help with the preparation of the bottle. She would direct the clinician to fill the bottle with just the right combination of hot and cold water to arrive at the right temperature for Nia. Charlene would test the water before giving it to Nia and sometimes would send the clinician back to adjust the water temperature at her direction. The clinician understood this interaction as reflecting an important expression of care and support that Charlene did not feel comfortable asking for with her own family, but was increasingly feeling able to ask of the clinician. In contrast to the collaborative experience that developed in sessions around the preparation of Nia's bottle, at home Charlene continued to find criticism and conflict. For instance, Charlene began to use the blender to make homemade baby food. On one occasion, when Charlene forgot to unplug the blender, her mother became so upset with her that she hid it from her and told her that she could no longer use it. This hurt and confused Charlene, who expressed anger at her mother.

As Charlene began to open up about her significant relationships, the clinician asked more directly about her experience of Nia's birth and the following months. She initially struggled to put words to her experiences and later said that she had never been asked much about herself. She said that her family did not talk about such things. Charlene said that the pregnancy was unplanned but said little else about Nia's father, Anthony. According to Charlene, Nia had seen Anthony only a few times since the birth and he was not involved in her life. Regarding Nia's difficult birth, Charlene said that Nia had stopped growing in utero and needed to be delivered via emergency surgery. She described feeling confused, overwhelmed, and alone and was convinced that both she and Nia might not survive the surgery. She described feeling physically and emotionally disconnected from Nia as she recovered in the NICU for several weeks. She continued to worry that Nia might not survive. In addition to struggling with depression, Charlene used avoidance as a response to the trauma of Nia's prematurity and fragility at birth, part of a pattern of attachment that fends off emotional closeness as a means of protection against the danger of loss and resulting emotional pain.

Charlene revealed a pattern of distant relationships with family. She described a pattern of important people disappearing from her life without explanation, including her two brothers and father. Charlene's father now lived nearby but had 12 children from several different partners. Charlene described feeling close to and protected by him when she was little but had few interactions with him in recent years. As Charlene continued to discuss the dynamics in her family, she expressed longing for a mother who could be there to support her in the way that she wanted. She painted a picture of her mother as a distant figure who rarely spoke with her or asked about her and whose support of her when she was growing up was limited to her athletic potential. Charlene got a scholarship to run track in college but a knee injury in her freshman year hampered her attempts to pursue that dream. She dropped out the following year and after a few years at home became pregnant. She said that her mother had stopped supporting her after she told her about the pregnancy, and often treated her as if she were a nuisance around the house. She said that she sometimes berated her and called her stupid.

Charlene said that she knew very little about her mother's history and family. She said that her mother had one sister who was mentally ill and who was apparently in a hospital somewhere. She also said that her mother had another sibling who lived nearby but whom Charlene barely knew and about whom her mother never spoke. Charlene revealed a culture of silence in her family, a culture in which members did not speak about important matters and showed little interest in or capacity for self-reflection. People who experience trauma often use avoidance and emotional distancing as a means of self-protection. The clinician modeled that knowledge can be safe. Putting words to feelings, encouraging greater capacity for self-reflection, and fostering a different kind of relationship between Charlene and her daughter became implicit goals of the evolving treatment.

As Charlene became more curious about her family during therapy, she asked her mother more questions at home. Each question was met with silence or rejection. One afternoon Charlene was in her mother's room when she uncovered personal papers on her mother's desk, one of which was her mother's birth certificate. The certificate had a different name listed for her mother's parents than she recognized, and her mother's birth date was the same but her maiden name was also different. Charlene confronted her mother with this information and her mother refused to address it, telling her to mind her own business.

The mystery surrounding her mother's identity and questions about why she had cut off ties with her parents stirred new questions and feelings in Charlene. The caring attention that she received in the therapeutic relationship caused Charlene to long for deeper relationships with the important people in her life. Charlene began to feel a kind of empathy for her mother, imagining that difficult things had happened to her when she was little that had impacted her ability to be the kind of mother that she wanted to be. She attempted to tell her mother how she felt about their relationship and how she would like their relationship to be. At one point, with the help of the clinician, she wrote a letter to her mother saying that she would like to do more things together and fight less.

These attempts to reach out to her mother led her to seek greater closeness in her relationship with Nia and to vow that things would be different between them. She was increasingly able to better care for herself and her daughter. As she began to understand and express her own relational needs, she was more able to be attentive and engaged with Nia, seeming to take pleasure in Nia's ever-changing development. Nia, now nearly 9 months old, was steadily gaining weight. Although still delayed due to her prematurity, she was sitting up and making gains developmentally. Charlene's affect appeared brighter too. She seemed to enjoy our sessions and to feel safe to speak about the things in her life that concerned her.

Another sign of the strength of the growing therapeutic relationship was that when Charlene was mistakenly given a referral to a home visiting program offering similar therapeutic services, Charlene expressed confusion and declined to follow up on the referral telling the referring social worker that she already had a therapist. Charlene said, "I told her this is where we come to talk about things now."

A Disruption in Treatment: Experience of Trauma

When Nia was 10 months old, Charlene who had always been consistent in attending sessions, suddenly did not show up or call for the scheduled session. The clinician called and left a message on her phone but did not hear back from her. Later in the afternoon, the clinician received a call from the Child Protective Services worker, a clinical social worker, saying that Charlene had been attacked by Anthony while she was holding Nia during a visit to his home.

Charlene did not come to therapy for the next two weeks and did not return the clinician's phone calls expressing concern. When she arrived for the session the following week, the faint outline of a black eye was still visible. Charlene was wearing her earphones again and avoided eye contact. Nia was screaming inconsolably in the waiting room and Charlene appeared tired and withdrawn. She said that she had lost Nia's pacifier. Charlene sat down with a blank expression. She complained about Nia's unending screams. The clinician told Charlene that he had been concerned about them and that he had wondered where they were and how they were doing when he did not hear from them. Charlene did not respond. The clinician told Charlene that he had heard from the social worker that something terrible had happened and that Anthony had attacked her while she was with Nia. Charlene nodded. She said that he "got off a cheap shot while I wasn't looking." She described how she tried to defend herself and to protect Nia by putting her down on the bed so that Nia would not be hurt.

Charlene expressed feeling angry, betrayed, and confused. She described calling the police and filing a report. She said that she fled without Nia, leaving her in Anthony's apartment so that she could call the police. She said it was all that she could do. She explained that she feared for her life. The clinician acknowledged how difficult it must have been for both of them and how scared they both must have been. Nia calmed down but appeared exhausted and on edge.

It became apparent over the next few sessions that Charlene's depressive symptoms had returned and that her growing capacity to think about and care for Nia was being threatened by the recent trauma. At the start of one session, she left Nia in the waiting room while she went to the bathroom, leaving Nia screaming. Charlene expressed that she could no longer tolerate Nia's cries and that she did not know why Nia was crying or what to do about it. The clinician asked, "I wonder if she was frightened when she didn't see you. She must have wondered where you went and when you would be back. With her cries she was saying, 'Where did my mommy go? Who are these people I don't know.'" This led Charlene to reflect on her own feelings of distrust in other people and her desire to keep to herself and not leave the house. She revealed a history of verbal and emotional abuse from Anthony. She said that, when they were together, Anthony frequently called her stupid and told her she was worthless.

Despite such abuse, Charlene explained that she wanted Nia to know her father and to have a good relationship with him. She explained that this is why she sought him out for the visit that led to the violence. Charlene could not understand what caused Anthony to attack her. She wondered if he was using drugs or was mentally ill. The clinician continued to link Charlene's feeling of overwhelm, anxiety, and intolerance for Nia's cries with her experience of the violence, working to normalize her heightened affect by putting it in the context of the trauma.

After the trauma, Nia's sleep difficulties returned and Charlene withdrew further from her relationships with her family. During one session, as she was discussing the trauma, Charlene said quietly, "I'm having a moment." When the clinician asked what this meant, she said that it is a phrase she used when she felt upset and it helped her to calm down. The clinician asked where she felt this upset feeling and Charlene pointed to the core of her body. She said that she had been having this since the attack and that she worried that she was "going coo coo." The clinician worked to normalize this response to the trauma and explained the way that such stressful events can affect one's body. Despite the fact that this was frightening for Charlene, the clinician understood this revelation as a sign that Charlene's reflective function was improving, an important aspect of secure attachment relationships.

The clinician also worked to link Charlene's frustrations with Nia's cries with her scared and dysregulated feelings in the aftermath of the domestic violence. During one session, Charlene said, "She gets so upset when I am making the bottle. She gets so angry at me." The therapist said, "I think she is letting you know how hungry she is." Charlene said, "But she can't go on having a short temper like this. People will think she's crazy." The clinician linked this fear that others would think that Nia was crazy with her concerns that she would be "like Anthony" who had surprised her by becoming violent with both of them. Charlene said she was worried that Nia would be an angry person, that she would blame Charlene for what happened, and that she would treat Charlene the same way her father did.

During one session in which Charlene was discussing the impact of the violence, and Nia, 11 months old now, was particularly fussy, the clinician turned to Nia and said, "Your mommy told me that your daddy hit your mommy while she was holding you, and you were so little, and scared and couldn't do anything to stop it." Nia became very still and looked at the clinician with rapt attention and then turned back to her mother, burrowing her face in her shirt. Charlene said, "Do you think she remembers what happened? Nia, mommy is so sorry. Mommy loves you." She hugged Nia close. This exchange created the opportunity to reflect on Nia's experience of the trauma and to discuss how children her age remember scary experiences.

As the clinician and Charlene continued to discuss her feelings about the assault, Charlene expressed deep shame at being attacked in front of her daughter and at having her daughter see her as weak and helpless. She felt that she abandoned Nia when she left her with Anthony. Still, her ambivalent feelings about Anthony and her desire for Nia to know her father made it difficult for her to want to pursue charges against him. She eventually decided to proceed, saying, "He needs to learn that he can't hurt us like that." Anthony was convicted and sent to county jail. Charlene felt proud of herself for setting an example for her daughter but also felt fearful of Anthony's reaction once he was released.

Putting words to these and other feelings seemed to give Charlene great relief but her "moments" continued, especially when she was reminded of the trauma. To more concretely address Charlene's anxiety, the clinician offered to show her several mindfulness-based breathing exercises and progressive relaxation designed to increase her ability to regulate her body when she became anxious or upset. After experimenting with these techniques at home, Charlene said that they helped her to calm herself down including after having a difficult exchange with her mother. Charlene would later remember to use the same techniques when feeling nervous before a job interview and reported them being helpful.

Re-experiencing the Trauma

After Anthony was sent to jail, his mother began to reach out to Charlene and to express an interest in seeing her granddaughter. Charlene was hesitant at first, but as they began to see more of each other, Charlene began to trust this maternal figure who expressed more warmth and concern for her than her own mother. This growing relationship was complicated when Anthony was released from jail and began coming to his mother's house. He also began calling Charlene to express interest in seeing Nia, which was a violation of the restraining order. Charlene resisted Anthony's attempts to get in touch with her and was clear that she did not want to see him.

One afternoon, when Nia was 13 months old, Charlene was startled when Anthony answered the door at his mother's house as she arrived with Nia for a visit. Charlene was terrified. She described later that her heart began to race and she began to sweat as she had visions of the assault. She was so flustered that, in an instant, she decided to leave Nia at the house for the visit and to go on a walk in the neighborhood to calm down. Later in session, the clinician and Charlene discussed Nia's reaction to being left with Anthony; Charlene was unsure. She was so flooded with feelings herself that she did not notice her daughter's state. The next week Charlene reported that Nia was fussy the whole week and that she was not sleeping well. The clinician wondered aloud if this was Nia's way of saying what it was like for her to see her father and that she, like her mother, was affected by seeing him. Charlene said she was not sure what Nia remembered about what happened or what she thought of her father. Later Charlene admitted that she was scared and was able to make a connection between Nia's fussy behavior after the visit and her own feelings about seeing Anthony. After the session, Charlene called Anthony's mother to tell her that she did not want to see Anthony during the visits, as seeing Anthony was a violation of the restraining order and upsetting to her and Nia.

During this time, the clinician spoke directly with Nia, now over a year old, about seeing her daddy and about being with him without her mommy. When the clinician spoke to Nia about this, Nia would look at the clinician intensely. During one of these moments Charlene said, "I think she understands what you are saying. She remembers. She knows who she was with." The clinician understood this to be an important sign that Charlene was making connections between Nia's emotional experience and her awareness of the trauma.

Other aspects of Nia's behavior began to trigger Charlene's memory of the trauma. When Nia hit her mother in what appeared to be an accidental or playful way Charlene reacted to her by yelling at her to stop. Charlene feared that when her daughter became upset that she was "crazy like her dad." Other times she worried that her daughter "doesn't like me." The clinician attempted to carefully link these attributions to the experience of the trauma, which helped Charlene continue to integrate and recover from the effects of the assault. Her concerns about her relationship with her daughter also led her to express her longing for the loving, supportive relationship with her mother that she always wanted.

Improvement and Consolidation

As the treatment progressed, the collaborative relationship between the clinician and the CPS social worker became a critical part of the ongoing treatment. It was important to be transparent with Charlene about any communications with the social worker. Similarly, when the pediatric staff asked for updates about the case, the clinician asked Charlene what information she felt comfortable being shared and tried to limit information that was relevant to Nia's health and well being. Throughout the treatment, the CPS social worker was actively involved in monitoring Nia's progress and yet remained respectful of Charlene's privacy.

As Nia's weight and development improved and the end of the CPS case was in sight, the CPS social worker began receiving calls from Charlene's mother stating that Charlene was endangering Nia at home. Although Charlene's mother would not give specifics, the social worker was concerned. After a series of visits to the home and calls to the pediatrician and the clinician, the CPS worker began to believe that it was the relationship between Charlene and her mother that needed attention. During a consultation with the clinician, the clinician suggested a meeting between Charlene and her mother to be facilitated by a therapist at CPS. The social worker and the clinician agreed that mother and daughter could use a place to talk about their relationship and that this would best be done with another therapist. Charlene agreed that she did not want her mother to come to her child–parent therapy, because she felt it would be an intrusion into the safe space that was created. She and the clinician prepared a written list of feelings and thoughts that she would like to communicate to her mother in the meeting including, "I would like us to spend more time together with Nia and go places like we did when I was little."

Charlene's mother cancelled the CPS meeting several times before attending a meeting. According to the social worker, Charlene's mother appeared angry and resentful of Charlene. She repeated her belief that Charlene was endangering Nia. She said that she did not clean up after herself and played loud music in her room at home. When Charlene invited her mother to meet regularly with the CPS appointed therapist and read her the list she had prepared, her mother was evasive. Finally, she agreed to meet the following week but did not show for the meeting. Charlene expressed sadness and confusion about this in her own therapy. Still, much to Charlene's relief, the social worker indicated that there was no reason for CPS to keep the case open any longer.

When the CPS case was finally closed, Charlene called the clinician to leave a celebratory message on his voicemail even though she knew he was out of town. Despite occasional setbacks, Charlene and Nia seemed to be recovering from the trauma. A significant shift occurred as Nia, initially delayed in her gross motor skills, began to crawl—and, later, walk—in the therapy room. As Nia explored the space, the clinician suggested to Charlene that they move to the floor so that they could interact more readily with Nia. The clinician also wondered what Nia might like to play with and invited Charlene to help choose toys that she thought Nia would enjoy. Charlene appeared reluctant at first but as she moved to the floor, it became clear how much Nia enjoyed this newfound attention and focus on her.

Charlene enjoyed this change as well, remarking that she wished that Nia could be so relaxed at home and saying that she wished she had more toys that she could play with there. The clinician and Charlene brainstormed about ways that Charlene could create developmentally appropriate toys for Nia out of common household items and Charlene experimented with this at home reporting that she and Nia had spent time together that was enjoyable and free of worry and stress.

As the work continued, Charlene's guilt and confusion about Nia's prematurity and early feeding problems, which were exacerbated by the domestic violence, occasionally led her to feed Nia whatever she wanted in order to reassure herself that she was a good mother. The clinician continued to work with Charlene to develop insight into these feelings. Also, as Nia became more mobile and moved into toddlerhood, Charlene struggled to set limits with her out of fear of upsetting her. Charlene disclosed that she tried to give Nia whatever she wanted because, when Nia got upset, Charlene worried that Nia would be a sad and angry person the rest of her life. With some well-timed developmental guidance, Charlene came to understand that limit setting was actually healthy for Nia and would eventually lead her to feel safer and more relaxed.

As Charlene gained confidence as a parent, she saw greater possibility that things could be different at home. Being able to observe Nia become more curious about the objects and toys in the office and to see her interactions and smiles at the clinician allowed Charlene to think of Nia differently. Similarly, as Charlene's relationship with the clinician grew, her ambivalence and conflict about Nia's attachment and need of her receded. Her growing ability to experience trust and safety in another person continued to increase her capacity as a mother.

The mutual decision to move to the floor during sessions was especially significant because it helped to facilitate Charlene's acknowledgment of Nia's separateness as a person with interests, capacities, and ideas of her own—an awareness that was greatly impeded by the trauma. This was especially important because it challenged an intergenerational pattern in which Charlene had been treated by her mother as an extension of her mother's unfulfilled potential rather than as an individual with her own needs and desires. She was treated as the child who would fulfill her mother's dreams of going to college and of succeeding in ways that she never felt that she could.

Charlene's depression receded over the course of the treatment. She took appropriate steps to enroll Nia in daycare, sought training for new employment and got a job. She started saving money and looking for a place of her own where she hoped that she and her daughter would create an environment that would be more hospitable and nurturing of their relationship. She talked of returning to school to finish college in order to study sports psychology so that she could help young athletes succeed in their careers. Charlene's relationships with women also began to improve. She developed a trusting relationship with Anthony's mom and a relationship with her paternal aunt.

Nia's language capacities steadily developed which decreased her frustration. Charlene followed through on pediatrician referrals for speech and language evaluation, as well as a nutritionist visit to learn how to foster healthy eating habits. Most importantly, Charlene's capacity to reflect on and express a full range of feelings with respect to herself and her daughter markedly improved. Her work with the clinician helped her to better care for herself and her baby, both of which were impaired by the depression and her unresolved attachment relationships and compounded by the trauma. Although Charlene had faced serious challenges from her postpartum depression, the trauma of the domestic violence and lack of family support, her work with the clinician helped her have a different relationship with her daughter than she had with her mother.

Conclusion

Trauma damages the capacity to connect with others and to access one's internal resources (Lieberman and Amaya-Jackson 2005; Lieberman and Van Horn 2008). Charlene had never been in therapy and had had little opportunity to cultivate self-awareness. Her unresolved attachment relationship with her mother and postpartum depression caused her to have difficulty forming trusting, intimate relationships, including with her own daughter. Her feelings of abandonment by her mother put her at risk of repeating this dynamic with Nia. Prior to therapy, she continued in an abusive relationship that reinforced a depressive sense of herself. As the abuse escalated and then turned into violence, Charlene's relationship with her daughter became impaired as both suffered the effects of the trauma.

The relationship with the clinician facilitated the repair of the trauma and allowed Charlene to strengthen her relationship with her daughter, improving her capacity to protect and nourish her and to become a secure base for her growing explorations, all key goals of child–parent psychotherapy (Busch and Lieberman 2007; Lieberman and Van Horn 2008). By developing a strong attachment relationship with the clinician, Charlene was able to better understand and express her feelings of hurt, disappointment, and anger about her relationship with her mother and to begin to trust another person. Her growing reflective capacity in the context of this relationship allowed her to make meaning of the trauma without it further damaging her relationship with her daughter. This in turn allowed her to develop closer relationships and to return to work.

Although the referral to child protective services was a source of rupture between the pediatrician and Charlene, Charlene later proudly celebrated Nia's weight gain with her, highlighting the importance of the gradual repair of the attachment relationship with her child's doctor, whose referral to CPS may have otherwise caused Charlene to leave the clinic.

When Charlene finally moved out of her mother's home, she did so in order to gain some independence and to create a safer emotional environment to raise Nia. One unintended consequence of the move was that Nia could no longer be seen at the clinic using the state-funded health care plan that required her to get care in her county of residence. Rather than simply referring her to another provider, Nia's pediatrician and the clinician worked together to ensure that Nia could continue to receive services at the clinic and to benefit from the trusted relationships that she had established there. While it remained a source of sadness for Charlene that repair was not possible in her relationship with her own mother, she used her growing internal resources to continue to make positive changes for herself and her daughter.

Recommendations for Practitioners

Families and children who experience trauma stand to benefit from the thoughtful, cross-disciplinary collaboration of medical and mental health providers in unconventional settings such as the community pediatric clinic (Groves and Augustyn 2011). In the case example, the clinic-based treatment and ongoing collaboration with the pediatrician allowed the clinician to support the mother as she navigated the complexities of the relationships between the doctor, her daughter, her extended family, and the CPS social worker. This collaboration helped to preserve the mother's fragile relationship with the pediatrician whose referral to CPS was initially experienced as such a betrayal. Had the patient been seen at another clinic, communication about the patient's care may have faltered, raising the possibility of further CPS intervention.

The co-location of physical and mental health services in community health settings acknowledges the fact that psychological problems are often the greatest barrier to physical wellbeing. Practitioners of various disciplines hear different stories and hold different aspects of the families they serve. Bringing such differing perspectives together, in coordination of care, benefits families as well as the systems that serve them. Social workers and psychologists seeking innovative ways to engage high-risk families from socio-economically marginalized communities may consider closer collaboration with pediatricians. Pediatricians can also benefit from maintaining a heightened awareness of the impact of trauma on the health and well being of their patients (Burke et al. in press; Groves and Augustyn 2011). The trauma screen developed at BCHC is a useful tool to engage families in a conversation about the emotional and psychological consequences of trauma that put their children at risk for disease later in life. The screen de-stigmatizes the trauma, creating a dialogue about a topic that is often experienced as shameful.

The use of multi-disciplinary rounds is an effective way of mitigating the long-term effects of secondary traumatization and brings clarity to the referral process through direct consultation and the sharing of resources and expertise. The multi-disciplinary rounds process also relieves the pediatrician of the responsibility of delving into traumatic material with the patient. Medical doctors often are reluctant to ask about the emotional impact of trauma for fear of eliciting emotional material for which they have little training about how to respond (Groves and Augustyn 2011). Social workers and psychologists can support the community-based medical community by becoming engaged in forging closer alliances with doctors and nurses and by advocating for the use of a comprehensive trauma screen. Such alliances serve to mitigate the impact of trauma on children's physical, emotional, and psychological development. Trauma–focused interventions such as child–parent psychotherapy increase parents' ability to respond to their children's needs, and are effective in engaging hard to reach families cross-culturally (Lieberman 1990; Lieberman and Van Horn 2008; Gosh Ippen and Lewis 2011). At a time when medical and psychological services are increasingly specialized, this integrative model of cross-disciplinary collaboration provides an effective attachment-based treatment for children and families affected by trauma while strengthening our ability to support and learn from each other.

References

Brazelton, T. B. (1992). *Touchpoints: Your child's emotional and behavioral development*. Reading: Addison–Wesley.
Bronfenbrenner, U. (1977). Toward and experimental ecology of human development. *American Psychologist, 32,* 513–531.
Burke, N. J., Hellman, J. L, Scott, B. G., Weems, C. F., & Carrion, V. G. (2011, in press). The Impact of adverse childhood experiences on an urban pediatric population. *Child Abuse and Neglect.* doi:10.1016/j.chiabu.2011.02.006.
Busch, A. L., & Lieberman, A. F. (2007). Attachment and trauma: An integrated approach to treating young children exposed to family violence. In D. Oppenheim & D. F. Goldsmith (Eds.), *Attachment theory in clinical work with children: Bridging the gap between research and practice* (pp. 139–171). New York: Guilford.

Cicchetti, D., & Lynch, M. (1993). Toward and ecological/transactional model of community violence and child maltreatment: Consequences for children's development. *Psychiatry: Interpersonal and Biological Processes, 56,* 96–118.

Cohen, J. A., Kelleher, K. J., & Mannarino, A. P. (2008). Identifying, treating, and referring traumatized children: The role of pediatric providers. *Archives of Pediatric and Adolescent Medicine, 162,* 447–452.

Devore, W., & Schlesinger, E. G. (1981). *Ethnic-sensitive social work practice.* St. Louis: C.V. Mosby.

Diller, J. V. (1999). *Cultural diversity: A primer for the human services.* Belmont: Wadsworth.

Felitti, V. J., Anda, R. F., Nordenberg, D., et al. (1998). Relationship of childhood abuse and household dysfunction to many of the leading causes of death in adults: The adverse childhood experiences (ACE) study. *American Journal of Preventive Medicine, 14,* 245–258.

Figley, C. R. (1996). *Compassion fatigue: Coping with secondary traumatic stress disorder in those who treat the traumatized.* New York: Brunner/Mazel.

Fraiberg, S. (Ed.). (1980). *Clinical studies in infant mental health: The first year of life.* New York: Basic Books.

Freud, S. (1959). Inhibitions, symptoms and anxiety. In J. Strachey (Ed. & Trans.), *The standard edition of the complete psychological works of Sigmund Freud* (Vol. 4, pp. 87–156). London: Hogarth. (Original work published in 1926).

Gaensbauer, T. J. (1995). Trauma in the preverbal period: Symptoms, memories, and developmental impact. *The Psychoanalytic Study of the Child, 50,* 122–149.

Gosh Ippen, C., & Lewis, M. L. (2011). They just don't get it: A diversity-informed approach to understanding engagement. In J. D. Osofsky (Ed.), *Clinical work with traumatized young children* (pp. 31–52). New York: Guilford.

Groves, M. B., & Augustyn, M. (2011). The role of pediatric practitioners in identifying and responding to traumatized children. In J. D. Osofsky (Ed.), *Clinical work with traumatized young children* (pp. 313–335). New York: Guildford.

Groves, M. B., & Augustyn, M. (2004). Identification, assessment, and intervention for traumatized children within a pediatric setting. In J. Osofsky (Ed.), *Young children and trauma.* New York: Guilford.

Hernandez Dimmler, M., Gutiérrez Wang, L., Van Horn, P., & Lieberman, A. F. (in press). Dissemination and implementation of child–parent psychotherapy: Collaboration with community programs. In A. Rubin & David W. Springer (Eds.), *Programs and interventions for maltreated children and families at risk.*

Kiefer, Christie W. (2000). *Health work with the poor: A practical guide.* New Brunswick: Rutgers.

Lieberman, A. F. (1990). Culturally sensitive intervention with children and families. *Child and Adolescent Social Work, 7,* 101–119.

Lieberman, A. F. (2004). Traumatic stress and quality of attachment: Reality and internalization in disorders of infant mental health. *Infant Mental Health Journal, 25,* 336–351.

Lieberman, A. F., & Amaya-Jackson, L. (2005). Reciprocal influences of attachment and trauma: Using a dual lens in the assessment and treatment of infants, toddlers, and preschoolers. In L. J. Berlin, Y. Xiv, L. Amaya-Jackson, & M. T. Greenberg (Eds.), *Enhancing early attachments: Theory, research, intervention, and policy* (pp. 100–124). New York: Guildford.

Lieberman, A. F., & Van Horn, P. (2005). *Don't hit my mommy!: A manual for child–parent psychotherapy with young witnesses of family violence.* Washington, DC: Zero to Three.

Lieberman, A. F., & Van Horn, P. (2008). *Psychotherapy with infants and young children: Repairing the effects of stress and trauma on early attachment.* New York: Guildford.

Lieberman, A. F., & Van Horn, P. (2009). Giving voice to the unsayable: Repairing the effects of trauma in infancy and early childhood. *Child and Adolescent Psychiatric Clinics of North America, 18,* 707–720.

Lieberman A. F., Ghosh Ippen, C., & Van Horn, P. (2006). Child–parent psychotherapy: 6-month follow-up of a randomized controlled trial. *Journal of the American Academy of Child and Adolescent Psychiatry, 45,* 913–918.

Lyons-Ruth, K., & Jacobvitz, D. (1999). Attachment disorganization: Unresolved loss, relational violence, and lapses in behavioral and attentional strategies. In J. Cassidy & P. R. Shaver (Eds.), *Handbook of attachment: Theory, research, and clinical application* (pp. 520–554). New York: Guilford.

McCann, L., & Pearlmann, L. A. (1990). Vicarious traumatization: A framework for understanding the psychological effects of working with victims. *Journal of Traumatic Stress, 3*(1), 131–149.

National Center for Infants, Toddlers and Families. (2005). *Diagnostic classification of mental health and developmental disorders of infancy and early childhood* (DC:0–3R) (revised). Washington, DC: Zero to Three.

Northern California Council for the Community. (2004). Community health assessment: Building a healthier San Francisco. Accessed from: http://www.hospitalcouncil.net/sites/main/files/file-attachments/sfdph.2004_community_needs_assessment.20041.pdf.

Renschler, T. S. (2009). Sleeping on the couch: Interpretation-in-action in infant-parent psychotherapy. *Journal of Infant, Child, and Adolescent Psychotherapy, 8,* 145–155.

Sanders Thompson, V. L., Bazile, A., & Akbar, M. (2004). African Americans' perception of psychotherapy and psychotherapists. *Professional Psychology: Research and Practice, 35,* 19–26.

Scheeringa, M. S., & Zeanah, C. H. (1995a). Symptom differences in traumatized infants and young children. *Infant Mental Health Journal, 16,* 259–270.

Scheeringa, M. S., & Zeanah, C. H. (1995b). Symptom expression and trauma variables in children under 48 months of age. *Infant Mental Health Journal, 16,* 259–70.

Scheeringa, M. S., & Zeanah C. H. (2001). A relational perspective on PTSD in early childhood. *Journal of Traumatic Stress, 14,* 799–815.

Seligman S., & Pawl, J. H. (1984). Impediments to the formation of the working alliance in infant–parent psychotherapy. In J. D. Call, E. Galenson, & R. Tyson (Eds.), *Frontiers of infant psychiatry*. (Vol. 2, pp. 232–237). New York: Basic Books.

Silverman, R. C., & Lieberman, A. F. (1999). Negative maternal attributions, projective identification, and the intergenerational transmission of violent relational patterns. *Psychoanalytic Dialogues, 9,* 161–186.

St. John, M., & Lieberman, A. F. (in press). The "talking/playing/doing cure" in the parent–child matrix: Child–parent psychotherapy in the treatment of infants and young children. In P. Luyten, L. Mayes, P. Fonagy, M. Target, & S. J. Blatt (Eds.), *Handbook of contemporary psychodynamic approaches to psychopathology*. New York: Guilford.

Tough, P. (21 March 2011). The poverty clinic. *The New Yorker,* 25–32.

Williams, T. M. (2008). *Black pain*. New York: Scribner.

The Essential Role of the Body in the Parent–Infant Relationship: Nonverbal Analysis of Attachment

Suzi Tortora

This chapter focuses on the imperative role of body/movement experience, nonverbal understanding, nonverbal expression, and the felt-experiential nature of interpersonal exchange in early childhood development. It explores how a mental and emotional sense of self is linked to an experiential bodily felt state on both an intrapersonal and interpersonal level. The concepts in this chapter follow the dissolution of the Cartesian theory of a mind–body dualism (Damasio 1994/2005), instead working from the concept that a continuum exists between the mind, the body, and the emotions (Tortora 2006).

Nonverbal movements are a powerful communication tool (Tortora 1994, 2004, 2006). The therapist gains insight into a patient's sense of self through observing personal nonverbal styles. The therapist obtains key information about the developing attachment relationship between an infant and parent through observing their dyadic nonverbal exchange (Tortora 2006, 2010, 2011).

The focal point of dance movement psychotherapy philosophy and intervention methodology is the role of the body, nonverbal communication, and movement experiences in development of self (Bartenieff and Lewis 1980; Levy 2005; Tortora, 1994, 2004, 2006, 2010, 2011). This chapter explains the relationship between dance movement psychotherapy and infant mental health, through the *Ways of Seeing* psychotherapy program developed by this author. It provides a comprehensive review of specific infancy mental health theories and attachment research, highlighting current thinking about the essential role the body, movement, and nonverbal experience play in the development of the emotional self. An introduction to the nonverbal parent–child attachment relationship analysis system developed by this author called Dyadic, Attachment-based, Nonverbal, Communicative Expressions (D.A.N.C.E.) exists elsewhere (Tortora 2010, 2011); this chapter will focus on its application.

D.A.N.C.E.'s observation method offers a systematic way to organize nonverbal interactions between individuals, especially parents and infants. It provides a means

---

S. Tortora (✉)
Dancing Dialogue: Healing and Expressive Arts, New York, NY, USA
e-mail: suzitortora@mac.com

J. E. Bettmann, D. D. Friedman (eds.), *Attachment-Based Clinical Work with Children and Adolescents,* Essential Clinical Social Work Series,
DOI 10.1007/978-1-4614-4848-8_7, © Springer Science+Business Media New York 2013

of communication and understanding through nonverbal movement analysis and dialogue between the therapist, the child, and the parent, when used within the context of the psychotherapeutic milieu.

Experiences Outside of Verbal Conscious Awareness

There is a growing interest among infant mental health researchers, psychoanalysts, and theorists in understanding the infant's experience occurring outside of verbal conscious awareness (Boston Process Change Study Group 2010; Stern 1985, 2004, 2008, 2009, 2010; Malloch and Trevarthen 2009; Trevarthen 2009). The infant's nonverbal experiences have been analyzed to explain his/her experience of self and other in the developing attachment relationship. Specifically, the authors have explored how the infant learns to process information during the development of a sense of self (Stern 2004; Boston Process Change Study Group 2010)—infant memory (Gaensbauer 2004, 2011)—and how this information can inform parent–infant psychotherapy (Boston Process Change Study Group 2010; Downing 2005, 2008; Trevarthen 2009; Malloch and Trevarthen 2009).

Notably, the authors describe the nonverbal realm of our personal and social lives differently: "lived experience" (Pally 2001, p. 72), "body to body, biology to biology" (Pally 2001, p. 72), "lived interactions and implicit experiencing" (Boston Process Change Study Group 2010, p. 195), "social connectedness" (Meltzoff and Brooks 2007, p 149), "implicit knowing" (Stern 2004, p. 112), "moment-to-moment implicit processes" (Beebe and Lachmann 2002, p. 210), "intersubjectivity" (Trevarthen 1979, p. 521), and "perceptual–cognitive–affective–sensory-motor schemata" (Gaensbauer 2004, p. 29).

Pally (2001) proposes "... language ... causes a rupture between what one says and how one feels, the verbalizable self and the experiencing self" (p. 73). This quote highlights the experiential nature of interactions which occur beyond the realm of verbal conscious understanding. Pally (2001) advocates for analysts to increase their awareness of nonverbal communication during therapeutic exchanges. She draws a distinction between language and nonverbal cues. She places value in the abstract reasoning and self-reflective capacities of the verbalizing self. Pally (2001) states that the nonverbal nature of the experiential self facilitates empathic exchange, emotional expressivity, and physiologic and affective self-regulation. This process occurs without words.

Embodied Experiences

Movement is the primary language in dance movement psychotherapy. Nonverbal actions communicate thoughts, emotions, feelings, and sensations within self and between self and other. The dance therapist is trained to carefully observe the specific details of the patient's nonverbal cues and analyze them within the context of the patient's unique personal movement repertoire. The dance therapist considers movement actions to be forms of expression, revealing the patient's intra- and inter-personal style of relating. The dance therapist develops movement and dance activities in the therapeutic session to experientially explore the patient's emotional life. In the early 1940s and 1950s, the founders of dance movement psychotherapy initially came to this understanding through their personal dance experiences and while working with other dancers through creative and modern dance techniques (Bernstein 1979, 1981; Chace 1953, July 1964, 1968; Chaiklin 1975; Levy 2005; Pallaro 1999; Sandel et al. 1993; Schoop and Mitchell 1974, 1986; Whitehouse 1977, 1999).

Dance therapists now find support for the relationship of movement and self from philosophy, phenomenology, neuroscience, infant mental health, and embodiment and enactment research (Berrol 2006; Bloom 2006; Koch and Fischman 2011; Tortora 2004, 2006, 2010). The philosopher Sheets-Johnstone (2010, p. 2) discusses "the dynamic congruency between emotions and movement..." stating that "moving is a way of knowing" (1998, p. xv) and is at the core of our sense of agency. Dance movement therapists use the term embodiment to describe the relationship between thought, emotional experience, and the felt-body experience in interaction with the surrounding environment (Bloom 2006; Koch 2006; Koch and Fischman 2011). This perspective brings the mind and body together: "unifying perception and action, creativity and recognition, cognition and emotion... [it] reminds us that our existence is related to our own ways of experiencing" (Koch and Fischman 2011, p. 66). Embodiment theory views the integration of different aspects of self, including multisensory, cognitive, and emotional, as developing through the experience of the body (Bloom 2006). From an embodiment perspective, the body-and-body movement, including gestures, postures, and actions through space occur in response to internal and external stimuli (Bloom 2006).

In a dance movement psychotherapy session, a distinct edge arises between the verbalizable and experiencing self, a phenomenon discussed by Pally (2001). The immediacy of the felt experience during the dance/movement exploration exists in the moment. The immediate felt experience is an embodiment of thinking, sensing, and feeling. During dance/movement activities, there is simultaneity between reflection and experiencing. The dance therapist creates dance/movement explorations to support the patient/mover's specific nonverbal expressions and communicates a sense of knowingness about self and body. During the verbal processing aspects of the session, the patient/mover shifts out of the immediacy of the felt moment to engage in the mental task of searching for words to accurately describe and reflect upon the experiential activities in the session. Moving freely across the edge that joins embodied experiencing and verbal reflecting is very powerful. This movement facilitates a deep sense of self as a whole, integrating thought, body, and emotion. Viewing embodiment within the psychotherapeutic process as a way to learn about one's self mirrors the early stages of self-awareness and self and other relationships in infancy and early childhood.

Embodiment and the Attachment Relationship

Infants begin life in embodied experience. Thoughts, sensations, and feelings are one for infants. The mind, body, and emotions are all aspects of self that become known more deeply over the course of development. Nonverbal embodied experience plays a key role in the development of the early attachment relationship.

Winnicott (1971, 1982) addresses the embodied experience between self and other in his statement, "When I look, I am seen, so I exist" (p. 114). Being "seen" (1971, p. 114), in Winnicott's eyes, refers to the infant's subjective experience of seeing self, reflected in the mother's expressive responses toward the infant during their two-way process of engaged looking. Stating that the psyche and soma work together, Winnicott (1972, p. 16) postulates that a sense of self "is naturally placed in the body"and emerges through the infant's experiential explorations with the environment.

Winnicott emphasizes the role of the mother's face as the precursor of the mirror in this first stage of emotional development. The infant's sense of self emerges as early experiences lead to a differentiation between "the not-me from the me" (Winnicott 1971, 1982, p. 111). Stern's work takes this concept further by stating, "Infants are not lost at sea in a wash of abstractable qualities of experience" (Stern 1985, p. 67). He argues that infants establish a differentiated consistent sense of self quite early in development as they systematically begin to order components of experience into "self- and other-invariant constellations" (Stern 1985, 2000, p. 67). Stern describes this early self as developing from two primary senses of self—the emergent self and the core self—which unfold through experiences that are predominantly derived from palpable actions, perceptions, and body sensations.

The attachment theory work of Bowlby (1969) resonates with the physical, experiential nature of infant emotional growth emphasized by Winnicott and Stern. He also states that the communication between the mother and infant occurs through a variety of experience-dependent components, including the tempo of actions that are jointly created through facial expressions and posture, the tone of voice, and gestural exchanges. Bowlby highlights the primary role of the mother providing a safe container for the infant through dynamic, spontaneous nonverbal interactions, which create mental representations that organize the experience for the infant.

Dance Movement Psychotherapy and Infant Development Literature

A key dance movement psychotherapy principle which states that all individuals need to be seen (Bernstein 1979, 1981; Levy 2005; Tortora 2006) reflects Winnicott's (1971) ideas. Being seen implies that all persons have a desire to be known for whom they are as individuals with needs and unique ways of existing. Beginning at birth, this desire manifests through nonverbal expression and experience and helps to define the individual's true authentic self (Tortora 2006; Whitehouse 1999). In a dance movement psychotherapy session, the implications of the need to be seen are both literal and metaphoric. The dance therapist gleans much of her understanding about the patient/mover she is working with through careful detailed analysis of the patient/mover's nonverbal actions. The dance therapist translates information from these observations into communicative dialogues between the dance therapist and the patient/mover through movement, dance, and sensory-based explorations that heighten body awareness and nonverbal self-expression. An individual feels listened to and understood through the dance therapist acknowledging and responding to nonverbal actions as forms of communication. As the patient/mover experiences her nonverbal expressions reflected back, the clarity about herself emerges.

The Winnicottian perspective references the experience of looking and being seen through silent responsive communication between mother and baby as the focus of primary identification (Abram and Hjulmand 2007). Freud (1923) defined primary identification as the initial emotional state in which the infant experiences significant others (most often the parent) as part of self, occurring as a precursor to the ability to make a distinction between self and other. Primary identification is the initial form of emotional attachment within the sequential process of individuation between self and other in the healthy infant. It is how the infant learns about self as separate from other; it enables the infant to feel real and alive (Abram and Hjulmand 2007; Winnicott 1971). The infant feels seen when the mother adapts to his needs (Winnicott 1971).

In dance movement psychotherapy, the process of seeing and being seen does not place emphasis on a primal lack of self-identification as in the Freudian perspective, but rather on the emergence of self through embodied exploration with other. This idea aligns with Stern's concept acknowledging the role of the early body and movement experiences in the emergence of a sense of self (Stern 1985, 2000, 2004, 2008, 2009, 2010). The belief that supporting one to quite literally experience their moving self enables the patient/mover to both discover aspects of self that exist or are evolving is the basis of this concept (Tortora 2006).

Dance movement psychotherapy uses the term dance in its broadest sense (Bloom 2006; Levy 2005; Sandel et al. 1993; Pallaro 1999; Tortora 2006; Whitehouse 1977, 1999). Dance emphasizes the emotionally imbued aspects of all actions and references—the whole spectrum of actions including stillness and internal body sensations such as attuning to the flow of one's breath pattern to very active movements across the space. Dance-in-dance movement psychotherapy accentuates the powerful self-expressive and communicative power of dance. All movements have the potential to be communicative, both to the dancer and the observer (Tortora 2006).

The dance therapist first dialogues with the patient/mover by adapting, mirroring, and attuning her movements to match those of the patient/mover. Dance movement psychotherapy differentiates between mirroring and attuning (Tortora 2006). Mirroring is defined as exactly matching the affective expression, the specific physical actions, and the qualitative feeling tone of the patient/mover's movements (Tortora 2006). As the dance therapist embodies the patient/mover's actions through mirroring, both the therapist and the patient/mover experience the patient/mover's nonverbal communicative references about self. In attunement, the dance therapist does not exactly follow the actions of the patient/mover, but rather responds by complimenting a quality of the patient/mover's actions to create a spontaneous dialogue that can expand the patient/mover's nonverbal vocabulary (Tortora 2006).

A brief case example will illuminate some of these ideas. A 4-year-old toddler had become withdrawn and despondent after the birth of his baby sister. Lying on a pile of pillows, the toddler begins to softly kick his legs in a pulsing rhythm as I approach him. I nod my head to the beat of the toddler's leg kicks. The toddler responds by increasing the speed of his kick. I rock my whole body toward and away from the child, matching the tempo of his kick. The toddler adds more strength to the kick, followed by me embodying this strength in my rocking by making it more vigorous and larger and by adding a leg kick. The toddler stands up, providing more power to his kick by transforming it into a full-body stomping and marching dance. I put on a selection of music that matched the rhythm of his actions and begin to narrate our actions, commenting on how strong and determined the toddler is. The toddler responds by saying, "Yes, I am the king, and no one can come into my kingdom unless I say so!" This sequence was the start of a continued movement play supported by verbal dialogue during which the toddler began to explore his feelings of anger and sadness about the birth of his sister.

The above vignette portrays how a single body action—leg kicking—can transform into a whole mind–body-emotional experience through a nonverbal exchange with the therapist. The embodiment of strength evolves through the jointly created nonverbal exploration. The toddler first fully sensed his feelings of anger in a controlled, organized, and safe manner through the unfolding movement sequences. The therapist saw his display of strength by initially exploring his emotional experience physically; the child then found the words and imagery to explore his feelings through physical expression. As the toddler developed physical and emotional comfort, he learned how to express his feelings of anger while simultaneously regulating his emotions. In the case example above, mirroring and attuning brought aspects of self into heightened conscious awareness for both the patient/mover and the therapist, enabling the patient/mover to own aspects of self that are emerging due to development, that may have been unknown, that were lost due to earlier experiences or trauma, or that were new.

Nonverbal Communication in the First Relationship

Using movement as communication with young children is natural for them. Nonverbal dialogue through attunement and mirroring is how our first relationships begin. Communication between infant and parent occurs through facial expressions, postures, tone of voice, and gestural exchanges, all of which manifest into a jointly created tempo (Bowlby 1981; Papoušek 2007, 2011; Papoušek and Papoušek 1987; Stern 1985, 2000, 2004; Trevarthen 1979, 1980, 2009). The infant begins to make sense and organize these events into predictable action-based sequences between the infant and significant people in the infant's life through the nonverbal exchange, which creates a "shared framework of meaning" (Stern 1985, 2000, p. 125). Repeated nonverbal experiences generalize into presymbolic representations described as "expectancies of actions sequences" (Beebe and Lachmann 2002, p. 212).

The infant feels cared for, seen, and understood through the parent's contingent and reliable responses to the infant's nonverbal cues. A sense of self-efficacy evolves, supporting the development of positive symbolic forms of self and a secure relationship with the parent. Dynamic, spontaneous nonverbal interactions create mental representations that organize the experience (Bowlby 1969). These "moment-to-moment" (Beebe and Lachmann 2002, p. 210) interactive experiences that are co-created and co-organized by the parent and infant give rise to the creation of a healthy bond.

Healthy engagement requires a certain level of regulation within and between each participant. Regulation established between the parent and infant is created as each partner maintains their own level of self-regulation. Each individual stays engaged with the partner through self-regulation of mental thought, sensations, and emotions (Beebe 2004; Beebe et al. 2005). Self-regulation occurs as each individual learns to organize internal and external input, constructing inner and interactive stability. The level of individual stability affects the individual's own behaviors and the dynamics of the dyadic relationship (Beebe 2004). Two minds become one in this co-created relationship between parent and infant (Seligman 2009).

Implicit Knowing, Mirror Neurons, and Intersubjectivity

Experiential body-to-body dialogue in the immediate nonverbal moment creates communication (Pally 2001; Stern 2004, 2008, 2010). The conversation occurs without a word expressed and often occurs outside of conscious awareness. The communication is multisensory, action-based, felt, and filled with emotion. It exists through tones, rhythms, and textures of expression that are sensed and known deep in the body, more than understood in the explicit declarative mind (Tortora 2006).

This sensorial, body-to-body language is the core method of conversational exchange for dance movement psychotherapists (Bloom 2006; Levy 2005; Pallaro 1999; Tortora 2006). During psychotherapeutic interactions, the dance therapist shifts into a receptive open place, attuning and mirroring his own actions, postures, and gestures to the nonverbal expressions of his patient. The nonverbal dialogue establishes a dance of relating both in emotional spirit and in physical actuality. As described in the vignette above, these dances may be as basic as a simple gestural exchange, an improvisational spontaneous dance-play, or a choreographed dance to music chosen to match the patient/mover's mood and expressive impulse. During the session, the dance therapist stays attuned to the patient, being present by listening through the whole body, by deeply attending to the multilayered sensations, feeling states, and images that arise within him as he observes the patient moment-to-moment (Tortora 2006). This type of listening and presence is called "embodied resonance" (Tortora 2009, p. 78). The therapist learns a great deal about the patient through attuned embodied resonance.

Infant mental health literature describes the body-to-body, sensory connection between self and other as occurring through implicit procedural knowledge (Boston

Process Change Study Group 2010). Implicit knowledge is nonverbal, non-symbolic, and unconscious and occurs through body-based experiences (Stern 2004, 2008). How an infant first experiences exchanges between self and other is based on this implicit way of knowing, interacting, and learning. It is also how the infant comes to know the difference between self and other on a primary body level.

The infant develops expectations through repeated sequences of experiences between self and other, which creates patterns within the relationship that form dependable ways of being with each other (Boston Process Change Study Group 2010). When the newborn lying alone in her bassinet becomes distressed, she cries while flexing and extending her limbs and shaking her head. She is able to settle as soon as she is placed in her mother's arms. The infant quickly comes to know the scent of the mother and the feel of her embrace. She learns to settle and regulate her distress through the familiar comfort she experiences from the mother.

As the dyad begins to play, creating games through facial, touch, and movement exchanges, this kinesthetic knowing develops further (Brazelton and Cramer 1990). The 5-month-old baby's smile at her mother is followed by a large smile from the mother and a gentle stroking of her baby's belly. The baby responds by kicking her legs in a short, pulsing manner. The mother caresses her baby's feet, assisting the leg pumps that evolve into bicycling motions. They both begin to giggle. This sequence will continue to develop into numerous variations, becoming a favorite greeting game as each member contributes new actions to the series of movements. The dyadic participants begin to learn about their ability to contribute to relational dialogues as each receives a response to their nonverbal contribution. The baby develops a sense of self-agency through this experience.

The discovery of mirror neurons in the 1990s provides evidence of a neurological basis for this nonverbal way of understanding the connection between self and other (Gallese et al. 1996, 2007; Gallese 2005). Mirror neurons are premotor neurons that fire within an individual's brain when both observing an action performed and when actually executing the action (Gallese 2005; Gallese et al. 1996, 2007). Neural mirroring in the brain causes a simulated body "resonance" mediated by a functional mechanism described as "embodied simulation" (Gallese 2009, p. 523). The observer experiences and understands the multisensory sensations, actions, intentions, and emotions of others through embodied simulation, creating a shared "body-state" (Gallese 2009, p. 524).

Such experience supports the development of intersubjectivity. The multilayered, body-based, socially-shared neural mapping is at the root of the motivational system present at birth that compels infants to create a joint social consciousness and identification with self and other (Gallese 2009; Trevarthen 2009). Gallese describes this aspect of intersubjectivity as "intercorporeity," which he defines as "the mutual resonance of intentionally meaningful sensory-motor behaviors—as the main source of knowledge we directly gather about others" (Gallese 2009, p. 523). We experience comparable sensations and emotions that are the fundamental organizing basis for empathy through our sensory-motor systems. Intersubjective social wiring begins at birth and underlies the motivation infants have to seek engagement and coordinate with others by participating in reciprocal nonverbal communications

(Trevarthen 1979, 1980, 2009). The infant comes to know the psychological state of other by matching or complimenting affect and feeling tones, using perception and proprioception.

The video-microanalytic research of Papoušek and colleagues details the key elements of infant learning about the interrelatedness between themselves and their parents (Papoušek 2007, 2008, 2011; Papoušek and Papoušek 1987). They emphasize early pre-verbal communication as the medium from which the parent–infant system develops and intersubjective learning takes place. The research uses video analysis to closely observe the pre-verbal dynamics within the dyad to detect parent's intuitive competence (Beebe and Lachmann 2002; Downing 2005, 2008). Intuitive parenting involves the parent's ability to create contingent responses to his infant by adjusting the nonverbal qualities of his actions and prosody of speech. The nonverbal qualitative adjustments include decelerating, exaggerating, varying, and simplifying her style to compliment the infant's changing capacities to self-regulate and relate on a multisensory, motoric, and proprioceptive level (Papoušek 2007; Papoušek and Papoušek 1987). Papoušek uses the term "angel's circle" (Papoušek 2011, p. 36) to describe these positive exchanges between parent and baby. She proposes that these sequences promote positive reciprocal exchanges which regulate the parent–infant interaction, providing moments of intersubjectivity.

Embodied Resonance and Authentic Movement in Psychotherapeutic Intervention

The literature cited above locates the transmission of emotion, thought, and sensation from self to other in a different realm than the spoken word. Embodied attunement, somatic attunement, and embodied resonance describe the therapist's felt experience of connection to the patient (Fogel 2009). By attuning to this aspect of self, the therapist's own sensorial experience provides kinesthetic empathy, co-regulating and containing the patient's experience. Embodied simulation describes the neural basis for the ability to simulate actions resulting in a shared body resonance, creating understanding and connection of body states of others in relation to one's self (Gallese 2005; Gallese et al. 2007).

The dance therapist attunes to the dynamic forms of expression and experience of the individual and the dyad through embodied resonance. The therapist comes to understand the nonverbal indicators that reveal the infant and parent's experience and feelings at the core of their attachment relationship. The therapist's ability to differentiate his own felt subjective experience from the experiences of those he is engaged with through observation or actual movement dialogue is at the heart of embodied resonance in dance movement psychotherapy.

A practice called authentic movement (Adler 1987, 2002; Chodorow 1999; Levy 2005; Pallaro 1999; Tortora 2006; Whitehouse 1977, 1999) is a prominent method used in dance movement psychotherapy to identify subjective experience. In authentic movement, one person takes on the role of the mover and the other the witness forming a dyad. The dance therapist asks the mover to close her eyes, quiet her thoughts, and simply listen to her body. In this listening state, the mover waits for an impulse from the body to move, with stillness included as an active action. A form of movement meditation arises as the mover waits to be moved rather than directing the movement actions from conscious thought. From this deep place of listening, one's personal movement repertoire unfolds. Idiosyncratic patterns arise, revealing pre-conscious and unconscious personal patterns, which may include pre-verbal sensations and images (Chodorow 1999).

The witness' job is to observe the mover from a perspective of open receptivity. The witness maps the details of the mover's actions objectively and descriptively, separating out personal references, thoughts, emotions, and bodily felt reactions as the witness' own experience evoked by observing the mover. D.A.N.C.E. separates these impressions into three distinct self-observation components: *witnessing* refers to the objective mapping and immediate thoughts that arise; *kinesthetic seeing* notes the witness' bodily and sensorial reactions; and *kinesthetic empathy* refers to personal emotional reactions that arise while observing the mover (Tortora 2006). The witness attunes to her own reactions, paying close attention to somatic references. After the mover moves for a set period of time, both the witness and mover dialogue about their individual experiences. The witness describes the movement elements she observed, owning her own reactions as personal references. In her reflections back to the witness, the mover describes her own experience. The witness and the mover realize places of intersubjective union through this process. It is a profound experience, to be seen without judgment or projection while finding a common place of meeting in the shared experience.

Bringing Embodied Resonance into the Therapeutic Space

The therapist creates a container to hold and reflect the patient's experience (Fogel 2009) through embodied attunement. The dance movement psychotherapist carefully and spontaneously develops improvisational multisensory activities, movement, dance, and play from this felt place of conscious attunement. The dance therapist strives to capture the patient/mover's essence, matching and complimenting the qualities that are sensed from the nonverbal realm.

Infant and parent learn about their individual tolerances and needs, building self-regulatory and co-regulatory capacity supporting attachment, through the use of movement action as nonverbal expression in therapy. Both parent and infant achieve a sense of efficacy as they experience resonance between self and other. Being with the other attuned in "now moments" (Boston Process Change Study Group 2010, p. 12) enables the emergence of creative ways of being together. They experience the intersubjective sense of being seen, heard, felt, and understood. Both Papoušek (2007, 2010) and Boston Process Change Study Group (2010) discuss close analysis of the nonverbal dialogue in parent–infant psychotherapy to capture and extend these moments of meeting to create fresh relational possibilities. The therapist can restore intersubjective emotionality by tapping into the parent's intuitive competence reflected in these moments (Papoušek 2007, 2008, 2011).

The Message Is in the Movement

Nonverbal exchanges are very compelling. They are at the root of human emotional connection and communication, even though what is actually being expressed is difficult to describe in words. From the beginning, multisensory experiences shape a baby's development and are revealed through the child's personal nonverbal movement style. When dialoguing with the qualitative elements of a person's expressive actions, mutual connection occurs. A shared experiencing self is expressed without words. In these moments, a knowing and relating between self and other is present and the connection seals the relationship, enabling each mover to share his or her personal experience. The past, present, and future all exist in these moments of shared experience. This author uses the term "sense of body" (Tortora 2004, 2006, 2009, 2010) to highlight how our embodied experiences are the core mechanism from which we learn about our surroundings, connect to others, and express ourselves.

"Body movements tell affecting poetic or musical 'stories' about happenings outside 'here and now,' outside the subjective Self" (Trevarthen 2009, p. 509). Trevarthen emphasizes the creative nature of personal actions that become communications within a cultural and communal narrative. His work highlights the innate human motivation from birth to seek appreciation, connection, and understanding within a collective world created by community, culture, and attachment relationships. Musicality is the term Trevarthen (1980) uses to describe the shared consciousness that develops between parent and baby, regulated by joy and love, and experienced through the rhythm of movement and imitative sound.

Stern (2009) notes, "The key for human beings is movement. It is the primary experience. Everything builds upon movement. Movement has four daughters: time, space, directionality, and force". The importance of movement is again highlighted in Stern's quote about early infancy experience. These "four daughters" Stern refers to are based on the Laban nonverbal movement analysis system (Stern 2009, 2010).

Finding the Right Words to Describe This Wordless State

Seligman and Harrison (2012) assert:

> The infant relies on motor activity, affect, and sensation to communicate with and make sense of his or her relationship with the caregiver. In the past, researchers and therapists (e.g. Piaget) have often underestimated or over-simplified these basic dimensions of experience... Affect, proprioceptive, kinesthetic, somato-sensory, and autonomic experiences are integrated into an early sense of self in infancy... Models of nonverbal patterns of behavior and interpersonal experience are increasingly at the core of accounts of personality development and psychopathogensis. (p. 241)

Seligman and Harris cite the coming together of cognitive and affective neuroscience, infancy developmental research and psychology, phenomenology, non-linear dynamic systems theory, pediatrics, psychiatry, and psychoanalysis as contributing to this newly heightened acknowledgment (Seligman 2009; Seligman and Harrison 2012). Clinicians and researchers are in an exciting dialogue, which supports a more precise and solid base of understanding, strengthening approaches in practice and research. But still, how do we best articulate the unspoken experience that so dominates interpersonal interaction?

Laban Movement Analysis (LMA) and Ways of Seeing D.A.N.C.E.

The Laban Movement Analysis (LMA) system is one of the systems dance, psychotherapy uses to analyze the nonverbal experience (Bartenieff and Lewis 1980; Levy 2005; Tortora 2004, 2006, 2010, 2011). The salient feature of LMA is its emphasis on specific qualitative elements of movement action, which provide descriptive information about how the action is performed, what body parts execute the action, and where the actions occur in reference to self, others, and the surrounding spatial environment (Bartenieff and Lewis 1980; Laban 1975, 1976; Laban and Lawrence 1974; Tortora 1994, 2004, 2006, 2010, 2011). The observer hones in on intricate details of an individual's expressive actions using LMA's objective descriptors. When looked at as a whole, the descriptive elements create a unique picture of the mover, with the specific details adding texture, color, and tone to an individual's movement experiences. These qualitative elements are uniquely combined in an individual's movement repertoire to create personal nonverbal expressions that affect the dyadic dialogue. The LMA system is based on five qualitative elements: space, body, shaping, effort, and phrasing (Bartenieff and Lewis 1980; Laban 1975, 1976; Laban and Lawrence 1974; Tortora 1994, 2004, 2006).

Based on the Laban system (Bartenieff and Lewis 1980; Laban 1975, 1976), D.A.N.C.E. introduces specific nonverbal analysis elements that are assessable and teachable to those not trained in the Laban system (Tortora 2010). LMA is an observation method of dance movement psychotherapy and the foundational system used in the *Ways of Seeing* program (Levy 2005; Tortora 2006). The *Ways of Seeing* program adapts these elements to create a systematic nonverbal-analysis method, D.A.N.C.E., to observe individual and dyadic interactions with particular attention to which nonverbal elements most influence the developing attachment relationship. (See Tortora 2006, 2010, 2011 for a detailed description of the application of LMA in the *Ways of Seeing* program). The therapist directs particular attention toward observing each individual's nonverbal style within the context of the parent–child relationship. The therapist identifies self-regulatory and dyadic co-regulatory patterns in the dynamics that unfold through the analysis, elucidating what each person is experiencing on a body-based level.

The specific qualitative nonverbal elements defined in D.A.N.C.E. were chosen for their fundamental role in the embodied, sensorial, and action-oriented pre-verbal communications that influence the quality of the developing attachment relationship. The information obtained from D.A.N.C.E. provides insight into each mover's implicit and intersubjective experience and clarifies how each dyadic member affectively attunes to one another on a nonverbal and multisensory level. D.A.N.C.E. can be used to analyze any significant dyadic relationships in a young child's life.

The therapist watches the dyadic dance of relating by paying detailed attention to the specific body actions and shapes made with the body, spatial aspects of the actions, and the rhythm, timing, and phrasing of the movements created individually and in relationship to each other. The therapist analyzes the specific nonverbal elements of these categories in dynamic relationship to each other, not individually, to determine the nature of the attachment. The therapist ascertains a complete picture of the attachment relationship only by a thorough analysis of how the qualities of each individual's nonverbal style are executed within the context of the dyadic engagement, looking at the parts as they relate to the whole interactional style. There are 10 nonverbal categories in D.A.N.C.E. that guide the observation of the interaction: body, facial expressivity and quality of eye gaze, body shapes, use of space, quality of movement actions, quality and frequency of physical contact, tempo of nonverbal movement style, vocal patterns, regulation/co-regulation, and coherence. Detailed descriptions of the categories are not within the scope of this chapter; however, regulation/co-regulation and coherence bear some discussion because of their commonality with infant psychotherapy.

Regulation/Co-regulation

In this category, the therapist observes how each individual's interactional nonverbal behaviors support self-regulation within the context of the relationship, paying particular attention to each person's level of arousal as it may affect the quality and reciprocity of the dyadic engagement. The therapist analyzes how each person responds to their partner's arousal and engagement through their nonverbal actions. This includes whether the nonverbal qualities create contingent or non-contingent interactions. The therapist considers how the interpersonal dialogue does or does not support co-regulatory behaviors. The therapist observes how the nonverbal experience during the interaction may influence the infant's neuro-physiological development and the attachment relationship as it is unfolding.

Coherence

The therapist reviews the overall sense of harmonious connection within the dyad. The therapist analyzes the qualitative details of the movement actions that contribute to a contingent or non-contingent dialogue to decipher if and how the nonverbal communication creates a balanced exchange. The coherence category is an overview providing a comprehensive description of the dyadic nonverbal interaction pattern. The therapist is specifically looking at what, how, and if the elements of the dyad's nonverbal interaction form a give-and-take discourse reviewing the patterns of turn-taking, pausing, the manner of touch each partner engages in, the compatibility and frequency of each partner's use of space to explore, create distance, or seek closeness, and other responses that demonstrate compatibility, sensitive listening, and receptive engagement. Does the couple create a sense of congruency forming a simpatico relationship? Does their nonverbal dialogue demonstrate an attitude of contingent responsiveness? The coherence category describes the overall sense of discord or resonance within the dyad.

Attunement Versus Discord

The nonverbal analysis using D.A.N.C.E. provides a way to identify the subtle qualitative elements involved in attuned moments of meeting within the parent–infant dyad. The therapist uses the self-observation analysis to decipher how her personal lens may be influencing what she is observing. Sensing, dialoguing, and creating safe moments in the therapeutic space requires the ability to exist within that edge between the verbalizing self and the experiencing self. The therapist connects to the interactive dynamic of the parent and infant relationship, while also staying attentive to her own thoughts, sensations, and emotions. The therapist needs to stay within the experiencing mode while simultaneously attending to self-observations. These observations dialogue with the experiencing self, influencing subsequent moments of interaction with the dyad. The more aware the therapist is of this dynamic, the better able she will be to engage the dyad in a clear way. When the therapist is able to attune with the dyad, a shared sense of connection occurs. Her verbal and nonverbal interactions with the dyad enable each to feel seen. The experience of feeling seen supports the parent's own intuitive connection with her baby. Shared attunement does not always occur in the dyad; the therapist may detect dissonance in the dyad through this process.

The therapist uses the detailed D.A.N.C.E. analysis to identify the qualitative characteristics that may be causing discord in the dyad. The therapist attends to personal impressions in tandem with the felt experience within the therapeutic moments and this reveals how the disharmony within the interaction is occurring. It is the qualitative aspects of the nonverbal interaction that create the essence of shared meaning. When a member of the dyad does not feel seen by the other, a lack of resonance is experienced. This causes a rupture in shared meaning making and understanding. If this occurs continuously without repair, two separate subjective experiences develop, fracturing the intuitive and innate motivation for shared consciousness. Each member does not feel understood or seen. The intersubjective link feels lost. These out-of-sync experiences mount up, creating new patterns of interaction. Partners then focus on self-preservation and personal need. The need to stay tuned to self creates a loss of connection of the feeling tones of the other person. The root of discord in intimate relationships begins in this subtle yet profound dissonance.

   The therapist feels and observes the dissonant state through the nonverbal qualitative dynamics of the interaction. The therapist feels it when he tunes into his reactions while observing the pair. Identifying the nonverbal qualities that create this experience provides a key to repairing the dyadic dynamic in dance movement psychotherapy treatment. The dance therapist attunes to and mirrors his own body actions to these nonverbal qualities as he engages with the parent or child. He also incorporates these nonverbal qualities into the movement, dance, and dance-play activities with the couple, enabling them to explore new ways to relate to each other.

Case Vignette

The case vignette below illustrates these dynamics. The vignette describes an interaction from an early dance movement psychotherapy session, depicting a typical dynamic of this mother–infant dyad. The child was referred to treatment at age 16 months by his parents. They described their child as very smart and verbally precocious but emotionally fragile, fearful, and exceedingly anxious. She had a difficult birth experience and first year of life, including issues with regulation evidenced in disruptive sleep and poor food intake. She lacked motor-skill curiosity, did not crawl, and was fearful of tunnels at the playground. Problems within the attachment relationship emerged in the treatment over time, influenced by undiagnosed postpartum depression. The author changed identifying details for confidentiality. In the description below, the mother's name is Ariel and the infant's name is Jessica.

   Jessica, age 16 months, and her mother are playing together in a dance movement psychotherapy session. A bit unsteady on her feet, Jessica stands very vertically, pointing off to the left side, away from Ariel. Ariel sits to Jessica's right on the floor shaping her body around her legs as she hugs them toward her chest quietly looking at Jessica. Jessica and Ariel are positioned apart. They pause in this stance in their own private spheres of space. They do not touch and cannot reach each other unless they shift their whole body stance. From this position, Ariel leans slightly forward, extending her arm out and gently stroking Jessica's foot. Jessica responds by slowly bringing her arm to her side as she looks down at Ariel's gesture and then gazes to the right, away from Ariel, then back across to the left, continuing to not look at Ariel. Ariel brings her arm back to hug her legs, resuming her own private contained sphere of space. She quietly watches Jessica, with focused visual attention and an open, light facial expression. Jessica momentarily looks at Ariel directly, brightens facially and begins to make a strong clicking sound, which Ariel mirrors with an exaggerated open-mouth smile. Jessica continues her clicking, disengages her eye contact, and walks further away.

   Ariel, now sitting behind Jessica, shifts her body weight back, orienting herself toward Jessica, and hugs her legs in closer with bound tension matched by slightly increased tension in her facial muscles. She visually follows Jessica's actions but her gaze appears inwardly focused. Jessica, with her back to Ariel, discontinues her clicking sound, taps and then waves playfully at a large ball, creating a similar rhythmic pulse to her clicking, and then turns her body with her back fully toward Ariel. She walks directly to another large ball that she pushes for a moment and then turns around and walks directly toward Ariel again with a neutral facial expression. Jessica stops herself in front of Ariel once more out of arm's distance, creating her own separate spherical container. Ariel immediately brightens, responding with a warm open smile, and tilts her head back, looking directly at Jessica. Looking away from Ariel, Jessica re-initiates the clicking vocal game. Looking directly at Jessica, matching her daughter's tone with her own vocalizations, she shifts her weight backward onto her unfolded arms, reorienting her whole body diagonally toward Jessica. As she does this, Jessica bypasses Ariel's eyes and looks down at Ariel's legs, which are now crossed in an open position with her arms on her lap. Jessica continues her wandering gaze now, up and away from Ariel to Jessica's right. Jessica has a neutral facial expression.

The moment of connection is fleeting, and Jessica is off again, walking away from Ariel. Ariel looks over her shoulder, visually following her daughter's path for a moment and then she too looks away as her smile fades into a facial quality of neutral bound tension. She looks back at Jessica and then away again toward me, bringing her hands together on her lap.

D.A.N.C.E. Analysis of the Case Vignette

While watching this couple, I am struck by one immediate thought: I sense that Jessica is on her own and Ariel is alone too. At 16 months, it is natural for Jessica to be exploring, but I am sensing something more than meeting this developmental milestone. What is it, and why do I feel this way? I reflect on my kinesthetic responses. Emotionally, I experience a level of yearning and sadness. I feel heavy and weighted in my body. As if I want to move forward but cannot. Tension and weight hold me back. I look more deeply into their nonverbal dance to decipher what I am responding to. I start by noting their strengths, followed by what I experience as dissonance in their relationship.

The feeling tones of their movements compliment and match each other. They both approach time with a sense of caution and slowness. Their spatial approach is also attuned. They are able to look directly at each other and orient their gestural and full-body actions towards each other. They have similar body tension from bound to neutral, with some flow in their small gestures that extend into the mid- to far-reach areas of their personal space. LMA uses the term kinesphere to describe the three-dimensional personal sphere of space surrounding the body that is reachable by extending any limb from the torso out to the periphery (Laban 1976).

Vocally Ariel also attunes to her daughter, matching the tone, slightly exaggerating Jessica's clicking sounds and exclaiming with joy within a range that compliments Jessica's vocalizations. Ariel also follows Jessica's tempo, stopping when Jessica does, creating periods of silence. Their utterances are within a qualitative range that is compatible with their actions and gestures.

The tempo and phrasing quality of their actions are often in synchrony or complimentary. They both exhibit an "action and pausing" phrasing style, starting and stopping within moments of each other. As Jessica walks away, Ariel shifts her body back. Both Jessica and Ariel pause. When Jessica moves again, Ariel maintains her position, following Jessica's actions visually with little full-body action. She becomes animated and responsive when Jessica directs her actions toward her and quickly shifts away, dropping her heightened affective expressions when Jessica leaves.

Individually they are self-regulated, and Ariel demonstrates the ability to respond contingently to Jessica's actions. There is a fragile quality to Jessica's actions. She explores slowly and moves cautiously. Ariel attunes well to Jessica's style. She adjusts her actions, moving slowly within her own body boundaries without startling Jessica. She pauses when Jessica pauses and stays behind Jessica, allowing her to explore. There is an overall sense of co-regulation. In spite of these strengths, I do not get a sense of harmonious coherence in their relationship. Rather my kinesthetic empathic sensation is one of caution. "Tread lightly," I witness myself internally saying. I do not experience playful spontaneous engagement between them. I am aware that my actions become direct, controlled, and focused. The key to this impression becomes evident when looking at their eye gaze and facial expressivity, and how they individually shape their bodies and engage each other spatially.

Jessica looks directly at Ariel for only short periods of time, often slowly shifting into a joyful expression that emerges from a more neutral facial action. More frequently she gazes away from Ariel, creating an attitude of gaze avoidance and wandering, diminishing her bright expression back to neutral or gentle expressive interest as she focuses on an object in the room rather than Ariel. Ariel does provide solid eye contact when Jessica is facing her, but her face quickly shifts into a tense, sad expression when Jessica is not oriented towards her. Several times following engaged eye contact, Ariel and Jessica direct their gazes in opposite directions rather than follow each other's gaze.

It is their use of space, the shape of their postures, and their lack of physical contact that are most revealing. Jessica and Ariel create relational space that is separate and self-contained. They each stay in their own private kinespheric space for the whole sequence. Ariel maintains a closed posture for most of the interaction, shaping around her legs or keeping her arms on her lap. Jessica holds her body very vertically aligned, stopping her actions before she comes close to Ariel. This stopping action before coming into close proximity draws my attention. What stops Jessica each time? The interactional spaces they create through their actions predominantly occur using the whole room rather than in close proximity and are filled with pauses before and without physical contact. The essence of their embraced space (defined as the quality or essence emanating between the couple that keeps them connected through and regardless of their actual spatial distance (Tortora 2011)) is about coming and going without direct or extended contact. There is a sense of distance, and approach and withdrawal, from both Ariel and Jessica.

Dance Movement Psychotherapy Intervention for the Case

The qualitative elements become the focus of the intervention activities. We begin to create dance-play "attachment games" with the common theme of moving toward Ariel, culminating in a warm embrace, followed by playful separations through varying spatial distances. We play with the timing of these actions, approaching Ariel through space, through these improvisational dances. We also explore lengthening the timeframe of their embrace. Jessica both improves her motor coordination and feels a sense of agency in being able to reach Ariel through these activities. Jessica and Ariel stay engaged, mingling, and overlapping their kinespheric spaces for longer periods of time. We create lively circle dances to rhythmic and melodic music, dancing together into the center of the circle and then back out again, always emphasizing joyful eye contact throughout the dance. We establish connection through joint attention during our dances, which develops into true reciprocal interaction as Ariel and Jessica take turns leading new dance steps all over the room.

I also focus on helping Jessica experience an embodied sense of agency during our sessions. I support Jessica to soften her vertical stance by having her explore the relationship between her upper and lower body and left and right sides of her body through somersaults, log rolls, and gliding across the floor while lying supine and pushing from her legs. I am very aware of the quality of my touch and my posturing as I support her. My touch is firm yet responsive to her actions. I listen to her body actions through this touch, assisting her initiations of each movement. She embodies her actions more effectively, building her sense of body and efficacy. She develops more confidence in her mobility as she becomes more coordinated physically, moving from and off of center. She explores an experiential sense of stability and fluidity of movement through space as she successfully reaches her mother. I move with enhanced coordination, shaping my body around her while still maintaining clear body boundaries. We establish a co-regulatory nonverbal dialogue through our jointly created actions and responsive interactive physical contact. Jessica can kinesthetically experience a sense of self and other awareness.

I begin individual dance movement psychotherapy sessions with Ariel in tandem with these dyadic sessions. Ariel shares her history and the difficulties of her attachment with her own mother and father during these sessions, how hard she worked to do what they expected of her, but not feeling she was successful in meeting these expectations. She explains that she did not feel seen, accepted, or understood. She comments that Jessica seems to feel more bonded to her father. She is relieved to know Jessica does have an attachment, quietly adding, "I assume she does not need me." I feel this statement deep in my heart. My thoughts reflect on her still quiet presence in sessions—how little she initiates, and how often she waits for Jessica to come to her, only to feel Jessica approach and withdraw before experiencing the emotional warmth of a mommy–baby hug.

We focus on body awareness activities in our sessions that help her both stay in touch with her feelings and create a sense of calm presence. We work on breathing more fully through her whole body to help her feel her presence. She dances to music that matches her mood and explores how to let her breath support her full body actions with flow and fluidity. We use rhythmic music sensing her full body weight, as she moves in synchrony with the beat. She experiences her ability to listen to herself, take a stance, and voice her needs. As I reflect on my felt experience in both my private sessions with Ariel and our parent–baby sessions, I realize I must hold them both through my embodied presence, my actions, and my words, as well as the dance-play activities we create together. Ariel must experience her ability to be present for her daughter that she can be a capable mother and that her daughter needs her. Jessica must experience her own agency in reaching and connecting to Ariel both emotionally and physically, through her embodied self-discovery.

Ariel lies down and Jessica retreats, becoming very solemn at one point in our parent–baby session. Ariel reveals to me in her private session that during the height of her depressive state she slept a great deal. In our next parent–baby session, we develop "The Night, Night Game." Ariel lies down pretending to sleep. Jessica comes over to her, draping her body over Ariel, exclaiming, "Wake up!" with a bright smile and a warm hug. The whole family plays this game at home as well.

Ariel and Jessica begin to create new felt-sense experiences that expand their nonverbal relational repertoire through activities such as these. Jessica is "seen" in the Winnicottian sense. As they try on each other's movements, a shared-body state (Gallese 2005, 2009) and resonance occurs, enabling emotional dialogue. Gallese's (2009, p. 524) term intercorporeity describes the multilayered, body-based, shared neural wiring of sensory-motor systems that enables individuals to experience and relate to similar actions, intentions and emotions of one another. Ariel and Jessica learn about each other in this very primary way during their multisensory motoric conversations. They begin to create a new nonverbal vocabulary and a new way to be with each other through dance, play, and rhythmic interactions. Jessica and Ariel are able to talk to each other through body-to-body exchange through the interactive dance-play activities. The experiences create a fresh moment-to-moment musical story in the Trevarthenian (2009) sense, which enhances both self-organization and co-constructed regulation, thus building and repairing their attachment relationship.

Conclusion

The case vignette demonstrates how to use nonverbal dialogue and analysis as a therapeutic tool to repair the attachment relationship. The author underscores throughout this chapter the role body-based movement experience plays in the developing attachment relationship. Expression through movement is at the core of human relationships. Martha Graham asserts, "Dance is an absolute. It is not knowledge about something but is knowledge itself . . . movement never lies" (Graham 1973, p. 270). Dance movement psychotherapy places great emphasis on observing the nonverbal movement style of an individual. The therapist pays alert attention to the specific qualitative details of the mover's action and nonverbal style of moving, as a vital form of communication and expression. Recent research, especially in the fields of infant mental health, development, and psychology and cognitive and affective neuroscience, provides a wealth of information that informs dance movement psychotherapy practice.

These fields of research are beginning to discuss how multisensory sensations, actions, intentions, and emotions are experienced, creating a shared body state (Gallese 2005) between self and other. Intercorporeity is at the root of intersubjectivity, the motivational system present at birth that compels infants to create a joint social consciousness and identification with self and other (Gallese 2009; Trevarthen 2009). The researchers state that the origins of empathy come from one's ability to be intersubjective. Trevarthen (2009) emphasizes the innate motivation of all humans, beginning in infancy, to create a communicative narrative of meaning through nonverbal action exchanges.

Dance movement therapists use empathic embodied attunement to learn about their patients and to create experiential therapeutic interactions. Dance, movement, and body experience are key elements used in dance movement psychotherapy clinical methodology. The therapist derives insight into each mover's implicit and intersubjective experience from information analyzed through D.A.N.C.E. The therapist uses the self-observational component of D.A.N.C.E. to also attune to her own reactions, thoughts, and multisensory sensations as they may be affecting her interactions with the parent–baby couple.

The author developed D.A.N.C.E. to provide a bridge between colleagues of diverse early childhood and adult treatment fields and dance movement psychotherapy to support a team approach to treatment. D.A.N.C.E. encompasses the fields of infant mental health, neuroscience, nonverbal movement analysis, and dance movement psychotherapy. The author created the D.A.N.C.E. method with multifaceted motivations. The author created it first to continue to support the inclusion of dance movement psychotherapy within the psychotherapeutic treatment team. Second, dance movement psychotherapy has much to contribute to the fields of infant mental health, development, and psychology due to the deeply experiential body sensing and nonverbal nature of its approach. Third, in the current climate of "evidenced-based practice," the creative arts therapy fields suffer from a lack of research substantiating clinically-based success (Haen 2009; Johnson 2009). Interestingly, Trevarthen (2009) states that current empirical methodologies are too mechanistic and objective. They fail to successfully explain and examine the rhythmic, embodied, emotional dialogues rooted in nonverbal sensation and exchange that inform our innate human motivation for shared communication, consciousness, and understanding.

Future Research

The lack of research in the field of dance movement psychotherapy and other creative arts therapies have hindered their growth. There is a need for more quantitative and qualitative studies following the behavioral and social science research methods of inquiry to demonstrate the effectiveness of the creative arts approaches to those unfamiliar with the field. However, there is also a need to look beyond these traditional research methods as the only accepted methodologies, for the need to accommodate to the structure of these forms of inquiry has also hindered the creative artistic process. There is a new form of artistic inquiry developing through the creative arts fields that is emerging as a viable research methodology (Hervey 2000). As he notes:

> Artistic inquiry is defined as research that (1) uses artistic methods of gathering, analyzing, and/or presenting data; (2) engages in and acknowledges a creative process, and (3) is motivated and determined by the aesthetic values of the researcher(s). (p. xiii)

Expanding the research methodology to include artistic inquiry will further the collaborative potential of the creative arts in therapeutic fields.

Recommendations for Clinicians

The creative arts therapies have a long-standing collaborative relationship with other human service fields, including mental health, social work, psychology, psychoanalysis, education, and medicine (Hervey 2000). Greater awareness of the clinician's embodied experience as described in this chapter will enhance the clinician's understanding of nonverbal phenomenon and provide deeper insight into the personal counter-transference material that arises. A common language to describe nonverbal phenomenon would also greatly benefit clinicians and enhance collaboration within and between each field. It is my hope that D.A.N.C.E. can provide a common systematic language to discuss nonverbal phenomenon and interactional experience. Establishing a language between our fields can provide direction on a map to further understanding, research, and collaboration. The map can simultaneously serve the interests of all the related fields. It supports the effectiveness of dance movement psychotherapy; provides insight into the essential role the body, movement, and nonverbal experience play in relationships; and further informs our understanding of the embodied essence of implicit knowing and intersubjectivity in early childhood development.

References

Abram, J., & Hjulmand, K. (2007). *Language of Winnicott: A dictionary of Winnicott's use of words* (2nd ed.). London: Karnac Books.

Adler, J. (1987). Who is the witness? *Contact Quarterly: Dance Journal, XII 1*, 20–29.

Adler, J. (2002). *Offering from the conscious body: The discipline of authentic movement*. Rochester: Inner Traditions.

Bartenieff, I., & Lewis, D. (1980). *Body movement: Coping with the environment*. New York: Gordon & Breach Science.

Beebe, B. (2004). Co-constructing mother–infant distress in face-to-face interactions: Contributions of microanalysis. *Zero to Three, 24*, 40–48.

Beebe, B., & Lachmann, F. (2002). *Infant research and adult treatment: Co-constructing interactions*. Hillsdale: The Analytic Press.

Beebe, B., Knoblauch, S., Rustin, J., & Sorter, D. (2005). *Forms of intersubjectivity in infant research and adult treatment*. New York: Other Press.

Bernstein, P. (1979). *Eight theoretical approaches in dance-movement therapy*. Dubuque: Kendall/Hunt.

Bernstein, P. (1981). *Theory and methods in dance-movement therapy*. Dubuque: Kendall/Hunt.

Berrol, C. (2006). Neuroscience meets dance/movement therapy: Mirror neurons, the therapeutic process and empathy. *The Arts in Psychotherapy, 33*, 302–315.

Bloom, K. (2006). *The embodied self: Movement and psychoanalysis*. London: Karnac.

Boston Process Change Study Group. (2010). *Change in psychotherapy: A unifying paradigm*. New York: W.W. Norton & Company.

Bowlby, J. (1969). *Attachment and loss. Vol. 1: Attachment*. New York: Basic Books.

Brazelton, T. B., & Cramer, B. T. (1990). *The earliest relationship: Parents, infants, and the drama of early attachment*. Reading: Addison-Wesley.

Chace, M. (1953). *Use of dance action in a group setting*. Paper presented for the American Psychiatric Association, Los Angeles, CA.

Chace, M. (July 1964). Dance alone is not enough . . . today's dance therapy demands special skills and training. *Dance Magazine, 7*, 58–59.

Chaiklin, H. (Ed.). (1975). *Marion Chace: Her papers*. Columbia: American Dance Therapy Association.

Chodorow, J. (1999). To move and be moved. In P. Pallaro (Ed.), *Authentic movement: Essays by Mark Starks Whitehouse, Janet Adler, and Joan Chodorow* (pp. 267–278). Philadelphia: Jessica Kingsley.

Damasio, A. (1994/2005). *Descartes' error: Emotion, reason, and the human brain*. New York: Penguin.

Downing, G. (2005). Emotion, body and parent-infant interaction. In J. Nadel & D. Muir (Eds.), *Emotional development: Recent research advances*. Oxford: Oxford University Press.

Downing, G. (2008). A different way to help. In A. Fogel, B. King, & S. Shanker (Eds.), *Human development in the 21st century: Visionary ideas from systems scientists*. New York: Cambridge University Press.

Freud, S. (1923). *The ego and the id*. New York: W.W. Norton & Company.

Gaensbauer, T. J. (2004). Telling their stories: Representation and reenactment of traumatic experiences occurring in the first year of life. *Zero to Three, 24*, 25–31.

Gaensbauer, T. J. (2011). Embodied simulation, mirror neurons, and the reenactment of trauma in early childhood. *Neuropsychoanalysis, 13*, 91–107.

Gallese, V. (2005). Embodied simulation: From neurons to phenomenal experience. *Phenomenology and the Cognitive Sciences, 4*, 23–48.

Gallese, V. (2009). Mirror neurons, embodied simulation, and the neural basis of social identification. *Psychoanalytic Dialogues, 19*, 519–536.

Gallese, V., Fadiga, L., Fogassi, L., & Rizzolatti, G. (1996). Action recognition in the premotor cortex. *Brain, 119*, 593–609.

Gallese, V., Eagle, M., & Migone, P. (2007). Intentional attunement: Mirror neurons and the underpinnings of interpersonal relations. *Journal of the American Psychological Association, 55*, 131–176.

Graham, M. (1973). *The notebooks of Martha Graham*. New York: Harcourt Brace Jovanovich.

Haen, C. (2009). Introduction to the special issue. *The Arts in Psychotherapy, 36*, 59–60.

Hervey, L. W. (2000). *Artistic inquiry in dance/movement therapy: Creative alternatives for research*. Springfield: Charles C. Thomas.

Johnson, D. R. (2009). Commentary: Examining underlying paradigms in the creative arts therapies of trauma. *The Arts in Psychotherapy, 36*, 114–120.

Koch, S. C. (2006). Interdisciplinary embodiment approaches. Implications for creative arts therapies. In S. C. Koch & I. Bräuninger (Eds.), *Advances in dance/movement therapy. Theoretical
perspectives and empirical findings* (pp. 17–28). Berlin: Logos.

Koch, S., & Fischman, D. (2011). Embodied enactive dance/movement therapy. *American Journal
of Dance Movement Therapy, 33*, 57–72.

Laban, R. (1975). *The mastery of movement*. Boston: Plays.

Laban, R. (1976). *The language of movement: A guidebook to choreutics*. Boston: Plays.

Laban, R., & Lawrence, F. C. (1974). *Effort*. Boston: Plays.

Levy, F. (2005). *Dance movement therapy: A healing art* (revised edition). Reston: American
Alliance for Health, Physical Education, Recreating and Dance.

Malloch, S., & Trevarthen, C. (Eds.). (2009). *Communicative musicality: Exploring the basis of
human companionship*. New York: Oxford University Press.

Meltzoff, A. N., & Brooks, R. (2007). Intersubjectivity before language: Three windows on preverbal sharing. In S. Bråten (Ed.), *On being moved: From mirror neurons to empathy* (pp. 149–174).
Philadelphia: John Benjamins.

Pallaro, P. (Ed.). (1999). *Authentic movement: Essays by Mark Starks Whitehouse, Janet Adler, and
Joan Chodorow*. Philadelphia: Jessica Kingsley.

Pally, R. (2001). A primary role for nonverbal communication in psychoanalysis. *Psychoanalytic
Inquiry, 21*, 71–93.

Papoušek, M. (2007). Communication in early infancy: An arena of intersubjective learning. *Infant
Behavior and Development, 30*, 258–266.

Papoušek, M. (2008). Disorders of behavioral and emotional regulation: Clinical evidence for a
new diagnostic concept. In M. Papoušek, M. Schieche, & H. Wurmser (Eds.), *Disorders of
behavioral and emotional regulation in the first years of life* (pp. 53–84). Washington, DC: Zero
to Three Press.

Papoušek, M. (2011). Resilience, strengths, and regulatory capacities: Hidden resources in
developmental disorders of infant mental health. *Infant Mental Health Journal, 32*, 29–46.

Papoušek, H., & Papoušek, M. (1987). Intuitive parenting: A dialectic counterpart to the infant's
integrative competence. In J. Osofsky (Ed.), *Handbook of infant development* (Vol. 14, 2nd ed.,
pp. 669–720). New York: Wiley.

Sandel, S., Chaiklin, S., & Lohn, A. (1993). *Foundations of dance/movement therapy: The life and
work of Marion Chace*. Columbia: The Marion Chace Memorial Fund of the American Dance
Therapy Association.

Schoop, T., & Mitchell, P. (1974). *Won't you join the dance? A dancer's essay into the treatment of
psychosis*. Palo Alto: Mayfield.

Schoop, T., & Mitchell, P. (1986). Reflections and projections: The Schoop approach to dance therapy. In P. Lewis (Ed.), *Theoretical approaches in dance/movement therapy* (Vol. 1). Dubuque:
Kendall/Hunt.

Seligman, S. (2009). Anchoring intersubjective models in recent advances in developmental psychology, cognitive neuroscience and parenting studies: Introduction of papers by Trevarthen,
Gallese, and Ammaniti & Trentini. *Psychoanalytic Dialogues, 19*, 503–506.

Seligman, S., & Harrison, A. (2012, in press). Infant research and adult psychotherapy. In G. Gabbard, B. Litowitz, & P. Williams (Eds.), *The Textbook of Psychoanalysis* (2nd ed.). Washington,
DC: American Psychiatric Publishing.

Sheets-Johnstone, M. (1998). *The primacy of movement*. Philadelphia: John Benjamin.

Sheets-Johnstone, M. (2010). Why is movement therapeutic? *American Journal of Dance Therapy,
32*(1), 2–15.

Stern, D. (1985). *The interpersonal world of the infant: A view from psychoanalysis and
developmental psychology*. New York: Basic Books.

Stern, D. (2004). *The present moment in psychotherapy and everyday life*. New York: W.W. Norton
& Company.

Stern, D. (2008). The clinical relevance of infancy: A progress report. *Infant Mental Health Journal,
29*, 177–187.

Stern, D. (2009). *Early interpersonal experience and intersubjectivity.* Paper presented at the meeting of Zero to Three 24th National Training Institute, Dallas, TX.

Stern, D. (2010). *Forms of vitality: Exploring dynamic experience in psychology, the arts, psychotherapy, and development.* New York: Oxford University Press.

Tortora, S. (1994). Join my dance: The unique movement style of each infant and toddler can invite communication, expression and intervention. *Zero To Three: Bulletin of National Center for Clinical Infant Programs, 15,* 1–12.

Tortora, S. (2004). Our moving bodies tell stories, which speak of our experiences. *Zero to Three, 24,* 4–12.

Tortora, S. (2006). *The dancing dialogue: Using the communicative power of movement with young children.* Baltimore: Paul H. Brookes.

Tortora, S. (2009). Case Study. In A. Fogel (Ed.), *The psychophysiology of self-awareness: Rediscovering the lost art of body sense* (pp. 77–79). New York: W.W. Norton & Company.

Tortora, S. (2010). Ways of seeing: An early childhood integrated therapeutic approach for parents and babies. *Clinical Social Work Journal, 38,* 37–50.

Tortora, S. (2011, April–September). Beyond the face and words: How the body speaks. *Journal of Infant, Child, and Adolescent Psychotherapy, 10,* 242–254.

Trevarthen, C. (1979). Communication and cooperation in early infancy. A description of primary intersubjectivity. In M. Bullowa (Ed.), *Before speech: The beginning of human communication* (pp. 521–571). London: Cambridge University Press.

Trevarthen, C. (1980). The foundation of intersubjectivity: Development of interpersonal and co-operative understanding in infants. In D. Olsen (Ed.), *The social foundation of language and thought* (pp. 316–342). New York: Norton.

Trevarthen, C. (2009). The intersubjective psychobiology of human meaning: Learning of culture depends on interest for co-operative practical work—and affection for the joyful art of good company. *Psychoanalytic Dialogues, 19,* 507–518.

Whitehouse, M. (1977). The transference and dance therapy. *American Journal of Dance Therapy, 1,* 3–7.

Whitehouse, M. (1999). Creative expression in physical movement is language without words. In P. Pallaro (Ed.), *Authentic movement: Essays by Mark Starks Whitehouse, Janet Adler, and Joan Chodorow* (pp. 33–40). Philadelphia: Jessica Kingsley.

Winnicott, D. W. (1971). *Playing and reality.* New York: Tavistock.

Winnicott, D. W. (1972). Basis for self in body. *International Journal of Child Psychotherapy, 1,* 7–16.

Winnicott, D. W. (1982). *Playing and reality.* London: Routledge.

Gems Hidden in Plain Sight: Peer Play Psychotherapy Nourishes Relationships and Growth Across Developmental Domains Among Young Children

Rebecca Shahmoon-Shanok, Ozlem Bekar, Emily Fried and Miriam Steele

Human rights begin, "in small places, close to home—so close, so small they cannot be seen on any maps of the world. Yet they are the world of the individual person … such are the places where every man, woman and child seeks equal justice, equal opportunity, equal dignity without discrimination. Unless these rights have meaning there, they have little meaning anywhere" (Roosevelt 1958).

Introduction

Research in developmental psychology shows that the experiences which young children have with each other are frequently growth-promoting (Coolahan et al. 2000; Fantuzzo et al. 2004). Equally important in the resource-constrained world of mental health and related supports for young children with challenges, peers are an abundant natural resource, gems to be mined. Nonetheless, peers are usually overlooked in psychotherapeutic considerations for children aged 2 through 5. Both the large corpus of attachment research which usually refers to parent–child relationships and the theory and practice of psychotherapy with young children have largely ignored peer relationships as a possible source of therapeutic progress. Thus, our chapter responds to two questions: What may we learn by focusing greater attention among interventionists and researchers upon relationships between and among peers? Which principles and

R. Shahmoon-Shanok (✉)
Institute for Infants, Children and Families, Jewish Board of Family
and Children's Services, New York, NY, USA
e-mail: rsswork@gmail.com

O. Bekar
Department of Psychology, The New School for Social Research, New York, NY, USA

Relationships for Growth and Learning Program, JBFCS, New York, NY, USA

E. Fried
Early Childhood Center, Albert Einstein College of Medicine, Bronx, NY, USA

M. Steele
Department of Psychology, New School for Social Research, New York, NY, USA

J. E. Bettmann, D. D. Friedman (eds.), *Attachment-Based Clinical Work with Children and Adolescents,* Essential Clinical Social Work Series,
DOI 10.1007/978-1-4614-4848-8_8, © Springer Science+Business Media New York 2013

therapeutic processes enable children to become positive, even psychotherapeutic change-agents for each other?

Following from the general acceptance of attachment theory and research among professionals, clinicians, and clinical researchers across relevant disciplines recognize and utilize individual psychotherapy and child–parent psychotherapy as the dominant modes of intervention for young children. Child–parent psychotherapy stands out amongst early interventions for its strong evidence base with five randomized controlled trials (Cicchetti et al. 1999, 2000, 2006; Lieberman et al. 1991, 2005). For too many children, however, individual treatment and parent–child psychotherapy are unavailable, impossible to get, otherwise impractical (Osofsky and Lieberman 2011; Tolan and Dodge), or resisted by parents for a range of reasons. Thus, the vast majority of preschool children with mental health problems in the United States do not receive the services that they need (Gilliam 2005).

Prevalence rates of mental health problems in children aged birth through 5 range from 16 to 21 % (Egger and Angold 2006; Lavigne et al. 1996). Although 8–10 % of preschool children have a diagnosable mental health disorder (Roberts et al. 1998), only 6 % of preschool children who are in need of these services actually receive them (Kataoka et al. 2002). Further, approximately 0.7 % of preschool children in the United States (more than 5,000 children between the ages 3 and 5) are expelled from preschools due to behavioral problems every year (Gilliam 2005). This rate is three times higher than that of older school children, indicating that the preschool years are an especially risky period. Importantly, the risk of expulsion increases significantly for those children whose preschool setting does not provide access to on-site mental health services (Gilliam 2005).

Evidence indicates that early childhood mental health problems constitute a significant risk factor for later psychopathology, if not treated or prevented effectively (e.g., Kagan and Zentner 1996). Moreover, early childhood mental health problems create serious obstacles for learning and school readiness (National Scientific Council on the Developing Child 2008). According to kindergarten teachers, 35 % of American children reach kindergarten unprepared to learn (Boyer 1991). Therefore, it is critical to have an effective, economical, viable, and available approach to meet the mental health needs of preschool children.

Why include this chapter in a book about attachment? Based on our clinical and research experience (Halpern et al. 2004a, b; Shahmoon-Shanok et al. 2005a, b), we assert that relationships with peers can exert a powerful force toward generative development across developmental lines (Freud 1965). We also endorse the prevailing perspective that the nature of each child's attachment relationship to a caregiver has a defining effect on mental health, social emotional wellness, the ability to interact with others and learn in school.

Bowlby (1973, 1980, 1982b) described child and caregiver dyads where the optimal scenario is one where parents offer sensitive and responsive caregiving, especially in times of distress. These experiences form the building blocks of the child's "internal working models" or "blueprints" for future relationships. As the partner in the relationship who is "older, wiser and stronger" (Bowlby 1980), the parent provides the child with a secure base from which to explore the world. This describes the optimal, secure attachment pattern; particular ongoing disruptions within the parent–child relationship account for the insecure and disorganized patterns of attachment. While children need caregiver attachment relationships, peer relationships also can become critical, organizing attachment relationships. Indeed, peer attachment relationships can assist children in improving the regulation of affect and the internalizing of interactions that become generalized patterns influencing how they experience other relationships going forward (Aikins et al. 2009; Armsden and Greenberg 1987; Howes 1987; Hughes and Dunn 2007; Laible et al. 2000; Wilkinson 2004).

This chapter presents the view that, under certain conditions, small psychotherapeutic peer playgroups accelerate development across domains while also promoting the growth of higher order defenses. In this model, peer attachment relationships can be a vital extension of psychotherapeutic intervention options. Indeed, even with very young children ages 2 through 5, the presence of peers can be harnessed in psychotherapy as an energizing incentive for growth. In therapeutic peer playgroups, children's presenting challenges diminish while their flexible new resources come to dominate. These resources then generalize to their classrooms and homes (Halpern et al. 2004a, b; Shahmoon-Shanok 2000, 2005a, b; Shahmoon-Shanok et al. 2005a, b; Shanok et al. 1989).

We begin by highlighting some of the research suggesting the value of toddler and preschool peers as growth-promoting agents for each other. This chapter then discusses the literature on group play psychotherapies for young children. It describes a continuous peer play psychotherapy (PPP) program for at-risk and diagnosable preschool children offered in public daycare, Head Start settings, and preschool programs across socio-economic groups. We next consider the conditions required to facilitate peers so they can become generative change agents for their group-mates. Then, we present an account of two children in the same playgroup, highlighting their growth-enlivening interactions. We also elaborate on the role of reflective supervision for PPP. Finally, we examine the cases presented in light of PPP's conceptual base and attachment theory.

Review of the Literature

Research on Peers

Bowlby (1982a) wrote that human beings are born with the capacity to engage in relational interactions with caregivers in order to maximize survival. For example, neonates only an hour old can imitate some facial behaviors (Meltzoff and Moore 1977), while infants respond to maternal facial and vocal cues and act on relational contingencies at 4 months (Beebe et al. 1997). These early, preverbal interactions with primary caregivers bring about a relatively stable set of beliefs and expectations in the infant about his self and environment, which by about 9 months of age form the basis of what Bowlby (1982a) termed "internal working models". Internal working models are the representational systems that underlie attachment classifications and have significant effects on attentional, perceptual, emotional, and behavioral mechanisms in later years (Bowlby 1973; Kobak et al. 2006; Sroufe et al. 2005).

Peer relationships, a central area of interpersonal functioning during the preschool years (Hay et al. 2004), are also affected by these internal working models. Cassidy et al. (1996) found that perceived parental rejection was associated with expectations of hostile intentions from peers. Furthermore, insecurely attached children had more negative representational schemas of their peers than the securely attached children. These negative representations of peers predicted fewer reciprocated friendships at school. Therefore, internal working models generated through interactions with caregivers generalize to relational representations of peers and are acted out in relationships with each other.

Peer relations are not only affected by internal working models, but also have the potential to influence these models (Aikins et al. 2009). While the bulk of a child's attachment security is formed through interactions with the primary caregiver during the first year of life (Bowlby 1973), the child's internal working model remains open to external influences. Examples of such influences include variables outside the parent–child sphere such as negative life events (Fraley 2002; Waters et al. 2000; Weinfield et al. 2000). Aikins et al. (2009) found that low friendship quality during early adolescence is related to unresolved attachment representations at age 16, highlighting a possible pathway reaching to attachment security from peer relationships.

Complementary and reciprocal social play appears when children are 1 year old, with social pretend play emerging around age 2 in typically developing children (Howes 1988). In toddlerhood, it has been shown that peer interactions are frequent, long, and positive (Lokken 2000). By age 3, the typical child can interact with peers, engage in pretend play and build stable peer relationships (Hay et al. 2004). Vaughn et al. (2001) found that 60 % of preschool children have at least one, usually same-sex, reciprocated school friend by the age of 4. Thus, establishment of healthy peer relationships is an essential and age appropriate developmental stage for preschool children (Hay et al. 2004).

In peer relationships, children negotiate domains such as aggression, cooperation, fairness, empathy, and rivalry (Gagnon and Nagle 2004; Hay et al. 2004; Spinrad et al. 2004). Developing adaptive peer relationships during preschool years is associated with better social competence (Lindsey 2002), self-regulation skills (Ramani et al. 2010; Vaughn et al. 2001), and with better academic performance (Coolahan et al. 2000; Fantuzzo et al. 2004). By contrast, anxiety-prone and fearful preschool children who tend to be low in emotion regulation are more likely to engage in solitary play activities and are more likely to be rejected and maltreated by peers later (Spinrad et al. 2004). Such social–relational difficulties during preschool years are predictive of both internalizing and externalizing problems in early and later adolescence (Bornstein et al. 2010).

Research on Group Play Psychotherapy

Group play psychotherapy is not a widely researched treatment modality for young children (Bratton et al. 2005). Yet, some evidence shows that it is an effective treatment modality for those who suffer from widely varied problems such as victimization by domestic violence (Smith and Landreth 2003; Tyndall-Lind et al. 2001), homelessness (Baggerly 2004), reading disabilities (Bills 1948), speech difficulties (Danger and Landreth 2005; Wakaba 1983), depression, anxiety and low self-esteem (Baggerly 2004), and social isolation (Fantuzzo et al. 1996).

The group play psychotherapy approach on which this chapter is based, *Relationship for Growth & Learning (RfGL)*, is a program run by the Institute for Infants, Children and Families, part of Jewish Board of Family and Children's Services (JBFCS), a large, non-sectarian, not-for-profit mental health, social service agency in New York City. A longitudinal study of the model's efficacy indicated that children who received PPP from the Fall to Spring semesters caught up with their non-playgroup peers in eight different domains (Halpern et al. 2004b).

Another group play psychotherapy model, the Resilient Peer Treatment (RPT) Program (Fantuzzo et al. 1996) also uses low socio-economic preschool environments to deliver early interventions through a peer play modality. RPT is consistent with *RfGL*'s PPP as they both utilize a developmental–ecological foundation on which they base their intervention modalities. In RPT, resourceful children (called play buddies) are paired with target children who play together in their classrooms during regular class time. A longitudinal study evaluating the efficacy of RPT showed that socially withdrawn children in the experimental group developed significantly better interpersonal and self-control skills, engaged in fewer solitary play activities and displayed significantly less internalizing and externalizing behavior problems as compared to the 'attention control' group after the intervention (Fantuzzo et al. 1996).

The literature on peer relationships reveals that psychotherapeutic interventions which make use of peer relationships in preschool settings are promising. These components fit within a developmental–ecological perspective; interventions should be compatible with the child's natural environment and developmental level for them to reach their potential effectiveness.

The Program Model

Rationale for Peer Play Psychotherapy

When children enter preschool they are expected to play, make friends, and learn to follow the classroom routines while maintaining good behavior and listening to teachers. PPP is used to support those children who are unable to participate in age-expected ways, who appear unable to progress. All children want to interact with other children (Hay et al. 2004). This motivation to connect is a huge incentive for the PPP playgroup to be an "irresistible medium for growth and meaning, learning and belonging" (Shahmoon-Shanok 2000, p. 244). The children both provoke and befriend each other over time and internalize therapeutic interventions. The deep desire to be with and interact with each other becomes a robust muscle empowering developmental unfolding.

PPP incorporates a psychosocial process that facilitates personal growth (Sweeney and Homeyer 1999) by combining play as the work of children (Slavson 1979) with the development of peer relationships. Play serves as a child's primary means of communication (Johnson and Clark 2001) and a tool to make sense of the world around him (Koplow 2007). Since young children, especially those with challenges, have usually not yet developed the language or reflective capacities that allow communication about emotional experiences, they use play to develop focus and shared attention to work through aggressive impulses, traumatic experiences, conflict, and to differentiate and gain mastery over internal affective states. Play therapy is indicated when a child cannot play or when their usual play does not enable mastery over her or his challenges (Koplow 2007).

Landreth (2002) describes group play therapy as "a psychological and social process in which children, in the natural course of interacting with each other in the playroom, learn not only about other children but also about themselves" (p. 42). Young children are social beings who seek interpersonal interactions that are dyadic and reciprocal, beginning from the first day of infancy and continuing throughout development (Howes 1987). They learn through group play psychotherapy ways in which they can negotiate interpersonal relationships and naturally extend these skills outside the playroom to other social situations (Brusiloff and Witenberg 1973; Greenspan and Wieder 1998; Pressman and Blumenfeld 1981; Shahmoon-Shanok 2000; Shanok et al. 1989; Sweeney and Homeyer 1999). That the children in *RfGL*'s PPP readily develop across several developmental domains implies that attachment-based fundamentals of mental and developmental health are strengthened by this intervention (Halpern et al. 2004b; Shahmoon-Shanok et al. 2005a, b).

Relationships for Growth and Learning

While most JBFCS and *RfGL* services and training are located in New York, *RfGL* training and resulting services have reached many practitioners and several agencies across the United States, most notably in Central Florida. Established in 1968, *RfGL* successfully addresses the full range of diagnoses from those that have environmental etiologies, including trauma, moderate body-based developmental challenges, and a combination of both (Halpern et al. 2004a, b). PPP-treated diagnoses exclude full-blown psychosis and autism, since such children are rarely tolerated in daycare, Head Start, or other preschools.

RfGL provides a two-year, interdisciplinary intensive training program for professionals from numerous related fields, primarily social work, psychology, early childhood, special education, occupational therapy, speech-language therapy, the arts therapies, and psychiatric nursing (Shahmoon-Shanok et al. 2006). This training program supports delivery of all the clinical work with children, their parents, and teachers on-site within daycare, Head Start centers, as well as preschools, by each preschool-based *RfGL* team. Teams are led by a mental health consultant called Clinical Coordinator. *RfGL* Clinical Coordinators provide weekly reflective individual and group supervision for each of their own team members and lead weekly seminars for team members from all of the current childcare centers served as part of the formal, two-year intensive training program. Reflective supervision has been defined as a relationship for learning in a mutually created, emotionally safe space where strengths are cherished and vulnerabilities are partnered (Fenichel 1992; Shahmoon-Shanok 2006, 2009; Shanok 1991/1992; Shanok et al. 1995; Siegel and Shahmoon-Shanok 2010).

RfGL staff, trainees, and students learn to view themselves as guests in someone else's home and as people who share the daycare staff's primary goal of helping children to be successful when they arrive in kindergarten. With the Clinical Coordinators' guidance, they actively interact with all center-based staff, including the director, teachers, family workers, office building, and kitchen staff members.

Which Concepts Govern RfGL?

Infant and early childhood mental health have been articulated as the capacities to grow and love well, express, experience, and regulate emotions and recover from dysregulation, form trusting relationships and repair conflict, explore and learn within society's values, and manage fear and frustration (Lieberman 2006). Tolstoy once noted, "One can live magnificently in this world if one knows how to work and how to love . . . " (Tolstoy 1856, as cited in Troyat 1967, p. 158). Themes of love and labor are central to some of the most influential theories of psychological well-being (Erikson 1963; Freud 1930). Similarly, *RfGL* recognizes that to assist children in the related developmental domains of relationship (love) and learning (work), we must help them attain certain primary capacities. A list of seven attributes envisioned as the fundamental goals for all children of kindergarten age were established by the cross-disciplinary board and staff of Zero to Three, the National Center for Infants, Toddlers and Families. Figure 1 lists those seven precious objectives.

Developmentally and relationally, children who possess these seven capacities are on their way to attaining maturity. They are able to work with regularity, cooperation, and satisfaction while establishing and maintaining loving relationships. They are children who succeed in school both academically and socially. These are the seven attributes which *RfGL* aims to foster in the children who participate in its PPP groups and receive ancillary services.

RfGL team members work closely with teachers and the center director to screen all of the center's children in August, September, and October to identify those children who have not attained the emotional objectives. These are the children who

THE EMOTIONAL FOUNDATIONS OF SCHOOL READINESS

SELF – CONTROL
The ability to modulate and control actions in age-appropriate ways.

RELATEDNESS
The ability to engage with others based on the sense of being understood by and understanding others.

CAPACITY TO COMMUNICATE
The wish and ability to verbally exchange ideas, feelings and concepts with others. This is related to a sense of trust in others and of pleasure in engaging with others, including adults.

INTENTIONALITY
The wish and capacity to have an impact, and to act upon that with persistence.
This is clearly related to a sense of competence, of being effective.

CONFIDENCE
A sense of control and mastery of one's body, behavior and world; the child's sense that he is more likely than not to succeed at what he undertakes, and that adults will be helpful.

CURIOSITY
The sense that finding out about things is positive and leads to pleasure.

COOPERATIVENESS
The ability to balance one's own needs with those of others in a group activity.

These characteristics equip children with a "school literacy" more basic than knowledge of numbers and letters. It is the knowledge of how to learn.

Fig. 1 The emotional foundations of school readiness. *Zero to Three* National Center for Infants, Toddlers and Families (1992), p. 7

do not seem to be growing or functioning well within the daily program of their center; the quiet, lost, constricted or joyless children on one end of the continuum, and the wild, disruptive, aggressive, equally despairing children, on the other. All children at each site are screened and then, through *RfGL*-facilitated case discussions by relevant *RfGL* team and center staff members (e.g., the director, teacher and family worker), they are assigned to intervention levels 1 through 4, that is, individualized, targeted, expanded, or inclusive (see Fig. 2).

After children are observed in classrooms and evaluated, their parents are offered an opportunity for their child to participate in a peer psychotherapy playgroup, meaning intervention levels 2, 3, or 4. We believe that a child not progressing in the place where s/he is spending most waking hours five days a week is reason enough for intervention. Research confirms that the *RfGL* approach to selecting children is successful in picking up those who are lowest functioning (Halpern et al. 2005a, b; Halpern and Rinks 2004). Thus, evaluation including parents prior to treatment is bypassed in favor of evaluation during the first weeks of playgroup and continuing

Relationships for Growth & Learning

INTERVENTION LEVELS FOR CHILDREN

Intervention Level 1: *Individualized*

- At the *universal*, or preventative, level, each child is observed by several childcare and *RfGL* staff members in the classroom and participates in varied screening and assessment procedures.
- Impressions and results are aggregated and shared by a team made up of the childcare teacher, family service provider, *RfGL* trainers, and others as appropriate.
- Each child is considered, planned for and followed in conferences over the school year.

Intervention Level 2: *Targeted*

- At the *targeted*, or intervention, level, individual children are selected to participate in peer playgroups.
- When playgroup intervention is recommended, the child's parents and other significant adults are integrated into the process.
- Children are selected for this intervention because they have emotional, social, behavioral, cognitive, communicative, developmental, or health vulnerabilities that may be already severe (diagnosable) or may lead to severe problems. Over 35 percent of children entering preschools may be in this category. (Boyer, 1991; Carnegie Corporation of America, 1994).

Intervention Level 3: *Expanded* (Part C)

- The *expanded*, or referral, level is for children who have had or who warrant Part C evaluation or diagnosis (required to be at least 10 percent of children entering Head Start) for developmental challenges.
- Children in this category are included in a peer playgroup when it will enhance their individual treatment plans or help their parent accept referral to Part C.

Intervention Level 4: *Inclusive*

- This inclusive level of intervention includes Levels 1: *Individualized* and 2: *Targeted* as described above plus other services such as Level 3: *Expanded* (Part C); parent-child psychotherapy; and/ or other services.

Fig. 2 Intervention levels for Children. (Shahmoon-Shanok, Lamb-Parker, et al., 2005a, p. 411)

thereafter. This strategy saves time and adds weeks or months to service delivery. Simultaneously, it eludes the parental resistance frequently provoked by typical approaches to evaluation, diagnosis, and referral for a child with mental health or developmental problems.

In order to get children into services quickly, the *RfGL* program does not require that parents participate. Instead, *RfGL* has honed outreach techniques to parents. Most parents do become involved in the program either initially or over time. To begin establishing relationship and communication about a child, the PPP therapist might send good news notes in the parent's favorite mode of communication, such as a text or voicemail or the therapist might walk a parent to the subway and, with permission, even get on the subway with her or him. The therapist might instead meet somewhere near the parent's workplace. Although they understand that the services are offered under the auspices of a mental health agency located elsewhere, between 90 % and 98 % of parents offered *RfGL* services, agree to their child's participation in PPP (Shahmoon-Shanok et al. 2005a, b).

Apparently easier for parents to accept than other forms of psychotherapeutic referrals, *RfGL* uses small playgroups consisting of two to five children under the leadership of a respectful, responsive psychotherapist, or co-therapists. Playgroups meet two times a week for 1 h over 8 to 10 months, sometimes continuing into a second year. Children are picked up by their therapists from their classroom who walk with them to their sessions in a separate playroom or dedicated area. The small playgroup space is furnished with toys and books, a few pillows and a rug. Each item is selected to encourage children to relax and relate their stories either symbolically or more concretely, as they become able. The playthings provided include dress-up clothes, cars and trucks, dolls, play-dough, crayons or markers, blocks, pillows, soft balls or beanbags, animals, puppets, a dollhouse and family figures, cash registers, play money, pretend food, plates and utensils, and scarves and sheets to cover children or drape over the table to fashion an outfit, or quiet enclosure, a hiding space, or symbolic place such as home or a car. These materials provide children with opportunities for solitary and cooperative play, interaction, relatedness, as well as exploration and telling, either concretely or symbolically, of their stories. The deeply attuned listening that each child receives from the therapist helps him/her organize stories. Also, high-intensity affective interchanges (Schore 1994) with peers in an ongoing family-like system gradually helps children come to know themselves and their ideas, as well as become interested in the ideas, emotions, and stories of others (Brusiloff and Witenberg 1973; Pressman and Blumenfeld 1981; Shahmoon-Shanok 2000; Shahmoon-Shanok et al. 2005a; Shanok et al. 1989).

Children with contrasting dispositions are grouped together. For example, internalizing, depressed children are not placed with several others like them. Similarly, children who are predominantly dysregulated are not placed in the same group. By offering children personality styles different from their own, each child is provided with alternative emotional, personality, and defensive pattens with which to engage, struggle, identify, play, and learn over time. Such groupings seem to enhance a child's reflective capacities as each is faced with trying to comprehend what might motivate the behavior and thoughts in a child who has thoughts, feelings, and intentions which can be similar to or different from themselves. Nudging each child's curiosity about the mind of the other is a hallmark of an approach aimed at enhancing reflective capacity.

The reasons that PPP groups, facilitated by an attuned adult, are developmentally helpful to young children have been identified and organized as 16 enabling agents (Shahmoon-Shanok 2000; Shanok et al. 1989). Within this framework, the therapist works toward development of relationship and basic safety as s/he values each child and the group-as-a-whole (Shahmoon-Shanok 2000). S/he promotes, even cherishes, each child's growing sense of individual self and of the individuality of others within the context of the group (and naturally evolving sub-groupings within it). When the therapist exclaims over the absence of a group member, "I wonder what Jeremy would say about that truck if he were here . . . ," she furthers the children's development of object constancy while reinforcing the irreplaceable role each child has in the group as a whole. The child is also repeatedly provided with a model of what it looks like to be reflective. The frequent use of words like "I wonder" conveys that the mind of the therapist is engaged with thinking about the mind of the other, in this case, Jeremy.

Co-creation of meaning and the development of rituals and narratives advance the sense of belonging among the members of the group (Shahmoon-Shanok 2000). The therapist facilitates the development of particular shared rituals and routines that are meaningful to individual group members. The rituals and routines that evolve from the children's interactive activities elevate their sense of safety and security within the group. Shared rituals, cohesive group procedures, and narratives thus provide a fundamental sense of a home-base for each group member's sense of belonging and the deepening of his or her relationships. Over time, the children co-create meaning and a sense of group cohesion and power through the shared activities, play, and rituals that they evolve. For example, the group may begin to run ahead of the therapist every time, slam the door in her face and gleefully hide for her to find them: each knows that this is a game. Group members develop a history and evolving narratives about themselves as a group ("Let's get ahead and hide!" or "Hey, let's build that boat again so Oscar can fall out and get saved!" or "Remember when Elena started to talk? We were happy that day"). In so doing, they fashion a deep sense of belonging to an entity with a mutually understood identity, similar to that of a robust family.

The habitual ways of being together, in a therapeutic context, described here as rituals are akin to patient–therapist relationships which are formed in individual treatment. Each therapeutic dyad, for example, dances a dance as they start a session, but each finds slightly different steps which then become theirs to repeat and vary together. The verbalization of past shared experiences exemplified above with the conjoined meaning-exclamation "remember when . . . " are akin to aspects of parent–child attachment-facilitating behavior. For example, this kind of interaction has been described previously in the context of newly adopted children where the parent–child attachment was facilitated by adoptive parent's spontaneously bringing up recent shared experiences (Steele et al. 2007). The use of the word "remember" manifests meta-cognitive processes related to reflective functioning that emerge in many of the children as they internalize their therapists and their friends.

Smaller than the classroom, the group becomes a symbol for family, as well as the locus to re-work family dilemmas, emotions and roles. The character and mood of each PPP group, created with guidance from the therapist through the development of relationships, is also similar to that of a family system (Shahmoon-Shanok 2000). As infants enter the world within a family system, they have a deep and dramatic effect on every member of their family system. This impact causes growth and change in each parent and sibling, even as those family members affect the development of their baby and growing child over time. Indeed, children make waves in their families and within each family member and thus they come to feel felt (Winnicott 1987; Siegel 2007, 2010). Similarly, the PPP system is responsive to each of its elements as significant modifiers. Each child experiences the momentum which emerges from causing a difference in someone else. In that process, the children experience both strength and weakness in relationships, while simultaneously exerting a dynamic impact on everyone else. At the same time, the children feel their emotional needs being heard, felt, digested, and respected.

Peers as Generative Change Agents in PPP

Group dynamics in PPP are similar to those of other psychotherapeutic groups: Children unconsciously assign themselves roles as extensions of their problems and play out awareness of their roles or fantasies of desired roles (Slavson 1979). Stimulation in PPP provides children with the opportunity to provoke and absorb from each other while developing novel symbolic play routines, thereby broadening their capacities for self-expression (Slavson and Schiffer 1975). Thus, the relationships that emerge within the therapeutic group process enable children to help each other overcome difficult emotional experiences and express affective states in increasingly appropriate ways. When small groups of diagnosable or at-risk children are together with few rules, intense rivalries, longings and affects about the entire range of human themes burst forth. In PPP, children commonly experience and encounter states of high affect, massive motivation to connect with each other even in rivalry, plus enormous ambition to emulate each other which provokes penetrating practice, discovery, and learning.

Within peer playgroups, led by a psychotherapist who adheres to certain principles and is supported in reflective supervision (Murphy et al. in press; Shahmoon-Shanok 2006, 2009; Shanok 1991/1992; Shanok et al. 1995; Siegel and Shahmoon-Shanok 2010), something powerful happens among the children which exerts a pull toward growth along multiple developmental lines (Freud 1965). What then, are the required conditions for children to promote each other's development? In playgroups, the therapist consistently gives the following message to the children: "Our one rule is that people and things need to always be safe." When partnered over time with a relationally oriented adult partner who has the primary goal of helping the children to feel safe, children begin to work out and exercise their relational skills with each other. The therapist invites wide open expression of emotions, activities, words, ideas, and play. Ruptures are common and often extreme. In response, the therapist models strategies for repair, helping each child's needs to become known, communicated, and represented.

These frequent rows become the occasions around which negotiation and repair sequences serve to fortify a child's sense of self-with-strengths (Shahmoon-Shanok 2000). Such bumpy encounters are very much akin to the ruptures and repairs described in the relational psychotherapy process (Safran and Muran 2000). In PPP, the therapist models the abilities to hear, respect, and appreciate each child's unique desires. The therapist also helps those who need it to negotiate multiple points of view and communicate their own. For example, with permission a therapist might place a hand on the shoulder of the child for whom s/he is speaking and then also do it for the other child in the fight, going back and forth, speaking for each. Group members develop first the ability to stand still, then to listen, then to tolerate, and later to empathize with points of view different from their own. This process enables children to gain the ability to communicate and negotiate in the midst of conflict. Just like in typical family systems as each child discovers herself, "each 'I' grows in the context of meaningful other 'I's'" (Shanok et al. 1989, p. 87) and as a part of the "We." In this process, children appear to deepen their capacities for reliable and secure attachment.

As Jordan (1985) notes about intersubjectivity in adult relationships,

> In a mutual exchange one is both affecting the other and being affected by the other. There is both receptivity and active initiative towards the other ... Intersubjectivity carries with it some notion of motivation to understand another's meaning system from his/her frame of reference and ongoing and sustained interest in the inner world of the other .... (p. 2)

Jordan anticipated the recent turn in relational psychotherapy and psychoanalysis and several related fields, for example theory of mind (Bretherton and Beeghly 1982), innate intersubjectivity which was termed mother–infant bi-directional exchange (Trevarthen 1979, 1989), mentalization (Fonagy and Target 1997), reflective function (Fonagy et al. 2002; Schore 1994), mindsight (Siegel 1999), and interpersonal neurobiology (Siegel 1999, 2008).

Intensively and inherently interpersonal because of its nature, the *RfGL* therapist emphatically and empathically represents the perspective of each child until he is able to do it for himself. The therapist viscerally enacts a synchronous sense of each child's self and of the other. In those interactions and the negotiation and repair sequences which follow, each child experiences the caring attunement of the therapist. Occasionally, children may also sense or stumble into strong emotions evoked within the therapist. With many recurring, gut level interchanges experienced, witnessed, and always mediated by a therapist dedicated to repair, children's relational capacities are advanced.

The diagram which follows (Fig. 3) summarizes the PPP model and the assumed intrapsychic links fueling PPP's interventions. PPP, embedded in *RfGL*'s 16 enabling agents (Shahmoon-Shanok 2000), strongly influences adaptive affective skills (i.e., capacity for mentalization; flexibility in, and a range of emotions; and positive peer representations), behavioral skills (i.e., interactive play behaviors), social skills (i.e., having reciprocated friendships), and the acquisition of improved gestural–verbal communication and other pre-academic skills. Just as these capacities underlie attachment security in typically developing children, these skills are fed by and feed into attachment security in PPP children and finally result in their improved school readiness. As readers digest the intertwining case story of two children which follows, it may be useful to return to this figure and reflect upon the abrupt, insistent circles of communication (Greenspan 1993) between the children, Samantha and Simon.

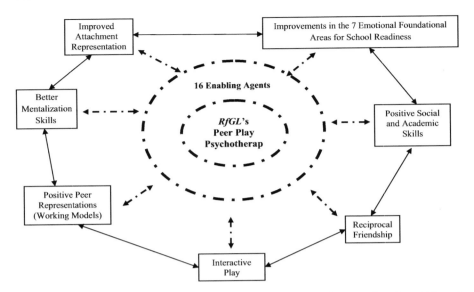

Fig. 3 *RfGL*'s enabling agents foster both will and vision for growth across domains within and among the children in PPP

Two Case Examples[1]

Simon, a 3.6-year-old, second-generation Hispanic–American boy lived with his mother, father, and twin brother. Prior to entering the public preschool in which he was treated, Simon's mother had removed him and his twin brother from their former preschool due to reports from the director that other children were terrified of Simon. He displayed self-destructive behaviors that we later understood were reactions to his sensory sensitivities activated by noise, commotion, and touch. Whenever his surroundings were loud or busy, Simon would throw violent tantrums. He fell to the ground, screamed, cried, banged his head, and bit his hand until he drew blood. As an apparent response to his inability to control internal sensations, Simon had also developed many compulsive behaviors, like closing and opening each door he saw, in a futile attempt to gain some sense of control. A tantrum would ensue every time Simon was not permitted to try to control his surroundings in this and other habitual ways. Yet Simon was physically aggressive towards others only if they came too close to his body, as he misperceived touch as a threat, or if they tried to take a toy away from him. Deemed the "bad twin" by both his family and school, Simon had internalized an injured, anguished self-image.

At home, Simon's mother had tremendous difficulty setting limits and did not know how to help him control his fierce outbursts. Seemingly desperate for help, she

---

[1] All identifying information has been changed. The story is told from the perspective of his therapist, the third author.

immediately accepted the referral for Simon to participate in *RfGL* and in weekly individual sessions for her to develop tools to manage his behavior and her own anxiety. Over time, Simon's mother reported an intergenerational pattern in which she and her mother were unable to control their anger and verbal aggression. She also reported that Simon witnessed occasional verbal arguments between herself and his father, but denied incidents of abuse or domestic violence.

Simon did not have friends anywhere and his brother, who had grown frustrated with his many outbursts, stopped playing with him in order to develop separate friendships. In his class, Simon was unable to negotiate with peers and, when urged to share or take turns, his aggressive tantrums intensified other children's intense dislike. He often yelled at teachers and refused to follow routines. Diagnosed by the team with a Regulation Disorder of Sensory Processing Type B, Negative/Defiant using *Diagnostic Classification: 0–3R* (Zero to Three Press 2005), Simon's needs extended beyond mental health. He received speech-language therapy, occupational therapy, and had a special education itinerant teacher (SEIT) in his classroom. Guided by my supervisor, I kept close contact with each of his service providers and supported communication among, as well as between, each of them and his parents.

Simon participated in PPP with Samantha, a first generation, Spanish-speaking child living with both parents and her two older siblings. The youngest of three children, Samantha was treated like a princess. She was given whatever she wanted, whenever she wanted it; sharing or turn-taking were never demanded of her. Generally compliant with adults, her parents reported having no concerns regarding her behavior at home. Although they had noticed that she was bossy with her siblings and cousins, it had not occurred to them that she might have difficulty adjusting to school.

Samantha entered daycare speaking only Spanish and was placed in a class where the teachers and a few children spoke Spanish as well. Nevertheless, it quickly became evident that Samantha experienced severe separation anxiety that impeded her ability to regulate, learn, and form peer relationships. Dropped off at school each morning by either her mother or father, she cried for 1 to 3 h and sometimes for the entire day. Diagnosed as having a Separation Anxiety Disorder consistent with *D C: 0–3R* (Zero to Three Press 2005), Samantha was unable to focus or attend to classroom activities, did not communicate with teachers or interact with other children, and typically appeared sad and withdrawn when she was not crying. Her teachers were increasingly concerned and her parents, also worried, readily accepted the referral to enroll her in *RfGL*. Her desolation lasted over a month before Samantha began PPP and continued in the classroom after she started for about another month.

Prior to being placed together in a playgroup, Simon and Samantha were placed in two separate PPP groups. The other children in Simon's group were Ashley, a seemingly angry child with underdeveloped play skills, and Ryan, a selectively mute boy. In this group, Samantha seemed afraid and consistently refused to go to the playroom with her assigned therapist and the group. My supervisor noticed that she was developing a classroom bond with Ryan, the selectively mute boy in Simon's group which I led. Ryan and Samantha offered each other comfort. They both experienced difficult adjustments to beginning school but seemed to feel comfortable communicating only to each other, in Spanish. My supervisor realized that Samantha might be more receptive to playgroup if Ryan was present and suggested that I spend time interacting with Ryan in their classroom with the hope that Samantha would gradually begin to feel comfortable with me.

After 2 weeks of three time weekly visits to their classroom, Samantha sat in a chair next to me. While resting my forearm on the table, Samantha walked two fingers up my arm and then quickly withdrew her hand with a tiny smile. She then prompted me to reciprocate by pointing to my hand and then to her arm. Following her lead, this back-and-forth lasted several minutes, until she stopped and pointed to a picture of a bunny on her shirt and said "conejito." I replied by simply smiling at her and saying "bunny." Samantha nodded, smiled, and walked away.

Hesitantly, Samantha came with Ryan to the next session. Although Simon's inability to engage with peers had become evident with a severe tantrum in the first session when another child tried taking a toy from him, his tantrums were happening less often. Oscillating between solitary, parallel and to cooperative play at first only with Ryan, Samantha was able to return to playgroup each session. It was evident that she did not like Simon. She ignored his fledgling attempts to engage and became very irritated by his tantrums.

As the group's therapist, I often felt helpless and ineffective. I relied greatly on the support of my supervisor and our *RfGL* team to help me understand what I could do to calm down myself in order to assist him and the other children. After a few months noticing my interventions with Simon, other group members began to comment on what triggered his aggressive behavior: "Oh, he didn't like those loud noises!" They began to develop an understanding of his underlying positive intentions and subsequently began to create roles for him in their increasingly cooperative play schemes.

When the other children in the group graduated from preschool a few months later, Samantha and Simon remained as a group of two. Through the first few weeks together without others, Samantha successfully ignored Simon and made evident her continued dislike for his belligerent, loud behavior. However, over time Samantha appeared to realize that if she were to expand her play schemes, she would have to include Simon. Evidencing her strong will, Samantha used her speedily expanding English to communicate her reasoning for why she would not play with him. As Simon grew more tolerant of her, Samantha increasingly challenged him. Rather than giving Simon a toy that he had wanted, Samantha held on and made him wait. As we helped Simon control his aggressive impulses and express them through symbolic play, it became obvious that he was very intelligent with strong play skills that had been rendered invisible by his reactivity.

Both Simon and Samantha were acquiring emotionally relevant lexicons, often using a feeling face chart that I repeatedly offered. Scrutinizing my interventions with Simon, Samantha began to decipher the positive intentions behind his behaviors. Although she did not always tolerate the behaviors, she became more accepting of Simon as a playmate. Samantha entered Simon's play more frequently and, together they developed more complex play routines. Samantha also began to use the face chart when surveying and reflecting aloud on Simon's conduct and affective experiences.

Approximately 1 year after his group began and in the midst of playing with Samantha, Simon looked up at the clock that he had broken a few months prior and said "I broke that. I was angry. I was really, really angry and I broke the clock." It appeared that, once he was no longer distracted by his belligerent reactivity to sensory stimuli, Simon could acquire and use language to describe the emotions that fed his actions. At around the same time, Simon also developed an imaginary play scheme where he was a monster that destroyed the playroom. The "Simon Monster" aggressively dumped all the toys onto the floor, knocked over chairs, growled at Samantha and me, and held up his hands as claws. Through reflective supervision, I began to understand that Simon felt like there was a monster inside of him that he had been unable to control, but could now express symbolically.

Three months later, the "Simon Monster" returned, but in a different form. Simon hid behind a puppet show curtain and growled and he reached claw-like hands through the curtain, until he emerged and said that he was a monster. Rather than aggressively destroying the room, he made large, slow movements, knocked over chairs and dumped bins of toys with smooth, controlled body movements. Samantha initially responded by throwing soft balls at Simon in an attempt to protect me. She then narrated his behavior. For example, when he shook the curtain she exclaimed, "He's shaking my room." When he growled, she announced, "No habla" and interpreted his feelings, stating that he was "mad." Simon recruited Samantha to be a monster as well, indicating his dawning ability to initiate symbolic play with peers. I exclaimed, "Wow, Simon has really learned how to control that monster!" Using their experiences with the newly evolved "Simon Monster," Simon and Samantha generated a ritual in which they ran ahead of me to the playroom for each subsequent session and hid behind the curtain, joyously affiliative monsters conspiring together to playfully attack me.

Two months prior to my departure from the preschool, I began the termination process with Simon and Samantha. Simon initially responded that he was sad and drew a picture of a sad face. One month later, Simon introduced an elaborate symbolic play scheme where he and Samantha plotted together to kill me, their departing therapist. During the termination process, Samantha began refusing to leave the playroom at the end of each session. My supervisor helped me recognize the parallels of separations from her mother in the morning and the separations from me at the end of each session which she knew were leading up to our permanent separation. Empathizing with her emotions, I allowed her to bring a toy along for the walk back to the classroom with the understanding that she would return it to me prior to entering its door. Initially, Samantha responded well, but soon began bolting back to the playroom instead. Sometimes I had to set physical limits and carry her to the classroom. Simon, accustomed to the limits on his antagonistic behavior months before, now began to set limits on Samantha's by exclaiming, for example, "You're not allowed to run!"

On the day of their final session, Samantha and Simon dumped every bin of toys onto the floor and into a large pile. Samantha explained that I would have to clean up the toys alone. When I reflected back to them that it would take a long time without help, they explained that it will take me "forever" to pick up the toys so I could never leave. Simon and Samantha's increasingly resourceful relationship enabled them to work together to impart their affection, distress, and anger about my leaving. At the end of the session, Simon and Samantha hid in the playroom closet. After a few minutes, I opened the door and found Simon softly crying with Samantha's arm around him providing comfort.

Discussion with my supervisor enabled me to cope with my own sad feelings and past experiences of separation and loss. The interactions through the termination process, leading up to and including what occurred between the children in the closet, indicated Simon's growing ability to use relationships with other children to help him experience and express feelings that otherwise might have been too onerous to endure. His new sense of control extended outside the playroom: He was better able to follow the classroom routine, listen to teachers and decrease the frequency and intensity of tantrums in school.

Children who had previously avoided Simon now sought him out as a popular playmate. His behavior at home also improved and his mother became better able to set firm, appropriate limits without yelling in an uncompromising, angry tone. Similarly, Samantha's progress in the playroom generalized to the classroom, as she began to utilize her strong negotiation skills when interacting with other children. She no longer cried and was able to speak about her feelings upon separation. She seemed cheerful most of the time and engaged both with other children and with the range of classroom activities and materials. Samantha's sarcastic sense of humor surfaced, yet she was not ever mean. Simon and Samantha completed the school year as best friends in the classroom, soon graduated, and moved on to kindergarten.

Discussion and Conclusion

The vignette of Simon and Samantha illustrates how PPP utilizes peer relationships to promote individual and interpersonal growth within the small context of the group and the larger context of the preschool classroom. The reader can glimpse here two children who, though different in character and developmental level, experienced an ardent relationship which propelled their robust, intersubjective process. The therapist began by trying to establish a relationship with each individual child and with the group-as-a-whole and facilitated "a secure and accepting environment in which the child feels safe to explore thought and feelings" (Johnson and Clark 2001, p. 247). Simon, who was faced with constant threats to and through his sensory system, was unable to symbolically express his impulses through play or language. Like many other children with over-responsive systems, aggressive dysregulation became a maladaptive pattern for him. Disintegrating into inner- and outer directed aggression was initially his best defense against his helplessness and vulnerability. Despite social repercussions, he came to use this self-protective force to cope and feel some power (Johnson and Clark 2001; Koplow 2007; Lieberman and Van Horn 2008; Willock 1983).

Simon's psychotherapist observed and reflected aloud on his behaviors and emotions and established a sense of permissiveness in the playroom. This provided him with the opportunity to ventilate in a safe space while also receiving feedback from peers, thus offering them the ability to help modify his behavior over time (Schiffer 1969). The sense of permissiveness established by the therapist enables children in PPP to inherently know that the playroom is a different space where they are safe to express whatever they need and feel, as long as the safety of everyone present is not threatened (Johnson and Clark 2001). Simon was encouraged to use the space and time to develop skills to cope with and master experiences of dysregulation, disappointment, anxiety, fear, insecurity, and confusion that led to maladaptive self-destructive and hostile behaviors (Shahmoon-Shanok 2000, p. 217–237).

In PPP, children are often in fervent competition with each other for the attention of the therapist, especially at the outset. Indeed, children sometimes feel themselves to be in actual danger in PPP, both because of their inner worlds and outer reality, as well as because of the real threats the other children sometimes pose. Like a primary maternal figure with an infant, the therapist keeps the children safe over time, moving into the role of an attachment figure. Perhaps because they have rivals and because the therapist must make herself very clear in her positions, the children have an accelerated and magnified set of interactions with the therapist. The children see how the therapist functions in terms of her utter loyalty to each child. Simultaneously, she manifests her commitment to keep them all safe by being fair, but different, in her handling of every child in the group.

With young and often primitive children, PPP can be very taxing psychologically and emotionally for staff and trainee therapists. Intense transferential patterns are evoked by each of the children, as well as by sub-groups and by the entire group. It is not unusual, for example, for a therapist to experience gut-wrenching feelings of being left out that bring up long-forgotten echoes from school or family-of-origin experiences. Transmuting such reactions into useful awareness and empathic interventions is essential and requires a system of reflective individual and group supervision.

With ongoing support from her reflective supervisor and her *RfGL* team, Simon's therapist provided meaningful, caring interventions that redirected his aggressive and self-destructive behaviors without denying either his underlying emotions or impulses. By accepting Simon's experience of affective-bodily states, his therapist enabled him to possess the sense that he could be understood and attended to, rather than rejected, even when he was totally dysregulated. As the therapist observed and reflected upon other children's behaviors and feelings, Simon, in turn, slowly became able to notice and draw on the observations of other children in the playgroup. They, in their turn, were able to present him with more appropriate alternatives because none were as dysregulated as he.

By posing questions to the group such as, "What can we do to fix this?" the therapist also displayed and encouraged his use of negotiation and repair (Safran and Muran 2000; Shahmoon-Shanok 2000). In the latter part of treatment, Simon and Samantha were able to reflect on their therapist's past efforts to form a plan to resolve conflict, which always included both children's desires, and then develop such solutions for themselves. Simon was learning what Samantha already knew: Tolerating delay of gratification is worth it because being with the other is at least equally desired. Each child developed the sense of being effective with and useful to others. They also developed a moral sense or conscience, the experience of what it takes to live generatively with others within society (Shahmoon-Shanok 2000).

Through the formation of peer relationships, preschool age children "report on the behavioral characteristics of their peers" and "tend to make negative judgments about peers who escalate rather than self-regulate aggression" (Howes 1987, p. 263). Accordingly, when Samantha rejected Simon's aggressive behaviors, he grew more aware of her and, eventually, began to modify his own behavior (Shahmoon-Shanok 2000; Slavson and Schiffer 1975). The intense group dynamics inherent in PPP provoked Samantha to provide Simon with immediate, uncompromising feedback regarding his behavior, essentially teaching him what is socially acceptable (Johnson and Clark 2001).

Children develop reciprocity as they formulate creative solutions to help each other when experiencing difficult emotions. Like Samantha, children in PPP become "auxiliary therapists" as they "have an unusual capacity to assess correctly the reasons for another child's behavior, sometimes even pointing out underlying meanings" (Slavson and Schiffer 1975, p. 374). In these powerful interchanges, emotions and words become conjoined, eminently meaningful and powerfully evocative (Shahmoon-Shanok 2000). These types of interactions rarely occur in individual psychotherapy, which is usually characterized by the regulating effect of a calm psychotherapist. Additionally, the therapeutic interventions in PPP occur in real time, meaning that affect-laden events are addressed as they happen. This is quite different from children who experience peer relational challenges but relay the incident later in a therapeutic or other reflective context.

Children in the playgroup illustrate appropriate behaviors and responses to each other (Shechtman and Ben-David 1999). When Simon watched others negotiate, take turns, share, and engage in cooperative play, he was learning vicariously. Later, he developed ways to problem-solve with Samantha rather than act on his impulses. Simon also benefited from Samantha's growing ability to notice his positive intentions, although expressed through negative behavior, which helped him neutralize aggressive feelings by accepting his behavioral reenactments (Shanok et al. 1989). This concept is related to both Simon and Samantha's growth in reflective functioning, which "permits the child to respond not only to other people's behavior, but to his *conception* of their beliefs, feelings, hopes, pretense, plans, and so on" (Fonagy and Target 1997, p. 679, [italics in original]). Simon and Samantha's development of reflective functioning allowed them to understand and ascribe underlying mental states and behaviors as predictable and meaningful (Fonagy and Target 1997; Slade 2002). We can see Simon's early steps in developing reflective awareness when he said that he had broken the clock because he had been very angry. And when Samantha said that the "Simon Monster" was mad, she demonstrated achievement of a higher level of reflective functioning that allowed her to recognize that Simon's inner world fueled his behavior. Able to accurately identify (with) his underlying emotion, she responded in a sensitive, emotionally attuned manner (Slade 2002).

By "practicing reticence" (Trevarthen 1979, p. 343) in her own role, the therapist enabled Samantha to further her role as an "auxiliary therapist" (Slavson and Schiffer 1975, p. 374). In this role, Samantha asserted herself and set limits for Simon's inappropriate behavior while communicating why she would not tolerate his behavior. By finding her own strong voice in the face of a boy who had intimidated her in the past, Samantha helped maintain the safe space of the playroom while developing self-knowledge as a clear, resourceful, emotionally intelligent little person who could have a generative impact on another human being. She learned that she could accomplish these tasks while successfully setting limits to further her own sense of safety.

At many of these junctures, reflective supervision played a critical role for the therapist. As she hovered with the impulse to step in, she remembered her supervisor's voice gently but strongly urging, "Step back ... look, linger and marvel." In group supervision and videotaped PPP sessions used in *RfGL* training seminars, her supervisor modeled restraint in her own clinical work. This had a profound effect on the therapist: she slowed down, learned to listen and see more deeply, discerning the children's own potentials within their interactions. With this stance, her respect for the children's own capabilities blossomed. She increasingly tried to intervene non-verbally unless a verbal intervention is required. For example, "Both of you want that car so much! How can we work this out?"

The therapist's commitment to promoting feelings of safety and security served as a catalyst in the development of secure attachment representations. Samantha's difficulty finding security in interpersonal relationships outside her enmeshed family caused her resistance to leaving the classroom with her first assigned therapist. The initial goal then became helping Samantha feel safe enough to come to the playroom. Her new therapist worked at becoming a familiar presence in the classroom. Through the course of treatment, the therapist reflected to the playgroup on Samantha's struggles with separations and helped draw parallels to the emotions experienced by her peers. This normalized Samantha's affective experiences and provided opportunities for the therapist and the children to demonstrate alternate ways of coping.

PPP acts as a self-reinforcing and sustaining modality. Opportunities for consolidation of therapeutic gains are readily available with the very same partners outside of the therapy room (Shahmoon-Shanok 2000; Shanok et al. 1989). As children become better able to show or verbalize their needs and feelings, most teachers and parents become more successful at understanding and providing for them. Not only can these children move toward developmental and relational growth, but their home and school environments can usually change to accommodate and fortify those shifts (Shahmoon-Shanok et al. 2005a, b).

Due to the unique contribution of positive peer relationships to improved academic and social functioning (Coolahan et al. 2000; Fantuzzo et al. 2004; Howes 1987; Lindsey 2002), group play interventions lie at the heart of the successful early developmental trajectories. Enhanced attachment representations and mentalization capacities also play significant roles in predicting the content of representational schemas and the quality of peer interactions. PPP, while cognizant of the effects of the family on each child's development, makes use of available resources, making the most of readily available peer relationships to alter the internal working models of relationships in the minds of preschool children and promote growth. As the children begin to hold each other in mind, they experience their therapist and PPP colleagues simultaneously holding them in mind (see Pawl 1995; Slade 2002).

Despite the limited research on group play psychotherapy with very young children (Ginott 1958; Landreth 2002; Lomonaco et al. 2000), our experience suggests that group play psychotherapies are effective interventions and should be utilized frequently. Family cannot substitute for peer relationships. Starting young and continuing through life, friendships with peers are among the most significant of relationships.

Peers in PPP attract, provoke, demand, coax, wheedle, and squeeze growth out of each other in ways that a psychotherapist cannot. Within the safe space developed in PPP, what the children do with each other, no therapist, parent, or teacher could. When grouped together in the specific circumstances described in this chapter, peers emerge as potential therapeutic allies, gems previously hidden in plain sight. Within therapeutic conditions, the children become instruments of positive learning and growth for their friends and for themselves.

Acknowledgments Whatever vigor and potency this chapter holds is possible only given the enormous body of esteemed work by numerous colleagues, trainees, as well as the staff, children, and family members of numerous day care, Head Start and other preschool centers which have been part of the *Relationships for Growth & Learning (RfGL)* program, Institute for Infants, Children and Families, an arm of JBFCS in New York City over many years. The authors are deeply grateful for their loyalty, vivacity and the relationships for growth and learning each of them embody and engender.

Our gratitude and esteem goes out to Marybeth Logan, LCSW, *RfGL*'s Associate Director and both reflective and administrative supervisor of the Core Team as well as Vicki Katz, LCSW, *RfGL* Senior Core Team member, reflective and co-administrative supervisor. Vicki Katz supervised the cases presented in this paper. This chapter also benefitted enormously from the research partnership that *RfGL* has with the Clinical Psychology Program of the New School for Social Research, co-directed by Miriam Steele, PhD and Howard Steele, PhD. Their remarkable student, Ozlem Bekar, has served *RfGL* as researcher, statistician, team member, and communicator par excellence. With her leadership, several New School students helped with parts of the literature review. Warm and enthusiastic thanks to each of them! We acknowledge with immense gratitude the support by New York's Administration for Children's Services (ACS) which enabled a *RfGL* demonstration project at three Head Start centers over 5 years. The project included research on many aspects of *RfGL* intervention and training by the Mailman School of Public Health, Columbia University, with Principle Investigator Faith Lamb-Parker, PhD and Ellen Halpern, PhD as Co-Principle Investigator. We are deeply indebted also to three Head Start directors, Ronni Fischer, Veronica Klujsza, and Lenore Peay, who were active, wise and essential guiding members of the project's Steering Committee from 1999 through late 2004. With a great sense of appreciation, we also recognize all the many Head Start staff members, whose growing partnership and daily dedication were essential to the children's burgeoning growth. With a sense of abiding thankfulness and admiration, our hearts remain with the children's parents and all the children who participated.

References

Aikins, J. W., Howes, C., & Hamilton, C. E. (2009). Attachment stability and the emergence of unresolved representations during adolescence. *Attachment and Human Development, 11,* 491–512.

Armsden, G. C., & Greenberg, M. T. (1987). The inventory of parent and peer attachment: Individual differences and their relationship to psychological well-being in adolescence. *Journal of Youth and Adolescence, 16,* 427–454.

Baggerly, J. N. (2004). The effects of child-centered group play therapy on self concept, depression, and anxiety of children who are homeless. *International Journal of Play Therapy, 13,* 31–51.

Beebe, B., Lachmann, F., & Jaffe, J. (1997). Mother-infant interaction structures and presymbolic self-and object representations. *Psychoanalytic Dialogues, 7,* 113–182.

Bills, R. E. (1948). Non-directive play therapy with retarded readers. *Journal of Consulting Psychology, 14,* 140–149.

Bornstein, M. H., Hahn, C., & Haynes, O. M. (2010). Social competence, externalizing, and internalizing behavior adjustment from early childhood through early adolescence: Developmental cascades. *Development and Psychopathology, 22,* 717–735.

Bowlby, J. (1973). *Attachment and loss: Vol. 2. Separation: Anxiety and anger.* New York: Basic Books.

Bowlby, J. (1980). *Attachment and loss: Vol. 3. Loss: Sadness and depression.* New York: Basic Books.

Bowlby, J. (1982a). Attachment and loss. Vol. 1. Attachment (2nd ed.). New York: Basic Books.

Bowlby, J. (1982b). Attachment and loss: Retrospect and prospect. *American Journal of Orthopsychiatry, 52,* 664–678.

Boyer, E. L. (1991). *Ready to learn: A mandate for the nation.* Princeton: Carnegie Foundation for the Advancement of Teaching.

Bratton, S., Ray, D., Rhine, T., & Jones, L. (2005). The efficacy of play therapy with children: A meta-analytic review of the outcome research. *Professional Psychology: Research and Practice, 36,* 376–390.

Bretherton, I., & Beeghly, M. (1982). Talking about internal states: The acquisition of an explicit theory of mind. *Developmental Psychology, 18,* 906–921.

Brusiloff, P., & Witenberg, M. J. (1973). *The emerging child.* New York: Aronson.

Cassidy, J., Kirsh, S., Scolton, K., & Parke, R. (1996). Attachment and representations of peer relationships. *Developmental Psychology, 32,* 892–904.

Cicchetti, D., Toth, S. L., & Rogosch, F. A. (1999). The efficacy of toddler-parent psychotherapy to increase attachment security in offspring of depressed mothers. *Attachment and Human Development, 1,* 34–66.

Cicchetti, D., Rogosch, F., & Toth, S. L. (2000). The efficacy of toddler-parent psychotherapy for fostering cognitive development in offspring of depressed mothers. *Journal of Abnormal Child Psychology, 28,* 135–148.

Cicchetti, D., Rogosch, F., & Toth, S. L. (2006). Fostering secure attachment in infants in maltreating families through preventive interventions. *Development and Psychology, 18,* 623–649.

Coolahan, K., Fantuzzo, J., Mendez, J., & McDermott, P. (2000). Preschool peer interaction and readiness to learn: Relationships between classroom, peer play and learning behaviors and conduct. *Journal of Educational Psychology, 92,* 458–465.

Danger, S., & Landreth, G. (2005). Child-centered group play therapy with children with speech difficulties. *International Journal of Play Therapy, 14,* 81–102.

Egger, H. L., & Angold, A. (2006). Common emotional and behavioral disorders in preschool children: Presentation, nosology, and epidemiology. *Journal of Child Psychology and Psychiatry, 47,* 313–337.

Erikson, E. H. (1963). *Childhood and society* (2nd ed.). New York: Norton.

Fantuzzo, J., Sutton-Smith, B., Atkins, M., Meyers, R., Stevenson, H., Coolahan, K., & Manz, P. (1996). Community-based resilient peer treatment of withdrawn maltreated preschool children. *Journal of Consulting and Clinical Psychology, 64,* 1377–1386.

Fantuzzo, J., Sekino, Y., & Cohen, H. L. (2004). An examination of the contributions of interactive peer play to salient classroom competencies for urban head start children. *Psychology in the Schools, 41,* 323–336.

Fenichel, E. (Ed.). (1992). *Learning through supervision and mentorship to support the development of infants, toddlers and their families.* Arlington: Zero to Three: National Center for Clinical Infant Programs.

Fonagy, P., & Target, M. (1997). Attachment and reflective function: Their role in self-organization. *Development and Psychopathology, 9,* 679–700.

Fonagy, P., Gergely, G., Jurist, E. J., & Target, M. (2002). *Affect regulation, mentalization and the development of the self.* New York: Other Press.

Fraley, R. C. (2002). Attachment stability from infancy to adulthood: Meta-analysis and dynamic modeling of developmental mechanisms. *Personality and Social Psychology Review, 6,* 123–151.

Freud, A. (1965). *Normality and pathology in childhood.* New York: International Universities Press.

Freud, S. (1930). In J. Strachey (Ed.), *Civilization and its discontents* (Trans: J. Strachey). New York: W. W. Norton and Company.

Gagnon, S. D., & Nagle, R. J. (2004). Relationships between peer interactive play and social competence in at-risk preschool children. *Psychology in the Schools, 41,* 173–190.

Gilliam, W. S. (2005). *Prekindergartners left behind: Expulsion rates in state prekindergartner systems.* New Haven: Yale University Child Study Center.

Ginott, H. G. (1958). Play group therapy: A theoretical framework. *International Journal of Group Psychotherapy, 8,* 410–418.

Greenspan, S. I. (1993). *Playground politics: Understanding the emotional life of your school-age child.* New York: Addison-Wesley.

Greenspan, S. I., & Wieder, S. (1998). *The child with special needs: Encouraging intellectual and emotional growth.* New York: Da Capo.

Halpern, E., & Rinks, S. (2004). *Preschool therapeutic playgroup process: A theory accounting for its effectiveness.* Poster presented at the Head Start's 7th National Research Conference. Washington, DC.

Halpern, E., Lamb-Parker, F., & Grant, M. (2004a). *Relationships for growth: A preliminary look at social-emotional and cognitive outcomes.* Poster presented at the Head Start's 7th National Research Conference, Washington, DC.

Halpern, E., Lamb-Parker, F., Seagle, C., & Grant, M. (2004b). *Relationships for growth: Program evaluation.* Poster presented at the New York Zero-to-Three Network's Annual Meeting, New York, NY.

Halpern, E., Lamb-Parker, F., & Acra, C. (2005a). *Social-emotional functioning and academic risk: Cluster analysis of social-emotional measures differentiates academic functioning in Head Start children.* Poster presented at the Head Start's 8th National Research Conference: Serving Children through Partnership and Collaboration, Washington, DC.

Halpern, E., Lamb-Parker, F., Acra, C., & Jaspen, D. (2005b). *Cluster analysis of social-emotional data from the relationships for growth project.* Poster presented at the Head Start's 8th National Research Conference: Serving Children through Partnership and Collaboration, Washington, DC.

Hay, D., Payne, A., & Chadwick, A. (2004). Peer relations in childhood. *Journal of Child Psychology and Psychiatry, 45,* 84–108.

Howes, C. (1987). Social competence with peers in young children: Developmental sequences. *Developmental Review, 7,* 252–272.

Howes, C. (1988). Peer interaction of young children. *Monographs of the Society for Research in Child Development, 53,* 1–92.

Hughes, C., & Dunn, J. (2007). Children's relationhips with other children. In C. A. Brownell & C. B. Kopp (Eds.), *Socioemotional development in the toddler years* (pp. 177–200). New York: Guilford.

Johnson, S. P., & Clark, P. (2001). Play therapy with aggressive acting-out children. In G. L. Landreth (Ed.), *Innovations in play therapy: Issues, process, and special populations* (pp. 239–255). New York: Brunner-Routledge.

Jordan, J. V. (1985). *The meaning of mutuality*. Paper presented at a Stone Center Colloquium, Wellesley College, Wellesley, MA (Copyright 1986).

Kagan, J., & Zentner, M. (1996). Early childhood predictors of adult psychopathology, *Harvard Review of Psychiatry, 3*, 341–350.

Kataoka, S. H., Zhang, L., & Wells, K. B. (2002). Unmet need for mental health care among US children: Variation by ethnicity and insurance status. *American Journal of Psychiatry, 159*, 1548–1555.

Kobak, R., Cassidy, J., Lyons-Ruth, K., & Ziv, Y. (2006). Attachment, stress, and psychopathology: A developmental pathways model. In D. Cicchetti & D. Cohen (Eds.), *Developmental psychopathology: Theory & method* (Vol. 2). (pp. 333–369). Hoboken: Wiley.

Koplow, L. (2007). *Unsmiling faces: How preschools can heal* (2nd ed.). New York: Teachers College Press.

Laible, D. J., Carlo, G., & Raffaelli, M. (2000). The differential relations of parent and peer attachment to adolescent adjustment. *Journal of Youth and Adolescence, 29*, 45–59.

Landreth, G. L. (2002). *Play therapy: The art of the relationship* (2nd ed.). New York: Brunner-Routledge.

Lavigne, J. V., Gibbons, R. D., Christoffel, K. K., Arend, R., Rosenbaum, D., Binns, H., & Isaacs, C. (1996). Prevalence rates and correlates of psychiatric disorders among preschool children. *Journal of the American Academy of Child and Adolescent Psychiatry, 35*, 204–214.

Lieberman, A. F. (2006). *Addressing domestic violence as a risk to infant mental health: The theory and practice of child-parent psychotherapy*. Paper presented at the Annual Meeting of the American Academy of Child and Adolescent Psychiatry, Los Angeles, CA.

Lieberman, A. F., & Van Horn, P. (2008). *Psychotherapy with infants and young children: Repairing the effects of stress and trauma on early attachment*. New York: Guilford.

Lieberman, A. F., Weston, D. R., & Pawl, J. H. (1991). Preventative intervention and outcome with anxiously attached dyads. *Child Development, 62*, 199–209.

Lieberman, A. F., Van Horn, P., & Ippen, C. G. (2005). Toward evidence-based treatment: Child-parent psychotherapy with preschoolers exposed to marital violence. *Journal of the American Academy of Child and Adolescent Psychiatry, 44*, 1241–1248.

Lindsey, E. W. (2002). Pre-school children's friendships and peer acceptance: Links to social competence. *Child Study Journal, 32*, 145–156.

Lokken, G. (2000). Tracing the social style of toddler peers. *Scandinivian Journal of Educational Research, 44*, 163–176.

Lomonaco, S., Scheidlinger, S., & Aronson, S. (2000). Five decades of children's group treatment: An overview. *Journal of Child and Adolescent Group Therapy, 10*(2), 77–96.

Meltzoff, A., & Moore, M. (1977). Imitation of facial and manual gestures by human neonates. *Science, 198*, 75–78.

Murphy, A., Steele, M., & Steele, H. (in press). From out of sight, out of mind to in sight and in mind: Enhancing reflective capacities in a group attachment-based intervention. In J. Bettmann & D. D. Friedman (Eds.), *Attachment-based clinical work with children and adolescents*. New York: Springer.

National Scientific Council on the Developing Child. (2008). *Mental health problems in early childhood can impair learning and behavior for life: Working paper No. 6*. Accessed from Harvard University Center for the Developing Child website: http://developingchild. harvard.edu/index.php/resources/reports_and_working_papers/working_papers/wp6/

Osofsky, J. D., & Lieberman, A. F. (2011). A call for integrating a mental health perspective into systems of care for abused and neglected infants and young children. *American Psychologist, 66,* 120–128.

Pawl, J. H. (1995). The therapeutic relationship as human connectedness: Being held in another's mind. *Zero to Three, 15,* 1–3.

Pressman, P. S., & Blumenfeld, H. (Eds.). (1981). Group therapy with high risk preschool children: A thematic issue developed by the child development center. *Family and Child Mental Health Journal, 7.*

Ramani, G., Brownell, C. A., & Campbell, S. B. (2010). Positive and negative peer interaction in 3- and 4-year-olds in relation to regulation and dysregulation. *Journal of Genetic Psychology, 171,* 218–250.

Roberts, R. E., Attkisson, C. C., & Rosenblatt, A. (1998). Prevalence of psychopathology among children and adolescents. *American Journal of Psychiatry, 155,* 715–725.

Roosevelt, E. (1958, March). *In your hands.* Booklet presented to the United Nations Commission on Human Rights, United Nations, New York.

Safran, J. D., & Muran, J. C. (2000). *Negotiating the therapeutic alliance: A relational treatment guide.* New York: Guilford.

Schiffer, M. (1969). *The therapeutic play group.* New York: Grune & Stratton.

Schore, A. (1994). *Affect regulation and the origin of the self: The neurobiology of emotional development.* Hillsdale: Erlbaum.

Shahmoon-Shanok, R. (2000). Infant mental health perspectives on peer play psychotherapy for symptomatic, at-risk and disordered young children. In J. D. Osofsky & H. Fitzgerald (Eds.), *The WAIMH handbook of infant mental health* (pp. 199–253). New York: Wiley & Sons.

Shahmoon-Shanok, R. (2006). Reflective supervision for an integrated model: What, why & how? In G. M. Foley & J. D. Hochman (Eds.), *Mental health in early intervention: Achieving unity of principles and practice* (pp. 343–379). San Francisco: Jossey-Bass.

Shahmoon-Shanok, R. (2009). What is reflective supervision? In S. Heller & L. Gilkerson (Eds.), *A practical guide for reflective supervision* (pp. 7–24). Washington: Zero to Three Press.

Shahmoon-Shanok, R., Lamb-Parker, F., Halpern, E., Grant, M., Lapidus, C., & Seagle, C. (2005a). The relationships for growth project: A transformational collaboration between Head Start, mental health and university systems. In K. M. Finello (Ed.), *Handbook of training and practice in infant & preschool mental health* (pp. 402–424). San Francisco: Jossey-Bass.

Shahmoon-Shanok, R., Lapidus, C., Grant, M., Halpern, E., & Lamb-Parker, F. (2005b). Apprenticeship, transformational enterprise, and the ripple effect: Transferring knowledge to improve programs serving you children and their families. In K. M. Finello (Ed.), *Handbook of training and practice in infant & preschool mental health* (pp. 453–486). San Francisco: Jossey-Bass.

Shahmoon-Shanok, R., Henderson, D., Grellong, B., & Foley, G. M. (2006). Professional preparation for practice in an integrated model: The magic is in the mix. In G. M. Foley & J. D. Hochman (Eds.), *Mental health in early intervention: Achieving unity in principles and practice* (pp. 383–422). San Francisco: Jossey-Bass.

Shanok, R. S. (1991/1992). The supervisory relationship: Integrator, resource and guide. *Zero to Three, 12*(2), 16–19. (Reprinted in (1992). *Learning through supervision and mentorship* (pp. 37–41), E. Fenichel (Ed.), Arlington: Zero to Three: National Center for Clinical Infant Programs).

Shanok, R. S., Welton, S. J., & Lapidus, C. (1989). Group therapy for preschool children: A transdisciplinary school-based program. *Child and Adolescent Social Work, 6,* 72–95.

Shanok, R. S., Gilkerson, L., Eggbeer, L., & Fenichel, E. (1995). Reflective supervision: A relationship for learning. In *A guidebook and videotape.* Zero to Three: National Center for Infants, Toddlers and Families.

Shechtman, Z., & Ben-David, M. (1999). Individual and group psychotherapy of childhood aggression: A comparison of outcomes and processes. *Group Dynamics: Theory, Research, and Practice, 3,* 263–274.

Siegel, D. J. (1999). *The developing mind: Toward a neurobiology of interpersonal experience.* New York: Guilford.

Siegel, D. J. (2007). *The mindful brain: Reflection and attunement in the cultivation of well-being.* New York: W. W. Norton & Co.

Siegel, D. J. (2008). *The neurobiology of 'we'* [DVD]. USA: Sounds True.

Siegel, D. J. (2010). *Mindsight: The new science of personal transformation.* New York: Bantam Books.

Siegel, D. J., & Shahmoon-Shanok, R. (2010). Reflective communication: Cultivating mindsight through nurturing relationships. *Zero to Three Special Issue on Reflective Supervision, 31*(2), 6–14.

Slade, A. (2002). Keeping the baby in mind: A critical factor in perinatal mental health. *Zero to Three, June/July,* 10–16.

Slavson, S. R. (1979). Play group therapy. In C. Schaefer (Ed.), *The therapeutic use of child's play* (pp. 241–252). New York: Jason Aronson.

Slavson, S. R., & Schiffer, M. (1975). *Group psychotherapies for children: A textbook.* New York: International Universities Press.

Smith, N., & Landreth, G. (2003). Intensive filial therapy with child witnesses of domestic violence: A comparison with individual and sibling group play therapy. *International Journal of Play Therapy, 12,* 67–88.

Spinrad, T. L., Eisenberg, N., Harris, E., Hanish, L., Fabes, R. A., Kupanoff, K., & Holmes, J. (2004). The relation of children's everyday nonsocial peer play behavior to their emotionality, regulation, and social functioning. *Developmental Psychology, 40,* 67–80.

Sroufe, L. A., Egeland, B., Carlson, E., & Collins, W. A. (2005). *The development of the person: The Minnesota study of risk and adaptation from birth to adulthood.* New York: Guilford.

Steele, H., & Steele, M. (2008). On the origins of reflective functioning. In F. N. Busch (Ed.), *Mentalization: Theoretical considerations, research findings, and clinical implications* (pp. 133–158). Mahwah: Analytic Press.

Steele, M., Hodges, J., Kaniuk, J., Steele, H., D'Agostino, D., Blom, I., Hillman, S., & Henderson, K. (2007). Intervening with maltreated children and their adoptive parents: Identifying attachment facilitating behavior. In D. Oppenheim & D. Goldsmith (Eds.), *Clinical applications of attachment theory* (pp. 58–89). New York: Guildford.

Sweeney, D. S., & Homeyer, L. E. (1999). *The handbook of group play therapy: How to do it, how it works, whom its best for.* San Francisco: Jossey-Bass.

Tolan, P. H., & Dodge, K. A. (2005). Children's mental health as a primary care and concern: A system for comprehensive support and service. *American Psychologist, 60,* 601–614.

Trevarthen, C. (1979). Communication and co-operation in early infancy: A description of primary inter-subjectivity. In M. Bulloma (Ed.), *Before speech: The beginning of inter personal communication* (pp. 321–347). Cambridge: Cambridge University Press.

Trevarthen, C. (1989). Development of early social interactions and the affective regulation of brain growth. In C. von Euler, H. Forssberg & H. Lagercrantz (Eds.), *Neurobiology of early infant behavior* (pp. 191–216). London: Macmillan.

Troyat, H. (1967). *Tolstoy.* New York: Doubleday.

Tyndall-Lind, A., Landreth, G. L., & Giordano, M. A. (2001). Intensive group play therapy with child witnesses of domestic violence. *International Journal of Play Therapy, 10,* 53–83.

Vaughn, B. E., Colvin, T. N., Azria, M. R., Caya, L., & Krzysik, L. (2001). Dyadic analyses of friendship in a sample of preschool-age children attending Head Start: Correspondence between measures and implications for social competence. *Child Development, 72,* 862–878.

Wakaba, Y. Y. (1983). Group play therapy for Japanese children who stutter. *Journal of Fluency Disorders, 8,* 93–118.

Waters, E., Weinfield, N. S., & Hamilton, C. E. (2000). The stability of attachment security from infancy to adolescence and early adulthood: General discussion. *Child Development, 71,* 703–706.

Weinfield, N. S., Sroufe, L. A., & Egeland, B. (2000). Attachment from infancy to early adulthood in a high-risk sample: Continuity, discontinuity and their correlates. *Child Development, 71,* 695–700.

Wilkinson, R. B. (2004). The role of parental and peer attachment in the psychological health and self-esteem of adolescents. *Journal of Youth and Adolescence, 33,* 479–493.

Willock, B. (1983). Play therapy with the aggressive, acting-out child. In C. E. Schaefer & K. J. O'Connor (Eds.), *Handbook of play therapy* (pp. 386–411). New York: Wiley.

Winnicott, D. W. (1987). *Babies and their mothers.* New York: Addison-Wesley.

Zero to Three (2005). *DC: 0–3R: Diagnostic classification of mental health and developmental disorders of infancy and early childhood* (revised edition). Washington: Zero to Three Press.

Zero to Three: National Center for Infants, Toddlers and Families. (1992). *Heart start: The emotional foundations of school readiness.* Washington: Zero to Three Press.

The Impact of Intervention Points of Entry on Attachment-Based Processes of Therapeutic Change with Prepubertal Children

Geoff Goodman

Perhaps the central question asked by attachment researchers who have both studied and designed attachment-based early intervention programs for mothers and infants is, "Where should one intervene to improve the infant's attachment security?" Regardless of the researcher, two answers always seem to be offered: either (1) at the level of maternal mental representation, or (2) at the level of maternal behavior. For example, both van IJzendoorn et al. (1995) and Berlin (2005) present almost identical models of attachment transmission that predict that maternal mental representation of her attachment relationship to her parents influences her own maternal behavior, especially sensitivity and contingent responsiveness, which in turn influences the infant's attachment security. This developmental pathway simultaneously privileges the quality of the mother–infant relationship as the foundation of infant attachment security and later socioemotional adaptation (Weinfield et al. 1999) and illustrates the means by which the quality of attachment is believed to be transmitted intergenerationally.

All attachment-based early intervention programs seem to focus exclusively on the maternal mental representations or behavior as the agents of change. One group of researchers explained that "as an adult, the caregiver has more degrees of freedom in changing patterns of attachment–caregiving interactions than does the child" (Cooper et al. 2005, p. 141). This top–down approach to intervening in infant attachment security has become a core tenet of attachment theory (Sroufe 1985). The mother is believed to be providing emotional "training" to the infant "through her behavioral and emotional reactions to her baby [which] is thought to build the child's working model of attachment, and thus lays the foundation for the expectations the child has concerning his or her relationship with the mother" (Cassidy et al. 2005, p. 38).

De Wolff and van IJzendoorn (1997), however, questioned conceptualizing maternal sensitivity as the mediator between the maternal mental representation of her own childhood attachment experiences and the infant's attachment security. Explanations

G. Goodman (✉)
Clinical Psychology Doctoral Program, Long Island University,
Brookville, NY, USA
e-mail: Geoffrey.Goodman@liu.edu

J. E. Bettmann, D. D. Friedman (eds.), *Attachment-Based Clinical Work with Children and Adolescents,* Essential Clinical Social Work Series,
DOI 10.1007/978-1-4614-4848-8_9, © Springer Science+Business Media New York 2013

of the small statistical relation between maternal mental representations and infant attachment security identified by van IJzendoorn (1995) vary: inadequate assessment of maternal sensitivity, need for greater focus on constructs related to but not identical with sensitivity (e.g., reflective functioning, secure-base provision), inadequate theory, and infant temperament (Berlin 2005; Cassidy et al. 2005; Goodman 2002; Slade et al. 2005). As the child becomes older, his or her mental representations of parental relationships become increasingly resistant to change as past interactional experiences become habitual, expected, and reliable forecasters of future caregiver behavior (Bowlby 1980; Bretherton 1985; Main et al. 1985). Thus, when considering attachment-based intervention for children beyond preschool, do the assumptions of caregiver-focused interventions still apply? An attachment-based model for understanding potential intervention points of entry for prepubertal children is presented in Fig. 1. This model includes the two traditional intervention points of entry (A and D) as well as five other points of entry either recently targeted (B and C) or not targeted at all (E, F, and G) in current attachment-based early intervention programs (Bosquet and Egeland 2001; Slade et al. 2005).

The Impact of Parent, Child, and Therapist Characteristics on Intervention Points of Entry

Theoretical preferences often influence the selection of intervention points of entry. Researchers can empirically test the success of interventions through rigorous execution of intervention protocols and evaluation of the outcomes to be modified. Intervention evaluators ask two questions: (1) does the intervention modify the outcomes targeted by the therapist, and (2) which intervention points of entry are targeted most effectively for which parents and children? Attachment-based early intervention programs usually target maternal sensitivity and infant attachment security as variables to be modified (Cooper et al. 2005; Dozier 2003). More recent intervention strategies focus on maternal reflective functioning and maternal mental representations of the relationship with the child (Slade et al. 2005).

Attachment-based intervention programs with the prepubertal child, however, need to emphasize other outcomes such as the regulation of severely dysregulated affects, frustration tolerance and self-inhibition, autonomy, social competence, self-esteem, intellectual functioning, and academic achievement. Erikson (1950) identified industry versus inferiority as the prevailing psychosocial crisis of the prepubertal developmental period, with competence as the successful outcome and inferiority as the failed outcome. Thus, I am proposing that intervention strategies need to target psychological domains that enhance competencies particular to a psychosocial developmental period.

The intervention points of entry to be selected and outcomes to be modified also depend on the psychological characteristics of the parents and child as well as the therapist. The effectiveness of an attachment-based intervention program depends on the extent to which these psychological characteristics either facilitate or interfere

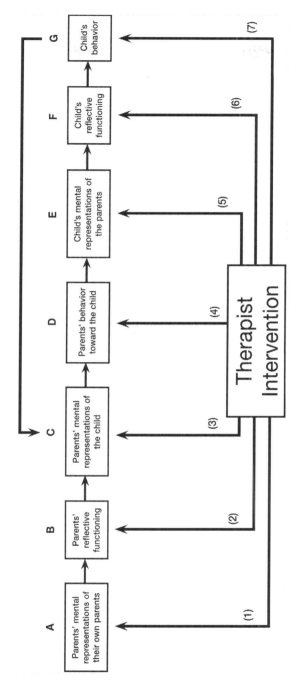

Fig. 1 Potential intervention points of entry based on attachment theory

with the implementation of the intervention. The intellectual functioning of both the parents and child should influence the selection of the intervention points of entry as well as outcomes to be targeted for modification. For example, some psychoanalysts (e.g., Clarkin et al. 1999; Kernberg et al. 1989) recommend insight-oriented therapy only to patients assessed as having average or higher intellectual functioning, while referring the rest to cognitive-behavioral therapy such as dialectical behavior therapy (Linehan 1993). It is believed that patients assessed as having higher intellectual functioning are more likely than others to have the capacity to engage in the kind of abstract reasoning and symbolic thinking required for insight-oriented clinical work.

Reflecting on the effectiveness of their intervention program that targets the improvement of reflective functioning in low-income, high-risk, first-time mothers, Slade and her colleagues (Slade et al. 2005) commented that reflective functioning "is linked to executive capacities such as planning and reasoning that are part and parcel of higher cortical functioning" (p. 171). In mothers assessed as having intellectual functioning in the borderline range, "we have at times had so much difficulty just getting them to hold onto an idea, let alone link it to other mental or objective phenomena, that we have had to lower our goals and expectations significantly" (p. 171). Considering my thesis that intervention points of entry need to vary with parental characteristics, I question whether the authors' selection of mothers' reflective functioning as the primary intervention point of entry was appropriate for everyone, given the serious intellectual limitations of some of the mothers. The same caution applies to the intellectually limited prepubertal child. A more behavioral intervention approach might therefore be indicated. Of course, the child's behavior reciprocally influences the mother's mental representations of the child in the form of behavioral expectations (see points of entry G to C in Fig. 1).

I am similarly proposing that the severity of psychopathology present in the parents and child should also influence the selection of the intervention points of entry as well as outcomes to be targeted. For example, Slade and her colleagues (Slade et al. 2005) identified severe psychopathology (notably, posttraumatic stress disorder [PTSD], and borderline personality disorder) among at least 40 % of the mothers enrolled in their attachment-based early intervention program. Because of the underlying personality disorganization, these mothers experienced particular difficulty in acquiring reflective functioning. The therapist working with such mothers must tend to both the daily chaos and upheaval in these mothers' lives as well as "the mothers' awareness of their babies' needs and intentions" (p. 172). Poverty, social deprivation, community violence, and the resultant sense of powerlessness might also be barriers to the acquisition of reflective functioning. One might conclude that severe psychopathology, like low-intellectual functioning, might pose formidable obstacles to the exploration of mental representations or the acquisition of reflective functioning in both parents and prepubertal children. Thus, a more behavioral approach might be considered for some of them.

Yet other researchers believe that a more intensive, psychodynamic intervention approach in which mental representations are explored and modified is especially indicated, while behavioral interventions are contraindicated. For example, in a discussion of the four principles that underlie their attachment-based early intervention program, Cooper et al. (2005) suggested that

> ... [T]eaching parents concrete behavior management techniques may be limited by a parent's problematic history and the resulting tendency to experience strong negative emotion (which may evoke defensive behavior) in response to particular signals from her or his child. Although a parent may cognitively learn about more sensitive responses, there may in fact be no increased likelihood of the parent applying those new responses when emotionally aroused by the child's signals. Our assumption is that applying these changes in a lasting manner requires changes in the parent's internal working models [mental representations], which are partially regulated by emotional reactions. (pp. 131–132)

In parents who experience strong negative emotion or "acute emotional arousal"–DSM-IV-TR (American Psychiatric Association (APA) 2000) criteria of borderline personality disorder, and PTSD, respectively–perhaps the only interventions that have any likelihood of modifying the prepubertal child's socioemotional outcomes target those points of entry that focus on parent and child mental representations or reflective functioning (see points of entry A–C, E, F in Fig. 1). Several studies (Egeland et al. 2000; Olds 2005; Spieker et al. 2005) concur that intensive attachment-based early intervention programs can be more effective with more psychiatrically compromised mothers than with those less compromised. Spieker et al. (2005) speculated that the fragility of their clinically depressed mothers elicited more care-giving responses from their therapists, while self-sufficient mothers were more frustrating to work with.

Research demonstrates that the prepubertal child diagnosed with serious emotional disturbance is more likely to benefit from an intensive, relationship-focused intervention approach than a less-intensive (fewer weekly sessions) approach (Fonagy and Target 1996; Target and Fonagy 1994a, b). Notably, less emotionally disturbed children respond equally well regardless of intervention intensity (frequency and duration of intervention). In fact, in a retrospective study of 763 child cases, less-intensive approaches resulted in negative outcomes for almost 60 % of the children with serious emotional disturbance, but positive outcomes for over 80 % of the less emotionally disturbed children (Fonagy and Target 1996; Target and Fonagy 1994a, b). These findings suggest that the selection of intervention point of entry might be more consequential for children with serious emotional disturbance than for children simply at risk for serious emotional disturbance. I am suggesting that intervention strategies must take into account (1) developmental period, (2) parental and child intellectual functioning, (3) parental and child socioemotional functioning (level of emotional instability), and (4) treatment phase. I am also suggesting that higher intellectual and socioemotional functioning increases one's intervention options with both parent and child. Conversely, lower intellectual functioning might limit the therapist to behavioral strategies, while lower socioemotional functioning might limit the therapist to relationship-focused strategies that identify underlying mental states (Clarkin et al. 1999; Egeland et al. 2000; Erikson 1950; Fonagy and Target 1996; Kernberg et al. 1989; Olds 2005; Slade et al. 2005; Spieker et al. 2005; Target and Fonagy 1994a, b).

In the following two clinical illustrations, I will demonstrate how I selected various intervention points of entry based on the conditions I have just reviewed. Both treatment cases have obvious similarities: two boys presenting with primary encopresis (their bowels were never trained), few peer relationships, and an aversion to the awareness of feeling states. Both patients also lived in intact family systems with two parents who were intelligent, reasonably successful, and living in middle-income, suburban neighborhoods. The mothers of both patients were highly emotionally reactive to this encopretic behavior, which compounded their children's problems. These two children, however, differed significantly in age and possibly in the etiology of their encopresis. The first child began to show an interest in using the toilet when two traumatic events occurred: the birth of a younger brother and shortly thereafter, a natural disaster that created significant emotional upheaval for him and his family. The second child was placed into full-time childcare at a very young age but experienced no known traumatic events. Finally, I hope to demonstrate that keeping all the possible intervention points of entry (see Fig. 1) firmly in mind during the treatment of prepubertal children will expand the therapist's options and thereby allow the therapist to fit the treatment to the patient and improve its effectiveness.

First Clinical Illustration

Maverick (a pseudonym) was a 4½-year-old boy who was experiencing toilet-training difficulties. He had bowel movements during the day and night in his underwear. These accidents occurred at school, on the school bus to and from school, and at home. Maverick could sit in his own products for hours and not seem uncomfortable. When a classmate asked him what that smell was, Maverick told him, "Just ignore it." He also experienced interpersonal difficulties. Maverick needed to control all his interactions with his peers as well as with adults. Other children did not want to socialize with Maverick because the play had to take place on his terms, with his choice of activity and his rules. The parents and teacher reported that Maverick often refused to follow directions, particularly when someone asked him to transition from one activity to another (e.g., watching television to going to bed, eating breakfast to leaving for school, playing with peers to sitting at circle time). After two years of once-per-week individual psychotherapy with me in which Maverick made only modest gains, I began four-times-per-week psychoanalysis in June 2003, recognizing Maverick's strong intellectual skills and stable family system. Maverick was now 6 ½ years old.

Most disturbing to his parents was Maverick's aggression directed toward his brother, who is 2½ years younger. When his brother wanted to inspect one of Maverick's toys, Maverick would hit him hard enough to make him cry. When Maverick's mother changed his brother's diaper, Maverick would sometimes hit his mother. Maverick's use of aggression was not limited to his brother or mother; sometimes he also hit his school peers when they refused to play his games by his rules.

This aggression was not always reactive. In school, Maverick once threw a live bunny against a wall for no apparent reason. When I asked about the incident in the following session, Maverick expressed anger that the teacher later refused to allow him to hold a baby chick. Maverick then demonstrated this sadistic impulse in vivo by gleefully knocking onto the floor a Russian matryoshka of cats, which he referred to as a mommy cat with her baby cats. He then took an action figure and got down on the floor to play with the cats. Maverick then narrated a fantasy story in which the baby cats got inside the mommy for protection from the bad guy action figure. He demonstrated with the figures that the bad guy overpowered the mommy and the baby cats fell out and died. They returned to life, however, and battled against the bad guy, who then died. Then other bad guys came and "touched the insides" of the cats, who were filled with "boiling hot liquid soap." Each bad guy was scalded and died. Then the baby cats got inside the mommy again for protection as before against the original bad guy, who had returned to life. He described that the bad guy then savagely attacked the mommy, who died along with her babies who had fallen out. At the end of the session, Maverick instructed me to clean up all the toys because "I like to order you around." To myself, I interpreted this play to mean that Maverick was feeling completely unprotected by his secure base—his mother. According to Bowlby (1988), infants form attachment relationships with individuals who are most likely to protect them from danger. In times of danger, the infant seeks proximity and maintains contact with that person who can maximize their feelings of security. Once the danger has passed, the infant again feels secure enough to explore the environment, provided the caregiver to whom the infant has formed this special relationship is nearby. This caregiver provides a secure base to the infant. Maverick's play suggests that he had no secure base—his mother could not protect him from danger. The frightening quality of this play also suggests that Maverick had formed a disorganized-attachment relationship. In a disorganized-attachment relationship, the child has no confidence in his or her caregiver; and therefore feels utter helplessness in the face of threat (Lyons-Ruth and Jacobvitz 1999).

During other sessions, Maverick demonstrated possible indications of trauma. While playing Uno or board games, Maverick would often upset the game board and fling all the pieces and the board itself all over the office without warning. He called this event "Hurricane Floyd." I later learned from his parents that at age 2½, Maverick and his parents had fled their home during Hurricane Floyd, which terrified him. When asked about this incident, Maverick reported that he remembered Hurricane Floyd and how loud the thunder and wind were. He described that he remembered his parents looking scared. He then made a statement that he immediately retracted: "God was trying to get me and my mommy." Maverick's baby brother was born only 4 months earlier, which I surmise placed stress on Maverick's mother. Maverick was probably experiencing this new brother as the loss of emotional closeness with his mother: The newborn baby required enormous amounts of attention that Maverick was no longer receiving. From an attachment theory perspective, Maverick might have perceived this new baby as a threat to his secure base. With the secure base less emotionally and physically available, Maverick was already probably feeling worried about his safety as well as angry toward this new intruder. The hurricane only exacerbated these feelings, making them more palpable. I believe that eventually, these feelings necessitated Maverick's retreat from a normal developmental line (toilet training) to his encopretic symptoms, which allowed Maverick to express simultaneously his needs for attention and his anger toward his unprotective parents.

Another intriguing aspect of Maverick's personality involved his making home-made greeting cards for his teacher and school peers. Some of them read, "I'll never hurt you again. Be my friend again." He also gave them stones he believed represented some value to them. I understood these behaviors as representing unsuccessful attempts at undoing, reflective of a sense of guilt over his mistreatment of them and his need to re-establish some sense of closeness to them.

In my early work with Maverick, I tried to contain his chaotic, hurricane-like feelings of anxiety and rage by empathizing with him (see point of entry F in Fig. 1). I made nonthreatening interventions such as, "Gee, that hurricane must have been really scary—you weren't feeling protected." Maverick responded to this containment by becoming more organized in his play; the hurricane-themed aggressive play eventually disappeared. Maverick's encopresis, however, continued unabated. Both parents expressed impatience and frustration with the lack of immediate results; they wanted these behaviors to stop as soon as possible. During a collateral parent session, Maverick's mother clearly articulated the emotional impact of this symptom on her: "I want to kill him!" Simultaneously with my treatment, Maverick's mother decided to take Maverick to a series of experts: an encopresis specialist, a gastrointesti-nal specialist, a neurologist for an EEG (which was negative) and psychostimulant medication (which was prescribed), a neuropsychologist, a school psychologist, a urologist, and a nutritionist. Maverick's mother noted that the neurologist suggested that Maverick had Asperger's disorder and therefore needed a different kind of treat-ment. She conducted some Internet research and drew the same conclusions. I told Maverick's mother that, although I am not a neurologist, I did not believe that the psychostimulant medication would be helpful (see point of entry D in Fig. 1). She snapped back, "Well, nothing else seems to be helping!" I empathized with her frus-tration and impatience—how humiliating and frustrating it must be to be changing Maverick's underwear at age 6 (see point of entry B in Fig. 1). I explained that Maverick did not have Asperger's disorder and sat down alongside her as I reviewed the diagnostic criteria in the DSM-IV-TR (American Psychiatric Association [APA] 2000) and discussed them with her. By the end of the collateral parent session, she agreed that Maverick did not have Asperger's disorder.

I was feeling intense pressure from this exasperated mother to solve the problem of the encopresis quickly; otherwise, she would surely end the treatment as Maver-ick suspected. In the session that followed, Maverick was preoccupied with saying "bye-bye" over and over again. I responded by stepping up my interpretation of the aggression I felt certain was unconsciously responsible for this boy's refusal to be toilet-trained (see point of entry G in Fig. 1). Simultaneously, I moved away from the relationship-building work (see point of entry F in Fig. 1) that proved so effective earlier in the treatment. Maverick responded by withdrawing from me—a kind of iatrogenic negative therapeutic reaction. I believe that I fell victim to his mother's projective identification of her own feelings of incompetence, inadequacy, and dis-illusionment partly because I was experiencing those very feelings in myself, partly due to my own conflicted mental representation of the attachment relationship with my father. My intrapsychic vulnerability was exploited by the mother's projection into me of unwanted aspects of her own parental representation.

In my own training analysis, I gained insight into these dynamics. I was also 2½ years old when my sister was born. According to my parents, my adjustment to her existence was difficult. My family often told me the story that soon after she was born, I bit her toe because she was "making too much noise." My father sent me to my room with no dinner—only one example of his inability to tolerate or understand my angry feelings. My interactions with Maverick's mother exerted pressure on me to identify with those aspects of my representation of my father and project my own self-representation of the resentful, spiteful brother onto Maverick. In other words, I colluded with Maverick's mother against her son, whom I began to perceive from my grown-up, "fatherly" perspective as an unacceptable version of myself.

The unconscious purpose of my confrontational interpretations was to coerce Maverick to start behaving properly (see point of entry G in Fig. 1) rather than to help him to mentalize his affects (see point of entry F in Fig. 1). Metaphorically, Maverick's mother and I were sending him to his room with no dinner. Fortunately, Maverick's desire to come to sessions never wavered; instead, he protected himself during sessions through withdrawal. He would play by himself in a corner. How could I empathize with his mother's frustration, impatience, and devaluation of the treatment (see point of entry B in Fig. 1), and not act on the pressure she was exerting on me to change my method of working with Maverick? This sort of tightrope walking became my primary challenge. Maverick began to interact with me once again and reveal his internal world to me, and his mother experienced less frustration and impatience. For example, he could once again allow me to assume the voice of the Lego robot he was building and interact with me through the Lego robot. This play had completely stopped during my confrontational phase.

Analysis of First Clinical Illustration

In this case, I concluded that Maverick was experiencing severe obsessive–compulsive and oppositional psychopathology that was adversely affecting his familial and social relationships. Maverick's severe psychopathology, coupled with high intellectual functioning, warranted an intensive, relationship-focused therapy that could activate the chaotic mental states in the therapist–patient relationship (see point of entry F in Fig. 1). In the early phase of treatment, this approach served a containing function for Maverick. He played the role of God, wreaking havoc on a scared, helpless child played by me. Rather than trying to re-establish control, I empathized with Maverick's scared, helpless feelings (see point of entry F in Fig. 1). This experience of containment facilitated Maverick's use of me as a secure base-someone who, like an attachment figure, could make him feel safe to explore his own mental contents as well as mine.

In the next phase of treatment, Maverick's mother introduced her interpersonal dynamics into my relationship with Maverick. The frustration and impatience that she was expressing to me resonated with my own interpersonal dynamics, producing a shift in my intervention strategy to point of entry G—essentially a behavioral intervention implemented through a coercive focus on Maverick's aggression. Through my own use of reflective functioning, I recognized this enactment and implemented the original intervention strategy directed at point of entry F. I attempted to contain his mother's feelings of helplessness and embarrassment produced by fragmented mental representations established in the context of her own childhood familial relationships (see point of entry A in Fig. 1).

In the final phase of treatment reported here, I resumed my relationship-building work with Maverick and redirected my intervention strategy at point of entry F. Maverick responded by orienting toward me again and using me as a secure base who was containing his chaotic mental representations. Maverick needed and benefited from intensive, relationship-focused therapy. I quickly learned that my shift in approach adversely affected the treatment. Because of my awareness of options, I was able to consider moving away from a focus on behavior back onto a focus on the child's mind. Like the baseball batter who experimented with a different stance at the plate and figured out it did not work for him and so returned to the old stance, I returned to the stance that had been working for me. I had options, and I exercised them.

Second Clinical Illustration

Dennis (a pseudonym) was a 5-year-old boy referred to me for outpatient psychotherapy by his parents. In the initial consultation in April 2005, Dennis's parents expressed exasperation at their son's reluctance and stubbornness, expressed in his refusal to use a toilet for defecation rather than his pull-ups. They feared that Dennis's toilet-training refusal was going to interfere with his self-esteem as he was beginning kindergarten in the fall. At the time of referral, Dennis was attending preschool for a full day, five days per week. Prior to this placement, Dennis had attended a different preschool for a full day, five days per week since age 2. His mother shared this information with me non-defensively, never having considered the possibility that a very young child might need more physical and emotional proximity to his secure base. I said nothing about this arrangement because both parents had already shared with me their need to work full-time. In the course of treatment, I also learned that the parents did not have relatives nearby such as grandparents (i.e., secondary attachment figures) with whom they could leave Dennis while at work.

Dennis's parents reported that he had never been toilet-trained. At the time of the initial consultation, Dennis had used a toilet "a handful of times," according to his mother. His parents reported that they had attempted toilet training since Dennis was 3, when they attempted rewarding Dennis for using a toilet with M and M's or toys, which had only a very temporary impact on his behavior. Out of exasperation, Dennis's father sometimes used threats to get him to conform to his parents' expectations of using a toilet. For example, his father sometimes said, "I'm going to put you down the drain." He also admitted to kicking Dennis in the buttocks after some accidents. However, his mother sometimes behaved in ways that allowed Dennis to receive gratification from the encopresis. At the time of the initial consultation, Dennis's mother was still cleaning up his accidents, wiping him, and putting new pull-ups on him. His parents' description of this routine strongly suggested that Dennis enjoyed playing the role of the baby with his mother, who readily shared her exasperation with me even with Dennis in the office. His parents also reported other symptoms suggestive of oppositional behavior and a need for control, such as refusal of food presented to him at the dinner table, resistance to getting dressed in the morning, and resistance to getting ready for bed. Dennis also had an obsession with toy monster trucks, monster truck rallies (which he attended with his parents), and monster truck video games. What was originally a father–son activity evolved into a devotion that far exceeded the father's interest. Dennis stated that he wanted to be a monster truck driver when he grew up.

In October 2007, Dennis's mother tearfully shared with me that her son wanted to wear her pantyhose and wanted her to purchase a tutu for him. This gender-conflicted behavior manifested itself intermittently over the next 3 years. In July 2010, at age 10½, Dennis convinced his mother to purchase tights that fit him from a girls' clothing website. He was also watching youtube videos of men wearing business suits who took off their clothes to reveal they were wearing pantyhose underneath. Dennis described to his mother feeling profoundly ashamed of this behavior and refused to talk about it at all. He shut down during sessions when I raised the issue, making himself unavailable for any interactions with me about it. He shared with his mother that his father should not know about this behavior because he feared that his father would ridicule him and call him a "sissy." This assessment of the situation was probably accurate. Although the contents of Dennis's mind with regard to this behavior remained opaque to me, I viewed this behavior as a desire to identify with a nonthreatening maternal figure. His father's occasionally scary demeanor might have made Dennis feel ambivalent about a masculine identity. His interest in feminine clothing might have been an attempt to establish contact with those parts of his gender organization split off from his paternally sanctioned hypermasculinity as exemplified by his fascination with monster trucks. In other words, Dennis might have felt that the only way to protect himself against his scary father was to identify with those aspects of his father that his father values. By identifying with these hypermasculine aspects, Dennis won the temporary approval of his father, yet something else was lost. I contend that this boy's feminine aspects were getting repressed under the weight of the monster trucks and other symbols of hypermasculinity. Like "the return of the repressed" (Freud 1896, p. 170), however, Dennis's femininity leaked through to the surface—in a rather crude form not well integrated with the rest of his personality.

I treated Dennis for five years in once-per-week individual psychotherapy. This therapy included working collaterally with his parents to agree on a uniform behavioral approach to Dennis's difficulties (see point of entry D in Fig. 1) and working with Dennis individually to allow him to express any feelings that might be motivating his reluctance to use a toilet (see point of entry F in Fig. 1). Since the initial referral, both parents made amazing progress in adjusting their behavioral approach to Dennis's toileting difficulties. His father stopped making threats, while his mother stopped cleaning Dennis after accidents, instead getting him to clean up after himself. Dennis began to express angry feelings in therapy sessions which coincided with his increased use of the toilet. During our psychotherapy, Dennis experienced some successes while sitting on the toilet and showed pride in these successes. Nevertheless, Dennis still experienced accidents, which prompted his parents to welcome the prospect of a more intensive, relationship-focused treatment. Thus, I began four-times-per-week psychoanalysis with Dennis in May 2010, when Dennis was 10 years old. The parents were enthusiastic about Dennis's beginning psychoanalysis. I decided against a behavioral approach because of Dennis's high intellectual functioning: I believed that he could eventually work with his symbolized mental contents such as monster trucks representing internal feeling states. I hoped that this work would eventually lead to Dennis's symbolized (i.e., verbal) expression of feelings and a reduced need to act out his feelings by having accidents.

Since the onset of psychoanalysis, Dennis expressed both excitement and eagerness to spend time with me and a resistance to emotional intimacy with me, characterized by endlessly playing competitive games with me in which he compulsively cheated. He could not tolerate losing. Dennis used the defensive processes of isolation of affect and omnipotent control to exert the maximum degree of control over his internal and external world. In other words, Dennis seemed to be able to put his feelings into a compartment and leave them there for long periods of time, which gave him an illusory feeling of control. He also behaved as though he was more powerful than others and could order them around. For example, I had to hold Dennis's monster trucks in a particular way; disobedience resulted in withdrawal and complete emotional unavailability. He seemed to use encopresis as a mode of distancing himself from others and forcing others to distance themselves from him when he or they were getting too emotionally close and therefore making him feel too emotionally vulnerable. Paradoxically, these distancing strategies also maintain emotional involvement, even though the involvement is now antagonistic. Dennis learned that fecal smells are an effective means of removing others from one's proximity, while keeping him emotionally present in their minds as an antagonistic figure. I perceived an intrapsychic conflict over his needs for emotional distance and invincibility that coexisted with his needs for emotional closeness and camaraderie with me. Getting too close to me emotionally put Dennis at risk of the potential for getting rejected or abandoned by me. These are some of the most painful feelings experienced by human beings. I surmise that Dennis experienced these feelings every morning before his parents dropped him off for a full day of childcare at age 2.

I understood Dennis's dysfunction as an anxious-avoidant attachment to his caregivers that has generalized to a mode of relating to his internal and external world, affecting both self-esteem and pleasure-seeking realms, beginning by toddlerhood (a time when toilet training is a prominent developmental task) and continuing through-out childhood. According to Ainsworth (1979), anxious-avoidant attachment is an infant's pattern of relating to his or her caregiver in which the infant paradoxically behaves as though he or she does not need a secure base even when danger is clearly present in the environment. Ainsworth believed that such an infant expects rejection and abandonment during such times and therefore protects himself or herself from the pain associated with these experiences by behaving as though the caregiver has no emotional importance to him or her. Dennis essentially behaved toward signif-icant adults as though he did not need them to survive. A corollary to developing this pattern of relating to others is the corresponding inference–formed far outside awareness–that one's own self is not lovable enough to be worthy of protection and comfort during such times. Dennis essentially experienced himself as inadequate to live outside of his defensive hiding place, and he was deficient in experiencing the feelings and strivings normally associated with preadolescent development (e.g., as-piring to be attractive, relating on a level of mutuality, contemplating a sexuality that involves real people). On the positive side, underneath his defenses, Dennis strongly yearned for human connection. Although greatly obscured by his sadomasochistic façade—inviting punishment from his parents by having accidents that he knew infu-riated them and also inviting the scorn of peers with his fecal smell—he was deeply attached to his parents and became increasingly so to me.

Dennis might have been securely attached during infancy; however, coincid-ing with the difficulties he experienced with toilet training, his parents' attitudes toward him probably became rejecting, which in turn stimulated defensive pro-cesses compatible with an anxious-avoidant attachment pattern such as narcissistic withdrawal—the retreat into his own private interests to the exclusion of significant emotional contact with others. One can observe a prototype of this defensive pro-cess as early as 12 months in the strange situation procedure (Ainsworth 1979), in which the infant snubs the mother and pretends she is not in the room after a brief separation, as if to be saying, "I don't need you. In fact, I am dismissing you from my mind."

Dennis's mother was also experiencing unbearable tension at her workplace, which might have distracted her from being an emotionally present mother. It is unclear whether Dennis's parents were rejecting of him during his infancy, but there is some evidence that they were rejecting of him during his toilet training at age 3. Notably, Dennis was separated from his parents for 40 h per week at a childcare center since age 2. Bowlby (1980) believed that these patterns of relating to care-givers form out of expectations of caregiving early in life and become increasingly resistant to change, and therefore, self-perpetuating over time. Causality was there-fore probably bidirectional: Dennis' toilet-training difficulties likely stimulated and were stimulated by rejecting parental behaviors. The fact that Dennis's parents left him in full-time childcare at such an early age, however, might provide clues about the ultimate direction of causality. Belsky and his colleagues have suggested that the effects of extensive exposure to non-caregiver childcare early in life can be both profound and long lasting. Children left in childcare centers more than 20 h per week are more likely to form an anxious-avoidant attachment than children left in home childcare or left for fewer than 20 h per week (Belsky and Rovine 1988), and they have more teacher-reported externalizing behaviors in later childhood (Belsky et al. 2007). Parents who choose such child-care arrangements might also have pre-existing characteristics (e.g., anxious-avoidant attachment patterns of their own) that could also predispose their children to later struggle with emotional intimacy.

Regardless of the direction of causality or the developmental period when Dennis became anxious avoidant with respect to his relationship with his parents (i.e., infancy vs. toddlerhood), the transference in the treatment strongly suggested this same attachment pattern with me. Dennis spent entire sessions trying to push me away through a variety of means such as flatulating, cheating in competitive games, devaluing me, not answering questions, adopting a know-it-all attitude, or simply denying that I had any impact on him. In some sessions, he chose to play video games that completely excluded me. Dennis once intentionally threw a ball at my face and hit me in the eye. When I pointed out that he had hurt my eye, he started making clucking noises that indicated that he thought I had stopped playing because I was a chicken, afraid of getting hurt.

On the other hand, Dennis was extremely protective of our time together. Dennis's father, who dropped him off on Friday evenings for session, occasionally liked to talk to me about his job, his weekend plans, and Dennis's recent challenges. When this chatting occurred (which I no longer participate in), Dennis scolded his father for taking up his therapy time. His father then usually made a self-deprecating joke and left. If I was 2-min late for session, Dennis let me know that I was 2-min late. It was obvious that Dennis valued the time that we spent together and was willing to assert himself to protect it. This behavior suggested that I became important to Dennis in spite of the anxious-avoidant defensive processes that he typically employed to protect himself against getting emotionally close to others and allowing others to become important to him.

My countertransference reactions were consistent with a therapist who was perpetually assigned a masochistic role to play : I felt helpless, disillusioned, ineffectual, frustrated, humiliated, dismissed, marginalized, and invisible. Typically, I did not feel all these feelings in the same session, but invariably, I felt at least one of these feelings in every session. My countertransference reactions were notable because unlike many of my other therapeutic relationships, I knew exactly what I was feeling in a session with Dennis. There was no ambiguity. In spite of my knowledge of the origins of Dennis's psychopathology, however, I still found my responses to these countertransference reactions at times challenging. For example, when he hit me in the eye with the ball, I felt not only angry but also too stunned to say anything other than to stop the play. Perhaps I was afraid of expressing my own anger—no matter how justified it might have been as a self-protective response.

Clarkin and his colleagues (Clarkin et al. 2006) identified three channels of communication available to patients in the therapy relationship—verbal, nonverbal, and countertransference. Verbal communication represents the patient's use of words to convey thoughts and feelings to the therapist. The patient uses words to symbolize mental states such as feelings. Nonverbal communication represents the patient's use of behaviors to convey their thoughts and feelings (typically used more often by patients with personality disorders). The patient does not use words to symbolize mental states. Countertransference communication represents the patient's use of the therapist's own feelings to convey the patient's thoughts and feelings (also typically used more often by patients with personality disorders). Again, the patient does not use words to symbolize mental states. The channel that Dennis most skillfully used with me was countertransference. Feelings of helplessness induced in me by Dennis led me at various points in the treatment to consider reducing treatment frequency to pre-psychoanalysis levels. Self-reflection, however, always helped me to analyze these moments of countertransference and to recognize them for what they were: self-protective attempts by Dennis to push me away and thus diminish his feelings of vulnerability. Disdain was perfectly suited to accomplish this self-protective goal. In those moments when Dennis was feeling disdainful of me, sometimes it was good enough simply to act as a container rather than a retaliator. Retaliation would only gratify his need for engagement through control without the dreaded experience of any accompanying feelings of vulnerability elicited by the risk of loss of control and by extension, risk of loss of me. Making me angry and getting me to punish him (e.g., by yelling at him or withdrawing from play with him) would represent to him my loss of control, not his. He could control me yet not risk having to face what it feels like to lose someone he loves and depends on for security and comfort. His controlling stance protected him from genuine contact with me based on feelings of mutual love and caring. These feelings require both persons in a relationship to risk feeling hurt by the other person and even risk losing the other person. Dennis felt too frightened underneath his façade to risk more genuine engagement with me. It was easier to provoke me into fighting with him—a controlling form of contact minus the emotional risk. Benjamin (1987) suggested that controlling persons demand recognition of their omnipotence, which they cannot admit to themselves because this very demand reflects controlling persons' need of another person, thus disproving their omnipotence. Dennis found himself squarely in the middle of this dilemma.

Against this backdrop of Dennis's tentative engagement with me while ensconced in a nearly impenetrable, self-protective shell, the treatment focused, on the one hand, on tapping into Dennis's object hunger to draw him out; on the other, on interpretively articulating the anxiety and other latent mental states, which thereby became manifest and accessible. The hope was that this process would motivate in Dennis capacities to cope with and adapt to being more fully in life and result in his developing enduring abilities ("structures"), making defensive retreats unnecessary. If he could get a taste of a reciprocal relationship in which I would allow him to show his vulnerability—his need for recognition and connection—he would want more of this experience and eventually realize that his need for self-protection was unnecessary. I was not going to drop him, no matter how smelly he was, so the risk of rejection and abandonment was lessened. I was creating a mental space for him to try out a different way of being in the world.

Early in the psychoanalysis, Dennis and I struggled to find a therapeutic alliance that could propel us on a path of mutual discovery. Perhaps trying to satisfy my own inaccurate perceptions of my clinical supervisor's expectations, I initially attempted an exclusively interpretive approach focused on Dennis's feelings. This strategy repeatedly failed as Dennis emphatically stated that he did not want to talk about his feelings. He even complained to his mother (who reported it to me) that I asked the same five boring questions in every session—all having to do with feelings. I eventually realized that an exclusively interpretive approach was not going to facilitate a therapeutic alliance. I gradually shifted from an attitude of looking for opportunities to make meaningful analytic interpretations to an attitude of looking for opportunities to make meaningful emotional contact with Dennis as a feeling, desiring person. This new stance also proved difficult. During the first half of this first year of analysis, Dennis erected roadblocks to the path of my discovery of his personhood. He incessantly played competitive board and card games in which he compulsively cheated to guarantee a favorable outcome. One time, in the only game I played with him in which he never cheated, I beat him in checkers. Afterward, I told him that I knew how he could change his strategy to beat me the next time (he had moved his back line too early) and that I could share this information with him. Dennis declined this offer and instead resorted to cheating in all future checkers contests. In Dennis's mind, lack of knowledge is equated with vulnerability; thus, Dennis knew everything. He therefore categorically denied any acknowledgment that I might know something that he did not know. I came to understand why an exclusively interpretive approach would not work with Dennis, at least in this early phase of treatment, because interpretation requires a patient who realizes that he or she is not omniscient and is therefore willing to consider the information given by the therapist. A standard psychodynamic interpretation such as, "You poop your pants to push people away so that you can be in control of rejecting feelings," implies that the listener (in this case, Dennis) does not already know this information about himself. Because Dennis knew everything, he did not need this information from me. Another therapeutic strategy would be necessary.

The equation, "knowledge equals power," and its corollary, "lack of knowledge equals vulnerability," made the therapeutic work especially challenging for me. Not only did Dennis deny that I possessed knowledge that could be beneficial to him, but also Dennis refused to share knowledge about himself with me, thus making me feel helpless. At times, it was almost impossible to learn anything about his life outside sessions—his home life, teacher and peer interactions at school, or friendships. Sometimes, Dennis actively refused questions about his life; at other times, he just ignored me altogether. One exception to this knowledge blackout was Dennis's only discernible passion: monster trucks. Dennis often spent entire sessions talking about monster trucks—their designs, the drivers, the tricks they perform, the winners in various categories of monster truck contests, and their sponsors. He also demonstrated an encyclopedic knowledge of monster truck trivia. At some point, I quietly entertained the idea that Dennis might have sub-threshold Asperger's disorder because of his markedly restricted repertoire of interests, but his frequent eye contact and physical affection initiated with both parents directly refuted this idea. In these sessions, I played the role of the interested, admiring pupil of the master teacher's vast knowledge and expertise. He was delighted and content to maintain a monotonous pattern of sharing facts about monster trucks. I felt marginalized in our relationship, unable to reach him. The extensive mirroring he received from me, however, might have allowed him to begin to form an image of himself in my mind as someone worthy of attention and admiration. The goal then was for Dennis, gradually, to identify with this new self-image with its own accompanying expectations of comfort and support from his family, friends, and me.

In January 2011, I tried to break up this monotony. Dennis was making a Lego house for a monster truck driver to live in. I started building a Lego monster truck, but Dennis instructed me to stop because the truck would be unable to fit into his Lego garage. I countered that I was going to build a truck called the (patient's last name) Express that I would make out of aluminum, an ultra-light metal that would "get some really sick air" (a colloquial expression I learned from Dennis that indicates that during a jump, the truck stays in the air for a long time). Dennis immediately refuted this claim because aluminum monster trucks were outlawed in 2000, and monster trucks also have to be a certain weight. I then told him that I was going to hide cinder blocks in my truck's secret compartment that the inspectors would never find, which I would take out after the pre-contest weigh-in. Dennis countered that there could be no secret compartments. In spite of its mildly antagonistic nature, we were engaged in a relationship. I was making contact with him by using my own imagination and getting him to engage with my mind (see point of entry F in Fig. 1).

Soon after this session, Dennis brought in his toy monster trucks in a customized suitcase, laid them out on the floor, set up ramps and obstacles, and directed each truck through the obstacle course with little variation—each truck performing identically to the previous one. I took a truck and began doing unconventional tricks with it. Dennis immediately dismissed my tricks as "impossible." I reminded him that my own truck, which was sponsored by the American Psychological Association, had already performed all these tricks in real life. Dennis responded to this tall story with vigorous denials. Yet as I watched him run each truck through his obstacle course in monotonous succession, something novel happened—he began performing more unconventional tricks with his own trucks. I settled into the role of an arena announcer, mirroring him by enthusiastically praising his unconventional tricks as "unbelievable," "incredible," and "unprecedented." Dennis allowed himself to smile when I pretended to be an arena announcer. He even joined me occasionally in the announcing duties by highlighting a special feature of a particular trick. We were collaborating for perhaps the first time in treatment. He was surreptitiously getting a taste of a relationship without having to defend against it with his characteristic anxious-avoidant defensive processes. My efforts at engaging him were unnoticed by him.

By making up tall stories, I was introducing myself as a person with my own intentions and feelings. Essentially, I was introducing Dennis to a separate person eager to engage with him on a series of adventures in fantasy, which he ultimately preferred to the monotony of his own ritualized play that characteristically shut me out. I chose story lines that mirrored his own stories, yet illustrated to him that I had a different understanding of them. For example, in my story, I too had a monster truck that competed with the others, yet my monster truck was built differently (perhaps a model of his disavowed, devalued self-representation) and performed unconventional tricks (perhaps a model of his idealized, exhibitionistic self-representation). I believed that Dennis had felt rejected by his parents from an early age and had consequently developed a mental representation of himself as not lovable enough to be worthy of protection and comfort. This self-representation might have led Dennis to feel different from other children, fueled by his interest in wearing girls' tights. In contrast, Dennis also craved recognition from both me and his parents. Session after session, he tried to impress me with his mastery of monster truck trivia. Now, I had created a truck built differently like him that could captivate the attention of an entire arena of fans.

Just as a mentalizing caregiver communicates his or her understanding of the infant's mental states through the process of marking—using exaggerated facial and vocal expressions to indicate that the caregiver is aware of the infant's mental state but is not experiencing what the infant is experiencing (Fonagy et al. 2002), so too did I use exaggerated storytelling to indicate to Dennis that I was aware of his mental state but was not experiencing what he was consciously experiencing. Thus, I was both attached to him as a secure base and separate from him. This stance simultaneously confirmed the existence of our relationship and challenged his need to dominate and control me, which deprived me of my subjectivity and thrust him back into his isolated, lonely position. Instead of declaring, "I'll make you hate me so that I'm in charge of hating," Dennis got a taste of a reciprocal relationship without the need to protect himself from rejection and abandonment by controlling me. Instead of sadomasochistically titrating his emotional distance to others through defecating in his pants–pushing others away through his smelliness while enraging his parents and thus maintaining a hostile connection to them–Dennis was now beginning to relate to me without the sadomasochistic defensive machinery he once needed.

My work with the parents during the past year was limited but effective. I believe that my ability to act as a container for their own frustration with Dennis's provocative behavior helped them to contain this frustration in their interactions with Dennis and perhaps allowed him, in turn, to risk relating to his parents in a more prosocial manner as well (see point of entry B in Fig. 1). An opportunity to practice my containment and thus facilitate their capacity for self-reflection came in the form of an e-mail message from Dennis's mother in September 2010: "I CAN'T TAKE IT ANYMORE!!!!!!!! Do you know of any good boarding schools or military schools or 'scared straight' programs? I am serious. If this is him at 10, I can't deal with this as he gets older." I responded that Dennis's expressing his anger more directly (verbal channel of communication) could lessen his need to communicate his anger through his behavior such as defecating in his pants (nonverbal channel of communication). And in November 2010, his mother expressed her frustration upon learning that Dennis's school was recommending that she get him a tutor: "I am SO ANGRY!!! [Dennis's father] and I finally have a few dollars put away and are saving so I can buy a new car next year. Now I have canceled my first therapy appointment as I can't afford that—his music lessons are also canceled. Here we go again—more money into 'fixing' [Dennis]!! Horrible for a mother to say about her son. This doesn't even count the braces he will need. I just look at my sister who has a child the same age as [Dennis]. No eyesight issue, no allergy issues, no toenail issues, no pooping issues, no academic issues, no weight issue, etc., etc., etc., it just goes on and on with him. I am crying as I write this—anger and guilt fill me. Have to stop and compose myself as I'm at work."

Almost 6 months after this message, Dennis's mother wrote: "From my point of view, [Dennis's] personality and attitude have changed. We see he has more empathy, is more appreciative and is more verbal. Overall, he seems much happier. This is great progress. Thank you." In a separate e-mail message, she shared that Dennis had neither worn nor expressed a desire to wear pantyhose since January. Although Dennis still occasionally had accidents, he was on his way to becoming a separate yet connected preadolescent who was about to face a series of new challenges presented by adolescence. Dennis and I continue to work together. I am excited to discover where this process will take us next.

Analysis of Second Clinical Illustration

In this case, I realized that an exclusively interpretive approach that would naturally include transference interpretations was failing to reach Dennis behind his primitive fortress protected by barbed wire and armed guards. Such interventions (see point of entry E in Fig. 1) were aimed at a symbolic level of thinking not yet sufficiently consolidated for therapeutic use. He also had the problem of knowing everything that would have defeated such a strategy. I gradually shifted to looking for opportunities to make meaningful emotional contact with Dennis as a feeling and desiring person. In doing so, I held in my own mind the image of a boy-in-the-making who is worthy of caring, attention, and admiration rather than yelling, rejection, and abandonment. Dennis could observe my attitudes and behaviors toward him and begin to identify with and perhaps internalize this nascent self-image, which was both similar to and different from his own image of himself. This approach emphasized mentalizing feelings, desires, and intentions (see point of entry F in Fig. 1), rather than articulating parental images located in the transference (see point of entry E in Fig. 1).

Bateman and Fonagy (2004b) suggest that treatment approaches that emphasize transference interpretations expect too much agentive thinking from the patient, which the patient could perceive as blaming. In contrast, a therapist practicing Mentalization-Based Treatment (MBT) "would not expect the patient to understand much of the discourse that the therapist might verbalize in relational terms" (Bateman and Fonagy 2004b, p. 117). Primitively organized patients such as Dennis experience widespread "symbolic failure, particularly associated with incongruent mirroring" (Bateman and Fonagy 2004b, p. 118). Thus, transference interpretations, particularly with severely disturbed patients, whose symbolic capacity has clearly failed, would be ineffective. Only after a primitive symbolic capacity has become activated should a therapist attempt transference interpretations with such patients. In other words, the verbal channel of communication must be online.

Bateman and Fonagy (2004b) instead recommend cognitively based mentalization—identifying the mental states in the patient and others and connecting mental states to behaviors—as the effective ingredient of treatment for such patients. "Retaining mental closeness" (Bateman and Fonagy 2004a, p. 44) is the therapeutic principle used to accomplish the enhancement of mentalizing capacities. Specific therapeutic interventions include

> ... representing accurately the current or immediately past feeling state of the patient and its accompanying internal representations and by strictly and systematically avoiding the temptation to enter conversation about matters not directly linked to the patient's beliefs, wishes, feelings, etc. (Bateman and Fonagy 2004a, p. 44)

Empathic attunement to changes in mental states, active differentiation of mental states, and discussion of the patient's mental states in relation to the therapist's and others' perceived mental states in the here and now are other specific interventions that facilitate mental closeness.

These therapeutic conditions represent the essential ingredients of an effective treatment for severely disturbed child patients. Perhaps a relationship-focused intervention approach for more severely disturbed child patients requires the temporary use of mentalizing interventions early in the treatment process that serve the treatment goals of alliance building and stabilization before more ambitious interventions such as transference interpretations are attempted. Child patients need to feel secure enough in the therapeutic relationship and skilled enough in their symbolic capacity to explore the contents of their own minds, particularly the split-off mental representations contained therein. In the case of Dennis, I believed that underneath the controlling, know-it-all attitude lurked a scared, wounded child that I needed to reach somehow through imaginative play. I made my differently built truck show off by doing its own thing: my truck was driving to the hum of a different engine. In the future, when Dennis becomes more vulnerable in sessions for longer periods of time, I might be able to sprinkle into my work some interpretations of the meaning of his patterns of relating to others. Speaking in an altered voice, I might pretend that my truck is talking to the other trucks: "Hey, you guys, I feel I'm different and so I'm afraid you all won't like me or play with me, but all I really want is to be friends with you guys." This interpretation, communicated in the context of the play, suggests that Dennis wants to engage with others but is afraid he will be disliked and rejected. I am hoping that Dennis will be able to view these trucks symbolically—not only belonging to the world of playthings but also connected to his internal world of feelings about himself and others. This interpretation would facilitate the feeling of mental closeness described by Bateman and Fonagy (2004a) and aid in reviving Dennis's own nascent capacity for mentalizing his own mental states and those of others.

Conclusions

In summary, attachment-based interventions with prepubertal children need to take into account the points of entry where the therapist can most effectively improve children's well-being. The selection of an appropriate intervention point of entry within the complex parent–child family system depends on a knowledge of the child's current psychosocial developmental tasks as well as the attachment histories of the key players—parents, child, and therapist. Other factors such as the intellectual functioning, severity of psychopathology of the parents and child, and treatment phase also require consideration in how and where to intervene. Some children classified with insecure attachment patterns experience primitive anxieties that predispose them to severe forms of psychopathology requiring intensive, relationship-focused therapy to modify the underlying fragmentation and affect dysregulation.

The effectiveness of attachment-based child psychotherapy depends on formulating intervention strategies that focus on the specific vulnerabilities associated with specific patterns of attachment. For example, Cooper and his colleagues (Cooper et al. 2005; see also Dozier and Sepulveda 2004) hypothesized that parents with insecure attachment patterns formed out of early childhood relationships with their own parents can feel either (1) less comfortable with their child's need for exploration, independence, and autonomy, or (2) less comfortable with their child's need for closeness, protection, and comfort. Parents in the first category might feel that their child is too independent and does not need them. The child, acting in accordance with the parents' fears, might miscue parents by acting needy or distressed at the prospect of moving away to explore, even when he or she might be interested in doing so. Conversely, parents in the second category might feel that their child is too clingy and dependent. The child, also acting in accordance with parents' fears, might miscue parents by acting self-sufficient or precociously autonomous, even when he or she might be experiencing a need for comfort. Such compromises enable both parents and child to gratify the attachment needs of the child while simultaneously protecting both parties against mutual discomfort elicited by closeness or separation.

In the case of Maverick and Dennis, both patients shared a tendency to act self-sufficient and precociously autonomous, which necessitated a dismissal of unpleasant affect states and a consequent desire to control all relationship outcomes to avoid the emergence of such states. Not coincidentally, both patients also shared a symptom, encopresis, through which they reflected a disconnection from unpleasant body-based sensations and a desire to isolate themselves from others, as well as enraging their parents. These behaviors thus insured the patients some level of proximity to their parents, albeit with a hostile, sadomasochistic tinge.

Both sets of parents, perhaps inadvertently, signaled their lack of comfort with their child's need for closeness, protection, and comfort. Maverick's parents had a new baby during Maverick's toilet-training phase while simultaneously struggling with the aftermath of Hurricane Floyd. I suspect that they were emotionally unavailable to Maverick during this time, which Maverick undoubtedly experienced as a rejection or abandonment. He responded by turning away—avoiding the experience and communication of his attachment needs that his overwhelmed parents might have ignored or even been irritated by. Dennis's parents placed him into full-time childcare at the age of two—also during Dennis's toilet-training phase. During the first two years of his life, Dennis's mother also faced enormous challenges at her workplace, which might have distracted her from being emotionally present. Like Maverick, Dennis also responded by turning away. In contrast to my experience with

Maverick's mother, I felt better able to contain Dennis's mother's frustrations with her son. Additional clinical experience of working with my countertransference as well as additional therapeutic work on myself probably account for this difference in response to these two mothers who shared a sense of profound hopelessness and helplessness.

The goal of both treatments consisted of my recognizing the latent needs for attachment and closeness and not allowing these patients to deceive me (as they had deceived their parents) into listening to the manifest content of their presentations, which could easily be summed up by the command, "Get away!" Dozier (2003) suggested that therapeutic interventions are most effective when the therapist provides a "gentle challenge" (p. 254) to the patient. By relentlessly pursuing emotional contact and intimacy with Maverick and Dennis even though they signaled distance, I was defying their expectation that I would be uncomfortable with their need for closeness, protection, and comfort. Instead, I was letting them know that these needs were acceptable to me, and therefore suggesting that they were acceptable to me. My patients' defensive needs to interact sadomasochistically were no longer necessary.

Because of both patients' compromised symbolic capacity (i.e., using the nonverbal channel of communication to act out their feelings rather than express them verbally), I chose in both cases to intervene at point of entry F—to help these patients to mentalize their affects rather than act them out in a bodily function (encopresis) from which they were emotionally disconnected. In the case of Maverick, I got sidetracked by his mother's anger and disapproval of my work, which activated an archaic paternal representation in me that I enacted with Maverick, temporarily shifting my intervention point of entry to G. After figuring out the nature of this enactment, I reset the treatment course back to its original point of entry F. In the case of Dennis, I initially felt a need to impress my clinical supervisor with interpretive work but realized that this need was mine and was in fact getting me nowhere with Dennis. Mentalizing affects with storytelling (see point of entry F in Fig. 1) can facilitate the child patient's perspective taking and theory of mind (Mar et al. 2010) and eventually pave the way for later exploration of mental representations (see point of entry E in Fig. 1). A mentalizing intervention approach such as the one suggested by Fonagy and Target (2000) can prepare more severely disturbed child patients for later interpretive approaches that include transference interpretations and exploration of parental and self-representations.

Another way of putting this idea is that the child needs to become aware that he or she has a mind with mental contents, and that others also have minds with mental contents, before the therapist can proceed to more symbolically advanced intervention points of entry. In a later treatment phase, the therapist can help the child understand the complexity of his or her internal conflicts, for example, that a symptom like encopresis exists because it protects the child from emotional vulnerability, specifically, from the risk of rejection and abandonment, by preemptively alienating others. Thus, in the therapist's selection of a suitable intervention point of entry—whether behavioral, mentalizing, or representational (see Fig. 1)—the treatment phase must always be considered.

Implications for Practice and Teaching

In the context of these cases, I assert that all patients need a measure of flexibility in treatment. Despite diagnostic similarities, these two patients' needs and responses to therapeutic interventions varied. To meet these diverse needs, I implemented intervention strategies tailored to the unique characteristics of each patient rather than boilerplate strategies designed for all patients such as those contained in a treatment manual. In this era of managed care and manualized treatments, therapists need to remember that one size does not fit all. Therapy needs to be tailor-made for the patient's needs, not vice versa. Therapists' awareness of the many intervention points of entry can serve to fit the treatment to the patient and thereby improve its effectiveness.

The clinical data suggested that I adjusted my technical approach spontaneously when I felt that my patients would benefit from a change in intervention strategies. These technical modifications did not come from a treatment manual but from clinical intuition—the reflection on my own countertransference reactions, or possibly a more broadly conceptualized empathic connection with my patients. This empathic connection included awareness of (1) the patient's developmental period, (2) parental and child intellectual functioning, (3) parental and child socioemotional functioning (level of emotional instability), and (4) treatment phase. This empathic connection is critical to treatment outcome because it communicates to the patient that he or she is not alone in their suffering. The therapist is making emotional contact with all parts of the patient's self, which permits the patient's exploration of the contents of his or her mind as well as the therapist's mind. Through this empathic connection, the therapist provides a mental secure base from which the patient can explore unknown territory and to which the patient can return when the terrain becomes too frightening.

Instead of training our students to be slaves to a treatment manual, we should be training them to be its master. Teaching treatment adherence to two or three broadly conceptualized treatment models (e.g., psychodynamic and cognitive-behavioral) that emphasize a variety of intervention points of entry (A–G) should become a vital aspect of child clinical training. However, teaching treatment adherence to narrowly focused treatment manuals such as bedtime noncompliance (Ferber 2006) ensnares our field in the "narcissism of minor differences" (Freud 1918, p. 199) and immerses our students in memorizing procedures rather than experiencing relationships. Inattention to "conditions on the ground," to borrow a currently popular political phrase, can spell disaster, as Castonguay and his colleagues (Castonguay et al. 1996) learned. Our students need to be empathically attuned to their child patients' unique treatment needs so that they can recognize when their intervention strategies become counterproductive and consider a shift to a different intervention point of entry. Training in global clinical skills such as empathy, countertransference awareness, and potential interaction structures (i.e., enactments) would more suitably position our students to become effective child therapists than simply training them how to apply a treatment manual. Students need to acquire a whole arsenal of artist's tools. In some situations, a therapist might need a chisel, while in others, a paintbrush will do. Our field needs fewer technicians and more artists. And one aspect of the artistry of conducting therapy is the selection of the appropriate intervention point of entry.

Acknowledgments The author gratefully acknowledges the assistance of Clovia Ng (clovia@cngraphics.com) in reproducing Fig. 1 in Adobe Illustrator, Marcia Miller, Chief Librarian at Weill Medical College of Cornell University—Westchester Division, in locating and obtaining reference materials, and Tina Lo for checking references. The author also gratefully acknowledges the clinical supervision of Thomas Lopez, Ph.D., on the two clinical cases presented here.

References

Ainsworth, M. D. S. (1979). Infant–mother attachment. *American Psychologist, 34,* 932–937.
American Psychiatric Association (APA). (2000). *Diagnostic and statistical manual of mental disorders* (4th ed., text revision). Washington, DC: Author.
Bateman, A. W., & Fonagy, P. (2004a). Mentalization-based treatment of BPD. *Journal of Personality Disorders, 18,* 36–51.
Bateman, A. W., & Fonagy, P. (2004b). *Psychotherapy for borderline personality disorder: Mentalization-based treatment.* Oxford: Oxford University Press.
Belsky, J., Burchinal, M., McCartney, K., Vandell, D. L., Clarke-Stewart, K. A., & Owen, M. T. (2007). Are there long-term effects of early child care? *Child Development, 78,* 681–701.
Belsky, J., & Rovine, M. J. (1988). Nonmaternal care in the first year of life and the security of infant–parent attachment. *Child Development, 59,* 157–167.
Benjamin, J. (1987). The decline of the oedipus complex. In J. M. Broughton (Ed.), *Critical theories of psychological development* (pp. 211–244). New York: Plenum.
Berlin, L. J. (2005). Interventions to enhance early attachments: The state of the field today. In L. J. Berlin, Y. Ziv, L. Amaya-Jackson, & M. T. Greenberg (Eds.), *Enhancing early attachments: Theory, research, intervention, and policy* (pp. 3–33). New York: Guilford.
Bosquet, M., & Egeland, B. (2001). Associations among maternal depressive symptomatology, state of mind and parent and child behaviors: Implications for attachment-based interventions. *Attachment and Human Development, 3,* 173–199.
Bowlby, J. (1980). *Attachment and loss: Vol. 3. Loss, sadness and depression.* New York: Basic Books.
Bowlby, J. (1988). *A secure base: Parent–child attachment and healthy human development.* New York: Basic Books.
Bretherton, I. (1985). Attachment theory: Retrospect and prospect. In I. Bretherton & E. Waters (Eds.), *Growing points in attachment theory and research. Monographs of the Society for Research in Child Development, 50* (1–2, Serial No. 209), p. 3–35.
Cassidy, J., Woodhouse, S. S., Cooper, G., Hoffman, K., Powell, B., & Rodenberg, M. (2005). Examination of the precursors of infant attachment security: Implications for early intervention and intervention research. In L. J. Berlin, Y. Ziv, L. Amaya-Jackson & M. T. Greenberg (Eds.), *Enhancing early attachments: Theory, research, intervention, and policy* (pp. 34–60). New York: Guilford.
Castonguay, L. G., Goldfried, M. R., Wiser, S., Raue, P. J., & Hayes, A. M. (1996). Predicting the effect of cognitive therapy for depression: A study of unique and common factors. *Journal of Consulting and Clinical Psychology, 64,* 497–504.
Clarkin, J. F., Yeomans, F. E., & Kernberg, O. F. (1999). *Psychotherapy for borderline personality.* New York: Wiley.
Clarkin, J. F., Yeomans, F. E., & Kernberg, O. F. (2006). *Psychotherapy for borderline personality: Focusing on object relations.* Washington, DC: American Psychiatric.

Cooper, G., Hoffman, K., Powell, B., & Marvin, R. (2005). The Circle of Security intervention: Differential diagnosis and differential treatment. In L. J. Berlin, Y. Ziv, L. Amaya-Jackson & M. T. Greenberg (Eds.), *Enhancing early attachments: Theory, research, intervention, and policy* (pp. 127–151). New York: Guilford.

De Wolff, M., & van IJzendoorn, M. H. (1997). Sensitivity and attachment: A meta-analysis on parental antecedents of infant attachment. *Child Development, 68,* 571–591.

Dozier, M. (2003). Attachment-based treatment for vulnerable children. *Attachment and Human Development, 5,* 253–257.

Dozier, M., & Sepulveda, S. (2004). Foster mother state of mind and treatment use: Different challenges for different people. *Infant Mental Health Journal, 25,* 368–378.

Egeland, B., Weinfield, N. S., Bosquet, M., & Cheng, V. K. (2000). Remembering, repeating, and working through: Lessons from attachment-based interventions. In J. D. Osofsky & H. E. Fitzgerald (Eds.), *Handbook of infant mental health/World Association for Infant Mental Health: Vol. 4 Infant mental health in groups at high risk* (pp. 35–89). New York: Wiley.

Erikson, E. H. (1950). *Childhood and society.* New York: Norton.

Ferber, R. (2006). *Solve your child's sleep problems* (rev. ed.). New York: Fireside.

Fonagy, P., & Target, M. (1996). Predictors of outcome in child psychoanalysis: A retrospective study of 763 cases at the Anna Freud Centre. *Journal of the American Psychoanalytic Association, 44,* 27–77.

Fonagy, P., & Target, M. (2000). Mentalization and personality disorder in children: A current perspective from the Anna Freud Centre. In T. Lubbe (Ed.), *The borderline psychotic child: A selective integration* (pp. 69–89). London: Routledge.

Fonagy, P., Gergely, G., Jurist, E. L., & Target, M. (2002). *Affect regulation, mentalization, and the development of the self.* New York: Other Press.

Freud, S. (1896). Further remarks on the neuro-psychoses of defence. In J. Strachey (Ed. and Trans.), *The standard edition of the complete psychological works of Sigmund Freud* (Vol. 3, pp. 157–185). London: Hogarth, 1961.

Freud, S. (1918). The taboo of virginity (Contributions to the psychology of love III). In J. Strachey (Ed. and trans.), *The standard edition of the complete psychological works of Sigmund Freud* (Vol. 11, pp. 191–208). London: Hogarth, 1961.

Goodman, G. (2002). *The internal world and attachment.* Hillsdale: The Analytic Press.

Kernberg, O. F., Selzer, M. A., Koenigsberg, H. W., Carr, A. C., & Appelbaum, A. H. (1989). *Psychodynamic psychotherapy of borderline patients.* New York: Basic Books.

Linehan, M. (1993). *Congnitive-behavioral treatment of borderline personality disorder.* New York: Guilford.

Lyons-Ruth, K., & Jacobvitz, D. (1999). Attachment disorganization: Unresolved loss, relational violence, and lapses in behavioral and attentional strategies. In J. Cassidy & P. R. Shaver (Eds.), *Handbook of attachment: Theory, research, and clinical applications* (pp. 520–554). New York: Guilford.

Main, M., Kaplan, N., & Cassidy, J. (1985). Security in infancy, childhood, and adulthood: A move to the level of representation. In I. Bretherton & E. Waters (Eds.), *Growing points in attachment theory and research. Monographs of the Society for Research in Child Development, 50* (1–2, Serial No. 209), pp. 66–104.

Mar, R. A., Tackett, J. L., & Moore, C. (2010). Exposure to media and theory-of-mind development in preschoolers. *Cognitive Development, 25,* 69–78.

Olds, D. L. (2005). The Nurse-family partnership: Foundations in attachment theory and epidemiology. In L. J. Berlin, Y. Ziv, L. Amaya-Jackson, & M. T. Greenberg (Eds.), *Enhancing early attachments: Theory, research, intervention, and policy* (pp. 217–249). New York: Guilford.

Slade, A., Grienenberger, J., Bernbach, E., Levy, D., & Locker, A. (2005). Maternal reflective functioning, attachment, and the transmission gap: A preliminary study. *Attachment and Human Development, 7,* 283–298.

Slade, A., Sadler, L. S., & Mayes, L. C. (2005). Minding the baby: Enhancing parental reflective functioning in a nursing/mental health home visiting program. In L. J. Berlin, Y. Ziv, L.

Amaya-Jackson, & M. T. Greenberg (Eds.), *Enhancing early attachments: Theory, research, intervention, and policy* (pp. 152–177). New York: Guilford.

Spieker, S., Nelson, D., DeKlyen, M., & Staerkel, F. (2005). Enhancing early attachments in the context of Early Head Start: Can programs emphasizing family support improve rates of secure infant–mother attachments in low-income families? In L. J. Berlin, Y. Ziv, L. Amaya-Jackson, & M. T. Greenberg (Eds.), *Enhancing early attachments: Theory, research, intervention, and policy* (pp. 250–275). New York: Guilford.

Sroufe, L. A. (1985). Attachment classification from the perspective of infant–caregiver relationships and infant temperament. *Child Development, 56,* 1–14.

Target, M., & Fonagy, P. (1994a). The efficacy of psychoanalysis for children: Developmental considerations. *Journal of the American Academy of Child and Adolescent Psychiatry, 33,* 1134–1144.

Target, M., & Fonagy, P. (1994b). The efficacy of psychoanalysis for children with emotional disorders. *Journal of the American Academy of Child and Adolescent Psychiatry, 33,* 361–371.

van IJzendoorn, M. H. (1995). Adult attachment representations, parental responsiveness, and infant attachment: A meta-analysis on the predictive validity of the adult attachment interview. *Psychological Bulletin, 117,* 387–403.

van IJzendoorn, M. H., Juffer, F., & Duyvesteyn, M. G. C. (1995). Breaking the intergenerational cycle of insecure attachment: A review of the effects of attachment-based interventions on maternal sensitivity and infant security. *Journal of Child Psychology and Psychiatry, 36,* 225–248.

Weinfield, N. S., Sroufe, L. A., Egeland, B., & Carlson, E. A. (1999). The nature of individual differences in infant–caregiver attachment. In J. Cassidy & P. R. Shaver (Eds.), *Handbook of attachment: Theory, research, and clinical applications* (pp. 68–88). New York: Guilford.

Attachment Processes in Wilderness Therapy

Joanna Ellen Bettmann and Isaac Karikari

Attachment is an integral part of human nature. Attachment theory presumes we are biologically predisposed to connect to others. Founder of attachment theory, Bowlby (1988) noted that attachment behavior "is seen in virtually all human beings (though in varying patterns)" (p. 27). Attachment theory describes the various ways in which we relate to each other based on our perceptions of human relationships. These perceptions we hold result from experiences gained earlier in life (Bowlby 1980, 1988). In formulating attachment theory, John Bowlby called attention to its biological base, noting that attachment

> ... emphasizes the primary status and biological function of intimate emotional bonds between individuals, the making and maintaining of which are postulated to be controlled by a cybernetic system situated within the central nervous system utilizing working models of self and attachment figure in relationship with each other. (Bowlby 1988, p. 120)

Attachment patterns begin in childhood but manifest throughout our lives. The manifestations of attachment behavior occur in different ways. In children, four attachment styles exist: secure, anxious-resistant, avoidant, and disorganized. Secure attachment is promoted by the ready availability and responsiveness of the caregiver to the child's needs. This serves as a guarantee of the caregiver's protection and support, and contributes in building the child's confidence and boldness in facing the world and adverse situations. In anxious resistant attachment, the caregiver's response to the child is characterized by inconsistencies. The caregiver is not always available. There is thus a lack of surety regarding the caregiver's availability. This breeds anxiety and makes the child fearful about exploring its environment. With anxious avoidant attachment the negative responses that often accompany the individual's care seeking behavior stirs up a desire to be emotionally self sufficient. This often becomes the case after repeated negative responses (Bowlby 1988).

J. E. Bettmann (✉) · I. Karikari
College of Social Work, University of Utah, Salt Lake City, UT, USA

J. E. Bettmann
Open Sky Wilderness Therapy, Durango, Colorado, USA
e-mail: Joanna.Schaefer@socwk.utah.edu

J. E. Bettmann, D. D. Friedman (eds.), *Attachment-Based Clinical Work with Children and Adolescents,* Essential Clinical Social Work Series,
DOI 10.1007/978-1-4614-4848-8_10, © Springer Science+Business Media New York 2013

In adolescence, attachment patterns typically reflect the relational patterns developed with one's earliest caregivers. This is due, in part, to self-perpetuating patterns of relating to others, introduced in the initial primary caregiving relationship (Bowlby 1988). While Bowlby claimed that initial attachment representations and subsequent relational and behavioral interactions are not part of what he defined as the "inborn temperament" (Bowlby 1969, p 127), attachment representations and relational constructs become more rigid and defined as a person ages. Thus, the likelihood internal working models will change after early childhood decreases (Bowlby 1973). Resulting cognitive, emotional, social and developmental manifestations from initial attachment schemas also become more rigid and less susceptible to external influence (Benoit and Parker 1994; Sroufe 2005; Main et al. 1985).

Attachment theory speaks specifically to the impact of separations on children. Attachment theory proposes that separations from one's attachment figures have a profound impact on young children. John Bowlby and his colleagues James and Joyce Robertson demonstrated this vividly in the 1969 film "John, aged 17 months, for 9 days in a residential nursery" (Robertson and Robertson 1969). The film tracks the institutional stay of a young British boy in an orphanage while his mother was in the hospital delivering a baby. The video clearly shows John's enormous distress at the separation from his parents, his resulting protests, and eventually despair and withdrawal. While the film tracks a toddler responding to separation from attachment figures, older children and adults can respond similarly to separations. Kobak and Madsen (2008) note that separations at any age constitute a threat to the caregiver's availability. They assert,

> Older children and adults are likely to perceive threats to a caregiver's availability when lines of communication are disrupted by prolonged absence, emotional disengagement, or signals of rejection or abandonment. As a result, disrupted lines of communication produce feelings of anxiety, anger, and sadness similar to those that have been documented in young children's reactions to physical separations (Kobak and Madsen, p. 24).

Such dynamics are relevant to wilderness therapy settings, which consist of adolescents' prolonged absences from their caregivers, emotional disengagement due to their isolation in wilderness environment, and potential signals of abandonment by being sent away to treatment.

Changes in Attachment

Attachment patterns developed during childhood can be modified significantly based on later experiences and encounters a person has in life (Bartholomew and Horowitz 1991; Bettmann 2007; Qi-Wu et al. 2010). While the majority of populations will remain relatively stable in regards to attachment classification, a minority experience life events which may change attachment security. Waters et al. (2000) demonstrated this phenomenon in a longitudinal study investigating the relationship between negative life events and changes in attachment classifications. They assessed the attachment styles of 50 adults between the ages of 20 and 22 years old. A previous attachment study assessed these adults at 12 and 18 months of age (Waters 1978). Waters et al. (2000) found that change from secure to insecure attachment classification occurred with loss of a parent, life-threatening illness of parent or child, parental divorce, parental psychiatric disorder, and physical or sexual abuse by a family member.

In another study, Iwaniec and Sneddon (2001) measured attachment in infants who experienced failure to thrive symptoms and measured the same participants at 20 years of age. They found that attachment classification changed from insecure to secure in participants who experienced positive changes in environmental circumstances: Six were removed from home environments and placed into stable foster care homes, one was adopted, and one child remained in the home environment, but the mother left the child's father and established a positive relationship with a new partner. Furthermore, in a review of findings from the Minnesota Longitudinal Study on risk and adaptation from birth through adulthood, Sroufe (2005) explored implications of negative and positive life events on attachment representations. He concluded that attachment representations may shift from secure to insecure and from insecure to secure, depending on life events. He asserted that attachment representations in infancy only probabilistically predict attachment representations in later life and that many layered complexities play a role in forming relational development.

Changes in Attachment Due to Clinical Intervention

Some research has explored shifts in attachment classification due to psychotherapeutic intervention (Fonagy et al. 1995; Korfmacher et al. 1997; Levy et al. 2006). Levy et al. (2006) evaluated changes in attachment representations among 90 people with bipolar disorder receiving 1 of 3 year-long group therapy interventions: transference focused psychotherapy (TFP), dialectical behavior therapy (DBT), and modified psychodynamic supportive therapy (SPT). Using the Adult Attachment Interview (George et al. 1996), results indicated a three-fold increase of participants classified as securely attached from pre to post in the TFP group (from 5 to 15 %). Researchers found no differences in attachment classification from pre to post in the DBT or SPT groups. Such findings indicate that attachment representations may indeed shift as a result of clinical intervention. Similar to attachment theory, TFP is rooted in psychodynamic theory. Both trace problems to internally held beliefs and cognitions and thus focus on positively altering negative or dysfunctional internal working models to enable clients improve conceptions of their relationships and interactions (Levy et al. 2006).

In a similar study using different measures, Travis et al. (2001) analyzed intake and discharge interviews in a clinical population with significant interpersonal problems. The authors rated interviews based on Bartholomew and Horowitz's (1991) rating system, using four attachment prototypes: secure, fearful, preoccupied, or dismissing. Participants in the study received a 25-session, time-limited dynamic psychotherapy group intervention. Of the 29 participants receiving treatment, none were classified as secure at intake. However, at discharge, seven participants were classified as secure (24 %). Notably, prior to treatment, 11 participants were classified as preoccupied, 16 as fearful, and 2 as dismissive. At post-treatment, 10 were classified as preoccupied, 8 as fearful, and 4 as dismissive. Overall, 19 (66 %) participants changed attachment classification from pre- to post-intervention. While, the small sample size of this study limits the generalizability of its findings, its results suggest the attachment classification can shift as a result of psychotherapeutic intervention. Similar to attachment theoretical approaches, the dynamic psychotherapy used in this study focuses on clients' relational patterns which manifest in sessions with the therapist. The therapist's relationship with the client is considered a key factor in effecting change. In this model, the therapeutic relationship serves as positive model in helping rectify the client's maladaptive schemas of relationships (Travis et al. 2001).

While wilderness therapy programs do not explicitly aim to change adolescents' attachment classifications, some such programs work on the familial attachment relationships of their clients (Bettmann 2007). Using intensive family therapy interventions, wilderness therapy programs aim to improve adolescents' familial relationships. Such improvement seems likely to impact those attachment relationships. Using an in-depth case example, this chapter will explore how attachment processes emerge and are worked through in the context of wilderness therapy settings. First, however, we must explore what wilderness therapy is. What is this treatment type which thousands of adolescents attend each year (Russell and Hendee 2000)?

History of Wilderness Therapy

We will begin by exploring its origins. The precursors of wilderness therapy include "tent therapy," a term coined in reference to the use of tents for housing patients outdoors (Williams 2000, p. 48). This approach was used by some mental hospitals in the United States in the early 1900s. The effects were favorable, and its proponents attributed its beneficial effects to the outdoor setting as well as the group interactions that occurred there (Williams 2000). In 1929, Campbell Loughmiller founded the first outdoor camping program; this program utilized adventure therapy and was aimed at underprivileged children in Texas. Loughmiller focused on socialization of clients through the use of small group cooperation (Russell and Hendee 2000).

Another historical contributor to wilderness therapy was the Outward Bound program, a pioneering effort in outdoor/adventure programs which held education as an integral component (Bandoroff and Scherer 1994; Gillis et al. 2008). Founder of Outward Bound, Kurt Hahn understood the wilderness experience as a catalyst for self-discovery, growth, and development (Kimball and Bacon 1993; Bandoroff and Scherer 1994). Kurt Hahn, to whom most authors link the beginning of contemporary outdoor and adventure education programs, created the first Outward Bound program for Blue Funnel Shipping line, a Britain-based company, in 1942. The month-long program had as its primary goal the fostering of participants' independence and resilience, as well as creativity and ingenuity (Russell 2006). The program was reestablished in the United States in 1962, and became incredibly popular over the decades that followed (Kimball and Bacon 1993).

The incorporation of wilderness survival skills in wilderness therapy can be traced back to the Department of Youth Leadership at Brigham Young University (BYU) in the 1960s. Desert survival classes developed by BYU instructors became quite popular with students. The creators noticed that students appeared to have improved levels of self-esteem, which led to the development of a program for struggling freshman students. Soon after, the curriculum was adapted for troubled adolescents, eventually leading to programs such as Aspen Achievement Academy and the Anasazi Foundation (Russell and Hendee 2000).

A national survey conducted in 2000 revealed that 116 wilderness therapy programs existed in the United States, of which 86 participated in the survey (Russell and Hendee 2000). The majority of the programs that participated in the survey identified as private pay programs for which parents pay out of pocket or utilize their own insurance (81 %), while programs for adjudicated youth constituted a smaller percentage (19 %). Approximately 9,100 clients attended the programs in 1999, with an average of a little over 100 clients in each program. The authors estimate that with the inclusion of non-participating programs, wilderness programs serve approximately 11,000 clients a year (Russell and Hendee 2000).

These days, wilderness therapy treatment is commonly used as treatment for a variety of individual and family issues. Adolescents ' presenting problems typically include oppositional defiant disorder, substance abuse, depression, anxiety, trauma, and varied behavioral and emotional disorders and issues (Russell and Hendee 2000). Wilderness therapy programs typically do not treat acute psychosis, sexual deviance, extreme suicidal behavior, severe forms of behavioral and conduct disorders, and certain medical complications (Clark et al. 2004; Somervell and Lambie 2009).

Definition of Wilderness Therapy

Wilderness therapy is a behavioral healthcare model and a distinctive approach to adolescent mental health treatment (Becker 2010; Russell 2003). Wilderness therapy falls under the general framework of wilderness experience programs, which are programs that are operated in outdoor locations with the goal of client improvement through therapy, recreation, leadership formation, and/or instruction (Friese et al 1998; Russell 2001; Russell and Hendee 2000). Wilderness therapy, however, has specific characteristics that set it apart from other wilderness experience programs (Russell 2001; Russell et al. 1999). First, wilderness therapy is generally conducted in isolated wilderness environments, separating the client from settings they are accustomed to (Bettmann and Jasperson 2008; Kimball and Bacon 1993; Powch 1994; Russell et al. 1999). Program sites do not have amenities like indoor plumbing or electricity, and clients do not have access to computers or cell phones (unless used for family therapy interventions). Programs typically last between 3 and 8 weeks, providing a lengthy experience of living in a wilderness environment. Length of treatment is determined either by program model or clients' progress on treatment goals.

Living in a wilderness environment allows participants to focus more completely on the experience at hand (Bettmann and Jasperson 2008). In wilderness therapy, clients learn and use primitive outdoor survival skills (Bettmann and Jasperson 2008; Kimball and Bacon 1993; Russell et al. 1999). For example, clients are often expected to make fire without matches or lighters, prepare meals over a campfire, prepare their own shelters using tarp and rope, etc. (Kimball and Bacon 1993). Many programs also include outdoor challenges, such as difficult hikes, rock climbing, river rafting, rappelling, etc. (Kimball and Bacon 1993; Crisp 1996). The length of wilderness therapy programs varies greatly (Kimball and Bacon 1993), but normally ranges from 3 to 8 weeks (Newes and Doherty 2007).

These programs are most often created for adolescent clients (Becker 2010; Williams 2000), although adult programming is also available (Bettmann and Jasperson 2008). Wilderness therapy programs are typically not used as the first-line treatment for adolescent mental health issues (Clark et al. 2004; Russell 2007). However, for adolescents who appear less receptive to traditional forms of therapy, wilderness therapy programs present one viable option (Clark et al. 2004; Russell and Phillips-Miller 2002). Russell and Phillips-Miller (2002) found that clients voiced various reasons for attendance at a wilderness therapy program, including: school difficulties, abuse of drugs and/or alcohol, lack of success in other treatment modalities, emotional issues, and the client feeling as though they "needed help" (p. 422).

Therapy in this unique setting is carefully structured and includes "a process of assessment, treatment planning, the strategic use of counseling techniques (including group dynamics which are often a component of outdoor education programs), and the documentation of change" (Berman and Davis Berman 2000, p. 1). Russell (2001) asserts that wilderness therapy programs employ licensed therapists who are trained in the program's specialties, can create and tailor treatment plans, and help to manage aftercare services for clients. Romi and Kohan (2004) make the assertion that wilderness programs are:

> ... a complex of components that impact on the participant and create a synergism that is greater than the sum of all separate influences. People and nature combine so that each pre-structured program becomes a unique creation, influenced by the personalities of the individuals involved—participant or professional—and by the terrain and the vicissitudes of natural phenomena (p. 133).

In its particular therapeutic approach, wilderness therapy does not attempt to force change. Rather, through its skilled personnel, it uses interventions such as psycho-educational lessons, outdoor activities, and group psychotherapy in a bid to help change identified behavior (Russell 2001).

What about wilderness therapy is particularly helpful to clients? Russell and Hendee (2000) studied this, exploring the variables that clients found most helpful in this treatment type. First, the adolescent participants cited solo time, which is a scheduled time designated for clients to be alone to reflect upon their lives. Solos typically last 2 to 3 days, where clients set up their own campsites within hearing, but out of sight of staff. Adolescents are expected to take care of themselves in their campsites: building their own shelters, cooking their own meals, and completing therapeutic assignments designed by the treatment team. The clients also described the importance of relationships with program staff and therapists. Specifically, clients cited "non-confrontive and caring" (Russell and Hendee 2000, p. 172) relationship styles as helpful in engaging them in working through personal issues. Although the adolescents noted the difficulty of living in wilderness environments, they also indicated that it was empowering to master skills like hiking, reflection, and observation of the natural beauty around them (Russell and Hendee 2000). Other researchers examining the positive effects of wilderness therapy cite similar critical factors, noting the centrality of the wilderness environment, positive group dynamics, challenging and engaging activities, and therapist–client relationships (Becker 2010; Russell and Phillips-Miller 2002; Somervell and Lambie 2009).

Families play a critical role in adolescents' wilderness treatment. The family is sometimes regarded as a contributing factor in the problems adolescents face and thus intervention with the family system is important (Bandoroff and Scherer 1994). Some programs integrate elements of family therapy with wilderness programs (Bandoroff and Scherer 1994), which is an element Russell (2001) cites as a core feature of wilderness therapy. Such interventions may include mailed written assignments for clients and their families, family therapy via phone calls, and weekly phone contact between the program therapist and clients' families (Bettmann and Jasperson 2008). Some programs incorporate family seminars that include family therapy, groups, learning and usage of primitive skills, and trekking at the end of the client's stay (Bandoroff and Scherer 1994). Including families in the wilderness therapy process also aids in prospects for aftercare, as families can incorporate the skills they learned in their homes, creating an environment that sustains improved family relationships (Bandoroff and Scherer 1994).

Theoretical Foundations of Wilderness Therapy

Russell (2001) posits that, although wilderness therapy programs stem from various theoretical perspectives, several prevalent themes exist. First, wilderness therapy seems to be a blend of the Outward Bound, cognitive behavioral, and family systems models. Clients are exposed to challenging wilderness environments and then process the experience through these therapeutic modalities. Natural consequences are another important theoretical concept. Staff members are encouraged to let adolescents learn lessons on their own through experiences with the environment. Thus, staff members are able to take a caring, compassionate, and calm approach with clients, as natural consequences take the place of punishments. For example, an adolescent who rushes to build his primitive backpack quickly may end up with his backpack falling apart later in the day, a natural consequence to his rushing the task. Similarly, an adolescent who builds a poorly constructed shelter may find that he gets wet one night when it rains. Staff permits such natural consequences to occur, while also stepping in to support students in building new skill sets when needed.

Finally, metaphors, rites of passage, and times for reflection are also incorporated into most programs, mimicking traditional cultural practices (Russell 2001).

Hill (2007) also notes a collection of concepts which form the philosophical foundations undergirding wilderness therapy. These concepts include "full value contract," which refers to a group's agreement to maintain positive regard for its members and their contributions (Schoel et al. 1988, p. 33). This mindset becomes evident in the interactions that take place within the wilderness therapy group. Notably, the contract happens in the form of encouragement, the setting of goals or targets, and the way in which confrontations take place. Wilderness therapy also incorporates concepts from diverse models of therapy such as Adlerian therapy, behavioral therapy and reality therapy. For instance modeling, behavioral reinforcement, behavioral rehearsal, and behavioral contracts are typical wilderness therapy interventions which derive from behavioral therapy. Wilderness therapy's strength-based and egalitarian interactions between counselors and clients have links with Adlerian therapy (Hill 2007).

Attachment Processes in Wilderness Therapy Settings

Wilderness therapy and adventure-based therapeutic programs offer participants opportunities to gain new perspectives (Kluge 2007) and develop positive relationships that help mitigate negative behavioral patterns (Black et al. 2010). As a mental health treatment modality (Russell 2001), wilderness therapy can address attachment-related issues (Bettmann et al. 2008). Yet the study of attachment processes within the context of wilderness therapy is a relatively unexplored terrain (Bettmann 2007; Bettmann et al. 2008; Bettmann and Jasperson 2008).

Notably, out-of-home treatments for adolescents present a distinct challenge for attachment-based clinical work. How can treatment enhance the attachment bonds between family members when the treatment is residential, by definition keeping the adolescent and his parent apart? Further, in wilderness therapy programs, adolescents are far from their familiar family and friends, evoking strong attachment needs and the need for new relationships within the treatment setting. The wilderness setting and its therapeutic community of strangers activates the attachment system. Bowlby noted that the attachment system is activated by "strangeness, fatigue, anything frightening and unavailability or unresponsiveness by attachment figure" (Bowlby 1980, p. 40). Wilderness therapy incorporates such elements (Berman and Davis-Berman 2000; Romi and Kohan 2004).

In wilderness therapy settings, adolescents enter an environment of strangers: typically joining a group of eight other same-sex peers and three staff in the wilderness. This will be the adolescent client's group for the next month or 2 and strong relationships will form between them. But at the start, the adolescent joins a group of strangers in the middle of nowhere. Thus, their attachment system is strongly activated by the strangeness of the wilderness setting and the unavailability of their usual attachment figures. For the next month or 2, adolescents will be able to write their parents, but will have no contact with peers from home. They won't be able to make phone calls, send emails, or text attachment figures. Separated from all attachment figures in their home lives, adolescents' attachment systems are strongly activated at the beginning of treatment.

Such activation leads to a range of adolescent behaviors, from withdrawal to acting out. Adolescents sometimes withdraw, speaking little and refusing to participate in daily activities. Others act out, by yelling, name-calling, becoming physically aggressive, running away, or exhibiting other behaviors. While most programs attempt to manage these varied behaviors with purely behavioral responses, we suggest that programs understand such adolescent conduct as reactions to the activation of their attachment systems. Reconceptualized, adolescents are simply responding to the threat that they perceive in the strangeness of the wilderness environment.

In the context of such activation, program staff needs to work hard to engage new adolescent clients in empathic, nurturing relationships. For the month or 2 that adolescents are in the wilderness, they will need new attachment relationships. They will need relationships which fulfill attachment functions, such as secure base and safe haven (Cassidy 2008). Staff or peers in wilderness therapy settings can fulfill such roles, but likely only if they are primed to do so. In-the-field training provided by such programs should coach staff to do this. Regular staff training should focus on alerting staff on how to attend to the critically important therapeutic relationships which evolve between staff and adolescent clients. Programs should provide mentoring for staff in order to develop these skills, encourage staff to observe therapy sessions at times, and encourage frequent debriefing of cases with program therapists. All of these approaches are likely help staff to recognize their critical positions as attachment figures. Staff who conceptualize their roles as attachment figures are likely to provide the attuned, attentive emotional responses to adolescent acting out which adolescents need.

Bowlby noted that it takes "a familiar environment and the ready availability and responsiveness of an attachment figure . . . touching or clinging, or the actively reassuring behavior of the attachment figure" to deactivate the attachment system (p. 40). Staff and therapists in wilderness therapy programs can provide such availability and responsiveness if alerted to the primacy of their clients' attachment needs. The case study below illuminates such relational dynamics between a client and her therapist in a wilderness therapy program.

Case Study

Amy[1] was a 15-year old Caucasian female who presented to treatment at a wilderness therapy program where I [JB] was the therapist. Raised in an upper middle class home in a suburban East Coast city, Amy was the 3rd of 4 children raised by her parents, who were now married for 21 years. In many ways, she was similar to her peers in the program: acting out at home, substance abusing, oppositional at home and sometimes at school.

---

[1] A pseudonym

However, my initial session with her was significantly irregular. Most of my clients in the wilderness therapy program were angry to be there, having been sent to treatment by their parents for problems that the adolescents themselves didn't see as problems. In our initial sessions, I was used to their angry narratives, long-winded diatribes against the stupidity of parents and adults in general. However, my initial session with Amy was absent of any dialogue.

When I was introduced to Amy, she was on her third day in the program. The three staff in her group of eight girls informed me that she had not yet spoken to anyone in the program. This was striking. I had not yet encountered such a client. I thought, "well, I'm the therapist. She'll definitely talk to me." After the introductions by staff, I invited Amy to an individual psychotherapy session with me. We sat about 150 feet from the staff and girls group, and I began the session as I generally did with other students by asking Amy how things were going and other opening questions. She was silent. I explained to her my role and who I was as a field therapist. She was silent. I explained to her how eager I was to get to know her and hear what she had to say. She was still silent.

I experienced strong countertransference in her silence. At first, I felt rejected, hurt by her unwillingness to open up to me at all. I felt inadequate as a therapist, assuming that my techniques were poor, my interventions inappropriate. However, I began thinking about what would make Amy silent. Using an understanding of attachment theory, I hypothesized that Amy was deeply wounded by her relationships with primary caregivers. I assumed that such wounds, if they existed, made it difficult or impossible for her to trust other adults. I conceptualized Amy as avoidantly attached, one whose style was to avoid close relationships. I considered the strategies of avoidantly attached individuals: the emotional withdrawal, the unease with intimacy, the over-regulation of emotion.

Using this knowledge, I approached our relationship cautiously, but with warmth. As the therapist and thus the treatment team leader, I encouraged the staff to respond to Amy with availability, empathy, and emotional responsivity. In short, I encouraged them to act as available attachment figures so that Amy might begin to engage and eventually to trust. On her fifth morning in the program, the previously silent Amy asked staff to pass her a piece of her clothing as she was packing up. The staff responded warmly and excitedly, pleased to begin engaging with Amy.

The therapists' schedule at this program placed therapists in the wilderness with the group of nine clients and three staff for two consecutive days each week. When I returned to the group the following week, I found Amy significantly changed. While she was still angry, her anger was directed at her family. She spoke eagerly with me, wanting to share her displeasure with her parents and to strategize how to leave the wilderness program early. I empathized with Amy's situation—being sent to treatment she believed she didn't need—and encouraged her to share her feelings with her family in letters. She was resistant to writing her family, but did so: long, angry letters filled with epithets, blaming, and threats. The Amy I had experienced in session, the Amy who was eager to share, was nowhere evident in her letters. I was enormously encouraged by her willingness to engage in a therapeutic relationship, but perplexed by the vitriolic language in her communication with her family.

In subsequent weeks, Amy continued to engage eagerly in a relationship with me and with the staff. She formed friendships with some of the girls in her group and made progress in moving through the level system of the program. However, her letters to her family continued to blame them and to threaten. Unusually, her anger was not limited to her parents, but spread equally on her three siblings as well. Adolescents in wilderness therapy programs are often angry at parents at the beginning of treatment, but tend to become less angry as treatment progresses and they see positive changes in themselves. I was concerned about the continued high level of Amy's anger at her family which seemed unusually long-lasting.

As per the program's protocol, I spoke weekly with Amy's family, giving them updates on her progress and encouraging them to be warm and responsive to her concerns in their letters back to her. I encouraged them not to respond to her anger with their own, but to allow her reflect her upset, and they were able to do this. However, I was troubled by Amy's inability to work through conflict with parents. She seemed able to work through conflict with peers in the program, for example, giving "I feel" statements to her peers when coached by staff when her peers did not do the dishes as assigned.

The program lasted 7 weeks; at the end of it, all families came to the wilderness site for 2 days of family therapy. Unlike all of her peers graduating that week, Amy refused to hug her parents when she first saw them after 7 weeks away. They were hurt by this and turned to me, asking for answers. I continued to be baffled by Amy's fierce anger and rejection of them, but conceptualized her anger as hurt. I understood her to be suffering from deep wounds with her primary attachment figures, her parents. What I didn't understand was what hurt her. I encouraged her parents to remain open and warm with her; this was difficult for them to do. Her parents tended to talk to each other, rather than risk her anger and disdain.

After they had spent 24 h together doing family therapy activities and some un-structured time, I met Amy and her parents for our first and last hour-long family therapy session in person. She was due to graduate the next day and to go home with her family. I resolved to spend the session helping Amy to amplify some of her wounds with her attachment figures. In this session, Amy began with her anger and blaming, but through my gentle questioning, quickly devolved into tears. I had seen her cry in sessions previously, but her parents hadn't seen her cry in years and they were shocked. I encouraged them to respond to her with empathy and warmth, even if they didn't understand the source of her distress. With encouragement, Amy spoke about her feelings of rejection by her whole family. In one critical moment, Amy spoke about an incident in which her parents and siblings went out for ice cream, but didn't invite her. She spoke about how isolated and lonely this made her feel. Her mother responded with surprise, explaining, "we didn't think you'd want to go. You never acted like you wanted to be with us." Amy described that similar incidents happened numerous times, resulting in her feeling of isolation and loneliness.

It appeared that Amy's hurt in her most important attachment relationships resulted in her complete withdrawal, until even those closest to her perceived that she didn't want to be with them. Amy's avoidant attachment strategies served to protect her from some hurt, but isolated her to an extreme extent. Her anger towards her family was apparently a cover for the hurt she felt. Amy's ability to explain her hurt feelings to her family was the beginning of a rebuilding relationship between them.

Amy left the wilderness program the next day, headed to a therapeutic boarding school for the next year. In this environment, she would receive therapeutic and academic support. Her family headed to their home some states away. Six months later, I received a letter from Amy describing her appreciation for being seen and heard clearly while in wilderness. She expressed pride in her progress and pleasure at her achievements. Her letter brought me into tears. In wilderness therapy, Amy experienced being heard and understood, her hurt feelings were identified and amplified. This experience helped her to reconnect with her family and begin to modify her expectations of relationships.

Conclusion

This article presented a reconceptualization of adolescent dynamics in wilderness therapy settings, exploring how acting-out adolescent behaviors can be best understood in the context of powerful attachment dynamics. Adolescents entering wilderness therapy programs or other out-of-home care settings encounter strangeness, separation, loss, and change. All these activate the attachment system, but in an environment where there are no familiar attachment figures. In the case of wilderness treatment, clients have little access to their primary attachment figures: only through letters can they connect. In such an environment, adolescents' behaviors should be reconceptualized as attachment-seeking behaviors, even when they look angry, rejecting, withdrawn or avoidant.

But can brief treatment—such as a 7-week wilderness therapy program—change our clients' attachment relationships? While brief treatment seems unlikely to change attachment classification, it may shift adolescents' expectations of what their attachment figures can provide.

In the case of Amy, it seemed likely that her experience of open, warm, empathic, and attuned staff in the wilderness therapy program had enabled her to believe that her relationships with others could be so. Program staff met her avoidant withdrawal, anger, and blaming with warmth and acceptance. It seemed that perhaps Amy's new relational experience with program staff and therapists enabled her unconsciously to hope for more in her primary attachment relationships. Such hope may have led to her sharing of her hurt with her family, a critical first step in rebuilding their attachment relationship.

Wilderness therapy programs are uniquely positioned to work with adolescents' attachment behaviors because the treatment environment itself is likely to activate the attachment system. In the context of such activation, programs need to understand adolescents' aggressive acting or withdrawn behaviors as deriving from unmet attachment needs. Programs should train their staff and therapists to recognize adolescents' attachment bids, hidden though they may be. This training may enable programs to make significant gains with their clients.

Social workers wishing to learn more about such programs can do so through the National Association of Therapeutic Schools and Programs (www. natsap.com) or the Association of Experiential Education (www.aee.org). Both of these trade groups gather together programs doing similar work. By attending conferences put on by these groups or learning about their member programs on their websites, social workers can begin to get familiar with the work of these programs.

As psychotherapy is primarily a relational enterprise (Norcross 2002), psychotherapy in the wilderness is even more so. Wilderness therapy programs need to provide their adolescent clients with stable, responsive, and attuned figures who can meet attachment needs while adolescents' primary attachment figures are unavailable. Wilderness programs that serve troubled or vulnerable youth generally serve both corrective and preventive functions. This happens with the diversion of attention away from dysfunctional behavior and the instructing of youth in healthier responses and choices (Berman and Davis-Berman 2000) by equipping them with skills in handling difficult situations (Romi and Kohan 2004). These activities happen in the context of psychotherapeutic relationships. Understanding acting-out adolescent clients as displaying attachment needs, and in need of figures who can meet those needs, allows wilderness therapy programs to perceive the drives underneath the behaviors. Such understanding will both deepen and improve the treatment.

References

Bandoroff, S., & Scherer, D. G. (1994). Wilderness family therapy: An innovative treatment approach for problem youth. *Journal of Child & Family Studies, 3,* 175–191.

Bartholomew, K., & Horowitz, L. M. (1991). Attachment styles among young adults: A test of a four-category model. *Journal of Personality & Social Psychology, 61,* 226–244.

Becker, S. P. (2010). Wilderness therapy: Ethical considerations for mental health professionals. *Child & Youth Care Forum, 39,* 47–61.

Benoit, D., & Parker, K. (1994). Stability and transmission of attachment across three generations. *Child Development, 65,* 1444–1456.

Berman, D., & Davis-Berman, J. (2000). *Therapeutic uses of outdoor education.* (Report No. EDO-RC-00–5). Charleston: Office of Educational Research and Improvement. (ERIC Document Reproduction Service No. EDD0036).

Bettmann, J. E. (2007). Changes in adolescent attachment relationships as a response to wilderness treatment. *Journal of the American Psychoanalytic Association, 55,* 259–265.

Bettmann, J. E., & Jasperson, R. A. (2008). Adults in wilderness treatment: A unique application of attachment theory and research. *Clinical Social Work Journal, 36,* 51–61.

Bettmann, J. E, Demong, E., & Jasperson, R. A. (2008). Treating adolescents with attachment and adoption issues in wilderness therapy settings. *Journal of Therapeutic Schools and Programs, 8,* 117–138.

Black, D. S, Grenard, J. L., Sussman, S., & Rohrbach, L. A. (2010). The influence of school-based natural mentoring relationships on school attachment and subsequent adolescent risk behaviors. *Health Education Research, 25,* 892–902.

Bowlby, J. (1969). *Attachment and loss: Volume 1: Attachment* (1st ed.). New York: Basic Books.

Bowlby, J. (1973). Attachment and loss: Separation (Vol. 2). New York: Basic Books.

Bowlby, J. (1980). *Loss: Sadness and depression.* New York: Basic Books.

Bowlby, J. (1988). *A secure base: Parent-child attachment and healthy human development*. New York: Basic Books.

Cassidy, J. (2008). The nature of the child's ties. In J. Cassidy & P. R. Shaver (Eds.), *Handbook of Attachment*, (2nd ed., pp. 3–22). New York: Guilford.

Clark, J., Marmol, L. M., Cooley, R., & Gathercoal, K. (2004). The effects of wilderness therapy on the clinical concerns (on axes i, ii, and iv) of troubled adolescents. *Journal of Experiential Education, 27*, 213–232.

Crisp, S. (1996). *International models of best practice in wilderness and adventure therapy: Implications for Australia*. Retrieved from Winston Churchill Memorial Trust website: http://www.churchilltrust.com.au/site_media/fellows/Crisp_Simon_1996.pdf.

Fonagy, P., Steele, M., Steele, H., Leigh, T., Kennedy, R., & Target, M. (1995). Attachment, the reflective self, and borderline states. In S. Goldberg, R. Muir, & J. Kerr (Eds.), *Attachment theory: Social, developmental and clinical perspectives*. Hillsdale: The Analytic Press.

Friese, G., Hendee, J. C., & Kinziger, M. (1998). The wilderness experience program industry in the United States: Characteristics and dynamics. *Journal of Experiential Education, 21*, 40–45.

George, C., Kaplan, N., & Main, M. (1996). *Adult attachment interview protocol* (3rd ed.). Unpublished manuscript, University of California at Berkeley.

Gillis, H. L., Gass, M. A., & Russell, K. C. (2008). The effectiveness of project adventure's behavior management programs for male offenders in residential treatment. *Residential Treatment for Children & Youth, 25*, 227–247.

Hill, N. R. (2007). Wilderness therapy as a treatment modality for at-risk youth: A primer for mental health counselors. *Journal of Mental Health Counseling, 29*, 338–349.

Iwaniec, D., & Sneddon, H. (2001). Attachment style in adults who failed to thrive as children: Outcomes of a 20 year follow-up study of factors influencing maintenance or change in attachment style. *British Journal of Social Work, 31*, 179–195.

Kimball, R. O. & Bacon, S. B. (1993). The wilderness challenge model. In M. Gass (Ed.), *Adventure therapy: Therapeutic applications of adventure programming*. Dubuque: Kendall-Hunt.

Kluge, M. (2007). Re-creating through recreating. *Journal of Transformative Education, 5*, 177–191.

Kobak, R., & Madsen, S. D. (2008). The emotional dynamics of disruptions in attachment relationships: Implications for theory, research, and clinical intervention. In J. Cassidy & P. R. Shaver (eds.), *Handbook of attachment* (pp. 23–47). New York: Guilford.

Korfmacher, J., Adam, E., & Ogawa, J. (1997). Adult attachment: Implications for the therapeutic process in a home visitation intervention. *Applied Developmental Science, 1*, 43–52.

Levy, K. N., Meehan, K. B., Kelly, K. M., Reynoso, J. S., Weber, M., Clarkin, J. F., & Kernberg, O. F. (2006). Change in attachment patterns and reflective function in a randomized control trial of transference-focused psychotherapy for borderline personality disorder. *Journal of Consulting and Clinical Psychology, 74*, 1027–1040.

Main, M., & Cassidy, J. (1988). Categories of response to reunion with the parent at age 6: Predictable from infant attachment classifications and stable over a 1-month period. *Developmental Psychology, 24*, 415–426. doi:10.1037/0012-1649.24.3.415.

Newes, S. L. & Doherty, T. J. (2007). *Evaluating wilderness therapy as an option for treatment resistant adolescents*. Paper presented at 2007 American Psychological Association Convention, San Francisco, CA.

Norcross, J. (Ed.). (2002). *Psychotherapy relationships that work: Therapist contributions and responsiveness to patients*. New York: Oxford University Press.

Powch, I. (1994). Wilderness therapy: What makes it empowering for women? *Women and Therapy, 15*, 11–27.

Qi-Wu, S., Kok-Mun, N., & Lan, G. (2010). The link between parental bonding and adult attachment in Chinese graduate students: Gender differences. *Family Journal, 18*, 386–394.

Robertson, J., & Robertson, J. (Producers) (1969). *John, aged 17 months, for 9 days in residential care [Film]*. London: Tavistock Clinic.

Romi, S., & Kohan, E. (2004). Wilderness programs: Principles, possibilities and opportunities for intervention with dropout adolescents. *Child & Youth Care Forum, 33,* 115–136.

Russell, K. C. (2001). What is wilderness therapy? *The Journal of Experiential Education, 24,* 70–79.

Russell, K. C. (2003). An assessment of outcomes in outdoor behavioral healthcare treatment. *Child & Youth Care Forum, 32,* 355–381.

Russell, K. C. (2006). Brat camp, boot camp, or . . . . . . ? Exploring wilderness therapy program theory. *Journal of Adventure Education and Outdoor Learning, 6,* 51–67.

Russell, K. C. (2007). Adolescent substance-use treatment: Service delivery, research on effectiveness, and emerging treatment alternatives. *Journal of Groups in Addiction and Recovery, 2,* 68–96.

Russell, K. C., & Hendee, J. C. (2000). *Outdoor behavioral healthcare: Definitions, common practice, expected outcomes, and a nationwide survey of programs* (Technical Report No. 26). Retrieved from Idaho University at Moscow Wilderness Research Center website: http://www.its.uidaho.edu/wrc/pdf/obhpublication.pdf.

Russell, K. C., & Phillips-Miller, D. (2002). Perspectives on the wilderness therapy process and its relation to outcome. *Child & Youth Care Forum, 31*(6), 415–437.

Russell, K. C., Hendee, J. C., & Phillips-Miller, D. (1999). How wilderness therapy works: An examination of the wilderness therapy process to treat adolescents with behavioral problems and addictions. In D. N. Cole & S. F. McCool (Eds.) (edited 2000), *Proceedings: Wilderness science in a time of change.* Proc. RMRS-P-000 (pp. 1–28). Ogden: U.S. Department of Agriculture, Forest Service, Rocky Mountain Research Station.

Schoel, J., Prouty, D., & Radcliffe, P. (1988). *Islands of healing: A guide to adventure based counselling.* Hamilton: Project Adventure.

Somervell, J., & Lambie, I. (2009). Wilderness therapy within an adolescent sexual offender treatment programme: A qualitative study. *Journal of Sexual Aggression, 15,* 161–177.

Sroufe, L. (2005). Attachment and development: A prospective, longitudinal study from birth to adulthood. *Attachment & Human Development, 7,* 349–367.

Travis, L. A., Binder, J. L., Bliwise, N. G., & Horne-Moyer, L. (2001). Changes in clients' attachment styles over the course of time-limited dynamic psychotherapy. *Psychotherapy, 35,* 149–159.

Waters, E. (1978). The reliability and stability of individual differences in infant-mother attachment. *Child-Development, 49,* 483–494.

Waters, E., Merrick, S., Treboux, D., Crowell, J., & Albersheim, L. (2000). Attachment from infancy to early adulthood: A 20-year longitudinal study of relations between infant Strange Situation classifications and attachment representations in adulthood. *Child Development, 71,* 684–689.

Williams, B. (2000). The treatment of adolescent populations: An institutional vs. a wilderness setting. *Journal of Child and Adolescent Group Therapy, 10,* 47–56.

Part III
Building Capacity for Attachment-Based Clinical Work

From Out of Sight, Out of Mind to In Sight and In Mind: Enhancing Reflective Capacities in a Group Attachment-Based Intervention

Anne Murphy, Miriam Steele and Howard Steele

In this chapter, we share our experiences of working with parents and children and training clinical students, including social workers, over the past five years in a group attachment-based intervention (GABI). We designed this intervention specifically for clinical work with marginalized, socially isolated parents and their children (aged 0 to 3 years). The therapeutic goal of the intervention is to prevent child maltreatment by developing secure parent/child attachment relationships, promoting infant mental health, and reducing parental stress and social isolation. The intervention targets the needs of parents whose personal histories include multiple adverse childhood experiences including physical abuse, neglect, sexual abuse, multiple foster care placements, parental substance abuse, incarceration, and domestic and community violence. Theoretical and research findings from an attachment perspective inform the clinical model. The intervention is part of a study investigating its clinical effectiveness using state-of-the-art attachment measures, including indicators of reflective functioning (Steele et al. 2010). Thus, the GABI approach is an example of engaging in translational research whereby the clinical work influences the research and the research influences the clinical work.

A further integral part of the intervention is to train new clinicians alongside more seasoned clinicians in how to deliver the intervention. The lead clinician (AM) holds supervision immediately after each 2-h group clinical session, three times per week. The lead researchers (MS & HS) conduct weekly university-based research discussions to review video-taped GABI sessions to further develop a clinical training manual that may serve as a basis for replication and assist in training/supervision. This chapter illustrates both these reflective activities with the aim of showing how affectively laden material, typically residing "out of sight" and "out of mind" can effectively become "in sight" and "in mind", to the benefit of all stakeholders in the process. Several examples will serve as descriptions of this process that enhances

A. Murphy (✉)
Department of Pediatrics, Albert Einstein College of Medicine, Bronx, NY, USA
e-mail: anne.murphy@einstein.yu.edu

M. Steele · H. Steele
Department of Psychology, New School for Social Research, New York, NY, USA
e-mail: steeleh@newschool.edu

J. E. Bettmann, D. D. Friedman (eds.), *Attachment-Based Clinical Work with Children and Adolescents,* Essential Clinical Social Work Series,
DOI 10.1007/978-1-4614-4848-8_11, © Springer Science+Business Media New York 2013

reflective capacities of clinicians and of parents involved in the intervention. This chapter highlights the use of reflective supervision in training alongside its central role in the successful delivery of GABI.

Background

A clear way to ameliorate the deleterious influences associated with poverty and the concomitant immediate and long-term risk factors (Felitti et al. 1998) is to intervene early in the life of the children at risk, preferably with a multi-method, theoretically driven intervention. An attachment framework offers a comprehensive underpinning to the intervention proposed with its rich theoretical base and solid empirical foundation (Cassidy and Shaver 2010). This research-oriented theoretical paradigm derives much of its heuristic power from its original grounding in clinical phenomena and the subsequent support found for its utility in understanding the nature of parent–child relationships in both normative and high-risk samples. The unifying theme over the span of Bowlby's work (e.g., Bowlby 1944, 1951, 1960, 1969, 1973, 1980, 1982) was the effort to provide a cogent theoretical explanation for the recurrent observation of severe developmental deviations and emotional problems in children deprived of maternal care. In this context, the significant surge of interest in the application of attachment theory–for decades the exclusive concern of developmental researchers–to clinical issues is striking and immensely promising (Cicchetti et al. 2000a; Lieberman et al. 2005; Hoffman et al. 2006; Heinicke and Levine 2008; Moran et al. 2008).

Attachment theory and research command the attention of clinicians because of the availability of an interview procedure that enables a reliable assessment of whether past experiences of trauma or loss remain the focus of ongoing grief, or are unresolved, in the mind of the interviewee. The interview—the adult-attachment interview (AAI) (George et al. 1996), together with companion-scoring procedure (Main et al. 2008)—assesses an individual's current understanding of their childhood experiences, and is a robust, reliable and valid indicator of parenting competence (Steele and Steele 2008a). Unresolved responses to the AAI correlate with independent concurrent measures of absorption and dissociation (Hesse and van IJzendoorn 1999), frightened or frightening behavior in the parenting role, and infant–parent patterns of behavior governed by fear (Lyons-Ruth and Jacobvitz 2008).

The concept of reflective functioning (RF) arose from the task we (MS and HS) undertook to rate nearly 200 adult-attachment interviews collected as part of the London Parent Child Project (Fonagy et al. 1991; Steele and Steele 2008b). We found evidence that one way of breaking the cycle of abuse was for the individual to demonstrate a capacity to monitor the contents of his or her mind alongside the perusal of the mind of the other. By putting oneself in the so-called shoes of the other, s/he can begin to understand the thoughts, feelings and intentions that motivate their thoughts and actions (Fonagy et al. 1991).

We define reflective functioning as (1) an awareness of the nature of mental states in the self and others; (2) the mutual influences at work between mental states and behavior; (3) the necessity of a developmental perspective; and (4) the need to be sensitive to the current context. Reflective functioning is a powerful antidote to the pernicious effect that trauma has on mental health and specifically on the quality of parenting. Interventions that target the client's reflective capacities can assist the individual in coming to terms with or resolving the disruptive influences of past abuse (Bateman and Fonagy 2006; Diamond et al. 2008). Higher incidences of RF are linked to improved adult-treatment outcomes (Bateman and Fonagy 2003; Diamond et al. 2003; Fonagy et al. 1995). We (Steele and Steele 2008b) found better mental-health outcomes in children whose parents have higher reflective functioning scores. Specifically, higher scores of RF assessed in the parent correlated with lower externalizing behavior problems for the child at age five years and more positive self-reported mental health indicators of the child at age 11 years as assessed by the strengths and difficulties questionnaire (Goodman 1997). We found that RF, particularly in parents who experienced significant adversity during childhood, was a marker of resilience in these parents and correlated with secure attachment patterns in their children (Fonagy et al. 1994).

This link between secure attachment relationships and reflective functioning underlies our understanding of therapeutic change in attachment-based interventions which significantly enhance the quality of the parent–child relationship in at-risk populations (Heinicke et al. 1999; Marvin et al. 2002; Toth et al. 2006). Interestingly, the strongest evidence appears to come from interventions delivered at the end of the first year of life and through the child's second year. Bakermans-Kranenburg et al. (2003) concluded from their meta-analytic report on the subject that interventions targeting parental sensitivity initiated after approximately 6 months of age are more effective than interventions with more global goals beginning during the early months. This suggests the best window of opportunity for beginning an intensive attachment-focused intervention may be at the end of the first year of life.

An important published intervention utilizing attachment theory is child–parent psychotherapy (CPP; Lieberman et al. 2005, 2008). Five randomly controlled trials examined CPP in different settings (Lieberman and Weston 1991; Lieberman et al. 2006; Cicchetti et al. 1999, 2000a, b, 2006). These studies comprise a persuasive evidence base showing that CPP is effective for families whose risk context includes maternal depression, poverty, domestic violence, mothers with trauma histories, and maltreated children known to preventive services. The findings show that this treatment approach results in reduced child and maternal symptoms, and improvements in the child–mother attachment relationship.

The idea of delivering a group-based attachment intervention arose from the careful evaluation of a myriad of interventions aimed at addressing child maltreatment. Though formal parenting education programs have existed in various forms for decades, save for rare exceptions, these programs have not been evaluated in terms of design, measurement, and analysis, and have not focused on parent and child outcomes (Shonkoff and Phillips 2000). Some impressive results exist for home visiting programs over the long term, such as the Nurse Family Partnership program (Olds et al. 1998) and Healthy Families New York (HFNY: DuMont et al. 2008).

However, these programs do not provide families with direct contact with peers with whom they could sustain relationships after the intervention is completed. Thus, such programs are less able to target the social isolation of the families. There is also the issue of the cost-effectiveness of home visiting interventions as highlighted by recent Canadian research (Niccols 2008). Niccols (2008) demonstrated the therapeutic benefits and cost-effectiveness of a group-based intervention with an attachment focus. In a randomized trial involving 76 mothers, Niccols (2008) found that a parent–child group was as effective as a home visiting program in improving infant–mother attachment security.

Training Clinicians

For clinicians and trainees working in a parent–child psychotherapy program aimed at preventing or reducing the recurrence of child maltreatment, the emotional challenges are significant, including the likelihood of secondary traumatization and the matter of maintaining balanced and sensitive judgments that indicate multicultural competence. The need to train and support clinical staff appropriately is critical. The question of how best to realize these goals is challenging to answer. In the case of training, how do we know that our attempts at passing along the clinical wisdom and skill of one generation can be imparted to the next?

Unique challenges arise in the context of training clinicians to do parent–infant psychotherapy. This is in part because trainees come from a wide range of orientations and disciplines including social work, clinical psychology, pediatrics, child psychiatry, and mental health counseling. The core challenge, however, concerns the central task of balancing one's capacity to hold in mind the experience of the parent while simultaneously holding in mind the experience of the child, in light of past, present, and anticipated stresses impacting the parent, the child, and the clinician herself. This is a daunting task for even the most seasoned clinician. The challenge we will address in this chapter is how to incorporate the specific frame of reference known as reflective supervision to the training and implementation of group clinical work with families in which trauma spans generations.

Reflective Supervision

The concept of reflection in psycho-dynamically informed clinical work and research appeared in the literature in the early 1990s (Weatherston et al. 2010) as reflective functioning (Fonagy et al. 1991) and reflective supervision (Fenichel 1992; Shamoon-Shanok et al. 1995). The use of techniques utilizing reflective capacities in conducting and supervising clinical work surely predates these citations; the concept is akin to earlier writings emphasizing the importance of psychological insight, psychological mindedness, and self-observing ego functions, historical roots that certainly go back to Freud (Steele and Steele 2008b). The difference with reflective functioning is that an operational definition of it has been developed, with reliable and valid outcome research (Fonagy et al. 1998). In parent–child work, reflective supervision demands of the supervising clinician that she both practice and encourage the paying of attention to (a) one's own inner experience, (b) the experience of the infant or child, (c) the experience of the parent and (d) the experience of the trainee.

Shanok et al. (1995) and Shamoon-Shanok (2006) provided us with a cogent account of how reflective supervision may be the framework for clinical work delivered in peer settings with young children. Their quote is illustrative of the transformational power of the approach:

> Observing a child in a variety of situations and then joining and aggregating each observer's perceptions and knowledge in a conference is a commonly accepted relationship-based and reflective joint endeavor. A joint endeavor becomes a conjoined, transformational enterprise whose meaning increases and deepens–thus affecting all parties across hierarchies–when each person's perspective is deeply valued over time and linked to case outcome and to mission. (Shamoon-Shanok et al. 2005, p. 461).

There is much to unpack in this quote that may be applied to parent–child work in a group setting. Reflective supervision involves gathering information about a child across a range of situations, building up a profile of the child as he or she engages with parents, peers, therapist/teachers, etc. This is critical in forming pertinent clinical judgments using the aggregation of several observers' perspectives. When trainees and supervisors sit together and sift over the clinical formulations presented so that they become amalgamated, the group often arrives at sense of shared meaning. This process is instrumental in consolidating the group of clinicians with its mix of more senior and junior colleagues. This process also provides the backbone of the supportive framework for the clinicians, both in and out of the clinical group. Ultimately, clinical discussions of an ongoing treatment of a family while the family is out of sight bring the family firmly into the minds of the clinicians, helping to reaffirm the overall orientation of the intervention. In reflective supervision, we are able to think through one's reactions to a parent's negative attributions about their child by working to put ourselves in the parent's shoes delving into why, for example, a young father may think his infant's swats at him signal abuse. Such thoughtful attention into the mind of the other brings to light insights to further explore in the work. This also provides mechanisms for conceptualizing treatment goals for future sessions. The team's role of observing, describing, and reflecting on the interactions of parents and children is central to the mission of any attachment-based intervention and is the fundamental conceptual and clinical framework for GABI.

Group Attachment-Based Intervention (GABI)

The Group Attachment-Based Intervention is a treatment for parents with significant past histories of abuse and neglect, present struggles with relationship violence, homelessness, partner incarceration, and substance abuse, and fears that their children's lives will be no better than their own. GABI is designed for families with children birth to three years old. GABI meets three times each week for 2 h. A licensed psychologist, together with a parent–infant psychotherapist clinician (possibly a social worker), assume leadership of each group. Four to five social work and psychology practicum students assist. The training offered in GABI is unique in two ways for trainees: (i) trainees work alongside the lead clinician who has the opportunity to directly observe the interactions that may later arise in supervision discussions; and (ii) the intensity of working with families several times each week. Such intense family work elicits trainees' deeply held, often unconscious feelings and beliefs about parent–child interactions, what is optimal and what is not. Trainees and lead clinicians work closely, intensively sharing the joys and frustrations inherent in the daily challenges of working with painfully stressed families. This intensity heightens the need for supervision but provides an emotionally rich training experience. The model allows for close observation of the lead clinician in action and close collaboration with GABI trainees. Trainees report high levels of satisfaction with the apprenticeship model and describe the value of the parallel process of working as a group under the guidance of the lead clinician and with other trainees simultaneously.

There are four essential components to GABI. First, the group begins with a 45-min parent/child psychotherapy session held in a group playroom. Second, there is a parent/child separation where parents participate in a parent group while children engage in a child group for 60 min. Third, the parent/child reunion occurs; this is the most important segment where parents return to their young children after being separated. Fourth, reflective supervision sessions take place immediately after the group ends to hold and process the many observations and reactions of lead clinicians and trainees.

The Conceptual Framework of GABI: REARING

The attachment concepts central to GABI are drawn from the literature and each plays a role in setting the framework for the therapeutic treatment goals for the intervention overall and for each parent–child dyad. The REARING acronym emerged out of the effort to consolidate the attachment concepts for clinicians/trainees to keep in mind when trying to understand their reactions to the parent, the child, or their relationship in the work.

- *R*eflective functioning
- *E*motional attunement
- *A*ffect regulation
- *R*eticence in therapeutic and parental relationships
- *I*ntergenerational patterns
- *N*urturing the parent and child and enhancing parent's nurturing of their children
- *G*roup support

Reflective functioning *(RF)* is the hallmark objective of GABI. As mentioned previously, RF is the ability to think about the thoughts, feelings, and intentions guiding or underlying the behavior of others as well as self.

Emotional attunement in GABI involves having the therapists engage the parents and children in a way that recognizes their emotional states and conveys a sense of being understood. Therapists try to facilitate the parents' emotional attunement towards of their children, a critical skill in secure attachment relationships.

Affect regulation is vital to mental health. Inability to do so with regularity and competence can result in a variety of symptoms and pathology. Reflective functioning and emotional attunement goals of GABI are fundamental because they promote the parent's and child's ability to regulate affect. GABI offers the participants unique opportunities to practice interacting with therapists who are sensitive to the expression of volatile feeling states. It also helps parents learn to understand themselves and their children in a way that turns uncontrolled emotional arousal into understandable feeling states.

Reticence Reticence allows parents and children the space to discover their own feelings and fostering self-efficacy. GABI utilizes the theoretical and research construct of reticence as posited by Trevarthen (1979, p. 343), whereby "good parenting is defined by reticence on the part of the parent." Waiting to intervene can provide the parent with important information that would otherwise be missed if one rushes to step in. This process helps dyads to become more aware of each other's intentions.

Intergenerational patterns refers to understanding the current caregiving situation in the context of the experience of being parented. Often the parents who utilize GABI are parents who experienced inconsistent parenting in their own childhoods. With the urgent, often expressed wish to do a better job, the parents attending GABI attempt to understand the intergenerational forces at work as they attempt to shift to attachment-enhancing interactions with their children.

Nurturance is fundamental to secure attachment, so GABI focuses on the clinician nurturing both the parents and children, and, in turn, promoting the nurturance of the children by their parents. The GABI sessions include many opportunities to provide parents, and encourage parents themselves to provide their children, nurturing behavior. For example, each session includes physical contact between parent and child that accompany the songs that begin and end each session and the therapist's practice of serving each parent a warm beverage during the parents-only group. Via discussion with parents in the parent-only sessions, clinicians frequently invite parents to imagine their children as the vulnerable toddlers they are with deep needs for nurturance. In this way, parents come to understand that nurturing includes holding in mind their relationships with their children.

Group support is fundamental to GABI in order to combat the inherent social isolation faced by the participants and to support trainees. The groups allow for relationships to develop which provide important sources of social support to the parents and facilitate peer relationships amongst the children, a critical set of social-emotional skills to ensure each child's eventual school readiness. The group provides a unique training experience for students as they work alongside the lead clinician. The trainees can observe how the lead clinician sensitively interacts and responds to parents and children.

Reflective supervision takes place immediately following the group. The lead therapists meet with trainees for 1 h immediately after the group to discuss the clinical issues. This component is necessary both for training and in order to provide the clinicians/trainees an opportunity to process their own reactions to the often stressful situations. Reflective supervision offers a much-needed opportunity to evaluate and revise individualized treatment plans each week for each family. This process requires identifying the strengths and needs of individual families and developing specific strategies for the parent–child and child sessions. Fundamental to the supervisor's approach is a non-judgmental stance. On account of this, trainees are encouraged to share their reactions to the work including stirred up feelings stemming from their own past or current parent–child relationships. The lead clinician works to encourage understanding and acceptance of these inevitable trans-generational transactional phenomena while turning attention to using this understanding to support the trainees in an effort to benefit the children and parents who are the focus of the clinical work.

Training Clinicians in the Goals of GABI

Immersing clinicians in all four parts described above comprises the rich training experience required to deliver GABI. The process encourages trainees to hone their clinical skills by paying close attention to the REARING model (reflective functioning, emotional attunement, affect regulation, reticence, intergenerational patterns, nurturance, utilizing the benefits of group support among parents and within the clinical team). Clinicians themselves keep in mind the essence of the REARING model in thinking about the many different relationships involved in the group intervention—interactions between the parents and their children, the parents and each other, the children and each other, and the therapists with all of the participants. A further critical element is for the therapists to be aware of their own reactions to the work in the context of the multiple nested relationships of GABI depicted in Fig. 1. The lead clinician works to contain the intensity of the trainees' reactions to the parent–child interactions. The therapist here is like the attentive parent who takes in strong reactions, modulates them, transforms them, gives them meaning; such containment (Bion 1961) calms the child, or in this case, the trainee. The supervisor hopes that the trainees, like the child, will begin to internalize this process and contain their own emotional reactions. Figure 1 provides an image of these multiple nested relationships.

As Fig. 1 illustrates, in GABI the lead therapist provides a holding, emotionally responsive environment for all of the others present in the group. Through the lead therapist's support, the parents are able to better provide sensitive nurturing to their children. The lead therapist also provides emotional support to the trainees, who can then assist him or her in creating a warm, therapeutic environment. These relationships are not unidirectional, and the parents' and the children's needs and wishes also contribute to the therapeutic environment.

Beginning clinicians in parent/child work often feel an immediate reaction and desire to protect young children from a parent who may not meet the emotional needs of the young child in a manner which seems appropriate. "How can she act like that?" is a frequent early response to observing an overly harsh or punitive parent. It

Fig. 1 Multiple nested relationships in group attachment-based intervention (GABI)

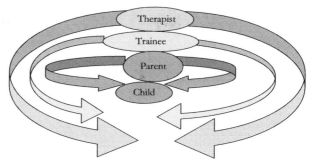

is important to acknowledge trainees' feelings of anger and frustration at parents and then help them build their capacity for reflective functioning for the parents. The lead clinician shares parent responses previously provided to AAI questions, for example, "What did you do when you were hurt or upset as a child?" thus, increasing trainees' abilities to imagine what their clients (the parents) experienced as children. It is sometimes shocking for trainees to hear the details of neglect and abuse experienced by the parents whose behavior, they realize, they may have been too quick to judge. If trainees can view parents as persons whose emotional and physical needs were never or inconsistently met as children and understand their struggles, they are less likely to judge and freer to facilitate the parents' ability to work through some of their past difficulties and meet their children's needs more effectively.

Initially frustrated trainees also often question the parents' life choices (multiple pregnancies, reliance on public assistance, choices in partners). It is helpful in facilitating the therapeutic work to ask "why might she be acting as she is?", rather than to judge. When we judge, we have only two choices: guilty or innocent. When we ask "why," we have countless avenues to explore and multiple opportunities for understanding. It is important, however, that the clinicians and trainees can openly express their feelings even if they are initially punitive or judgmental regarding the families and the work; and that the lead therapist can contain and explore those feelings in a supportive way. The lead therapist creates an accepting, non-judgmental climate allowing for the trainees to freely process their reactions to the ongoing work and derive energy to address afresh the needs of the families participating in the intervention.

Enhancing Reflective Capacities in Clinicians

Below is a list of three vital considerations in supervision work aimed at modeling and enhancing reflective capacities; these are (i) monitoring one's emotional availability, (ii) understanding that change happens slowly; and (iii) the vital role of observation.

Monitoring One's Emotional Availability

Just as we think about how intrusive or uninvolved parents can be with their children, the same observation fits to certain interactions clinicians have with the parents. Often there is a rush to intervene or say the "right thing". However, subtle scaffolding and one or two gentle questions can result in therapeutic action. Sometimes the therapeutic action comes just from the presence of the therapist. It is extremely important that therapists learn to be present without having to do something. The need to do or say something, often comes from the anxiety aroused within the therapist by the patient and/or situation. Being aware of his/her own feelings gives the therapist the chance to see moments unfold and watch the families find their own solutions supported by the nurturing environment.

Understanding that Change Happens Slowly

Creating a new parenting paradigm that involves shifts in the nature of internal models of how relationships work amounts to a profound change and takes time. Reassuring trainees that change is a slow process diffuses some of the urgency to make change happen too quickly through forced interventions. For example, too much talking can impede rather than facilitate change. The clinicians also have to accept the possibility that not all of the changes they might think are necessary will happen. For this reason, the idea of "good enough" parents (Winnicott 1971) is kept in mind as it provides support to clinicians aiming to help parents living in a context of often unpredictable life stressors, violence and trauma.

The Role of Observation

Using video footage of the clinical work is an invaluable tool in training. Observing the complexity of therapeutic interactions as they unfold throughout the 120 min can inform the clinical process immeasurably. Viewing video footage during supervision is useful both in terms of facilitating the therapeutic work and facilitating a reflective stance in the trainees. Observing one's self working helps trainees learn to observe and re-construct sequences of interpersonal interactions in their minds. This is important in the service of learning how to process clinical affect-laden experiences. Crucial information is gleaned from an individual's inability to remember or articulate what happened in a session. Coming to an understanding of what is difficult to remember leads to a discussion of why it is so hard, which can ultimately improve the therapeutic process. Clearly these are important considerations for the quality of therapy delivered to the families in the GABI intervention.

Reflective Supervision Session

Supervision begins tentatively, with the trainees usually being the ones to start the sessions with any salient issues they wish to bring from the recently completed clinical treatment session. Each clinician/trainee experienced something different and all are invited to share impressions in a non-judgmental format. The lead clinician models a non-judgmental stance as the approach with which to focus on the descriptions of the interactions with the parents and children. Often trainees will begin to talk about an episode and construct verbatim with the help of other trainees what they observed or heard with regard to a particular dyad. It is always important for the lead clinician to show curiosity and reflect on why a particular episode is discussed from among 120 min of interactions. The lead clinician shows acceptance for the variety of emotions which may accompany the processing of events including anger, laughter, sadness, and fear.

The clinician facilitates the reflective capacities by asking "why the tears, why the laughter?" The emphasis on the trainees' experience of the material in the here and now is meant to help in better understanding the possibility of avoidance/dismissiveness as a response to the often painful clinical material. Strong emotions might suggest ambivalence in the clinician and the need to process an encounter at a deeper level. Issues trainees bring to supervision usually concern something a parent has done or said. Usually the trainee has some strong feeling or a judgment about this issue or interaction. Exploring the interaction and the trainee's judgment gives way to a potentially useful reflective process involving the discussion of thoughts, consequences, limits and opportunities.

Clinical Vignettes

As part of our ongoing efforts to demonstrate the efficacy of GABI, we produced a manual of the treatment program[1]. The manual consists of descriptions of the intervention framework and was based on over 100 hours of videotaped footage of the actual clinical work. This video gave us the opportunity to observe in careful detail aspects of the therapeutic action as it unfolded in the intervention. In order to provide clinical examples, we endeavored to elucidate the content of the manual at a level of description potentially more detailed than high-quality process notes. This is because the vignettes are arrived at through viewing and re-viewing the video footage of the actual clinical work. Here are two examples of vignettes from the manual.

---

[1] The manual has been developed over the last few years with many New School graduate students including Kiara Schlesinger, Ellie Figelman Neuman and more recently Jordan Bate, Kerri Chladnicek, Sarah Jackson, Hannah Knafo, Adella Nikitiades, Michael Kinsey, Carmen LaLonde, Jessica Retan, Sophia Hoffman, and Rie von Wowern.

Vignette 1: The Challenge of "Sharing is Caring"

The first vignette emphasizes working with the trainees' counter-transference, feeling empathic toward one child, while shifting toward an attempt to understand the context of a second child. The trainee comments on observing a child, 36-month Max, who had been referred to the group for his aggressive behavior, and his mother, Raven. At the time, Raven was clinically depressed and also had a newborn son, and the family was living in a domestic violence shelter.

Parent–Child Session Clinical Observation

Three-year old Max grabs Play-Doh and refuses to share with another child (Iris) sitting at a table with her mother. Raven, Max's mother, focuses on her new baby. Raven yells across the room for Max to share while another mother says, "Sharing is caring." Lead clinician comments, "Ah, you want him to share."

The lead clinician approaches Max, kneels down next to him and helps him secure the Play-Doh he has just grabbed back. Providing a protective barrier with her arms around him and the Play-Doh, says to him in a quiet slow manner, "You just cannot share today. You have had to share so much; all your toys are in storage, you even have to share your mom with your brother." Child begins to cry and buries his head on the clinician's shoulder who comforts him by saying, "I think you need your Mom." Raven comes over and embraces him. After this acknowledgement of his feelings by both mother and clinician, he then hands a piece of Play-Doh to the other child. Raven becomes tearful.

Reflective Supervision Session

Trainee 1:	I felt so uncomfortable when Max would not share the Play-Doh. Iris looked so sad. Even the parents commented, "What about sharing is caring."
Lead clinician:	"It is really hard to watch when one child will not share"
Trainee 1:	"I felt so bad for Iris. I mean shouldn't we make him share?"
Lead clinician:	"Let's think about Max for a minute, why do you think Max was acting like that?"
Trainee 2:	I know it is hard for Max to share, especially as his Mom seems so far away and busy with the new baby.
Lead clinician:	It is interesting that was the other parent who shouted out "sharing is caring." We certainly want the kids to share as an ultimate goal but we are not there yet, but let's try and see things from Max's point of view.
Trainee 3:	You gave Max an experience of a grown-up understanding him. It was helpful to him that you could say that you understand how angry, sad, frightened he might be feeling.

Lead clinician:	I also wanted to hold back and have it be his Mom who could come help with the repair. We can wonder about what the experience might remind the mother of?
Trainee 2:	Maybe she sees herself in her child and it triggers such pain for her that she has to share everything.
Lead clinician:	Yes, we could have said to Raven, "It seems it is hard to see your child so angry and that he cannot share."
Trainee 3:	In the Parent-Only Group Raven cried as she told the group how difficult it is for them since all of their things are in storage and how she came from the hospital with the new baby to the shelter.
Lead clinician:	This mother commented how she never imagined she would live in a shelter with her babies and how guilty she feels; she cannot even provide a home for them, she questions what kind of a mother she is. We asked in the group today; "Has anyone else ever felt like this?"
Trainee 1:	The other mothers in the group really helped her as they re-counted their own hard stories and how they didn't ever believe they would be living the way they are living.
Lead clinician:	And another mother tearfully explained how she sees Raven as an amazing mother and how leaving an abusive relationship was very brave. I think it is also important to think about the parent's concern with "Sharing is caring" and how they feel the kids need to learn this for school and on the playground. We know that it is important and we can see the value they see in sharing, but it is important to explore why might Max be struggling.
Trainee 2:	I felt so bad for Iris, who wanted the Play-Doh, I mean aren't we supposed to be teaching them to share?
Lead clinician:	It was very painful to watch.
Trainee 1:	It was hard to wait and see what would happen, but we were lucky it turned out well and he did share.
Lead clinician:	Lucky, but let's try and think of these situations as likely to lead to various outcomes and what would have happened had he not shared and continued to grasp the Play-Doh?
Trainee 2:	Maybe we would have had to reflect longer with Iris on how bad we feel when someone does not want to share with us.
Lead clinician:	We would have the opportunity to express how much Max wants the Play-Doh for himself and how angry/sad that makes Iris. We might have then stated how badly everyone was feeling and show them we can tolerate their angry feelings in a safe manner.

This vignette touches on many different aspects of reflective capacities, in play or at work, both in terms of facilitating the process in the parents and children as well as trainees. We see here a rather routine incident that could easily unfold in many playgroups with children this age. The difference in the GABI intervention is the close monitoring of the sequence of interactions, and the explicit engagement with the participants in a therapeutic manner. Max was upset and perhaps expected a different response from the environment. He might have expected admonishment for not sharing. Instead, he experienced an adult labeling his feeling state and anchoring it as a legitimate response to his circumstances. Through this interaction, we presume he felt understood, that the adult had a sense of what was going on in his mind. Importantly, the therapist practiced reticence as she did not rush in to comfort Max, especially when he threw himself into her lap, but instead gave his mother the opportunity to engage in an affect-laden, attachment-relevant moment with her son. By not rushing in to fix the situation immediately for Max and Iris, the therapist offered an opportunity for the eventual repair to the rupture that had occurred between them. The trainees began the reflective-supervision session by expressing their empathy not initially for Max, but for Iris as the aggrieved child. An important process ensued where the lead clinician helped the group put Max's behavior into context and helped them metabolize their own feelings of frustration and sadness on Iris's behalf.

Vignette 2: Mother Instinct

The lead clinician and the trainees meet after the group for supervision and the conversation is left open to the trainees to discuss what resonated for them or felt important. The lead clinician then focuses on the discussion and provides specific information that is meant to widen the group members' perspectives and enhance their reflective functioning as they consider the individuals they are discussing. In this reflective-supervision session, the therapists begin by generally discussing the earlier parent group. During a brief pause, the lead clinician brings up one mother's use of the term "mother instinct." Importantly, she begins by recalling the mother's exact words.

Reflective Supervision Session

Lead clinician: Today Maria said ... what did she say? Janine, Rita, and Maria were talking about what they do when they're not in the mood for the kids and I was just really empathizing and saying it's really difficult even like playing with them when you're depressed and you're tired and you just don't want to hear it. And Maria–a mother who is very reluctant to play with her young son, often sitting across the room from him–said, "Yeah, but you can't do that. That's when the mother instinct has to come in. And you have to play."

Trainee 1:   That's good.

Trainee 2:   It's good, but at the same time...

Trainee 1:   Oh you don't believe her?

Trainee 2:   Its good, but at the same time it's not realistic.

Trainee 3:   I think there's a big difference between knowing what she should do and being able to do it. But then that's another source of guilt because then she can't do what she's supposed to do, so she just puts herself under pressure.

Trainee 2:   I don't even understand where the whole "nurturing" jumps in. It's very interesting that she used that word.

Lead clinician: (repeating verbatim the words that the mother used) The "mother instinct."

Trainee 2:   So does she have to worry about it if it is just gonna jump in and then I don't have to worry? It's not an active thing that I have to do. It's just very interesting.

Trainee 3:   The counterpart to that, I think, is it happens with everybody. There are days when you aren't in the mood and you can't play. You say, "Mommy can't play today." But they (the mothers in the group) can't imagine that. It happens, what's the problem? If you are okay with your own feelings, it's normal to feel exhausted. You are rejecting, somewhat yes, but it's tolerable.

Lead clinician: She could not take that issue, she was sort of. . .

Trainee 3:   Because she's not able to play as well. That's what's happening. She's really saying the opposite of what she said. She's saying she doesn't have "mother instinct." Or maybe she has it, but she's so depressed that it doesn't surface. So for her, she's saying the opposite.

Trainee 4:   I think it would have been interesting to ask Maria what she meant by "mother instinct." My fantasy is that seeing how she is, going through the motions of daily care without being able to be a playful parent, maybe it was something about eating, bathing, clothing, that's the "mother instinct."

Trainee 3:   If you think about instincts in general, it almost just happens impulsively, like it's natural, it's there, you don't do anything to bring it on.

Lead clinician: She had her first baby at thirteen. And if we think "mother instinct," she had that baby [the lead clinician provides background on how Maria became pregnant]. But you can imagine, a little thirteen-year old. You know, "mother instinct," I mean, do you have it at thirteen when they take a baby away from you? I mean. You kind of imagine.

Trainee 3:   I think she was the child, not the parent. She probably just gets what someone told her. Maternal instinct. Everybody has that. She has to believe, she has to. Otherwise, what else can happen? Maybe it was too painful, the conversation was just too painful.

Lead clinician: See, I'm seeing Maria now that we're talking. It's almost like a thirteen-year-old doesn't even really want to play anymore. Do you know what I mean?

In this session, the lead clinician demonstrates the clinical usefulness of practicing reticence and reflective functioning, two key components of reflective supervision. By allowing trainees' impressions to unfold naturally, the lead clinician creates a sense of safety for the group and promotes a nuanced, developmental understanding of the situation being discussed. The lead clinician is not in a rush to connect the dots for the trainees but slowly allows them the space and comfort to freely think out loud. The lead clinician is careful to remember the particular context of the conversation and the exact words that were used. By stopping to think for a moment and asking herself, "What did she say?" the lead clinician models for the other therapists the importance of being precise and remaining non-judgmental when conveying information about the families. The lead clinician demonstrates reflective functioning as she monitors her own memory and speech when recalling the moment she wishes to share with the group and she gently urges the trainees to do the same.

Furthermore, when Trainee 2 interprets "mother instinct" as "nurturing," the lead clinician guides her back to the original term Maria used. Throughout the discussion, the lead clinician simply reiterates Maria's reaction in the parent group. By repeating what Maria said and did, rather than providing her own perspective, the lead clinician encourages the trainees to delve further into not only what "mother instinct" means, but also why having a "mother instinct" may be important to this mother.

Toward the end of this segment, the lead clinician provides background information about Maria. The timing and use of this background information is important, because it serves to help the clinicians further understand the particular moment they are discussing. Using reticence, the lead clinician holds back in sharing Maria's history so trainees can express their own impressions first and then pulls the whole story together with the trainees' help. As a result, the group draws together a more sophisticated picture using what they were able to share together to generate a developmental understanding of how a few words of speech by a mother in the clinical group may reflect a deeply held state of mind about attachment, in this case "the mother instinct". We begin to see how this mother expects she should have some "mother instinct" which would enable her to play with her child. This vignette illustrates a shared motive among parents participating in GABI: to provide their children with what they themselves did not receive.

Supervision for the Supervisor

Supervisors need emotional containment from their professional peers, to obtain relief from all of the responsibilities and overwhelming experiences that arise in supervision inherent parent–child psychotherapy (Yerushalmi 1999). It is essential for the group leader to have peer supervision, because the leader is responsible for the well-being of the group members and their children, as well as the trainees (see Fig. 1). Responsibility for providing a "holding environment" (Winnicott 1965) for the expressed and unexpressed thoughts, behaviors and feelings of the many people involved including the parents, children, trainees and clinicians, each with different needs requires sensitivity and mechanisms for processing the often affect-laden interactions. At times in the GABI intervention, there are families with whom we have significant concerns regarding child welfare. The group leader needs a place to share clinical concerns and keep a balanced perspective, as the high-risk nature of the families for which this intervention is designed is demanding.

Conclusion

This particular attachment intervention incorporates the rudiments of Bowlby's theory on the nature of attachment relationships, as well as important attachment research findings from developmental psychology, and core elements of child–parent psychotherapy. The clinical vignettes illustrate the way in which these various threads come together when delivering the intervention. First and foremost, the treatment aims to facilitate reflective functioning in the parents, and nearly all aspects of it are directed toward this end. We see this as vital to therapeutic action. Importantly, it is the role of the lead clinician to also promote this capacity in the other clinicians who train in this modality, to create an environment that supports positive change in the children and parents. The vignettes illustrate how the current context families find themselves in, as in the case of Max, necessitates a loosening of the usual dictates of a pre-school setting, such as "sharing is caring" in favor of a more dynamic and ultimately therapeutic approach, taking into account the individual child's current perspective. This involves the clinicians' ability to reflect on each family's situation of living in a shelter and the meaning of this for each family member. In Max's case, the conflict over the clump of Play-Doh provided an opportunity to affirm Max's deep need for the experience of having something for himself, painful as that awareness might have been for Max, the sense of being understood and his intentions valued would surely give him psychological and social strength in the long run. The clinician stating in a quiet way that he or she appreciates the intentions underlying behavior is frequently more important appreciation for intentions underlying behavior is frequently more important than simply declaring the conventional value of "sharing is caring."

The second vignette provides further guidance in how paying close attention to the language of our patients may be a vital way to understand what they are meaning. Most of attachment research is observation and/or narrative based, which demands paying close attention to discrete behavior or language. There is much a clinician can learn from the main tenets of attachment-based research about how close observation of behavior and narrative can provide important windows into the nature of the patient's internal world. The lead clinician's artful display of reticence and patience, evidenced by not simply jumping to demanding that Max share or especially in the second case where she held off from disclosing important features of the mother's history until they could formulate their own meaning about what this mother might be feeling and thinking.

These features of the GABI approach are common in many forms of parent–infant psychotherapy. Apart from child–parent psychotherapy (CPP) which is distinguished by having the most rigorous evidence base, other attachment-based intervention are burgeoning, for example, Circle of Security (Hoffman et al. 2006) Minding the Baby (Slade et al. 2005) ABC intervention (Dozier et al. 2008) to name but a few. The variations among these interventions highlight the commitment clinicians working with parents and children have to an attachment framework and attest to the need to offer a range of interventions that will serve the wide range of clinical contexts.

It is an exciting time to be involved in parent–infant psychotherapy work as it seems to have come of age with more emphasis on prevention as well as intervention and a confluence of ideas concerning how to demonstrate treatment effectiveness. The need for these interventions is clearly great, if not overwhelming. With the focus on how to bring about change that moves troubled families training and toward attachment security, and how to put reflective functioning to work in both delivery of the intervention, we can make a contribution to future generations, one intergenerational family at a time.

References

Bakermans-Kranenburg, M. J., van IJzendoorn, M. H., & Juffer, F. (2003). Less is more: Meta-analyses of sensitivity and attachment interventions in early childhood. *Psychological Bulletin, 129,* 195–215.

Bateman, A., & Fonagy, P. (2003). The development of an attachment-based treatment program for borderline personality disorder. *Bulletin of the Menninger Clinic, 67*(3), 187–211.

Bateman, A. W., & Fonagy, P. (2006). *Mentalization-based treatment for borderline personality disorder: A practical guide,* Oxford: Oxford University Press.

Bion, W. R. (1961). *Experiences in groups.* London: Tavistock.

Bowlby, J. (1944). Forty-four juvenile thieves: Their characters and home-life. *The International Journal of Psychoanalysis, 25,* 19–53.

Bowlby, J. (1951). Maternal care and mental health. *Bulletin of the World Health Organization, 3,* 355–533.

Bowlby, J. (1960). Separation anxiety. *The International Journal of Psychoanalysis, 41,* 89–113.

Bowlby, J. (1969). *Attachment and loss: Vol. I. Attachment.* London: Hogarth Press and the Institute of Psycho-Analysis.

Bowlby, J. (1973). *Attachment and loss: Vol. II. Separation.* London: Hogarth.

Bowlby, J. (1980). *Attachment and loss.* New York: Basic Books.

Bowlby, J. (1982). Attachment and loss: retrospect and prospect. *American Journal of Orthopsychiatry, 52,* 664–678.

Cassidy, J., & Shaver, P. (2010). *Handbook of attachment.* New York: Guilford.

Cicchetti, D., Toth, S. L., & Rogosch, F. A. (1999). The efficacy of toddler-parent psychotherapy to increase attachment security in offspring of depressed mothers. *Attachment and Human Development, 1,* 34–66.

Cicchetti, D., Toth, S., & Rogosch, F. (2000a). *The development of psychological wellness in maltreated children.* Washington, DC: Child Welfare League of America.

Cicchetti, D., Rogosch, F., & Toth, S L. (2000b). The efficacy of toddler-parent psychotherapy for fostering cognitive development in offspring of depressed mothers. *Journal of Abnormal Child Psychology, 28,* 135–148.

Cicchetti, D., Rogosch, F., & Toth, S. L. (2006). Fostering secure attachment in infants in maltreating families through preventive interventions. *Development and Psychopathology, 18,* 623–649.

Diamond, D., Levy, K., Clarkin, J., & Stovall-McClough, C. (2003). Patient-therapist attachment in the treatment of borderline personality disorder. *Bulletin of the Menninger Clinic, 67,* 227–259.

Diamond, D., Yeomans, F., Clarkin, J., & Levy, K. (2008). The reciprocal impact of attachment and transference-focused psychotherapy with borderline patients. In H. Steele & M. Steele (Eds.), *Clinical applications of the adult-attachment interview* (pp. 339–385). New York: Guilford.

Dozier, M., Peloso, E., Lewis, E., Laurenceau, J-P., Levine, S. (2008). Effects of an attachment-based intervention on the cortisol production of infants and toddlers in foster care. *Development and Psychopathology, 20,* 845–859.

DuMont, K., Mitchell-Herzfeld, S., Greene, R., Lee, E., Lowenfels, A., Rodriguez, M., & Dorabaw-ila, V. (2008). Healthy Families New York (HFNY) randomized trial: Effects on early child abuse and neglect. *Child Abuse & Neglect, 32,* 295–315.

Felitti, V. J., Anda, R. F., Nordenberg, D., Williamson, D. F., Spitz, A. M., Edwards, V., Koss, M. P. & Marks, J. S. (1998). Relationship of childhood abuse and household dysfunction to many leading causes of death in adults: The adverse childhood experiences (ACE) study. *American Journal of Preventive Medicine, 14,* 245–258.

Fenichel. (Ed.). (1992). *Learning through supervision and mentorship to support the development of infants, toddlers, and their families*: A source book. Washington, DC: Zero to Three Press.

Fonagy, P., Leigh, T., Steele, M., Steele, H., Kennedy, R., Matoon, G., Target, M., & Gerber, A. (1996). The relation of attachment status, psychiatric classification, and response to psychotherapy. *Journal of Consulting and Clinical Psychology, 64,* 22–31.

Fonagy, P., Steele, M., Steele, H., Moran, G., & Higgitt, A. (1991). The capacity for understanding mental states: The reflective self in parent and child and its significance for security of attachment. *Infant Mental Health Journal, 12,* 201–218.

Fonagy, P., Steele, M., Steele, H., Higgitt, A., & Target, M. (1994). The Emmanuel Miller memorial lecture 1992. The theory and practice of resilience. *Journal of Child Psychology and Psychiatry, 35,* 231–257.

Fonagy, P., Target, M., Steele, H., & Steele, M. (1998). *Reflective-functioning manual, version 5.2, for application to adult attachment interviews*. Unpublished document, University College London and New School for Social Research.

George, C., Kaplan, N., & Main, M. (1996). *Adult attachment interview* (3rd ed.). Unpublished manuscript, University of California at Berkeley.

Goodman, R. (1997). The strengths and difficulties questionnaire: A research note. *Journal of Child Psychology and Psychiatry, 38,* 581–586.

Heinicke, C. M., Fineman, N. R., Ruth, G., Recchia, S. L., Guthrie, D., & Rodning, C. (1999). Relationship-based intervention with at-risk mothers: Outcome in the first year of life. *Infant Mental Health Journal, 20,* 349–374.

Heinicke, C. M., & Levine, M. S. (2008). The AAI anticipates the outcome of a relation-based early intervention. In H. Steele & M. Steele (Eds.), *Clinical Applications of the Adult Attachment Interview* (99–125). New York: Guilford.

Hesse, E., & van IJzendoorn, M. H. (1999). Propensities towards absorption are related to lapses in the monitoring of reasoning or discourse during the adult attachment interview: A preliminary investigation. *Attachment & Human Development, 1,* 67–91.

Hoffman, K. T., Marvin, R. S., Cooper, G., & Powell, B. (2006). Changing toddlers' and preschoolers' attachment classifications: The circle of security intervention. *Journal of Consulting and Clinical Psychology, 74,* 1017–1026.

Lieberman, A. F., & Van Horn, P. (2005). *"Don't hit my mommy!" A manual for child-parent psychotherapy for young witnesses of family violence*. Washington, DC: Zero to Three.

Lieberman, A.F., Ghosh Ippen, C., & Van Horn, P. (2006). Child-Parent Psychotherapy: 6-Month Follow-up of a Randomized Controlled Trial. *Journal of the American Academy of Child & Adolescent Psychiatry. 45(8),* 913–918.

Lieberman, A. F., Weston, D. R. and Pawl, J. H. (1991). Preventive Intervention and Outcome with Anxiously Attached Dyads. Child Development, *62,* 199-209.

Lieberman, A. & Van Horn, P. (2008). *Psychotherapy with infants and young children: Repairing the effects of stress and trauma on early attachment*. New York: The Guilford.

Lieberman, A., Van Horn, P., & Ippen, C. G. (2005). Toward evidence-based treatment: Child-parent psychotherapy with preschoolers exposed to marital violence. *Journal of the American Academy of Child and Adolescent Psychiatry, 44*, 1241–1248.

Lyons-Ruth, K., & Jacobvitz, D. (2008). *Attachment disorganization: Genetic factors, parenting contexts, and developmental transformation from infancy to adulthood*. New York: Guilford.

Main, M., Hesse, E., & Goldwyn, R. (2008). Studying differences in language use in recounting attachment history. In H. Steele & M. Steele (Eds.), *Clinical Applications of the Adult Attachment Interview* (pp. 31–68). New York: Guilford.

Marvin, R., Cooper, G., Hoffman, K., & Powell, B. (2002). The Circle of Security project: Attachment-based intervention with caregiver-pre-school dyads. *Attachment & Human Development, 4*, 107–124.

Moran G., Neufeld Bailey H., Gleason K., Deoliveira C., Pederson D. (2008). Exploring the mind behind unresolved attachment: Lessons from and for attachment-based interventions with infants and their traumatized mothers. In: Steele H, Steele M, eds. *Clinical applications of the adult attachment interview*. NY: Guilford Publications; 371–398.

Niccols, A. (2008). Right from the start: Randomized trial comparing an attachment group intervention to supportive home visiting. *Journal of Child Psychology and Psychiatry, 49*, 754–764.

Olds, D., Henderson, C., Kitzman, H., Eckenrode, J., Cole, R., & Tarelbaum, R. (1998). The promise of home visitation: Results of two randomized trials. *Journal of Community Psychology, 26*, 5–21.

Shamoon-Shanok, R. (2006). Reflective supervision for an integrated model: What, why, and how? In G.M. Foley & J.D. Hochman (Eds.), Mental health in early intervention: Achieving unity of principles and practice (pp 343-379). San Francisco: Jossey–Bass.

Shanok, R.S., Gilkerson, L, Eggbeer, L, & Fenichel, E. (1995). Reflective supervision: A relationship for learning. A guidebook and videotape. ZERO TO THREE: National Center for Infants, Toddlers and Families.

Shamoon-Shanok, R., Lapidus, C., Grant, M., Halpern, E., & Lamb-Parker, F. (2005). Apprenticeship, transformational enterprise, and the ripple effect: Transferring knowledge to improve programs serving young children and their families. In K. Moran Finello (Ed.), *The handbook of training and practice in infant and preschool mental health* (pp. 453–486). San Francisco: Jossey-Bass.

Shonkoff, J., & Phillips, D. (2000). *From neurons to neighborhoods: The science of early childhood development*. Washington: National Academies Press.

Slade, A., Sadler, L., Dios-Kenn, C. D., Webb, D., Currier-Ezepchick, J., Mayes, L. (2005). Minding the baby: A reflective parenting program. *The Psychoanalytic Study of the Child, 60*, 74–100.

Steele, H., & Steele, M. (2008a). *Clinical applications of the Adult Attachment Interview*. New York: Guilford.

Steele, H., & Steele, M. (2008b). On the origins of reflective functioning. In F. Busch (Ed.), *Mentalization: Theoretical considerations, research findings, and clinical implications* (pp. 133–158). New York: The Analytic Press.

Steele, M., Murphy, A., & Steele, H. (2010). Identifying therapeutic action in an attachment based intervention. *Journal of Clinical Social Work, 38*, 61–72.

Toth, S. L., Rogosch, F. A., Manly, J. T., & Cicchetti, D. (2006). The efficacy of toddler-parent psychotherapy to reorganize attachment in the young offspring of mothers with major depressive disorder: A randomized clinical trial. *Journal of Consulting and Clinical Psychology, 74*, 1006–1016.

Trevarthen, C. (1979). Communication and cooperation in early infancy: A description of primary intersubjectivity. In M. Bullowa (Ed.), *Before speech: The beginning of human communication* (pp. 321–347). London: Cambridge University Press.

Weatherston, D., Weigand, R., & Weigand, B. (2010). Reflective supervision: Supporting reflective supervision as a cornerstone for competency. Zero to Three, *31(2)*, 22–30.

Winnicott, D. W. (1965). The maturational processes and the facilitating environment. *International Psycho-Analytic Library, 64*, 1–276. London: The Hogarth Press and the Institute of Psycho-Analysis.

Winnicott, D. W. (1971). *Playing and Reality,* London: Tavistock.

Yerushalmi, H. (1999). The roles of group supervision of supervision. *Psychoanalytic Psychology, 16*, 426–447.

Implementing Attachment Theory in the Child Welfare System: Clinical Implications and Organizational Considerations

Susanne Bennett and Wendy Whiting Blome

Researchers and practitioners alike recognize the value of attachment theory to explain the relational dynamics, behavioral disorders, and long-range developmental sequelae of abused and neglected children who are involved in the child welfare system. Foster/adoptive families and new child welfare professionals frequently receive education about attachment as part of their training (Nilsen 2003). Clinicians often refer to attachment theory in decisions about parent–child relationships and permanency planning and in discussions about behaviors of children who have been abused, neglected, or removed from their homes (Barth et al. 2005; Berlin et al. 2005; Gauthier et al. 2004; Oppenheim and Goldsmith 2007; Redding et al. 2000). Clinicians use attachment concepts to understand the distress that foster children experience in the visitation process following removal from biological parents (Haight et al. 2003; McWey and Mullis 2004). Additionally, researchers use attachment measures to focus on the empirical link between disorganized attachment and the mental health issues of abused and neglected children (Fish and Chapman 2004; O'Connor and Zeanah 2003; Walker 2007). Researchers and clinicians together design attachment-based interventions to enhance the relationship of children with their biological or foster parents (Ackerman and Dozier 2005; Dozier et al. 2002a, b). Attachment theory and research is "arguably the most popular theory for explaining parent-child behavior by professionals involved with child welfare systems" (Barth et al. 2005, p. 257).

Nevertheless, the internal and external pressures on child welfare agencies often impede the implementation of attachment-based programs, despite the theory's popularity. To serve vulnerable populations, to compete for grants, and to meet Federal Performance Improvement Plans, managers and workers within the child welfare system are investing funds in training and devoting time to implementing practices determined effective by intervention research. Toward that end, attachment theory (Bowlby 1969, 1973, 1980, 1988; Cassidy and Shaver 2008) has attracted the attention of administrators interested in intervention research that promotes positive parent–child relationships and permanency planning. The theory emerged from

S. Bennett (✉) · W. W. Blome
National Catholic School of Social Service, The Catholic University of America,
Washington, DC, USA
e-mail: BENNETTS@cua.edu

J. E. Bettmann, D. D. Friedman (eds.), *Attachment-Based Clinical Work with Children and Adolescents,* Essential Clinical Social Work Series, DOI 10.1007/978-1-4614-4848-8_12, © Springer Science+Business Media New York 2013

an expansive body of research, and some attachment-based interventions are now empirically-supported treatments (Cassidy and Shaver 2008). However, translating attachment research into direct practice in clinical settings has been difficult (Nilsen 2003).

This chapter will explore some of the challenges in implementing in child welfare agencies the well researched, broadly accepted theoretical and practice base underlying attachment. Following a summary of the numbers of children and families served by child welfare, the chapter will present an overview of five attachment-based practice models that hold promise for addressing the needs of the child welfare population. The chapter will also present an examination of factors that encumber or support the implementation of attachment-based models in child welfare settings and a discussion of the goals of child welfare services and factors particular to child welfare organizations. The chapter will conclude with recommendations for practitioners and organizations in the child welfare field.

The Scope of Child Welfare

A federally mandated service implemented by the states, child welfare is part of the safety infrastructure of communities. Its mission is to prevent or ameliorate the abuse, neglect, dependency, and exploitation of children (Busch and Folaron 2005). While each state writes individual definitions based on standards set in federal law, the Department of Health and Human Services defines child abuse and neglect as "any recent act or failure to act on the part of a parent or caretaker which results in death, serious physical or emotional harm, sexual abuse or exploitation; or an act or failure to act which presents an imminent risk of serious harm" (U.S. Department of Health and Human Services (USDHHS) Administration for Children and Families, Administration on Children, Youth and Families, Children's Bureau 2010, p. vii). The four types of maltreatment—neglect, physical abuse, psychological abuse, and sexual abuse—can occur separately but often take place simultaneously. All forms of maltreatment have serious implications for a child's attachment patterns and emotional development (Baer and Martinez 2006; Strijker et al. 2008).

The National Child Abuse and Neglect Data System (NCANDS) collects data on child abuse and neglect rates from the states, while the Adoption and Foster Care Analysis and Reporting System (AFCARS) reports foster care and adoption data. In fiscal year 2009, hotline workers received an estimated 3.3 million allegations of child maltreatment, representing over 6 million children. State child protective service agencies accepted approximately 62 % of these referrals for a response (USDHHS 2010), and investigations determined that 78.3 % of children suffered neglect, 17. 8% experienced physical abuse, 9.5 % were subjected to sexual abuse, and 7.6 % faced psychological maltreatment (USDHHS 2010). (Children can suffer from multiple types of maltreatment; therefore, the percentages add up to more than 100 %.) Among victims of child abuse and neglect, 48.2 % were girls and 51.1 % were boys (less than

1 % gender unrecorded). Of the victims, 87 % were among three races or ethnicities—White (44 %), African–American (22.3 %), and Hispanic (20.7 %) (USDHHS 2010). Particularly children from birth to age one who are vulnerable to abuse and neglect, had the highest rate of victimization at 20.6 per 1,000 (USDHHS 2010). This has implications because the foundation of attachment develops in the first years of life (Cassidy 2008; Marvin and Britner 2008). Further, longitudinal research on high-risk populations confirms that attachments in infancy have predictive value for future functioning (Weinfield et al. 2008).

Although most children remain in their homes with supportive services to ensure safety, in 2009 child welfare workers placed one-fifth (20.8 %) of child victims in foster care following an investigation (USDHHS 2010). As of September 30, 2009, there were 423,773 children in foster care in the United States, and the median length of stay was 15.4 months (AFCARS 2010). When in foster care for an extended period or in multiple substitute care placements, the child experiences a greater risk for attachment disorders (Dozier and Rutter 2008; Putnam 2005; Strijker et al. 2008).

In 2009, a majority (51 %) of children placed in substitute care returned to their families or exited care to live with relatives (8 %), but workers placed 20 % of children exiting foster care in adoptive homes (AFCARS 2010). Adoption is the goal of choice for children not able to return to their families or to live in an appropriate kinship placement; however, it may present an additional attachment complication for many children (Deklyen and Greenberg 2008; Dozier and Rutter 2008). As of September 30, 2009, there were 114,556 children in the US child welfare system waiting for adoption. During 2009, public child welfare agencies assisted in the adoption of 57,466 US children, and the majority of children waiting for an adoptive placement had been in care for more than 2 years (AFCARS 2010). Children waiting for an adoptive placement were of median age 4.1 when they were removed and placed in foster care, and the waiting children were of median age 7.5 (AFCARS 2010). These figures are significant because the age of the child at adoption and the length of time a child is in out-of-home care create risk factors for attachment disorders (Deklyen and Greenberg 2008; Dozier and Rutter 2008; Putnam 2005). The following section reviews the implications of these statistics on attachment patterns for children affected by abuse and neglect.

Attachment Implications for Abused and Neglected Children

There is the potential for a concerning developmental trajectory for maltreated children served by the child welfare system. Children who experience abuse, neglect, and multiple foster care placements often struggle to attach to new caregivers (Dozier and Rutter 2008; Strijker et al. 2008), are at risk for developing insecure or disorganized/disoriented attachment behavior (Baer and Martinez2006; Lyons-Ruth and Jacobvitz 2008; Main and Solomon 1990; Putnam 2005), and experience symptoms of psychopathology, particularly when they have an accumulation of risk factors (Putnam 2005). According to Putnam (2005), "a range of adult psychiatric conditions are

clinically associated with child abuse" (p. 86), including major depression, borderline personality disorder, bulimia, substance abuse disorders, dissociative disorders,
and Post-Traumatic Stress Disorder. As a foundation for discussing attachment-
based interventions and their implementation, the following describes the risks for
attachment disorders among abused and neglected children.

Disorganized/Disoriented Attachment

A large body of empirical research validates an association between child maltreatment and disorganized attachment (Baer and Martinez 2006; Lyons-Ruth
and Jacobvitz 2008; van IJzendoorn et al. 1999; Webster et al. 2009). Disorga-
nized/disoriented attachment is generally the outcome of "extreme circumstances,"
such as "the absence of an attachment relationship (usually due to institutional
rearing), severe abuse or neglect, or traumatic disruption or loss of an attachment
relationship" (Deklyen and Greenberg, 2008 p. 681). Based on empirical research,
Main and Solomon (1990) originally distinguished disorganized/disoriented attachment from the two forms of insecure attachment (avoidant and ambivalent/resistant)
and from secure attachment. Child attachment classifications emerged from observations and assessment of the child's behavioral response to separation and reunion
in the Strange Situation Procedure, Ainsworth's well-validated tool for measuring
attachment (Ainsworth et al. 1978). When parents reappeared after separations in the
Strange Situation, the behaviors of some children were incoherent, confused, and
seeming to lack observable goals or intentions. The children froze and showed signs
of incomplete, interrupted movement, plus odd, misdirected, and disorganized behaviors. Main and Solomon (1990) proposed that these children failed to develop an
organized strategy for self-regulation of their emotions during times of distress. They
gave contradictory, yet simultaneous signals of approach and avoidance when in the
presence of the parent and demonstrated their fright without a means of resolving
their apprehension.

Using the Strange Situation Procedure (Ainsworth et al. 1978), a recent comparative study of two high-risk, ethnically diverse groups of preschoolers showed
that maltreated children had lower rates of attachment security and higher rates of
disorganized attachment compared to nonmaltreated children (Stronach et al. 2011).
In two other studies, 82 % and 90 % of maltreated children had attachment systems that were disorganized (Lyons-Ruth and Jacobvitz 2008). Nevertheless, not
all maltreated children have disorganized/disoriented attachments and may instead
demonstrate behaviors that are insecure or even secure.

Main and Solomon's (1990) empirical classification of disorganized/disoriented
attachment differs from the clinical classification of Reactive Attachment Disorder (RAD) in the Diagnostic and Statistical Manual of Mental Disorders (DSM-IV;
American Psychiatric Association 1994), which primarily describes symptomatology. Expanding the empirical and clinical descriptions of disorganized attachment,

the classification system of Zeanah and Boris (2000) gives more attention to the context of disorganized behavior. They delineate three types of disordered attachment in early childhood: (1) "nonattachment," in which the child has no discriminated attachment figure, most common among children who have been institutionalized; (2) "disordered attachment," in which a child has selective attachment with disturbed behavior, such as self-harm or role reversal; and (3) "disruption of attachments," in which children demonstrate strong grief reactions due to disruptions in their attachment with a primary attachment figure (Deklyen and Greenberg 2008). These contextual distinctions are particularly important when considering the origins of attachment behaviors of abused, neglected, institutionalized, and foster children in child welfare. However, Deklyen and Greenberg (2008) state that "much more research is needed, particularly with respect to children in the child protective system, to clarify the forms that attachment disorders are likely to take and to inform the design of more effective interventions" (p. 654).

The Child–Parent Relationship

The quality of the relationship between the attachment figure and child establishes the foundation for the developing child's sense of security. Weinfield et al. (2008) point out, "Individual differences in these attachment relationships reflect differences in the history of care ... these patterns of interaction, rather than individual behaviors, reveal the underlying character of the relationship" (pp. 78–79). Children who have a secure history of interaction with their parents are able to turn to them for reassurance, even when parental behavior has been threatening. In contrast, distressed children develop insecure attachment when parents are repeatedly indifferent (leading to avoidant attachment) or inconsistent (leading to ambivalent/resistant attachment)—patterns considered adaptive, though not optimal. Severely maltreated children, however, develop "breakdowns in the organization of attachment behavior, or ... reflect striking episodes of disorientation" (Weinfield et al. 2008, p. 81) because they have had repeated interactions with caregivers whose own behaviors reflect disorientation, often due to their unresolved loss or trauma.

Abusive caregivers are frightening to children, especially infants. When the child feels frightened, yet has no place to turn for comfort, the dynamic disorganizes the child's attachment system. Van IJzendoorn and Bakermans-Kranenburg (2003) described the phenomenon:

> The best example of a disorganized attachment is the relationship between the abused child and the abusive parent. The abusive parent fulfills two incompatible roles. On the one hand, he or she is the child's attachment figure and the only potential source of safety in an uncharted threatening world. On the other hand, the abusive parent is the stressor who can suddenly and unexpectedly threaten the child with physical or psychological violence. The child is placed in an irresolvable paradoxical situation in which the only possible base from which to explore the world is at the same time the source of unpredictable abusive threat. (p. 314)

Long-Range Outcomes

Unfortunately, longitudinal studies show serious adverse outcomes for infants and young children with insecure and disorganized attachment as they develop into later childhood and adulthood (Bernard et al. in press; Weinfield et al. 2008). Disorganized attachment in infancy significantly predicts dissociative symptoms in adolescence and young adulthood (Lyons-Ruth et al. 2006; Ogowa et al. 1997) and places children at higher risk for dysfunctional externalizing behaviors (Lyons-Ruth et al. 1997). Numerous studies show correlations between disorganization in infancy and controlling/disorganized behavior in preschool and elementary school, affecting peer relationships and parent–child interactions (see Lyons-Ruth and Jacobvitz 2008). Two longitudinal studies have followed infants to young adulthood, allowing comparisons of attachment classifications between the infant Strange Situation (Ainsworth et al. 1978) and the Adult Attachment Interview (AAI) (George et al. 1984). One study found that 86 % of disorganized infants were more likely than secure infants to be classified as insecure on the AAI at age 19 (Main et al. 2005). Similarly, disorganized infants were more likely to be classified as unresolved on the AAI at age 26 (Sroufe et al. 2005).

There is additional evidence that children with insecure or disorganized attachment show elevated levels of the stress hormone cortisol, compared to securely attached children (Lyons-Ruth and Jacobvitz 2008), which "can cause long-term damage to certain brain regions" (Putnam 2005, p. 88). Neuroimaging research on the effect of trauma on children and adolescents has found that persons diagnosed with post-traumatic stress disorder (PTSD) had smaller brains due to atrophy, especially in the corpus callosum, the area of the brain that connects the two hemispheres (Putnam 2005). Findings indicate that brain atrophy and the degree and duration of the abuse are positively correlated. This is a particularly significant finding because antisocial behaviors are associated with abnormalities in the corpus callosum (Putnam 2005). In sum, children who develop disorganized attachment in response to their abuse and neglect appear to be at high risk for brain damage, physiological dysregulation, and consequent psychopathology.

In response to the serious developmental sequelae of child abuse and neglect, Putnam (2005) says, "Our recognition of the profound and often lifelong effects of early environmental stressors dictates that we develop programs at the public health scale to prevent these experiences from occurring to infants and children" (p. 93). Others share his view as evidenced by the attachment researchers who have turned their attention to the development of clinical interventions designed to prevent child abuse, treat traumatized children, and promote healthy parenting. The following discussion summarizes five programs that professionals have created and empirically evaluated in recent years.

Attachment-based Treatment with Child Welfare Involved Families

The creation, implementation, and testing of treatment models for children and adults with attachment insecurity has become a major focus of attachment researchers over the past 20 years (Berlin 2005; Cassidy and Shaver 2008). A small, but growing, number of interventions are labeled as "evidence-based" or "promising" for use with traumatized children and their families, based on the number and level of empirical research studies that have demonstrated the effectiveness of the intervention (Igelman et al. 2008, p. 37). Evidence based practice (EBP), which originated in the field of medicine, refers to the process of "... integrating individual clinical expertise with the best available external clinical evidence from systematic research" (Sackett et al. 1996, p. 71). In the field of child welfare the concept of EBP, in contrast to a process, refers to a practice model or intervention empirically linked to positive change among clients (Luongo 2007).

Researchers tested some of the models discussed in this chapter with children and families affiliated with the child welfare system, yet few interventions specifically address the needs of foster children, and public child welfare agencies have not fully implemented these approaches. The following is a brief review of models recommended by the National Child Traumatic Stress Network (NCTSN 2011) or by scholars who focus on interventions for traumatized children and families associated with child welfare (Berlin et al. 2008; Dozier and Rutter 2008; Igelman et al. 2008). Although not an exhaustive review of all current interventions, these five models represent creative approaches that hold promise for children and families referred to child welfare agencies.

Attachment and Biobehavioral Catch-up

Attachment and Biobehavioral Catch-up (ABC) is a well-known, attachment-based intervention (Dozier et al. 2005, 2006, 2009), originally designed for foster parents and the infants and toddlers for whom they provide care, with the goal of "guiding parents to help their children regulate emotions, respond effectively to the children's distress, and understand the children's signals" (Dozier and Rutter 2008, p. 712). This program consists of ten weekly one-hour home visits by master's level social workers trained to help foster parents provide nonthreatening nurturing. In this program, foster parents learn to follow the lead of the child, to place the child's needs over their own non-nurturing instincts, and to recognize how their personal histories sometimes interfere with the special challenges many foster children have in regulating negative emotions (Berlin et al. 2008). Foster parents essentially "learn to re-interpret children's alienating behaviors" (Dozier et al. 2009, p. 327). In preliminary findings, foster parents who received the training reported fewer behavioral problems for older foster children, and a majority of the children had lower levels of the stress hormone, cortisol, following intervention (Dozier et al. 2006). Comparative evaluations found that children whose foster parents received the ABC intervention were considerably less avoidant in their attachment than those who received an educational intervention (Dozier et al. 2009).

Researchers have modified ABC for use with birth parents and continue to test the manualized intervention in randomized trials. Dozier et al. (2005) have reported, "birth parents embraced the intervention enthusiastically" because they learned ways "to override their own propensities to be rejecting of their children" (p. 190). In a recent study of 120 biological parents involved with CPS in a large, urban, mid-Atlantic city, outcomes support the efficacy of the ABC intervention (Bernard et al. 2012). Prior to intervention, the researchers assessed the attachment patterns of the children with the Strange Situation Procedure (Ainsworth et al. 1978) and then randomly assigned birth parents to the intervention and control groups. Compared to children whose birth parents received the control intervention focused on parent education and children's cognitive and linguistic development, children whose parents received the ABC intervention had significantly higher rates of attachment security (52 % compared to 33 %) and lower rates of attachment disorganization (32 % compared to 57 %) after the treatment. Reportedly, this study's results suggest that ABC "is effective in promoting organized and secure attachment outcomes among a group of young children who are at risk for neglect," yet "more nuanced questions of how and for whom the intervention works remain to be addressed" (Bernard et al. 2012). Nevertheless, the ABC intervention is significant because it is a short-term treatment model with both foster parents and birth parents involved in the public child welfare system.

Circle of Security

Another treatment model that has gained attention in child welfare is Circle of Security (COS), a 20-week group intervention based on attachment theory and object relations (Cooper et al. 2005; Marvin et al. 2002; Marvin and Whelan 2003). Researchers originally implemented COS with birth parents of toddlers recruited from Head Start and Early Head Start. According to the protocol, a parent interview and a videotaped Strange Situation (Ainsworth et al. 1978) yield the parent and child assessment prior to the first parent group. During the group process, parents learn to read their child's attachment cues and miscues by viewing edited video clips of their own attachment–caregiving interactions observed in the Strange Situation (Ainsworth et al. 1978) and by watching the edited tapes of other parents. In an initial pre-post study of the manualized COS training, 80 % of the children were insecure prior to the intervention. After the intervention, 46 % were insecure and 54 % were secure (Berlin et al. 2008). To date, researchers have not tested the efficacy of the COS model with a randomized control group, but it is one of the few attachment-based interventions implemented by social workers in a public child welfare agency (Blome et al. 2010; Page and Cain 2009). In addition, it is in use as a dyadic intervention and has been an auxiliary treatment in a number of parent–infant intervention programs related to jail diversion (Berlin et al. 2008). Whether in a group or dyadic intervention format, the video-feedback in COS offers parents the opportunity to reflect more easily on their interactions and to see a video demonstration of their child's attachment needs.

Child–Parent Psychotherapy

In contrast to the previous brief treatment models, Child–Parent Psychotherapy (CPP) offers a 50-session model of treatment based on attachment, psychodynamic, developmental, cognitive, behavioral, and trauma theories (Lieberman and Van Horn 2008; Lieberman et al. 2005; Lieberman 2003, 2004). It focuses on how domestic violence affects the parent–child relationship. Recommended by NCTSN (2011) as a promising evidence based intervention, this dyadic treatment is reminiscent of Selma Fraiberg's classic work with mothers and young infants (Fraiberg 1980). Like Fraiberg's (1980) psychoanalytic approach, CPP helps parents address "old 'ghosts' that have invaded the nursery" (p. 61) and are negatively influencing present-day parenting. Lieberman et al. (2005) state that CPP is based on the premise that "the attachment system is the main organizer of children's responses to danger and safety in the first years of life," and "early mental health problems should be addressed in the context of the child's primary attachment relationships" (p. 1241). Following a manualized treatment protocol, the weekly joint child–parent CPP sessions, interspersed with individual parent sessions as needed, help the parent and child create a narrative about the traumatic events in their lives. The treatment "focuses on improving the quality of the child-mother relationship and engages the mother as the child's ally in coping with the trauma" (Lieberman et al. 2005, p. 1243). Graduate level practitioners trained in the CPP protocol implement the approach as a home or office based intervention (Berlin et al. 2008).

One of the benefits of CPP is that professionals have effectively used the approach with a wide range of ethnic/racial groups, including Latino and African–American families, as well as recent immigrants in urban settings. Findings from randomized trials support the model's efficacy with trauma-exposed at-risk children (Cicchetti et al. 2006; Lieberman et al. 2005; Weiner et al. 2009). It is one of the treatments of choice of the national team of consultants from Zero to Three: National Center for Infants, Toddlers, and Families, who work with the judicial system, CPS, and mental health on behalf of young children. A creator of CPP and weekly consultant to CPS in San Francisco's public child welfare system, Lieberman states that the model ". . . is an excellent treatment approach for infants and young children in foster care" (personal communication, July 10, 2011). She reports, ". . . approximately 40 % of the families receiving CPP in our program are either referred by CPS or involved in the dependency system" (personal communication, July 10, 2011).

Minding the Baby

Of similar length to CPP, Minding the Baby (MTB) is a long-term home visiting program designed for high-risk, first time mothers (Slade 2006; Slade et al. 2005). The interveners in the pilot study—dyads of clinical social workers and pediatric nurse-practitioners—visit the mother weekly beginning in the third trimester of pregnancy and biweekly throughout the first year of the infant's life. In this model, the dyad aims to provide a secure base for the mother. In the pilot test, 36 % of the mothers had experienced abuse as children and 55 % had a history of depression (Slade et al. 2005). Notably, these are similar demographic characteristics of families affiliated with child welfare. This intervention aims to increase the mother's reflective functioning, that is, to increase her capacity to be attuned to the mind of the baby. Preliminary analysis of the intervention's outcome suggested that the mother's reflective functioning increased significantly over the course of the baby's first 18 months, and 76 % of the infants were secure at 12 months (Berlin et al. 2008). Significantly, the child welfare agency received no reports of abuse or neglect on behalf of the children participating in the study. According to Slade, "... we are not an intervention geared in any direct way toward families with [child welfare] involvement, although we are, of course, touched by the system in many ways" (personal communication, April 10, 2011). Slade et al. (2005) recommend their approach for parents with "significant psychiatric and trauma history" because these parents "are the ones who most need and are most likely to benefit from the kind of intensive, integrated intervention MTB has to offer" (p. 172).

Chances for Children

Chances for Children (Mayers et al. 2008), a school-based project initiated in the New York City public schools, addresses the needs of another population served by child welfare agencies—teen mothers. With on-site daycare facilities for children whose adolescent mothers are students, this intervention takes a multi-dimensional approach through the provision of parent therapy, child play therapy, parent–child therapy, parent groups, and support from daycare staff. The theories of Fraiberg (1980), Lieberman and Pawl (1993), and Fonagy and Gyorgy (2002) informed the treatment model, as well as the parent–child interaction focus of Beebe (2003) and McDonough (2000). Although the intervention is "primarily a clinical program, not a research program" (Mayers et al. 2008, p. 326), outcome measures suggest that it improved the responsiveness and affective attunement of the mothers to their children and increased the interest of children in their mothers. Publications about the program do not specify how many of these teens were receiving services from the public child welfare system in New York while they participated in Chances for Children.

Program Highlights

In these five models, attuned practitioners strive to establish a secure base for parents to explore and reflect on their relationships with their children. Using home visits, in-school visits, or group process, these models aim to increase parental sensitivity and reflective functioning. Specifically, they seek to increase the parent's capacity to understand how the child is viewing him/herself and others. Through interactions with the practitioners, parents begin to understand their children's attachment needs. This process then enables the parent to address unresolved conflicts and meet the needs of his/her child. Through empathic connections, parents receive training to understand the child's attachment cues, which give clarification about the child's underlying emotional needs. It is important to underscore that these five models are comprehensive, multi-theoretical, and require skilled professionals trained in the treatment protocol to intervene with families. With the exception of ABC, the models are neither specifically for child welfare families nor are they an exhaustive summary of all attachment-based interventions for children and families. Potentially, these five creative approaches can meet the kinds of needs that are present in families involved with the child welfare system.

Child Welfare Services

Although the attachment-based treatment models discussed seem appropriate for children and families serviced by child welfare, there are federal policies and organizational issues that may impede their implementation. One major challenge to implementation is that the mission of child welfare is different from the focus of such comprehensive attachment-based interventions.

The Adoption and Safe Families Act of 1997—P.L. 105-89 (ASFA)—established child safety as the first concern guiding all child welfare services. Although the law asserts the right of children to the essentials needed for healthy development, including a sense of belonging, continuity of care, nurturing relationships, and access to opportunities (Lutz 2003), protection from abuse and neglect remains its primary focus. In addition to safety, the law mandates that child welfare agencies ensure permanency and stability in the child's living arrangements and preserve family relationships and connections. Legislation, beginning with the Adoption Assistance and Child Welfare Act of 1980—P.L. 96-272, puts the focus on preventing placement, through family centered practice and establishing permanency for children (Lutz 2003).

To achieve permanency, child welfare agency staff must determine if the child can remain in the home, with services as necessary, or if safety concerns require placement in foster care with relatives or unrelated adults. While workers receive training to discern clues about the parent–child relationship—for example, the child's reaction to the parent and the parent's sensitivity to the child's emotional needs—physical safety is often the most visible factor noted during an investigation. In other words, though abuse and neglect affects the parent–child attachment relationship (Baer and Martinez 2006), enhancing attachment is not the primary concern in the investigation and immediate provision of services. Safety, permanency, and well-being are the primary federally mandated goals for the child welfare system.

Permanency Planning

To meet these goals, caseworkers establish a permanency plan, which should include an assessment of the attachment of the child and parent. The child welfare worker must conduct the analysis on an ongoing basis by staying in regular contact with the child and the family. The organizational structure of child welfare, however, may thwart the ability of workers to spend time with families and understand the intricacies of the parent–child relationship. In child welfare systems, caseloads are often large, with one survey indicating that only 11 % of foster care caseloads meet the Child Welfare League of America national standards (Children's Defense Fund and Children's Rights 2007). Additionally, child welfare workers stay on the job an average of less than 2 years, and 90 % of states report difficulty hiring and retaining qualified staff (Children's Defense Fund and Children's Rights 2007). Staff with social work degrees are most likely to continue working in child welfare and to achieve permanency outcomes in the least time (Barbee 2005; Ellett et al. 2009; Jones 2002, Jones and Okamura 2000), yet "less than 30 % of child welfare workers have professional social work degrees (BSW or MSW)" (Social Work Policy Institute 2011, para. 4).

This job instability is critical because worker constancy can make a functional difference for children and families. A seminal study of child outcomes found that children who had experienced one worker achieved permanency in 74.5 % of the cases; two workers dropped the permanency rate to 17.5 %, and with a succession of three workers, the permanence rate was a mere 5.2 % (Flower et al. 2005). Further research associated caseworker turnover with an increased number of placements, longer stays in foster care, and fewer services offered to families (Children's Defense Fund and Children's Rights 2007). These troubling statistics have implications for the application of attachment-informed practices within public child welfare agencies. Without continuity of professionally educated workers, it is difficult to establish the level of connection with parents and children needed to assess and enhance attachment security. With increased frequency of placements—complicated by high staff turnover—children are at greater risk for disordered attachments (Strijker et al. 2008).

Parent–Child Visitation

Parent–child visitation is among the most important services when children are in substitute care. Research findings strongly link frequent visiting by parent(s) with permanency outcomes for children. In a study of state policies, the suggested visitation schedule for children and parents ranged from daily to monthly (Hess 2003b). Yet Kuehnle and Ellis (2002) ask:

> Because physical proximity is the key goal of the attachment system for infants and toddlers, and availability is the goal for other children, how could children of any age possibly maintain an affectional or attachment bond with a parent he or she visits every 30 days? (p. 69)

Although family visiting is a core reunification service, planning and implementing visits is time-consuming and limited agency resources may undermine the success of the service (National Resource Center for Family Centered Practice and Permanency Planning 2008). A Georgia study found that only 12.7 % of mothers and 5.6 % of fathers visited with children in care at least once every 2 weeks during an 18-month period (Hess 2003a). Infrequent visits, influenced by scarce agency resources, further affect the parent–child attachment. Hess (1987) astutely observed:

> Each visit of a child in placement with his or her parent begins with a reunion and ends with another separation, a separation that, in most cases, continues until the reunion that begins the next visit. It can be expected that parent-child attachment and the reactions to reunion and separation shape the interactions during each visit, as well as interactions over time. (p. 30)

In sum, the policy framework of child welfare services, the educational level and high turnover of staff, and the enormity of the workload test the capacities of child welfare agencies to protect and serve all children and families at risk of abuse and neglect. In addition, the nature of parent–child visitation for children in foster care complicates, rather than enhances, parent–child attachments. Furthermore, the decisions that child welfare workers make exist within an organizational structure subject to internal and external pressures that compound the implementation of attachment-based initiatives. The following explores these organizational complexities and their link to the implementation of intervention models.

Organizational Issues

Large, public agencies and their private, subcontractor partners carry out services to families at risk of child abuse and neglect. Of particular relevance to the discussion of implementing attachment-based programs is the reality that "the bureaucratic structure of public child welfare rewards more routinization and centralization, yet simultaneously seeks to fulfill missions through technologies that encourage greater worker discretion" (Yoo et al. 2007, p. 64). Consistency of practice is necessary in an organization that must monitor activities for federal and state reviewers, yet the problems brought by children and families engaged in the child welfare system call for sound worker judgment and flexibility. To provide consistency and best meet the needs of protecting vulnerable children from abuse and neglect, evidence based practice has become "the buzzword in child welfare today" (Blome and Steib 2004, p. 611).

Internal and External Influences on Implementation of Evidence-based Practice

Internal Factors

Despite the current emphasis on EBP, Blome and Steib (2004) point out that there is no uniform path to meet desired outcomes in child welfare. They report: "Unfortunately, no one evidence based program leads to faster reunification, more stable placements, or higher rates of recovery from addiction. Many programs and practices may affect these outcomes depending on a myriad of organizational and staffing issues" (Blome and Steib 2004, p. 611). The transition to an evidence based approach to structuring services is a cultural shift, albeit one that is seen as inevitable by administrators in the field (Jack et al. 2010; Luongo 2007). Diffusion of an evidence based practice assumes, first, that the agency has knowledge of and access to empirically supported approaches and, second, that the agency has the ability and willingness to adopt the change (Rogers 2002).

   Organizational culture and climate are two internal factors that influence attitudes towards the adoption of an innovative EBP model (Aarons and Sawitzky 2006). Organizational culture is the organization norms and expectations regarding how people behave and accomplish tasks within an agency (Glisson and James 2002). This includes the mission, goals, values, norms, leadership, communication flow, policies, and practices that shape all program activities (Luongo 2007) and the common history and experiences of the organization as a whole (Bryan et al. 2007). Organizational culture has many layers, with shared behavioral expectations in the outer, conscious layer and values and assumptions making up the inner, less conscious layer that members of an organization may not fully recognize (Rousseau 1990). For example, an agency may acknowledge the importance of attachment principles in family assessment, but not provide the supervision or training necessary to allow the practice to become part of the organizational way of working. On a conscious level, staff may receive encouragement to apply attachment principles in their work with children, but on a less conscious organizational level, supervisors or managers may not support the intervention. Both levels create a culture within a child welfare agency. Contrasting with organizational culture, organizational climate reflects the perceptions of individual workers of the psychological impact of the work environment on their wellbeing (Glisson 2002; Glisson and James 2002). In a study of organizational culture and attitudes toward EBP, researchers found that culture precedes and affects climate, therefore actions to improve organizational culture may lead to improvements in climate (Aarons and Sawitzky 2006). For example, if the organizational culture functionally supports implementation of an attachment-based intervention and workers can see substantive gains in the relationships of the parents and children they serve, the assessment of staff about the cost of the work on their wellbeing may improve.

Leadership is key to a positive organizational culture (Glisson 1989) and may be especially important to the implementation of the multi-dimensional attachment-based programs like the five models previously discussed. Transactional leadership builds on exchanges that occur between the leader and the follower in which the leader rewards the follower for meeting specific performance criteria (Aarons 2006). Because child welfare is a highly regulated endeavor, transactional leadership, with the focus on measureable goals and established benchmarks, is an expected approach. Transformational leadership that inspires staff and increases their intrinsic motivation through understanding the goals of the leader provides the greatest relationship with positive results (Aarons 2006). Paired together, transactional leadership and transformational leadership can promote a culture of enthusiasm, openness, and trust. For example, implementing a complex attachment-based approach requires sustained interest by managers and supervisors, as well as consistent tracking of the fidelity of the intervention. Teaming the transactional and transformational approaches is necessary to move an intervention from a pilot to an institutionalized approach to practice.

Leadership also occurs at the supervisory level, and in child welfare, supervisors may be responsible for maintaining consistent attention to practice fidelity. They are central to the successful implementation of new programs. For example, the implementation of the COS intervention in a public child welfare agency demonstrated supervisory commitment to an EBP approach (Blome et al. 2010; Page and Cain 2009). Timothy Page, the social work researcher who studied COS, stated that one mid-level supervisor was so impressed with COS—especially the model's emphasis "on strengthening parents' capacities for empathic responsiveness to their children"—that she "became the chief advocate for crossing the divide between appreciation of the program as good theory and application of the program in the agency service environment" (Blome et al. 2010 p. 437). She preferred the COS method of having parents observe their children via videotape, which she viewed as more effective than the common didactic methods of many parenting classes.

External Factors

Leaders championing organizational change must constantly assess the external forces that may assist or impede the change initiative (Fernandez and Rainey 2006). As child welfare is a highly politicized and scrutinized field (Blome and Steib 2007), the planning and implementation of change frequently occurs in full view of both supporters and detractors. The workers and managers in child welfare operate in a fishbowl of public inquiry. Media outlets may portray tragedies as the result of faulty decision-making or caseworker error (Smith and Donovan 2003). The decision-making environment is often reactive and crisis driven, resulting in the hasty development of policies and practices to address current, sometimes tragic, events (Jack et al. 2010). Additionally, an external political crisis may undermine an attachment-based program in the process of implementation.

Organizational change does not occur through a one-time staff orientation or a series of emails. "With each strategic change the organization decides to make comes an inherent risk, and that risk must be weighed against the potential return" (Allawi et al. 1991, p. 39). Yet, political trends may influence potential return. For example, some theorists point out that long-standing public organizations, like child welfare systems, may be in the stage of development where conservers take control of the organization and the pace of change decelerates (Fernandez and Pitts 2006). Other theorists find that public organizations change regularly due to frequent shifts in the political environment—a significant risk factor for the implementation and sustainability of a complex treatment program. As public system observers have noted, ". . . constant change makes it difficult to implement and sustain long-term change in the public sector" (Fernandez and Pitts 2006, p. 4).

Economic considerations also influence change. Fernandez and Pitts' (2006) study of the conditions under which public managers pursue organizational change revealed two findings that relate to readiness for change. Public managers with more financial resources at their disposal are more likely to favor change in their organizations, and the more a manager interacts with relevant actors in the external environment, the more likely the manager will have a positive attitude to change. Such findings are relevant for academic researchers who evaluate attachment-based models of intervention within child welfare agencies. If researchers actively develop professional relationships with child welfare managers and if the agency receives financial resources through grants, the organization may be more open to implementing new interventions.

The ability of an organization ". . . to recognize the value of new, external information, assimilate it, and apply it . . . is critical to its innovative capabilities" (Cohen and Levinthal 1990, p. 128). Prior knowledge of a related area may facilitate assimilation of new knowledge. For example, in social work programs, the curriculum includes theory courses on human growth and development and, in many schools, courses on attachment. The extent to which child welfare agencies have staff with this foundational knowledge may enhance the implementation of an attachment-based program. Similarly, the level to which individuals are familiar with research terms and processes may influence their openness to implementing empirically informed practices. Jack et al. (2010) found that decision makers were more likely to use research evidence if they had research courses during graduate school, had work experience outside of child welfare, had access to databases which compile research findings, and possessed critical appraisal skills and a personal dedication to inquiry.

In addition to the knowledge of individual staff members, an organizations' absorptive capacity depends on the transfer of knowledge across and among subunits of the agency (Cohen and Levinthal 1990). In child welfare, implementing an attachment-based program would require an appreciation of family connections, beginning with intake and assessment and continuing through placement and reunification decisions. Involving the continuum of service divisions within the organization requires a focused communication strategy that is consistent, integrated, and thorough to assure fidelity of implementation of the empirically based program.

Steps and Stages of Organizational Change

Preparing organizations for change involves a series of interconnected steps. While agencies may successfully adopt simple innovations without difficulty, attachment-based treatment models are complicated. Pertinent to the implementation of the programs discussed in this chapter, Simpson (2009) suggests that "as innovations and new procedures become more complex and comprehensive, . . . the process of change becomes progressively more challenging—especially in settings where staff communication, cohesion, trust, and tolerance for change are lacking" (p. 543). For these reasons, it is critical to plan and prepare for implementation and "to identify and address organizational deficiencies before facing decisions about innovations" (p. 543).

Various theorists have outlined steps in the organizational change process (Fernandez and Rainey 2006), such as the five stages of exploration, program installation, initial implementation, full operation, and sustainability (Fixen et al. 2005). The first stage, exploration, assesses the potential match between community requirements, evidence based practices and programs, and community resources in order to decide whether to proceed. Stakeholders exchange information to identify the need for an intervention, to assess the fit between the intervention program and community needs, and to prepare the staff and resources by mobilizing information and support (Fixen et al. 2005). The process of convincing individuals of the need for a change—such as the usefulness of implementing ABC into foster care training or referring children and parents to therapists trained in CPP—begins with a compelling vision for the new way of operating (Fernandez and Rainey 2006). "The most elegant and sophisticated of new practices will not be implemented if they are not embraced by potential users" (Kimberly and Cook 2008, p. 12).

Program installation, the second stage, is a set of activities in which administrators establish structural supports necessary to initiate the program. The agency hires or realigns staff to meet the qualifications required by the program and secures resources and technology, as needed. Initial implementation, the third stage, can be challenging as the compelling forces of fear, inertia, and investment in the status quo (Fixen et al. 2005) test confidence in the decision to adopt a program. Some initiatives fail at this point, the victim of internal and external influences. In part, the lack of success may stem from insufficient attention to the individual level of adoption, because personal innovativeness, attitudes towards the innovation, and peer usage affect the outcome (Frambach and Schillewaert 2002). The challenge to managerial leaders is to build internal support for change and reduce resistance through full participation in the change process (Fernandez and Rainey 2006). Fourth, full operation occurs when the agency gives the message that the innovation is the accepted way of business. It is no longer the new program within the organization. Currently, some child welfare agencies are pilot testing attachment-based approaches, such as ABC and CPP, but no known agency has moved into the organizational phase of full operation. The last stage, sustainability, occurs when the innovation survives the departure of well-trained staff, adjustments to funding streams, and changes in the political and social environment (Fixen et al. 2005). Organizational managers, staff, and external researchers need to pay careful attention to all five stages of organizational change for successful implementation and, ultimately, sustainability of attachment-based interventions.

Finally, it is important to underscore the importance of financial resources for training. A public child welfare agency may want to implement an attachment-based intervention but may lack the funds to hire professional staff and train them in the identified model. Programs often require staff with a minimum of a Masters of Social Work (MSW) degree and specific training in the protocol, but public child welfare agencies, in most states, do not have a full complement of caseworkers at the MSW level. Although many child welfare agencies have sophisticated training academies that offer pre-service and in-service training, additional support may be necessary to implement a program with the complexity of the attachment-based interventions discussed above. As Luongo (2007) has said, "training in child welfare, to be successful, must encompass a much broader view of training as facilitating ongoing development (of the individual and organization)" (p. 93). In other words, successful implementation requires significant financial resources for broad, yet protocol-specific training, in addition to mutual awareness among agency leaders and external researchers regarding organizational readiness and organizational stages of change.

Recommendations for Practitioners and Organizations

Of the five attachment-based models presented in this chapter, researchers and clinicians have implemented ABC, COS, and CPP as pilot projects in public child welfare agencies. To promote these models and similar attachment-based interventions in the future, professionals will need to engage in careful planning, frequent collaboration, and extensive training, in addition to securing sufficient funding. A summary of the organizational literature and research models discussed above lead to the following recommendations for clinical practitioners and child welfare organizations that attempt further implementations:

1. Clinical practitioners and child welfare professionals need to understand the terminology, differences, and context of various attachment patterns, rather than assume that all child behavioral symptoms are a result of an attachment disorder. Clinicians need to use classifications that describe attachment patterns judiciously and with understanding of the meaning of the terms. These classifications can stay with a child for years and may cause harm if the description is incorrect or shared with non-professionals. Clearly, a best practice approach is for professionals to maintain confidentiality about the child's attachment patterns.

2. Practitioners and researchers need to conceptualize attachment disorders using a common framework and typology. Currently, there is inconsistency between practitioners and researchers regarding the meaning and etiology of disorganized attachment in children. Fidelity of definition is important for all professionals

who try to create, implement, and evaluate models of intervention for children affected by maltreatment.

3. In keeping with the child welfare mandate to assure the well-being of children in the protective system, administrators must allocate funding to a wide-range of services, including attachment-based interventions. However, designers of attachment-based interventions should consider the organizational and funding realities that exist for public child welfare agencies. In a time of funding cuts, it is difficult for child welfare agencies to provide interventions that require long-term commitments of time and resources.

4. Attachment theory is complex and the clinical programs based on this theory call for professional staff trained in the model's protocol. Public child welfare organizations need to hire professionals with the credentials to implement and oversee attachment-based interventions.

5. Because child welfare is a public sector program, government policies mandate that all children and families at risk receive a consistent level of service. Yet, the strengths and needs of each child and family demand an individualized approach, driven by a well-trained professional worker. It is important that private clinicians and academic researchers appreciate these conflicting demands on child welfare workers. Otherwise, workers may feel misunderstood and criticized, which may challenge the collaborative process essential to implementing an empirically based intervention.

6. The high turnover among workers and administrators impedes the implementation and institutionalization of practice change in child welfare agencies. Organizations need tactics, such as increased numbers of social workers, adequate professional supervision, improved continuing education, and smaller caseloads, to retain staff in order to maintain change processes.

7. Child welfare agencies need transformational leaders to promote collaboration and cooperation among stakeholders and support innovative approaches to serving children and families. In preparing to implement an innovative program, child welfare administrators, external academic researchers, and community clinicians must collaborate frequently and respect each other's skills.

8. Children in the child welfare system have a right to expect that the professionals engaged in their lives will provide the most effective empirically based treatments available and will believe in their capacity to lead functional and productive lives. Similarly, professionals need to appreciate the hope and possibility of change that attachment-based modalities can offer the child and family.

Conclusion

Child welfare administrators and staff understand the need to serve children and families who have experienced the disruptive influences of abuse and neglect and the interruption of attachment relationships. To address concerns about trauma and separations, professionals must balance the appeal of attachment-based interventions with an understanding of the organizational factors that may support or impede the performance of the model. This chapter reviewed empirically validated models that address the attachment processes for at-risk children and families, including those in the child welfare system. However, all five models require highly skilled, trained professionals to serve families, as well as organizational commitment to fidelity and evaluation to assure the proper implementation of the model. To optimize the successful expansion of these models into the public child welfare arena, attention to organizational issues and environmental context is critical.

References

Aarons, G. (2006). Transformational and transactional leadership: Association with attitudes toward evidence based practice. *Psychiatric Services, 57,* 1162–1169.

Aarons, G., & Sawitzky, A. (2006). Organizational culture and climate and mental health provider attitudes toward evidence based practice. *Psychological Services, 3,* 61–72.

Ackerman, J. P., & Dozier, M. (2005). The influence of foster parent investment on children's representations of self and attachment figures. *Journal of Applied Developmental Psychology, 26,* 507–520.

Adoption and Foster Care Analysis and Reporting System (AFCARS) FY 2009 data (October 1, 2008 through September 30, 2009). Retrieved from http://www.acf.hhs.gov/programs/cb/stats_research/afcars/tar/report17.htm.

Ainsworth, M., Blehar, M., Waters, E., & Wall, S. (1978). *Patterns of attachment: Assessed in the strange situation and at home.* Hillsdale: Lawrence Erlbaum.

Allawi, S., Bellaire, D., & David, L. (1991). Are you ready for structural change? *The Healthcare Forum Journal, 34,* 39–42.

American Psychiatric Association. (1994). *Diagnostic and statistical manual of mental disorders (4th ed.).* Washington, DC:

Baer, J., & Martinez, C. D. (2006). Child maltreatment and insecure attachment: A meta-analysis. *Journal of Reproductive and Infant Psychology, 24,* 187–197.

Barbee, A. (2005). *Child welfare workforce development and workplace enhancement institute.* [Conference presentation]. Crystal City: Children's Bureau.

Barth, R., Crea, T., John, K., Thoburn, J., & Quinton, D. (2005). Beyond attachment theory and therapy: Towards sensitive and evidence based interventions with foster and adoptive families in distress. *Child & Family Social Work, 10,* 257–268.

Beebe, B. (2003). Brief mother-infant treatment: The microsynchrony of maternal impingement and infant avoidance in the face-to-face encounter. *Psychoanalytic Inquiry, 20,* 421–440.

Berlin, L. (2005). Interventions to enhance early attachments: The state of the world today. In L. Berlin, Y. Ziv, L. Amaya-Jackson, & M. T. Greenberg (Eds.), *Enhancing early attachments: Theory, research, intervention, and policy* (pp. 3–33). New York: Guilford.

Berlin, L., Zeanah, C., & Lieberman, A. (2008). Prevention and intervention programs for supporting early attachment security. In J. Cassidy & P. Shaver (Eds.), *Handbook of attachment: Theory, research, and clinical applications* (2nd ed., pp. 745–761). New York: Guilford.

Berlin, L., Ziv, Y., Amaya-Jackson, L., & Greenberg, M. (Eds.). (2005). *Enhancing early attachments: Theory, research, intervention, and policy.* New York: Guilford.

Bernard, K., Dozier, M., Bick, J., Lewis-Morrarty, E., Lindhiem, O., & Carlson, E. (2012). Enhancing attachment organization among maltreated children: Results of a randomized clinical trial. *Child Development, 83*(2), 623–636.

Blome, W., & Steib, S. (2004). Whatever the problem the answer is Evidence Based Practice—or is it? *Child Welfare, LXXXIII,* 611–615.

Blome, W., & Steib, S. (2007). An examination of oversight and review in the child welfare system: The many watch the few serve the many. *Journal of Public Child Welfare, 1,* 3–26.

Blome, W., Bennett, S., & Page, T. (2010). Organizational challenges to implementing attachment-based practices in public child welfare agencies: An example using the Circle of Security® model. *Journal of Public Child Welfare, 4,* 427–449. doi:10.1080/15548732.2010.526904.

Bowlby, J. (1969). *Attachment and loss: Vol. 1. Attachment.* New York: Basic Books.

Bowlby, J. (1973). *Attachment and loss: Vol. 2. Separation: Anxiety and anger.* New York: Basic Books.

Bowlby, J. (1980). *Attachment and loss: Vol. 3. Loss, sadness, and depression.* New York: Basic Books.

Bowlby, J. (1988). *A secure base: Clinical applications of attachment theory.* London: Routledge.

Bryan, K., Klein, D., & Elias, M. (2007). Applying organizational theories to action research in community settings: A case study in urban schools. *Journal of Community Psychology, 35,* 383–398.

Busch, M., & Folaron, G. (2005). Accessibility and clarity of state child welfare agency mission statements. *Child Welfare, 3,* 415–430.

Cassidy, L. (2008). The nature of the child's ties. In J. Cassidy & P. Shaver (Eds.), *Handbook of attachment: Theory, research and clinical applications* (2nd ed., pp. 3–23). New York: Guilford.

Cassidy, J., & Shaver, P. (Eds.). (2008). *Handbook of attachment: Theory, research and clinical applications* (2nd ed.). New York: Guilford.

Children's Defense Fund & Children's Rights. (2007). Promoting child welfare workforce improvements through Federal policy changes. Retrieved from http://www.childrensrights.org/wp-content/uploads/2008/06/promoting_child_welfare_workforce_improvements_2007.pdf.

Cicchetti, D., Rogosch, F. A., & Toth, S. L. (2006). Fostering secure attachment in infants in maltreating families through preventive attachment in infants in maltreating families through preventive interventions. *Development and Psychopathology, 18,* 623–649.

Cohen, W., & Levinthal, D. (1990). Absorptive capacity: A new perspective on learning and innovation. *Administrative Science Quarterly, 35,* 128–152.

Cooper, G., Hoffman, K., Powell, B., & Marvin, R. (2005). The circle of security intervention: Differential diagnosis and differential treatment. In L. Berlin, Y. Ziv, L. Amaya-Jackson, & M. Greenberg (Eds.), *Enhancing early attachments: Theory, research, intervention, and policy* (pp. 127–151). New York: Guilford.

Deklyen, M., & Greenberg, M. (2008). Attachment and psychopathology in childhood. In J. Cassidy & P. Shaver (Eds.), *Handbook of attachment: Theory, research and clinical applications* (2nd ed., pp. 637–665). New York: Guilford.

Dozier, M., & Rutter, M. (2008). Challenges to the development of attachment relationships faced by young children in foster and adoptive care. In J. Cassidy, & P. Shaver (Eds.), *Handbook of attachment: Theory, research, and clinical applications* (2nd ed., pp. 698–717). New York: Guilford.

Dozier, M., Albus, K., Fisher, P. A., & Sepulveda, S. (2002a). Interventions for foster parents: Implications for developmental theory. *Development and Psychopathology, 14,* 843–860.

Dozier, M., Higley, E., Albus, K. E., & Nutter, A. (2002b). Intervening with foster infants' caregivers: Targeting three critical needs. *Infant Mental Health Journal, 23,* 541–554.

Dozier, M., Lindhiem, O., & Ackerman, J. (2005). Attachment and Biobehavioral Catch-up: An intervention targeting empirically identified needs of foster infants. In L. Berlin, Y. Ziv, L. Amaya-Jackson, & M. Greenberg (Eds.), *Enhancing early attachments: Theory, research, intervention, and policy* (pp. 178–194). New York: Guilford.

Dozier, M., Lindhiem, O., Lewis, E., Bick, J., Bernard, K., & Peloso, E. (2009). Effects of a foster parent training program on young children's attachment behaviors: Preliminary evidence from a randomized clinical trial. *Child & Adolescent Social Work Journal, 26,* 321–332.

Dozier, M., Peloso, E., Lindhiem, O., Gordon, M. K., Manni, M., Sepulveda, S., & Levine, S. (2006). Developing evidence based interventions for foster children: An example of a randomized clinical trial with infants and toddlers. *Journal of Social Issues, 62,* 767–785.

Ellett, A., Ellett, C., Ellis, J., & Lerner, B. (2009). A research based employee selection protocol: Strengthening retention of the workforce. *Child Welfare, 88*(5), 49–68.

Fernandez, S., & Pitts, D. (2006). Under what conditions do public managers favor and pursue organizational change? Retrieved from http://aysps.gsu.edu/publications/2006/index.htm.

Fernandez, S., & Rainey, H. (2006). Managing successful organizational change in the public sector: An agenda for research and practice. *Public Administration Review, 66,* 168–176.

Fish, B., & Chapman, B. (2004). Mental health risks to infants and toddlers in foster care. *Clinical Social Work Journal, 32,* 121–140.

Fixen, D., Naoom, S., Blase, K., Friedman, R., & Wallace, F. (2005). *Implementation research: A synthesis of the literature.* Tampa: University of South Florida, Louis de la Parte Florida Mental Health Institute, The National Implementation Research Network.

Flower, C., McDonald, J., & Sumski, M. (2005). *Review of turnover in Milwaukee County: Private agency child welfare ongoing case management staff.* Retrieved from http://legis.wisconsin.gov/lc/committees/study/2008/SFAM08/files/turnoverstudy.pdf.

Fonagy, P., & Gyorgy, G. (2002). *Affect regulation, mentalization, and the development of the self.* New York: Other Press.

Fraiberg, S. (1980). *Clinical studies in infant mental health: The first year of life.* New York: Basic Books.

Frambach, R., & Schillewaert, N. (2002). Organizational innovation adoption: A multi-level framework of determinants and opportunities for future research. *Journal of Business Research, 55,* 163–176.

Gauthier, Y., Fortin, G., & Jéliu, G. (2004). Clinical application of attachment theory in permanency planning for children in foster care: The importance of continuity of care. *Infant Mental Health Journal, 25,* 379–396.

George, C., Kaplan, N., & Main, M. (1984). *Adult Attachment Interview protocol.* Unpublished manuscript, University of California at Berkeley.

Glisson, C. (1989). The effect of leadership on workers in human service organizations. *Administration in Social Work, 13,* 99–116.

Glisson, C. (2002). The organizational context of children's mental health services. *Clinical Child and Family Psychology Review, 5,* 233–253.

Glisson, C., & James, L. (2002). The cross-level effects of culture and climate in human service teams. *Journal of Organizational Behavior, 23,* 767–794.

Haight, W. L., Kagle, J. D., & Black, J. E. (2003). Understanding and supporting parent-child relationships during foster care visits: Attachment theory and research. *Social Work, 48,* 195–208.

Hess, P. (1987). Parental visiting of children in foster care: Current knowledge and research agenda. *Children and Youth Services Review, 9,* 29–50.

Hess, P. (2003a). *A review of case files of foster children in Fulton and Dekalb counties, Georgia.* New York: Children's Rights.

Hess, P. (2003b). Visiting between children in care and their families: A look at current policy. Retrieved from http://www.hunter.cuny.edu/socwork/nrcfcpp/downloads/visiting_report-10-29-03.pdf.

Igelman, R., Ryan, B., Gilbert, A., Bashant, C., & North, K. (2008). Best practices for serving traumatized children and families. *Juvenile and Family Court Journal, 59,* 35–47.

Jack, S., Dobbins, M., Tonmyr, L., Dudding, P., Brooks, S., & Kennedy, B. (2010). Research evidence utilization in policy development by child welfare administrators. *Child Welfare, 89,* 83–100.

Jones, L. (2002). A follow-up of a Title IV-E program's graduates' retention rates in a public child welfare agency. *Journal of Health & Social Policy, 15,* 39–52.

Jones, L., & Okamura, A. (2000). Reprofessionalizing child welfare services: An evaluation of a Title IVE training program. *Research on Social Work Practice, 10,* 607–621.

Kimberly, J., & Cook, J. (2008). Organizational measurement and the implementation of innovations in mental health services. *Administrative Policy in Mental Health, 35,* 11–20.

Kuehnle, K., & Ellis, T. (2002). The importance of parent-child relationships: What attorneys need to know about the impact of separation. *Florida Bar Journal, 76,* 67–70.

Lieberman, A. (2003). The treatment of attachment disorder in infancy and early childhood: Reflections from clinical intervention with later-adopted foster care children. *Attachment & Human Development, 5,* 279.

Lieberman, A. (2004). Traumatic stress and quality of attachment: Reality and internalization in disorders of infant mental health. *Infant Mental Health Journal, 25,* 336–351.

Lieberman, A., & Pawl, J. (1993). Infant-parent psychotherapy. In C. Zeanah (Ed.), *Handbook of infant mental health* (pp. 427–442). New York: Basic Books.

Lieberman, A., & Van Horn, P. (2008). *Psychotherapy with infants and young children: Repairing the effects of stress and trauma on early attachment.* New York: Guilford.

Lieberman, A., Van Horn, P., & Ippen, C. (2005). Toward evidence based treatment: Child-parent psychotherapy with preschoolers exposed to marital violence. *Journal of American Academy of Child & Adolescent Psychiatry, 44,* 1241–1248. doi:10.1007/s10560-005-0039-0.

Luongo, G. (2007). Re-thinking child welfare training models to achieve evidence based practices. *Administration in Social Work, 31,* 87–96.

Lutz, L. (2003). Achieving permanence for children in the child welfare system: Pioneering possibilities amidst daunting challenges. New York: National Resource Center for Foster Care and Permanency Planning. Retrieved from http://www.hunter.cuny.edu/socwork/nrcfcpp/downloads/achieving-permanence.pdf.

Lyons-Ruth, K., & Jacobvitz, D. (2008). Attachment disorganization: Genetic factors, parenting contexts, and developmental transformation from infancy to adulthood. In J. Cassidy & P. Shaver (Eds.), *Handbook of attachment: Theory, research, and clinical implications* (2nd ed., pp. 666–297). New York: Guilford.

Lyons-Ruth, K., Dutra, L., Schuder, M., & Bianchi, I. (2006). From infant attachment disorganization to adult dissociation: Relational adaptation or traumatic experiences? *Psychiatric Clinics of North America, 29,* 63–86.

Lyons-Ruth, K., Easterbrooks, M. A., & Cibelli, C. D. (1997). Infant attachment strategies, infant mental lag, and maternal depressive symptoms: Predictions of internalizing and externalizing problems at age 7. *Developmental Psychology, 33,* 681.

Main, M., & Solomon, J. (1990). Procedures for identifying infants as disorganized/disoriented during the Ainsworth Strange Situation. In M. Greenberg, D. Chicchetti, & E. Cummings (Eds.), *Attachment in the preschool years: Theory, research, and intervention* (pp. 161–182). Chicago: University of Chicago Press.

Main, M., Hesse, E., & Kaplan, N. (2005). Predictability of attachment behavior and representational processes at 1, 6 and 19 years of age. In K. E. Grossman, K. Grossman, & E. Waters (Eds.), *Attachment from infancy to adulthood: The major longitudinal studies* (pp. 245–304). New York: Guilford.

Marvin, R., & Britner, P. (2008). Normative development: The ontology of attachment. In J. Cassidy & P. Shaver (Eds.), *Handbook of attachment: Theory, research, and clinical implications* (2nd ed., pp. 269–294). New York: Guilford.

Marvin, R., & Whelan, W. (2003). Disordered attachments: Toward evidence based clinical practice. *Attachment & Human Development, 5,* 283.

Marvin, R., Cooper, G., Hoffman, K., & Powell, B. (2002). The circle of security project: Attachment-Based intervention with caregiver-pre-school child dyads. *Attachment & Human Development, 4,* 107–124.

Mayers, H., Hager-Budny, M., & Buckner, E. (2008). The chances for children teen parent–infant project: Results of a pilot intervention for teen mothers and their infants in inner city high schools. *Infant Mental Health Journal, 29,* 320–342. doi:10.1002/imhj.20182.

McDonough, S. (2000). Interaction guidance: An approach for difficult to reach families. In C. H. Zeanah (Ed.), *Handbook of infant mental health* (2nd ed., pp. 485–493). New York: Cambridge University Press.

McWey, L., & Mullis, A. (2004). Improving the lives of children in foster care: The impact of supervised visitation. *Family Relations, 53,* 293–300.

National Child Traumatic Stress Network (NCTSN). (2011). *Treatments that work: Promising practices.* Retrieved from http://www.nctsnet.org/resources/topics/treatments-that-work/promising-practices.

National Resource Center for Family Centered Practice and Permanency Planning. (2008). *Programs that provide services to support family visiting of children in foster care.* Retrieved from http://www.hunter.cuny.edu/socwork/nrcfcpp/downloads/PHPrograms visiting.pdf.

Nilsen, W. J. (2003). Perceptions of attachment in academia and the child welfare system: The gap between research and reality. *Attachment & Human Development, 5,* 303.

O'Connor, T., & Zeanah, C. (2003). Attachment disorders: Assessment strategies and treatment approaches. *Attachment & Human Development, 5,* 223–244.

Ogowa, J., Sroufe, L. A., Weinfield, N. S., Carlson, E., & Egeland, B. (1997). Development and the fragmented self: A longitudinal study of dissociative symptomatology in a non-clinical sample. *Development and Psychopathology, 9,* 855–1164.

Oppenheim, D., & Goldsmith, D. (2007). *Attachment theory in clinical work with children: Bridging the gap between research and practice.* New York: Guilford.

Page, T., & Cain, D. (2009). Why don't you just tell me how you feel?: A case study of a young mother in an attachment-Based group intervention. *Child and Adolescent Social Work Journal, 26,* 333–350.

Putnam, F. (2005). The developmental neurobiology of disrupted attachment: Lessons from animal models and child abuse research. In L. Berlin, Y. Ziv, L. Amaya-Jackson, & M. T. Greenberg (Eds.), *Enhancing early attachments: Theory, research, intervention, and policy* (pp. 79–99). New York: Guilford.

Redding, R., Fried, C., & Britner, P. (2000). Predictors of placement outcomes in treatment foster care: Implications for foster parent selection and service delivery. *Journal of Child and Family Studies, 9,* 425–447.

Rogers, E. (2002). The nature of technology transfer. *Science Communication, 23*(3), 323–341.

Rousseau, D. (1990). Assessing organizational culture: The case for multiple methods. In B. Schneider (Ed.), *Organizational climate and culture* (pp. 153–192). San Francisco: Jossey-Bass.

Sackett, D., Rosenberg, W., Gray, J., Haynes, R., & Richardson, W. (1996). Evidence based medicine: What it is and what it isn't. *British Medical Journal, 312,* 71–72.

Simpson, D. (2009). Organizational readiness for stage-based dynamics of innovation implementation. *Research on Social Work Practice, 19,* 541–551.

Slade, A. (2006). Reflective parenting programs: Theory and development. *Psychoanalytic Inquiry, 26,* 640–657.

Slade, A., Sadler, L. S., & Mayers, L. (2005). Minding the baby: Enhancing parental reflective functioning in a nursing/mental health home visiting program. In L. Berlin, Y. Ziv, L. Amaya-Jackson, & M. Greenberg (Eds.), *Enhancing early attachments: Theory, research, intervention, and policy* (pp. 152–177). New York: Guilford.

Smith, B., & Donovan, S. (2003). Child welfare practice in organizational and institutional context. *The Social Service Review, 77,* 541–563.

Social Work Policy Institute. (2011). *Professional social workers in child welfare work: Research addressing the recruitment and retention dilemma.* Retrieved from http://www.socialworkpolicy.org/research/child-welfare-2.html.

Sroufe, A., Egeland, B., Carlson, E. A., & Collins, W. A. (2005). Placing attachment experience in developmental context. In K. Grossmann, K. E. Grossmann, & Waters (Eds.), *Attachment from infancy to adulthood: The major longitudinal studies* (pp. 48–97). New York: Guilford.

Strijker, J., Knorth, E., & Knot-Dickscheit, J. (2008). Placement history of foster children: A study of placement history and outcomes in long-term family foster care. *Child Welfare, 87,* 107–124.

Stronach, E. R., Toth, S., Rogosch, F., Oshri, A., Manly, J. T., & Cicchetti, D. (2011). Maltreatment, attachment security, and internal representations of mother and mother-child relationships. *Child Maltreatment, 16,* 137–145.

U.S. Department of Health and Human Services (USDHHS) Administration for Children and Families, Administration on Children, Youth and Families, Children's Bureau. (2010). *Child Maltreatment 2009.* Retrieved from http://www.acf.hhs.gov/programs/cb/stats_research/index.htm#can.

van IJzendoorn, M., & Bakermans-Kranenburg, M. (2003). Attachment disorders and disorganized attachment: Similar and different. *Attachment & Human Development, 5,* 313–320.

van Ijzendoorn, M., Schuengel, C., & Bakermanns-Kranenburg, M. (1999). Disorganized attachment in early childhood: Meta-analysis of precursors, concommittants, and sequelae. *Development and Psychopathology, 11,* 225–249.

Walker, J. (2007). Unresolved loss and trauma in parents and the implications in terms of child protection. *Journal of Social Work Practice, 27,* 77–87.

Webster, L., Hackett, R., & Joubert, D. (2009). The association of unresolved attachment status and cognitive processes in maltreated adolescents. *Child Abuse Review, 18,* 6–23.

Weiner, D., Schneider, A., & Lyons, J. (2009). Evidence-based treatments for trauma among culturally diverse foster care youth: Treatment retention and outcomes. *Children and Youth Services Review, 31,* 1199–1205.

Weinfield, N., Sroufe, A., Egeland, B., & Carlson, E. (2008). Individual differences in infant-caregiver attachment: Conceptual and empirical aspects of security. In J. Cassidy & P. Shaver (Eds.), *Handbook of attachment: Theory, research and clinical applications* (2nd ed., pp. 78–101). New York: Guilford.

Yoo, J., Brooks, D., & Patti, R. (2007). Organizational constructs as predictors of effectiveness in child welfare interventions. *Child Welfare, 86,* 53–78.

Zeanah, C., & Boris, N. (2000). Disturbances and disorders of attachment in early childhood. In C. Zeanah (Ed.), *Handbook of infant mental health* (2nd ed., pp. 353–368). New York: Guilford.

Index

J. E. Bettmann, D. D. Friedman (eds.), *Attachment-Based Clinical Work with Children and Adolescents,* Essential Clinical Social Work Series,
DOI 10.1007/978-1-4614-4848-8, © Springer Science+Business Media New York 2013

Printed in Great Britain
by Amazon